Contents

Copyright 2001 by the Board of Regents of the State of Florida
Printed in the United States of America on acid-free paper
All rights reserved

06 05 04 03 02 01 6 5 4 3 2 1

Library of Congress Cataloging-in-Publication Data
Marting, Diane E.
The sexual woman in Latin American literature : dangerous desires /
Diane E. Marting.
p. cm.
Includes bibliographical references and index.
ISBN 0-8130-1832-3 (alk. paper)
1. Latin American fiction—20th century—History and criticism. 2. Women in
literature. 3. Women and literature—Latin America—History—20th century.
4. Sex in literature. 5. Sex role in literature. 6. Asturias, Miguel Angel—
Political and social views. 7. Lispector, Clarice—Political and social views.
8. Vargas Llosa, Mario, 1936- —Political and social views. I. Title.
PQ7082.N7 M354 2001
863'.6409352042'098—dc21   00-053267

The University Press of Florida is the scholarly publishing agency for the State
University System of Florida, comprising Florida A&M University, Florida
Atlantic University, Florida Gulf Coast University, Florida International
University, Florida State University, University of Central Florida, University
of Florida, University of North Florida, University of South Florida,
and University of West Florida.

University Press of Florida
15 Northwest 15th Street
Gainesville, FL 32611-2079
http://www.upf.com

The Sexual Woman
in Latin American Literature
Dangerous Desires

Diane E. Marting

University Press of Florida
Gainesville · Tallahassee · Tampa · Boca Raton
Pensacola · Orlando · Miami · Jacksonville · Ft. Myers

The Sexual Woman in Latin American Literature

Florida A&M University, Tallahassee
Florida Atlantic University, Boca Raton
Florida Gulf Coast University, Ft. Myers
Florida International University, Miami
Florida State University, Tallahassee
University of Central Florida, Orlando
University of Florida, Gainesville
University of North Florida, Jacksonville
University of South Florida, Tampa
University of West Florida, Pensacola

Illustrations

Preface

This book originally began as a logical extension of my research into two areas: contemporary Latin American women writers and the many recent feminist debates regarding sexuality. I had decided to explore issues of that debate through an analysis of women's novels about *women's* sexuality. To my surprise, the more I searched for women's novels with an explicit sex scene to analyze the more I was reduced to treating works of the late 1970s and after. Where were the serious treatments of the subject by women from the first half of the century? And from the sexy, radical '60s? Surely, many women novelists were being quite explicit about female sexuality by then, or so I had thought. But I was wrong. So this project evolved into one to figure out both *why* women—who were not timid otherwise—avoided the subject of explicit sex from a woman's perspective, and *when* women novelists generally stopped avoiding it in Latin America. Soon I also came to question the overall characterization of the Latin American Boom novel as full of explicit and exuberant sexuality and to wonder how the more female-authored and gynocentric Post Boom novel compared to it. I found that many critical statements about sexuality in novels from the 1960s to today are based only on representations of male sexuality, of sex from a male perspective, and of sex as a male prerogative. Should I have been so surprised by this? I already knew that most discussions about (sexuality in) Latin American literature have been based on discussions of male authors. My mistake was in presuming that in simply turning to female authors, I would be able to investigate their many varied representations of female sexuality, of sex from a female perspective, and of sex as a female prerogative. But prior to the 1970s explicit sex from the perspective of a female character can be found almost nowhere except in the works of certain male authors. Treating female sexuality evidently was dangerous for women authors: for their reputation, for their future as writers, for their personal lives.

Thus to understand the modern treatment of the sexual woman one must study largely male authors, but the subject is not any less interesting because of this fact. This thematization of women's sexual experience by overwhelmingly male writers is not merely an odd twist of fate or eccentric feature of the fiction of recent decades, but rather a result of social, philosophical, and literary systems of gender hierarchy and difference. Learning more about why and how the figure of the sexual woman was used as a symbol by men and women can teach us about the history of women's (and men's) favored topics; about women's improved and improving publishing opportunities relative to men; and about the subtle ways in which our contemporary world, seemingly so transparent, remains a clouded mirror precisely because we form part of it. Additionally, I think this book demonstrates that further research should be done on those lesser-known women who did write about sexuality before the 1970s. I am currently embarking on one aspect of this large project, and I hope others will, too. The many recent publications on lesbian novels in the post-1970s period at the least signals that novels of female sexuality from Latin America indeed have become significant topics in the new millennium.

The descriptions of female sexual pleasure I treat here from the decades of the 1960s, 1970s and 1980s have not been studied together before in large part because they disrupt and perturb certain traditional readers' expectations of female sexual abstention, self-sacrifice, and silence. The singular, radical works from these thirty years conceive of sexual women characters as a means to a new realism, a realism that abandons the antiquated illusion (or social imperative) that women lack sexual desire. In fact my most interesting finding may ultimately be that those who do narrate tales about modern sexual women usually also achieve something more than a restitution of female sexual desire to fictional discourse: they correct other false stereotypes or they strive for a utopian writing through which a better world may be imagined. These writers contemplate a future in which the New Woman enjoys an equality with men that encompasses not only the right to have and to express sexual desires, but who also gains economic parity, legal justice, and a freedom of movement such that society and its institutions become truly gender blind.

The freedoms that these new sexual woman characters represent have been part of an international discussion about women and literature that is independent of the sexuality controversies that brought me to study them. For instance, Catherine Clément and Hélène Cixous have proposed that writing itself can inscribe a freedom from the past and present that may benefit women, in the book translated as *The Newly Born Woman* (1986). Because of these similarities between the freedoms accessible through writing as envisioned by these two French theorists and the freedoms accompanying female sexuality in the novels I analyze here, I have dubbed this recent, Latin American utopian character the "newly sexed woman." It is for future critics to determine whether the newly sexed woman truly marks the birth of a new epoch in Latin American writing for women.

Acknowledgments

The writing of this book would not have been possible without the help of many others. The careful reading of drafts by Nancy Gray Diaz, Aristides Sergio Klafke, Nancy Paxton, Edward Baker, William Calin, John Scott, Margo Persin, Elizabeth Ginway, Debra Castillo, Naomi Lindstrom, Mary Berg, Deborah Harper, and others has been invaluable. Columbia University's Summer Grants for Research in the Humanities provided support for the writing of the introduction. The American Council of Learned Societies did not directly fund this project, but the chapter on Clarice Lispector changed substantially after I received ACLS support of my research on the Brazilian writer for a different book. I would also like to thank the various entities of the University of Florida that have supported the writing of the Asturias and Vargas Llosa chapters: the research arm of the university, ORTGE, for a summer grant; the College of Liberal Arts and Sciences for a 1998 summer Humanities Enhancement grant; and my department, Romance Languages and Literatures, for several grants in research aid. My thanks also to the countless people who have supported me in other ways: my dissertation director, Janet Walker; my parents and brothers; Susan Clarendon; and the many others too numerous to name.

A Note about Translations

In order to make this book accessible to those who know no Spanish or Portuguese, without sacrificing the quotations in the original language crucial to scholars of Latin American fiction, I have provided quotations from the published English translations within my main text, with the original quotations in brackets (when short) and in endnotes (when long). A capital *T* following a page number indicates this number is the page of the published translation. A translation of a title that is neither italicized nor in quotation marks indicates that no published translation is known.

Any translation without a page number from an existing translation is my own. Modifications of published translations are indicated; they are usually intended to render a more literal sense of an original where a translation has been free or has emphasized other aspects of the work.

|

Dangerous (to) Women

Introduction

> Sexuality is to feminism what work is to Marxism: that which is
> most one's own, yet most taken away.
> **Catharine A. MacKinnon**

Alluding to literature's ambivalent role in woman's emancipatory
struggle, Angel Rama once wrote: "Literature for the woman writer was
frequently a jail; when literature begins to transform itself into an instrument to reduce alienation, it is common for whoever wields it as a
weapon—still awkwardly—against an armed society, to be blown to
bits."[1] The Uruguayan critic made this remark in his prologue to a 1966
collection of erotic short stories by Latin American women, *Aquí la mitad
del amor* (literally, Here half of love), in order to emphasize the changing
relationship between literature and women writers. Previously an impris-
oning "jail," now a useful "instrument," literature is a weapon used by
women and against women in the twentieth century's gender wars in the
cultural arena.

Rama's military metaphor of literature as a double-edged weapon
women try to use against an armed society brings to mind Luisa Valenzuela's short story "Other Weapons" (1985; "Cambio de armas" 1982)
in her book of the same name. As with Rama's statement about literature
for the woman writer, in Valenzuela a woman tries and fails to use a gun
the way she wishes. Her intended victim, a colonel, becomes her torturer
and keeps her alive as his personal sex slave. Eventually, this colonel comes
to believe he has completely erased her personality and her memory of her
radical political beliefs. In preparation for the moment in which he wants
to make an escape from the impending military attack, he tries to convince
her that she owes him her life, since others had wanted to kill her. At this
moment of crisis, the colonel gives back to her the very revolver with

which she had tried to kill him. After this change of weapons, as he turns to leave, she picks up the loaded gun and points it. The story ends ambiguously at this juncture: Is she pointing the gun at him, as most readers assume? Will she shoot or won't she? She has the weapon again and will make a choice. Or can she? Will her desire to end the torture she has suffered cause her to turn the weapon on herself? Or has she lost the ability, temporarily or permanently, to use the weapon as she herself might wish, either against him or herself? Will she obey the colonel and use it as he wishes?

In the Valenzuela story, the colonel believes the woman will obey his commands without any further force to back them up. His words, together with her memory of the torture, he hopes, could control her by themselves. In this verbal coercion lies a second "change of weapons," from guns to discourse. Returning to literature as a weapon, how has the woman novelist used literature in the past and how does she use it in the present? Have male-centered discourses and master narratives functioned like the colonel in "Other Weapons," keeping women under control? Do stories about the sexual woman veil the threat that she who follows the path of attacking society will bring down upon herself the wrath of her society? Additionally, has the woman reader been coerced, so that she obeys in fear, attacking the women who produce critical discourse? When the gun is returned to her, when women do write the stories about woman's sexuality, do they pursue their own issues? Do they obey the colonel and defend him? Do they kill themselves? Do they aim the gun at the society that punished sexual women for so long?

Like other women writers from her generation, Luisa Valenzuela has been able to employ sexuality boldly as an element of social critique, and return unscathed from the fray; the weapon has truly changed hands. But many women writers in the past, as Rama correctly reminds us, have injured themselves socially or have represented sexual women characters as unintentionally hurting themselves, through this new weapon at their disposal: women's sexuality in (woman's) fiction. Today, when most writers, women and men, write frequently about sex, it is difficult to remember that sexuality has only recently become ubiquitous in literature; it is a very contemporary literary fashion.[2] For most of this century, a woman writer courted danger by writing about woman's sexuality. It was not until the 1960s that sexuality in novels arrived at this juncture for the Latin American woman writer, not universally but generally speaking. Rama testified in 1966 that eroticism was still a dangerous topic for the woman writer to undertake. The weapon of sexual fiction before the 1960s had harmed the woman writer who may have attempted to aim it at gender injustice or even merely at rules of propriety. Within the space of a decade, most of the hesitations keeping women from treating female sexuality disappear. Women, in even greater numbers, wield the "weapon against alienation" and survive.

Literature has been changed by the new ways sexual themes have been deployed by women. To understand this change in the production of a novelistic discourse of female sexuality and in its product, the literary history of the twentieth century must consider the importance of women writers, of women's themes *and* of sexuality more generally—the discourse about sex which Michel Foucault has called modernity's characteristic obsession—if it is not to suffer a fatal blindness. Additionally, for this study, the topic of female sexuality in literature has intersected with the role as social critics to which most Latin American novelists ascribe, and thus gives its readers a new and significant perspective on gender debates and literary feminism in contemporary Latin America. This literary history, while fascinating and illuminating, is largely untold. The present book alone cannot remedy this lack. I hope that through an in-depth examination of selected transitional novels in which this "change of weapons" can be observed, and a hypothesis regarding them, both a detailed knowledge of particular examples and a general sense of this complex history can be gained.

The Sexual Woman in Latin American Literature is intended to suggest the outlines of such a history of female sexuality in the Latin American novel since the early 1960s. That a novel represents sexuality as a defining element in the life of a female character is a minimum requirement of the works I discuss. My other criteria for inclusion were a pervasive theme of female sexuality; a complexity of thought and expression; and internal claims (either explicit or implicit) for female sexual pleasure as significant in social terms. These are novels that combine an explicit sex scene with sustained primary focalization in a female character. I have sought novels written by women and men which inscribe a "female" point of view on sexual practices. This book looks at sexualized power relations in novels where woman is a subject who desires rather than an object who is desired. Her body is the site of pleasure which she actively seeks and in some measure experiences. These works explore issues of love, sex, and the condition of women.

Without any pretense of writing a totalizing history—impossible always and misleading when attempted—this present book examines as case studies three novels whose historical representativeness depends on homologies between them and trends in a larger, yet-to-be-written history of female sexuality in Latin American discourse in the post-1950s period. The three chapters treating individual novels reflect and project moments of transition in social attitudes. In this introduction, in contrast, I lay out both the extreme before and after positions, as well as the nature of the changes reflected in the case studies. I hypothesize the general trends that the chapters detail.

Women novelists, compared to men, have tended to avoid the subject of sexual women, at least until the 1960s. Arguably one of the most important women novelists from the early twentieth century, the Venezuelan Teresa de la Parra, for instance, prefers subtle irony regarding love and marriage to representations of sex when she questions woman's femininity as a meaningful, satisfying life choice. Themes of female sexuality, while crucially linked to themes of social justice for women, were dangerous to undertake. Angel Rama wrote: "That is what happened with Delmira Agustini: women's arts are beginning to exist in Uruguay due to her. She died when two disparate functions, both imposed by the new society of the 1900s, enter into conflict inside her: the mystification of the conventional bourgeois woman and her independence as a being of amorous sensuality."[3] Murdered by her ex-husband, the poet Agustini represents an extreme case of victimization by Montevideo high society's particular juncture of patriarchal values. The ferociousness of the attack against Agustini was not typical, but her brave writing and tragic death illustrate in broad outline some of the difficult choices and negative consequences for women authors and artists who before the 1960s flaunted strictures regarding the woman writer and female sexuality. For every successful female artist associated with sexual freedoms in Latin America—like later Uruguayan novelist Armonía Somers or Mexican painter Frida Kahlo—there were many others who dared not, or preferred not to, take such risks.[4] Merely being taken seriously as a professional artist or writer was difficult enough for a (Latin American) woman until very recently.

This danger to a woman author from writing about sex has taken a great variety of forms, from the most violent physical attack, as happened to Agustini, to serious damage to a woman writer's social reputation, resulting in exclusion from her social circles or losing her (other) job, to harm to her literary standing. In "The Front Line: Notes on Sex in Novels by Women, 1969–1979," Ann Barr Snitow argues that in English "Women, for so long equated with sex, did not immediately leap at the chance to tell their side of the sex story" because it hurt their reputation as all-round writers, as fully capable authors (167). If a woman produced a novel about sex, she was a "woman writer"; if she wrote on other topics instead, she was a "writer" without the qualifier.

In 1980 Puerto Rican novelist, poet, and essayist Rosario Ferré speaks of women writing about female sexuality as a future event, not yet accomplished: "Women writers today know that if they want to become good writers, they will have to be women before anything else, because in art, authenticity is everything. They will have to learn to become acquainted with the most intimate secrets of their body and to speak without euphemisms about it. They will have to learn to examine their own eroticism and to derive from their sexuality a whole vitality that is latent and exploited on few occasions."[5] The reasons women have not done so before, in Ferré's opinion, are the limitations on her "material freedom" ["libertad material"], which "the feminist movement has confronted energetically throughout the last ten years" ["se ha enfrentado enérgicamente a lo largo de los últimos diez años el movimiento feminista"], and her "inner freedom" ["libertad interior"]. Inner freedom includes both "the emotional and psychological sanctions that society continues to place on her on the level of customs, and the sanctions that woman normally imposes on herself" ["las sanciones emocionales y psicológicas que, al nivel de las costumbres, la sociedad sigue imponiendo a la mujer y las sanciones que ella suele imponerse a sí misma" (13–14)], which together place obstacles of the most varied sort in her path. In an affirmation of female sexuality as a topic for the woman writer, Ferré asks: "Don't women have a right, the same as men, to profane love, to transitory love, to bedeviled love, to passion for its own sake?" ["¿No tiene acaso la mujer, al igual que el hombre, derecho al amor profano, al amor pasajero, incluso al amor endemoniado, a la pasión por la pasión misma?" (16)]. She asserts: "passion is the defining nature of woman, but that passion tends to be at the same time, her greatest strength and her greatest weakness" ["pasión es la naturaleza definitoria de la mujer, pero esa pasión suele ser al mismo tiempo, su mayor fuerza y su mayor flaqueza" (17)].

Debra Castillo notes that another motivation leading women to write about female sexuality may have been to escape from the popular domestic fiction to which they appeared condemned; but she underlines the escape brought with it its own problems. It was in fact a double bind (private communication, February 26, 1999). If a woman wrote on female sexuality, she was castigated for her audacity; if she did not, she was criticized for not being "feminine." In the opinion of many, woman's greatest strength—love, not sex—was the world that women knew best.

The best-selling Chilean author and journalist Isabel Allende, for example, has said she feared being categorized as a "woman writer" because she felt such a designation diminished her reputation, by reducing the sphere and scope of her efforts. When Allende was asked in an interview whether she had used the diary technique in *House of the Spirits* (1985; *La casa de los espíritus* 1986), for instance, "because this was a novel about women," Allende responded: "No. And if I had known it was a feminine technique, I wouldn't have used it." Pressed to explain herself, Allende adds: "Because I don't think literature has any gender, and I don't think it's necessary to come up with a plan to write like a woman, because that seems like a kind of awkward self-segregation to me" (Allende in García Pinto 30). Consciously writing women's literature Allende considers "self-segregation." By extension, one can presume she means not only the diary technique but themes of importance primarily to women. Rosario Ferré, who has an essay on "The Diary as a Feminine Form" ("El diario como forma femenina"), praises the abundance of women's diaries of all sorts and explains: "The diary is that secret place where a woman can find her authenticity, free of the prejudices of which she has always been a victim" ["El diario es ese lugar secreto donde ella encuentra su autenticidad, libre de los prejuicios de los que siempre ha sido víctima" (27)].

Thus the new female sexuality in literature, while a project shared by individuals of both genders, involved difficult risks for women and men before the 1960s, and was taken up by many women with greater hesitation than by men.[6] In the research for this book, I have been most fascinated to discover that when male novelists wanted to write about feminist issues, whether or not their stance was pro-woman, they often chose female heterosexuality as their theme; I have been frustrated to find that women writers largely avoid female sexuality during the same period. But the history of the woman writer has undergone a greater number of changes and more dramatic changes than that of the male writer. Once women writers begin to notice the successes of feminism in the 1970s and after, fewer of them avoid sexual topics. Perhaps the risks for women writers had been attenuated, but certainly the rewards if these women were successful would be greater. While some women turned independently to themes of female sexuality, other women writers learned sometime around the 1960s that publishers and readers had actively begun to look for books by women on virtually every topic. Consciously feminist writers, of course, were already reading their literary foremothers with pride and learning from them. Whether feminist or not, women could gain by speaking to women's interests. For recent writers, in fact, the themes and characters of female sexuality most attract those women writers who seek to further a female tradition, rather than, like Allende, elude it. These two groups of women, those aspiring to explore pro-woman issues, and those wishing to hop on the bandwagon as a publishing decision, are the earliest women to write the new sexual fiction.

In the 1960s the Buenos Aires publishing house Editorial Merlín began publishing collections of sexual fiction similar to Rama's 1966 Uruguayan anthology. One, *Prostibulario* (Prostibulary), centered on brothels and prostitutes; another was *El arte de amar: el hombre* (The art of loving: men).[7] Both appeared in 1967 and contained a number of short stories and one essay: the former compilation was penned by seven men and one woman; the latter, by seven women about male sexuality. Nira Etchenique, the only woman writer in *Prostibulario*, is mildly punished for writing about sexuality; the weapon she wished to use is turned against her. The editors describe her in the capsule biography as "too strong" in her writing for a woman ["excesivamente viril" (41)]. It is surprising that the anthologists would want to denigrate an author they were publishing, and thus whom they would be expected to promote. But even in 1967, sex was supposed to be off-limits for women writers; they should stick to more "feminine" topics. When Etchenique wrote about prostitution, the editors publicly reminded her that she was a woman and should act like one.

For good reasons, feminist studies have chosen not to dwell on the threats women writers have received from addressing certain topics, and to emphasize instead women's agency and accomplishments in literature despite the obstacles and the risks. Nevertheless the warnings to women and the exemplary punishments existed. A full understanding of the freedom which Latin American women writers enjoy (or not) today is impossible if one simply ignores the real consequences to women of taking up certain subjects.

One reasoning of those who, like the colonel in Valenzuela's story or Etchenique's editors, sought to control women's actions and prevent her from writing about sexuality, and especially female sexuality, was that if a woman wrote about such things, she must have experienced them. Portraying the sexual woman could dangerously reflect back upon the woman who wrote the portrayal. Hence a consequence of this particular danger to their reputation is that the women who risked writing about sexuality in the early years gave up on producing popular, simple stories about women like themselves. The portrayal could be too easily read as autobiographical, unless the writing clearly destabilized that kind of reading. Much of the history of the reception of women's writing taught women writers the cautionary tale that if they wished to sabotage simplistic identifications of their characters with their own life, they needed to use more radical modes, more revolutionary changes in conceptualization, and greater experimentation in writing gender than their male counterparts. Women writers often write about sexual women today, and with impunity in most cases. We do not assume that women who write about prostitution have experienced that world. But the freedom today's authors have has been won through efforts by women and men who used the weapon of discourse to change literature and the society in which they live. Allende's success as a popular writer was preceded and partially made possible by a history of increasing female freedoms in Latin America and in its literature.

While not denying the infrequency of interest in the subject of female sexuality by woman novelists compared to men, David William Foster has sought to remind us that women writers do not always act like "women." Women like Agustini and Etchenique have disregarded the warnings and written about prohibited sexuality. When they do, such writers successfully show, according to Foster, the artificiality of gendered sexual scripts: "If male authors and their narrators have yet to create an authentic erotic vision in Latin America, one would expect that the women authors, subject to even greater sociocultural restraints, would be even more circumspect on the subject. Yet the Latin American women writers who write unabashedly about erotic themes bear out the hypothesis that women artists may more effectively shatter such taboos and restraints because they are not of their own making but imposed on them by a male-dominated society" (*Alternate Voices* 130).[8] Foster's idea is that among the self-selected group of women who disobeyed and wrote about female sexuality, breaking the rules is done well and thoroughly. He links female sexuality to freedom, the "effective" shattering of "taboos and restraints," which appears stronger in works by women writers than in those by men.[9] Put in terms of Michel Foucault's theory, Foster argues that the literary establishment, the publishing industry, and society offered carrots and sticks which combined to produce a discourse of sexuality by women which implicitly or explicitly thematized their own rebellion in taking up the subject. I am suggesting that writing about female sexuality was part and parcel of a broader disobedience to master narratives (the colonel's imperatives) on the part of these female novelists; if they write about breaking sexual rules, it would be a *mise en abîme* of their own actions.

Considering only female sexuality as a topic, I have found such a link with freedom not to be limited to women writers, however, contrary to conventional wisdom. For example, the male Peruvian novelist Enrique

Congrains Martín protests against bourgeois morality through the sexual aggressiveness of his female protagonist in *No una, sino muchas muertes* [Not one, but many deaths] (Peru, 1967). In a 1971 interview he explained that in this novel he wanted "to denounce the situation of Peruvian women . . . and at the same time to make fun of conventional feminine models. . . . And at the same time I wanted to say, more or less, 'These are the true possibilities for women to relate' or 'A woman should dare to do anything, absolutely anything.'"[10] The freedom Congrains Martín associates with his protagonist Maruja's sexuality is rebellion against a puritanical morality of feminine purity, frigidity, and fragility. Primarily a storyteller, he works out his optimism about the way the world can be radically altered through (a sexual) woman's activities. Not only does Maruja achieve a "liberation" of sorts through or with her sexuality, but female sexual pleasure clears the way, the novel suggests, for a more general freedom and equality for the poor—perhaps even a new society.

Female sexuality, in its association with freedom, in fact is the common denominator among sexual fictions which fulfilled my conditions for thematizing sexuality from a female subject position and in social terms. The authors, male and female, claim their novels are about the search for liberty, and characters are made to speak in similar terms. Definitions of female sexuality differ widely, as do definitions of the freedom said to accompany it, but pairing of the two appears unquestioned. To take another example from anthologists of erotic short stories, Márcia Denser, the compiler of two collections of Brazilian erotic short stories by women authors, *Muito prazer* [It's a pleasure] (1982) and *O prazer é todo meu* [The pleasure is all mine] (1984), does not neglect eroticism's liberatory capacity, even as she advances the idea that by the 1980s feminist motivations for female eroticism in fiction have already been transcended. To Denser, the 1980s no longer need collective social movements: "now it is the individual's turn" ["agora é a vez do indivíduo"] in this time of so-called postfeminism ("Apresentação" *Muito prazer* 5).

The attitude of considering a preoccupation with the theme of women's sexuality in literature to be synonymous with a demand for greater freedom generally appears to originate in ideas of sexual repression, according to which woman, as the more repressed of the two sexes, doubly defies the rules, as we saw in Foster above. But some critics have extrapolated much beyond those consequences which Foster claims. In the 1974 introduction to his Mexican anthology, Enrique Jaramillo Levi asserts that transgressing against erotic taboos holds great potential as a symbolic first step toward a desire for freedom in other areas. In so doing, Jaramillo Levi greatly expands the claims made for sexuality's liberatory associations. If freed from its bounds, he believes sexuality can bring about a less aggressive society where war itself can be prevented: "In societies in which sexuality is a normal manifestation of life, there is less aggression, both on an individual level (murders, thefts, fights, etc.) and collectively (war)" ["En las sociedades en las cuales la sexualidad es una manifestación normal de vida, hay menos agresividad, tanto a nivel individual (asesinatos, robos, riñas, etcétera), como colectivo (guerras)" ("Prólogo" 14)].

Less extravagantly, the editors of *El placer de la palabra* (1991; *Pleasure in the Word* 1993), Margarite Fernández Olmos and Lizabeth Paravisini-Gebert, attribute a liberatory function to sexual discourse when written by women, especially in its ability to confer dignity on images of women degraded by oppression. For readers of Spanish, they write: "The erotic discourse of the Latin American woman writer opens new literary and cultural horizons in her use of the sexual as a vehicle for an audacious critique of sex and politics. It forms part of a revolutionary process whose object is to unmask the cultural categories of sex and gender in a search for a real liberation and raising of consciousness leading to the total restoration of dignity to the Latin American woman."[11] In the English edition published two years later, they express these ideas with different nuances: "The sexual discourse of contemporary Latin American women authors is innovative and groundbreaking work that uses the dimension of gender to produce a powerful critique of sex and politics. It is a constructive creative process that exposes the cultural constructs of sex and gender in its pursuit of genuine sexual liberation and consciousness, and ultimately, in the restoration of the total and unrestricted dignity and autonomy of the Latin American woman" (32). In Spanish, the weapon used for sexual critique is the sexual (*lo sexual*), a blunt instrument at best, but in English it is "the dimension of gender," which I take to mean "gender difference." In fact, it is the conjunction of the two, gendered sexuality (female sexuality), and not merely "the sexual" or gender alone that has the greatest capacity for critiquing the way the status quo affects women. Resistance, confrontation, and varieties of the two become immediately visible.

A second nuance differentiating the introduction to *El Placer de la palabra* from that to *Pleasure in the Word* comes when the anthologists write in Spanish that women's erotic writing participates in a revolutionary process ("proceso revolucionario"), whereas in English, they call it a "constructive creative process." Here we find literature's greater political importance in Latin America than in the United States. Within a Latin

American literary context, women's erotic literature displayed a *revolutionary* agenda, in contrast to the norms of the United States and England, where a determined antipolitical stance prevailed in most sexual fiction. Additionally, in the Spanish introduction, sexual literature by women restores the Latin American woman's dignity, but in the English introduction, the editors say that both her dignity and her autonomy are recuperated. In this last contrast, the addition of autonomy, the difference between the Spanish and English versions appears less cultural. This has likely been an afterthought in the later edition, a greater recognition that sexuality is one of a woman's links to other people, one of the fulcrums of power, a linchpin (to use Foucault's metaphor) in systems of control of and by a subject. Hence woman's sexuality can be a means to resistance and agency in discourse, precisely owing to the way power is deployed through it.

Today, in most of Latin America, merely writing about sex or sexuality no longer has serious social consequences for the professional writer, even young female ones, and fewer claims are made for its dangerousness as a weapon to provoke social change. That more male writers than female ones treat female sexuality is part of the genealogy of the topos, but the predominance of men becomes less and less true as the vast changes wrought by the second wave of feminism become less novel and more the norm. Clearly, the relative silence of women writers as compared to men on the subject of female sexuality has largely ended; since the 1960s, when both men and women increased their production of sexual fiction, women have been catching up. Indeed, writing about sex has become almost obligatory in urban environments for many journalists and professional writers.

In Isabel Allende's "Mis líos con el sexo" [My problems with sex] (1988), the novelist and journalist humorously details her energetic attempt to catch up with the sexual liberties of 1970s Venezuela, having suddenly arrived there from a more sexually conservative Chile under the dictator Augusto Pinochet. Allende had written about sex previously as an audacious professional, but now she pursues sexual liberation as a way of life and a subject that touches her personally. She writes that her daughter Paula had begun studying sexology at the university. Allende tried to be modern, too, by attempting contortions with her husband, learning about sex toys, and installing a mirror over the bed, until a few years later an awareness of AIDS suddenly brings her experimentation to a rapid close. But in emphasizing her sore muscles after new sexual acrobatics with her husband, Allende trivializes, perhaps unintentionally, the continuing problems of the many sexually active women across Latin America who must deal with the inaccessibility of divorce, abortion, and modern birth control. Even today, there is danger in the practices of heterosexuality and lesbianism, even though there is appreciably less hazard, and perhaps even a reward system now, for those educated, comfortable, urban women who write about sex in the course of their professional lives.[12]

In Latin America the association of the sexual woman with freedom became a powerful new metaphor to deal imaginatively with the urgent social and political crises of the 1960s, 1970s, and 1980s. Perhaps we can find harbingers of the "newly sexed woman" character who appeared in the 1960s among the songs, stories, movies, and novels of the Mexican Revolution, with its image of the *soldadera* (both the female, gunslinging fighter and the camp follower—a prostitute or girlfriend/lover/wife of a soldier). In *Easy Women: Sex and Gender in Modern Mexican Fiction* (1998), Debra Castillo discusses the estimate that "during the Mexican Revolution of 1910–1920 more than half of the women in Mexico were forced to turn to prostitution to survive" and concludes: "Whatever the exact numbers of female soldiers, *soldaderas*, and actual prostitutes (given the confusions of war, any estimates can be more or less speculative), there is general agreement that, in the period of tremendous social upset, women were largely on the loose and on their own in Mexico" (4–5). Certainly other signals of the changes occurring in Latin American societies can be found in such diverse phenomena as the passage of women's suffrage in most Latin American countries between the two World Wars, with the resulting attention paid to the new female electorate; in the excitement caused by the Cuban Revolution in 1959, with its image of the female *guerrillera* (female revolutionary); and finally the new legislation accompanying modernization processes promoting women's work outside the home and the rural sectors. In the 1960s, the Latin American sexual woman suddenly had many faces, rather than merely that of the Janus-like prostitute, both innocent victim and embodiment of corrupted evil.

Whatever the combination of causes, broadly speaking there emerged at this time a sexual woman character who could symbolize or be a metonymic figure for some of the more subtle—and intimate—aspects of the 1960s upheavals. Women were demanding not to be bound by the antiquated social mores that forgave men all transgressions and forgave women none of them. In ever greater numbers, writers began to create characters doing the same. In fact, to a large coterie of leftist and liberal novelists in Latin America—men and women—the sexual woman became a vehicle for speaking about more general hopes for a future with greater political and social freedoms, as well as sexual freedoms. Like the short-story writers and editors I have already mentioned, male and female novelists in the 1960s began to treat woman's acquisition of *sexual* independence as a worthy social theme. While the poverty of the many and the massive accumulation of goods and power by the few were clearly the major target of the attacks on the contemporary situation by most Latin American novelists, an important and growing minority saw female sexuality as a new topic with untested capacities for critique and for envisioning social transformation.

What is the nature of the female sexuality that makes it propitious for such a serious literary exploration of social justice? First of all, sex is gendered. Sex impacts men and women, boys and girls, differently; discourses of fertility, abortion, and childbirth, to mention only the most obvious topics, represent the inflection of gender on individuals, communities, and the state, and can be commented upon easily by sexual fiction. In "Sexual Skirmishes of Feminist Factions, Twenty-Five Years of Debate on Women and Sexuality," the introduction to *Feminism and Sexuality, A Reader* (1996), editors Stevi Jackson and Sue Scott report that:

> While making an analytical distinction between gender and sexuality, we recognise that the two are empirically related. Indeed it is the relationship between the two which makes sexuality a crucial issue for feminists. . . . The social distinction and hierarchical relationship between men and women profoundly affect our sexual lives. This is true not only for those of us who are heterosexual: lesbian and gay sexualities are also shaped by wider understandings of masculinity and femininity, as are heterosexual attitudes to other sexualities— for example, the idea that lesbians are not "real women." Gender and sexuality intersect with other social divisions such as those based on "race" and class, so that we each live our sexuality from different locations within society.[13] Hence women's experiences of both gender and sexuality are highly variable. Feminists have sought to understand both what we share in common as women and the differences between us. In the context of the women's movement, which aims to advance the interests of all women, these differences have become a crucial, and often highly contentious, issue. (Jackson and Scott 2–3)

Thus the study of sexuality, whether male or female, translates into the study of gender relations because of the normative role played by heterosexuality in most societies' attitudes toward the libidinal body. But this genderedness does not entirely explain why female sexuality should be so strongly correlated with themes of freedom in literary discourse since the 1960s.

Indeed, the normative role played by heterosexuality is always an incursion of power and the opposite of freedom. It limits human beings to the socially held, culturally defined parameters for the practice of sex and gender, by each sex. Power at all levels employs sex and gender categorizations for the control of subjects. For instance, authors Caroline Ramazanoglu and Janet Holland made a study of young women and the risk of AIDS, concluding: "When young women say yes to sex, they say yes to power differently from their male sexual partners. Both are caught in the general deployment of heterosexuality, but they are situated differently within it" (255–56). By deployment of sexuality Ramazanoglu and Holland mean the injunction to produce a discourse of sex, which is the opposite of repression. They conclude that Foucault's theory of power and discourse "enables us to find young women working hard at silencing their own desires, and supporting masculine domination of sexuality, through their careful constructions of feminine selves" (260). To quote Jackson and Scott again: "heterosexuality is constructed around a hierarchy of gender evident in its specifically sexual practices as elsewhere. Lesbianism is a potential escape from this, a more pleasurable and less risky [i.e., involving less direct risk of violence by men] alternative, yet lesbians are not immune from the heterosexual ordering of desire which shapes all our sexualities. What counts as erotic is itself socially constructed in terms of relations of dominance, to the extent that it is difficult even to think of sex outside of the patriarchal language and culture which shape our thoughts, desires and fantasies" (Jackson and Scott 17). Judith Butler has denominated gender and sexual categories "regulatory fictions," that is, socially constructed identities which appear essential and necessary, but which in fact are shifting and shiftable; given to each of us, but capable of being adopted; authentic within certain contexts for each of us and yet capable of being discarded by the same person within other contexts.[14]

Kadiatu Kanneh explains how heterosexuality can have an ambivalent effect on the complex and shifting meaning of identity for individuals, as either negative or positive:

> Feminism's response to heterosexuality has repeatedly been to dismiss it, to criticize it as a neutral or normalizing area, as a threat to women, as akin to capitalism and male dominance. The other story

which remains almost in the guise of feminism's guilty shadow, is that of solidarity with a community, loyalty to a history which still needs, cries out, to be honored. I think of the black and white lesbians whose emotional suffering rests on their feeling of exile from fathers, brothers, mothers, the warmth of familial acceptance, the joy of staying with ease within the boundaries of home. I am also . . . necessarily reminded of those women, like myself, who feel caught between two contradictory heritages, coerced alternatively into the context of one or the other, disqualified from forming an identity in harmony with both. The politics of identity do, of course, involve a mass of contradictions, lived as shocks and moments of acute anxiety, invisibility, that sickness of standing at one remove from the body. A mixed-race identity reads as a contradiction in terms. (Kanneh 173)

In Latin America, Kanneh's perspective, in which competing family, race, and community identities vie with each other and with that of gender, has largely predominated. In fact, class and race have usually prevailed over gender as the social variables of power located in its discourses of control and of resistance. At the same time, the problems of sexual violence, heterosexist coercion, and so forth have been central to Latin American women's search for social justice in this century.[15] Among Latin America's activists for women, there was a recognition that intimate relations with men placed women at risk, either from those men, or from her society. Precisely due to the vitality of family and community for women, activists worked with knowledge of the bidirectionality of this equation, the ambivalent charge of sexuality for women. In addition, the Latin American fictional image of heterosexuality—since the widely distributed novels before the late 1980s all ignore or hide lesbian activity, except in brief segments—as either dangerous to her world or dangerous to her, coincides with the analysis of large segments of North American feminists: "Heterosexuality has always been risky for women, whether in terms of the double standard and fears of loss of 'reputation' or of pregnancy, disease, violence and coercion" (Jackson and Scott 17).

Hence it is not the nature of either sexuality or gender differentiation that provided '60s radicals and writers with utopian visions of sex as a symbol of social change, but rather the comprehension that this situation of normative power could be altered. When Angel Rama found a link between women's liberation and female sexuality in the short stories in *Aquí la mitad del amor,* he recognized that the connection is not philosophically necessary; there certainly exist many discourses of female sexuality which are not empowering at all and only acrobatically can even be related to feminism. However, Rama writes, the chosen stories "progressively reveal to us women's independence, acquired after a struggle—one demanded and required—the Otherness of the amorous relation, the mirror broken into slivers" ["van develándonos, progresivamente, la independencia duramente adquirida, la requisitoria, la otredad de la relación amorosa, el espejo hecho añicos" (Rama 8)]. The ideas here are at least threefold. First, those stories portrayed love in the experience of women as distinguished from that of men. Second, the stories describe love as it relates to women's liberation, or female emancipation from masculine domination. Third, women's "independence" was paradoxically revealed in the joining of woman and man in sexual love; difference (from a masculine center, standard, or point of view) appeared in love's "broken mirror." The ideology of love given in female subjectivity conflicts with the ideology of patriarchy. Thus female sexuality has a special ability to reveal chinks in society's masculinist armor.

In literature, there is a movement whereby female sexuality becomes generalized into a representative female experience, a stand-in for many other aspects of women's lives not deriving from the female role in reproduction, but rather from the webs of association that cultures spin around reproductive functions in historical moments. The tendency to which I am referring is not the gender-transcending one by which the characteristics of sexuality found in men are assumed to apply to women, or vice versa. The generalizing process in fiction which usually occurs in fictions of female sexuality compares a woman's sex life to her whole life. Often a female character's sexuality defines literally and limits her socioeconomic status, as when a youthful heterosexual episode produces a child and thus changes the woman's life unequivocally. She usually becomes the (sole) caretaker of the child and may also lose her parental support, her employment, her home, or all three. Most often, however, sex for a woman character functions as a symbol. Her sexuality—its timidity or vociferousness, its attention to a single object or openness to serial lovers, her sexual victimization by others or sexual cruelty to them—not only defines her character and experience, but also provides the import and meaning of her story in society outside the novel. This type of generalization from sexual narrative to social ideology can happen for male characters, too, but for them, the likelihood is that his sexuality will be generalized to some social belief vis-à-vis all humanity, rather than to one pertaining only to his sex.

Furthermore, since female sexuality, like male sexuality, clearly remits to biological sex differences, and because female sexuality, unlike male sexuality, is so frequently generalized to comment on gendered life experiences rather than the human qualities of a character, it may become a metaphor for feminist issues of sexual inequality or female empowerment.

While meditating on the importance of Roland Barthes's ideas of the "pleasure of the text" and the *jouissance* of reading, Fredric Jameson distinguishes between pleasure that is progressive and political versus that which is neither. The difficulties inherent in distinguishing political and apolitical conceptions of pleasure that Jameson seeks to explain are crucial. The latter is "comfort, and comfortable, in Barthes' pejorative sense," that is, a "vision of bodily pleasure that . . . is not . . . a Utopian vision of another way of living," and which treats "my individual relationship with my own body—which is to say with Earth (Heidegger) or with what used to be called Nature." In contrast, progressive and political pleasure is concerned with "that very different relationship between myself or my body and other people—or, in other words, with History, with the political in the stricter sense" ("Pleasure" 70). Jameson continues:

> Whence the troublesome unruliness of the sexual question. Is it only that comfortable material question, or is it more irredeemably scandalous—as in sexual "ecstacy" (the strongest translation of Barthesian *jouissance*), or in that even more somber matter of the will to power in sexual domination? These are harder "pleasures" to domesticate, their political content more easily assimilable to religions, or fascism—yet another "pleasure," this last! Therapeutic puritanism thus seems to impose itself again; yet before embracing it, it may be desirable to see what happens if we try to historicize these dilemmas, and the experiences that produced them. Is not, for example, the aesthetics of ecstacy, Barthesian *jouissance,* a properly '60s experience? (71)

In other words, to the extent that even pleasure—the apparently unpolitical component of sexuality—resists the passivity of middle-class comfort and edges toward radical states and actions of the libidinous body in society, pleasure can be a political issue within a historical context: "Maybe indeed the deeper subject is here: not pleasure (against whose comfort and banalities everyone from Barthes to Edmund Burke is united in warning us), but the libidinal body itself, and *its* peculiar politics, which may well move in a realm largely beyond the pleasurable in that narrow, culinary, bourgeois sense" (69; emphasis Jameson's). Thus the politics of pleasure, like the politics of sexuality (i.e., within discourses of sex) and of the libidinal body are only visible within their historical and cultural contexts.

Many critics of literature rely on Michel Foucault for his analysis of microrelations of power or for his refutation of the Repressive Hypothesis (by which repressive power largely seeks to silence sexuality), but they frequently forget he wrote not a timeless theory but a *history*. Foucault's many insights and methodological innovations pervade modern theoretical analyses in many disciplines; for this book, however, it is most important that he argued that sexuality appears differently across time and place. Is this obvious today? Perhaps. But it also seems difficult to remember that in analyses of sexuality we are never speaking of timeless universals or essentials. Our subject matter is concrete discourses and discursive practices related to (also changing) biological and psychosexual realms. A society which considers certain bodies male or female, young or old, healthy or sick, one of its own or foreign to its community, following its own definitions and concepts, will become modified in time or will be modulated in contrast to other societies at the same time. The realm of the political is the conflictive, conflicted, and conflicting space of power relations within and among societies; sexuality that is political is a social issue. The criticism and fiction I discuss here are thus intended as examples of historical moments; they represent discourses on sexual pleasure and sexual pain as a political issue.

For instance, in *El arte de amar: El hombre* by Bosco and others, psychotherapist Eva Giberti concludes that Argentine men in the 1960s are "creating a form of love, of man-woman relation, much more free, less rigid and stereotyped; less in function of others and more in accordance with itself" ["creando una forma de amor, de relación hombre-mujer mucho más suelta, menos rígida y estereotipada; menos en función de los otros y más de acuerdo con él mismo" (40)]. According to Giberti, in the past, traditional Argentine men needed to exhibit their manhood ("hombría") in public sexual aggression toward women, whereas 1960s men ("el hombre actual") are more sincere, more loving, and better partners for Argentine women. The essay in *Prostibulario*, the other 1967 Merlín anthology mentioned above, provides a second perspective on this period of sexual transition in Argentina. Written by tango composer Cátulo Castillo, the text provides a nostalgic look at his adolescent visits to brothels, when he says he was still "unprejudiced" and "unworried about hygiene." Castillo's youthful explorations of the red-light district are told with affection, and his ruminations about the past lack any conception of the economic plight, health risks, and legal purgatory suffered by many of the women who provide paid sexual services to men. His goals appear to be to give what he believes to be an "honest" and "objective" view while entertaining the (presumed male) reader. Without any awareness of male complicity in the poor conditions in which prostitutes live and work, Castillo discusses—in the tone of "isn't this interesting"—international attempts to regulate the actions and movements of prostitutes, marketing ploys used by madams, and then gives a brief descriptive typology of Argentine *prostíbulos, quilombos, franeleros, chichisbeos, clandestinos,* and so forth in the preceding fifty years. Most important, Castillo details the customs of his youth as if prostitution were a throwback to a bygone age, as if it were disappearing (whereas it was merely changing). In his essay the paid female prostitute gains an aura of quaintness, viewed from afar by a generation of elder gentlemen and their supposedly liberated readers.

In Castillo's essay, a discourse of "liberated sexuality" and of the counterculture is present, but muted; the new sexuality is assumed to have convinced readers that male recourse to whores as a widespread cultural practice in Latin America would gradually die a natural death as more and more young women of the middle classes (in capitals like Buenos Aires, at least) act on their sexual desires.[16] Unfortunately, neither female prostitution nor the negative consequences of unmarried pregnancies disappeared with the advent of sexual permissiveness in large cities in the 1960s. Indeed, the enduring imperviousness of traditional bastions of male sexual power in Latin America have contributed to continuing female sexuality's place as a favored literary topic for social critique of the status quo. Narratives about sexual women are a discursive weapon wielded by a variety of writers because these stories highlight injustices in diverse circumstances.

Sexuality (not just female sexuality) serves easily as a theme of social critique in Latin American fiction for additional reasons. First, with its rich linguistic repertoire of allusions, insinuations, slang, and metaphor, sexual discourse provides the novel with new words for fighting ideological battles grown stale. Second, as Doris Sommer (in *Foundational Fictions*) and others have shown, the Latin American canonical novel long before the 1960s had already been involved in discursive struggles involving gender, race, and ethnicity through romance in quite sophisticated ways.[17] Third, in "Notes on the Presentation of Sexuality in the Modern Spanish American Novel" (1982), D. L. Shaw speculates that sexuality became important in Latin America in the 1960s because of the "falling fortunes of the old novel of protest in Latin America. Head-on criticism seems to have failed" (281).[18] Writers searching for alternative means of addressing concerns of poverty or injustice fell upon the new mode of sexuality, because sex's halo of unchanging biological naturalness had been summarily removed by the sexual rebellion taking place in urban centers of Latin America. In countries where censorship was strong or the risk to an author was great if a critique took direct aim at a dictatorship or entrenched interests, as was frequently the case with the repressive regimes of the Southern Cone in the 1970s, sexuality allowed writers to criticize the state or the elites from a position of relative safety, since censors often missed the metaphorical and lateral social commentary in sexual fiction.

Additionally, sexual themes since the 1960s have appeared to have the potential to question traditional sexual ethics, and thus ethics in general by extension. In other words, not only could the same issues be addressed with new words and in a new and safer way, but also new issues altogether could be the target of sexual fictions. Female sexuality had the further possibility of specifically protesting against or reflecting upon women's condition. Awareness among intellectuals of the way gender has negatively affected woman in her sexual life spread rapidly in Latin America, as it did elsewhere, after World War II. The increasing understanding of gender as not given and eternal but historical and cultural had immediate importance for (re)interpreting social phenomena like sexual practices and the discourses about them, both fictional and nonfictional. Given the political adroitness and ideological sophistication of novelists in the region, they sometimes were more ready than their First World counterparts to question the most simplistic versions of liberal personal politics of 1968 and the student movements. In their fiction, Latin Americans often would combine identity politics with an analysis of class and struggles for power at a variety of contested sites. The Latin American intellectual, male and female, already adept at contextualizing, hybridizing, and modernizing concerns about race, gender, and imperialism, could see gender as never entirely separate from those other identifications.

A Backward Glance

The specialist can never tackle eroticism. Of all problems eroticism is
the most mysterious, the most general and the least straightforward.
Georges Bataille, *Erotism*[19] (273)

In 1969 Argentine author Julio Cortázar published an essay ("/que sepa
abrir la puerta para ir a jugar") in which he asks why there has never been
a Latin American Henry Miller, Georges Bataille, or Jean Genet. The Latin
American writer, according to Cortázar, has been "impeded, except in the
poem form, which is privileged territory and does not replace narrative
except for reasons of failure, timidity, or hypocrisy, from making the formal and expressive leap toward the conquest and illustration of an eroticism of the word (*el verbo*), toward its natural and necessary incorporation; not only does this incorporation not debase the language of desire
and of love, rather it forces eroticism to change from its mistaken condition as a special topic at certain times and to articulate within the structure
of personal and collective life, in a more legitimate conception of the
world, of politics, of art, the profound pulsations that move the sun and
the other stars."[20] In Cortázar's view, the stance of avoiding both bourgeois morality and literary decorum had been readily adopted as a goal by
his contemporaries, yet Latin American prose writers had mistakenly
overlooked eroticism as an important avenue of experimentation by
which to achieve this double objective.[21] Cortázar lived abroad most of his
life and understandably could want to cajole Spanish American writers
into forsaking romance for *jouissance*, love for eroticism. Nevertheless,
his great influence as a novelist and critic has led early commentators to
overemphasize the undeniable if limited importation of foreign models for
sexual fiction. In fact, Latin American writers were already moving where
Cortázar wanted them to be; it is not surprising that authors whose literary canon involved a strong tradition of romance as the mode for fiction-
alizing national dilemmas should move from love themes to those of sex
and pleasure in a period of postnational capitalism and consumerism. The
Boom novel, a phenomenon beginning in the 1960s and 1970s, numbers
among the many indicators of the increasing internationalization of Latin
American culture. Additionally, Latin Americans have usually been more
knowledgeable about European and North American literatures than
their counterparts about Latin American culture. These factors—the tradition of romance, the new if spotty Latin American "postmodern condition," and the Latin American knowledge of cultural trends in the First

World—have led others, independently of Cortázar, to ignore the Latin American antecedents of '60s sexual fiction.

Most Latin American novelists and thinkers legitimately have felt the novel was and is an opportunity to make a difference, to take a stand; they have worried that the chance might be squandered frivolously on tales of unpolitical sexual pleasure or comfort. The best novels in Spanish America were expected to interpret significant political dilemmas, or at least to have the potential for participating in debates that mattered to a group rather than an individual, and not be primarily about apolitical physical intimacies. Before the realization that sexuality too could be a discourse of social critique, eroticism was bound to be less favored than love, but it was not ignored. The pleasures of reading as *transgressive* pleasures passed unperceived below the political register, much as were what today are called "personal politics," "micropolitics," or the "politics of the everyday." Eroticism was still avant-garde style experimentation for Latin American prose writers, according to Cortázar, because they lacked a native tradition of erotic prose to imitate. Certainly, the prose tradition most critics and authors do acknowledge leans toward a seriousness of political intent.

Like Cortázar, the brief introduction to *Cuentos de nunca acabar* [Never-ending stories](1988), a reference to the *Arabian Nights*, fails to recognize Latin American precedents; the precursors of eroticism mentioned by name in this anthology of erotic prose are not from Latin America: Guillaume Apollinaire, Louis Aragon, D. H. Lawrence, and Pauline Réage.[22] Though some Latin American authors could read these writers in English or French easily, the translations into Spanish which made Miller, Bataille, and other writers of sexuality easily available largely began only in the 1960s, when sexual themes already had a strong literary foothold. Georges Bataille appeared in 1964 from Sur in Argentina, and Henry Miller's novels, one after another, were best-sellers there during the same decade.[23] Today a large group of Latin American prose writers younger than Cortázar has tried its hand at telling sexy, artful stories after reading in translation D. H. Lawrence, Henry Miller, Georges Bataille, Jean Genet, or Anaïs Nin. But if these foreign models were the exclusive or primary genealogy of the erotic in Latin American fiction, then sexual fiction would have had its mass beginnings only in the 1970s. In fact, it began earlier and came from a variety of sources, including the foreign novelists mentioned.

In preparing the public and publishers to accept novels by women originally written in Spanish or Portuguese, the role of female foreign literary models, such as the Euro-American Anaïs Nin and the French Pauline Réage (Dominique Aury), has been more tangential than those by foreign men. Since women writers had special reasons to avoid *realist* fictions of female sexuality (the scandal of autobiographical taint), Nin and Réage, two writers of autobiographical (or supposedly autobiographical) fictions were doubly transgressive because they defied both the literary norms of sexual prose by placing female subjectivity at the center of the fiction, and the woman writer's historic need for distance and caution when treating female sexuality. Latin American women have rarely accepted this auto-biographical baton, and when looking abroad have instead fixed upon surrealist or avant-garde models of fictive complexity and irreality for their own erotic works.

In Cortázar's brief consideration of eroticism in Spanish American literature, he notes that erotic poetry, but not erotic prose, has already been widely recognized as constituting a major Latin American form. To a great extent, it is the neglected, early importance of erotic and sexual poetry in Latin America, added to the tradition of romance in prose, that explains how sophisticated treatments of the subject could suddenly appear in prose within a decade or two, from many different writers, separated by thousands of miles, personal styles, political goals, and national literary traditions. Rosario Castellanos—a feminist and a female member of the Mexican Generation of 1950—exemplifies this typical Latin American allocation of eroticism to poetry and its avoidance in prose. Audacious in form and subject, Castellanos's poetry comfortably plays with sex and sexual vocabulary in poems like "Ninfomanía" [Nymphomania] (284) and "Kinsey Report" (112–15; 317–19T). "Ninfomanía" speaks in the first-person using metaphors of sexual voracity and desire; "Kinsey Report" invents responses from wives and single women, heterosexuals and lesbians, virgins and sexually active women, to questions about sex in interview format. Castellanos's play "The Eternal Feminine"(1988; *El eterno femenino* 1975), a hybrid pastiche of poetry and prose, spares no one in its farcical treatment of honeymooners and prostitutes. In Castellanos's short stories, essays, and novels, however, the critical power of her sarcasm, irony, and black humor leave little room for *eros ludens*. Her prose takes aim at targets like machismo, ethnic and religious prejudice, and poverty as causes of female suffering. But sexual pleasure for women characters, certainly, and for men, usually, is silenced. As a woman writer, Castellanos had reasons for keeping explicit sexual themes from her realistic prose fiction, because as a professor and diplomat it was a weapon that could backfire and injure her reputation. But if we are to trace the broad outlines of a history of sexual prose by women as well as men, it is important to recognize, as Cortázar did, that poets, even women poets, treated sexual themes extensively before the 1960s began to open prose to these themes on a large scale.

In fact, the fiction that lies on the frontier between poetry and prose—lyric fiction—provides counterexamples to Cortázar's chronology for the Latin American prose erotic. An important work of this sort is *House of Mist* (1947; *La última niebla* 1935) by María Luisa Bombal (Chile, 1910–1980). Bombal's writing imbues Daniel's unloved, unattractive wife, whom those around her see as asexual, with an unsuspected sexual dimension. The unnamed heroine experiences strong sexual desire for years by remembering a single night with an anonymous, casual lover. Poetically evoked, the lover's absence is lamented constantly, making him ever present in the novel. Marriage without love causes the protagonist to see the lover in the embers of a fire and to feel him in the touch of plants in a forest pool. The early certainty of her memory of the sexual encounter gradually erodes, though, into an uncertainty about her lover's existence. This erotic novel is known today in feminist criticism as a classic early work that dared to transgress against the mores of marriage. Certainly the novel protested against the need for women of a certain class to marry, and against the lack of women's rights within marriage. *House of Mist* also suggests that men may not have control over their wives' sexualities even when the women outwardly conform. The significance of these issues was great for women of wealth, and thus for early-twentieth-century women writers who tended to come from this class.

The protagonist of *House of Mist* is a sexual woman punished for the "crimes" of sex: rejected by her society, victimized within her community, and defeated by her antagonists within the novel. Ultimately, her sexual pleasure is tied to her feelings of self-worth; her powers of imagination allow her to keep alive the hope that love from a man would validate her as a person worth loving. Her "crimes" against bourgeois morality are given a sympathetic rendering. Unlike the ironic Brazilian intellectual Mário de Andrade, or Mexican nationalist Federico Gamboa, who also wrote early novels of female sexuality, Bombal portrays female sexuality as Sapphic, bittersweet passion: society in *House of Mist* is configured as desiring individuals rather than groups with political or historical or class characteristics. Female sexual pleasure is the redeemed treasure denied in woman's abstention, passivity, and self-sacrifice; it compensates her for her social devaluation and isolation. Consequently, the novel's sexual ideology and politics of gender run counter to a politics of masculine domination. As I have argued elsewhere, the action of the novella, the "case" it argues, is, minimally, in favor of the recognition of women's desires, and maximally, in favor of female sexual liberation.[24] Without ever being able to imitate sister-in-law Regina's defiance of social propriety, Bombal's protagonist envies Regina, who had had a lover and attempted suicide for love (like Bombal herself).[25] Female sexuality here is dangerous to women, since both Regina and the protagonist are led to attempt suicide by the force of their desire.

At the time Julio Cortázar advocated for fiction the new road of eroticism, he probably aimed to set up a broad series of contrasts between a time earlier than the date when he was writing (1969) and the future. In so doing, I suspect he merely sacrificed exceptions like Bombal to this time line in the name of a clean and simple program for young writers. His essay's oversimplifications have also been noted by other critics who, like myself, agree with the basic lines of Cortázar's assessment, but disagree with specific points. In a 1979 article, Juan Bruce-Novoa took both Cortázar and the Mexican poet and essayist Octavio Paz to task for denying "the existence of erotic prose in Latin American writing" prior to 1970. Bruce-Novoa cites the prose writings of the Generation of 1950 in Mexico (Juan García Ponce, José Agustín, Gustavo Sainz, Salvador Elizondo, Inés Arredondo, Rosario Castellanos, and others) as evidence of a slightly earlier tradition. Still, Bruce-Novoa agrees that Spanish American erotic *narrative* is new to the second half of this century and that, when he was writing in 1979, it still struggled for recognition in Mexico as a body of literature of importance.[26]

In addition to the lyrical novel, another optic that allows one to find novels of female sexuality from before the Generation of 1950 is the avant-garde, like the intellectual, novels by Mário de Andrade (Brazil, 1893–1945) and Armonía Somers (Uruguay, 1920–1994). While both Andrade and Somers have connections to poetry, their novels are not truly lyrical. A third kind of exception needs to be made for Rachel de Queiroz (Brazil, b. 1910), whose protest against woman's inequality in sexual matters is central to her sociological novels.[27] Maria's self-induced miscarriage in *The Three Marias* (1963; *As três Marias*, Brazil, 1939) by Queiroz dramatizes the unequal treatment of the sexes. A boy and a girl have made love, but the girl suffers all the negative consequences.

The way sex is put into writing by these three novelists (Andrade, Somers, and Queiroz) is better categorized as the more general "sexuality" rather than as eroticism. These novels share a very modern yoking of sex and feminist issues, less from any lyric borrowings than from their head-on attack on literary tradition, middle-class mores, and the "sanctity" of femininity. The women writers, Somers and Queiroz, shared the desire to speak of love with a woman's voice. All three discovered ways to wield women's sexuality as a weapon to broadside what they saw as society's ills. To fully understand them, and their contemporary progeny, we need to consider female sexuality within the (largely but not exclusively poetic) avant-garde movements in Latin America, that is, within Brazilian Modernismo and Spanish American *vanguardismo*. For our purposes here, it is enough to note that nonpoetic female sexuality occurred in earlier novels nearly always for some of the same reasons the avant-garde in general came to the fore: the relentless search for the new, which supplanted the idea of perpetuating a tradition. Internationally, the avant-garde shares an iconoclastic mindset and a rejection of the generation preceding it, as Poggioli suggested in *The Theory of the Avant-Garde,* and Latin America was no exception.

In "More Notes on the Presentation of Sexuality in the Modern Spanish American Novel," Donald L. Shaw argues that for Spanish-speaking America, sexuality comes to be treated first as a reaction to Modernism. According to Shaw, the key figure is the Argentine Roberto Arlt (1900–1942), and the characterizing feature or correlative theme for most early writers of sexuality is violence and venality to parody religiosity and the Modernist idea of finding a soul mate when in love. My hypothesis that themes of female sexuality come from writers of anticanonical, antimoral, and avant-garde tendencies thus finds confirmation in Shaw's idea that there was a "virtual abandonment of references to sexuality as a means of conveying moral commentary" (126). In my Chapter 2, on a late novel by Miguel Angel Asturias, surrealism and the pursuit of avant-garde goals are shown to have left their mark on his treatment of female sexuality, even as late as the 1960s.

Where the history of female sexuality in Brazilian literature differs from the Spanish American, and where women writers differ from men, can often be seen in the way in which the avant-garde (and later its legacy) is embraced. For instance, Shaw finds "Many of Arlt's major characters share the yearning of the *modernistas* for the ideal as a counterbalance to anguish, but they utterly reject [Rubén] Darío's notion that the best way to find it was to 'unir carne y alma'" ["unite flesh and soul"] (116). However, when Shaw writes that there was a "general tendency to react against the *modernista* exaltation of sexuality as a road to new perceptions either about the self or the human condition. Sexual behavior as leading to self-liberation exists as a theme in the Boom, but only as a minority phenomenon, and even then it tends to be divorced from love" (126), he means male sexuality: the experiences of male characters. The treatment of sexuality in literature, in most literatures, is almost always gendered, and the gender most often treated is the male. When one speaks of "sexuality," then, it is important to consider this difference, or we may subsume female sexuality as a "minority phenomenon," which purely numerically it was. Female sexuality was less frequent in literature, and its distinct history has yet to be told. We shall see in the Brazilian work treated in chapter 3 and in the Peruvian Boom novel in chapter 4 that women's sexuality offers a utopian space for imagining a different world, in contrast to male sexuality used as a bludgeon to remind the reader of the problems of the world we do live in. When novels stop addressing questions of how the sexual woman lives the delicate balance of love and marriage in the domestic novel, in order to ask how sex unbalances the gender contract, they are likely to be pursuing avant-garde aesthetics and themes.

In Brazilian Modernism, even more than in Spanish American Vanguardism (its closest historical parallel), writers had a decidedly playful attitude, and welcomed the sexual quite early into a game of shocking the staid and the proper. As early as 1927, the important Brazilian intellectual Mário de Andrade called his first novel, an experimental work about clandestine prostitution, *Amar, verbo intransitivo, um idílio* [To love, an intransitive verb, an idyll]. By this title, Andrade appeals to our sense of humor, our appreciation of irony, and above all our skepticism because *to love* is not usually an intransitive verb.[28] Considered as a group of terms (love, desire, eroticism, sex, sexuality, and sexual practice), *to love* and its cognates normally express relations between desiring subjects and love objects; in the grammar of human activity, they function like prepositions to define relations to love objects, even when those relations may be narcissistic, masturbatory, or metaphorical. Despite Andrade's playful assertion in his title, loving at its best is transitive: there is both a lover and a beloved. Fraulein, Andrade's prostitute protagonist, for instance, makes love to little boys. The relational nature (the "transitivity") of sexuality, love, and eroticism in prose fiction is, indeed, the very structure that permits sexuality to become a metaphor of choice for other social and political relations in the novels I examine here. The displacement of gender issues to those of race and class can occur because sexuality is a micro-relation of power. If we consider this first half of the twentieth century, we find that authors who treated female sexuality seriously and at length usually signaled structural inequalities in other features of identity at the same time.

Nonerotic female sexuality in fiction had appeared frequently in Latin America before the 1960s in the figure of the prostitute. Naturalist treatments were common, and important canonical novels throughout the twentieth century exhibit traces of nineteenth-century scientism. The prostitute's place in society, furthermore, favored her character as a metaphor for the abusive, intimate relations between classes and ethnicities. This displacement of female sexuality onto other issues often occurred as allegory. In *Santa* (1903; the title is the protagonist's name) by the Mexican Federico Gamboa, for instance, a poor, young country girl named Santa has a miscarriage and is thrown out of her home. The victim of a calculated seduction by a soldier who quickly abandons her, Santa is ignorant and isolated. Her innocence foments her feelings of guilt and anger so that she sees only suicide or prostitution as her options. Either way she can satisfy her wish to punish herself. Mexico City's brothels welcome the pretty, dark-complexioned newcomer, first with degradation and marginality, afterwards with disease, poverty, and a slow, painful death. The novel pleads for Santa and for what she represents, Mexico City, both being devoured by the venal appetites of foreigners and the white ruling class. A social conservative, Gamboa idealizes love and religious belief, using Santa's descent as a moral parable of their inefficacy against the twin evils of sexuality unconsecrated by marriage and of hypocrisy within the churchgoing community. Largely ignored by Mexican critics since the Revolution (until recently), the novel has not only survived but been perennially popular with the reading public.[29]

In *Foundational Fictions,* Doris Sommer has pointed to the role of love in the canonical Latin American novels of the nineteenth and early twentieth centuries. Within the conventions of romance, love served the allegorizing needs of nation-building from at least as early as the nineteenth century. Marriage has continued to serve allegorizing functions, particularly in popular novels, because of continuing assumptions idealizing the union of male and female as "natural" opposites, capable of loving each other and producing a new American genesis: "Sexual love was the trope for associative behavior, unfettered market relationships, and for Nature in general" (Sommer 35). When the conventions of romance are abandoned for the experimentation of the avant-garde in the early twentieth century (at different times and in different ways in each country), sexuality does not become less important in the novel. Instead, the literary uses to which sex is put diversifies; no widely held social ideal of love or marriage confers upon the novel a unifying function in society. Sexuality also becomes a weapon with which to combat social convention and conservatism. It becomes fundamental for holdouts of naturalism, and for rebels like surrealists, neorealists, and feminists. ✓

Returning to *Amar, verbo intransitivo* from 1927, we see that Mário de Andrade points an accusatory finger both at oligarchic traditions and privilege and at the foreigners who come to Latin America in search of economic fortune, through his prostitute protagonist, Fraulein. *Amar* is set around the time *Santa* was published (the beginning of the twentieth century). Fraulein is a German immigrant who works as a live-in tutor to children of the landowning oligarchy. In addition to lessons in German and music, her job is to initiate the eldest son Carlos in the ways of love. She manipulates the boy—all for his own good, according to his father and to Fraulein. She deludes herself and seeks to convince others that her employment is a disinterested social service to the moneyed classes. Her erotic desires serve the goals of the traditional patriarchal family, to her mind, by educating sexually and thus molding the character of the scions of the richest families. Since Fraulein sleeps exclusively with virgins, the boy's first experience in sexual love can be without disease; since she will not run away with the boy or marry him, it is without public scandal. If she is to receive her bonus pay from his father, she merely leaves quietly after being "discovered."

In *Amar* as in *Santa,* prostitution is a social evil in and of itself, and it also constitutes a symbolization of the corruption and self-serving values of the middle class and the rich. Whereas Santa was no match for the society that ravished her, for the *señoritos* who made love to her then denied her in public, for the godless corruption of Mexico City, Fraulein coldly calculates the money she will make from seducing the next boy in order to be able to stop her "moonlighting" and return home to Germany. Unlike Gamboa's focus on Santa's victimization by more experienced and more powerful men, young Carlos is Fraulein's victim. Fraulein's sexual pleasure is intended to shock readers; she is a stern German tutor, a purveyor of strict morality and a believer in marital fidelity for women only. Prostitution in *Amar* is portrayed as an option for an unscrupulous, educated career woman, which to her regret leaves her marginalized, lonely, and without long-term employment. New families must inevitably be found and she must keep herself attractive to the boys even as she ages, to be able to win them to her bed. Implicated most especially in this ironic, Modernist critique of a "love idyll," even more than Fraulein herself, are Carlos's parents and a materialist and sexist society that could produce this philosophy regarding the benefits of a live-in prostitute, while ignoring the costs to the boy and his teacher.

The images of prostitutes that predominate in Boom novelists like Colombian Gabriel García Márquez, Brazilian Jorge Amado, and Peruvian Mario Vargas Llosa verge on the nostalgic and the anachronistic, and often occur within the special spaces of an underworld or a rural setting reminiscent of earlier times. The character of the sexually liberated woman, who may serve Fraulein's initiatory function for males without charging for her services, has, correspondingly, been on the rise. This change may explain in part why other kinds of transgressive sexuality successfully compete with prostitution as the predominant form of female sexuality in Boom texts. This increase in the frequency of the sexual woman character who does not charge may also help us to understand why in the return to realism in post-Boom novels prostitutes are often relegated to the hyperrealist hybrid form of the testimonial novel. Another reason is that post-Boom novels are much more often authored by women. In *Easy Women,* Debra Castillo notes that "the interest in fictional loose women has spilled over into a parallel publishing boomlet in the *testimonios* of actual loose women" in Mexico beginning in the 1970s (258 n. 2). The protest element of prostitution narratives can easily be salvaged in the *testimonio,* whereas in the fictions about the unpaid female sexual transgressor broader social problems are critiqued less directly. The rapes and seductions in post-Boom writer Isabel Allende, for example, still point to the problems of repressive societies where poverty and political repressions persist, but prostitution is not the primary way actively sexual women appear. Other works, like *One Hundred Years of Solitude* (1968; *Cien años de soledad* 1967) by Boom writer García Márquez, serve as cautionary tales against the new forms of female sexuality. They are "master" narratives warning that if women's desires are heeded the family and community are at risk. In the final chapters of *One Hundred Years of Solitude,* a "newly sexed woman" and her equally perverse partner abandon their baby, who is devoured by ants, and Macondo is finally destroyed.

In the antibourgeois intellectual climate of modernism and postmodernism, failed marriages often symbolize the inability of a given society to cohere without the violent repression of some elements. Sexuality as distinct from marriage and love indicates a rebellious, unconfined, dissenting, transgressive, uncontrolled, or uncontrollable spirit. Rather than a romantic union of male and female, where gender differences achieve harmony or at least stasis, gender difference in recent works about female sexuality is magnified and reflected back upon itself, so that each woman is not only supremely different from each man, but also her alliance with a man is no longer in her interest or an unquestioned norm. A female character's sexual experiences criticize marriage more and more frequently as a limitation on her actions. Furthermore, the "newly sexed woman" is portrayed as different from other women, especially from women of the past. Indeed, the most radical thinkers caught up in the illusions of the sexual liberation craze of the 1960s and 1970s predicted, in addition to the demise of prostitution, the end of marriage. Márcia Denser's precipitate words on the end of feminism as a movement, that "the eighties are the time for the individual," can also be understood to mean that women in erotic fiction are not marrying or choosing long-term partners. A signal of modernity, the "newly sexed woman" character verges on intransitivity as she seeks a way to secure her desired autonomy and freedoms.

During the first half of this century, however, the sexual woman character in Latin American novels metonymically represented a social group made up of victims or victimizers. She was a pitiful prostitute, like Santa, or a devouring one who threatens the male hero, like Fraulein. Santa exemplified the poor and the darker-skinned people who toiled in the countryside; Fraulein, the European immigrant. This novelistic lineage rejected sexual women characters as builders of the nation but could not resist a fascination with their story. The sexual woman was a symptom of a "problem," an illness in the social body. More than any other novel, Rómulo Gallegos's extremely popular *Doña Bárbara* (Venezuela, 1929) engages ideologically with the kind of dangerous threat to Latin American society the sexual woman was thought to represent. The moral superiority of the male hero, Santos Luzardo, is attributed to a "civilizing influence," à la Sarmiento, in contrast to her wild barbarism. Even though Bárbara is said to be a lusty man-slayer, her pleasure (or her daughter Marisela's) is never a focus of the writing. Bárbara's sexuality looms large as a feared evil; it is alluded to as a part of her past that haunts her in the present. The barbarous representative of the savage land and people needing a civilizing (male) authority, Bárbara criminally pursues her pleasures and destroys the society in which she steals and kills. She is a Dionysian maenad opposed to the Apollinian Pentheus, with the values reversed from those of Euripides.

Unlike Euripides' (and Nietzsche's) profound philosophical respect for the Bacchae and the death religions they represent, Gallegos's Venezuelan "tragedy" disdains the old religion incarnated in female frenzy in favor of Santos Luzardo's law of light and reason. By his mere presence, Santos Luzardo disables Bárbara's power and mesmerizes her, so instantaneously does Bárbara fall in love. But Santos Luzardo finds her utterly repellent; his distaste is also the narrator's. Ultimately Gallegos writes away the troubling sexuality of his protagonist as a "problem" which if ignored disappears by itself, like Bárbara at the end of the novel, never to be heard of again. Like Athene at the ending of Aeschylus's *Oresteia*, Gallegos's novel is "always for the male . . . and strongly on [the] father's side" (ll.737–39). Yet for many of my students, Bárbara is a victim who could not get justice from laws or people with authority; she was a rape victim, possibly justified, in their opinion, in at least some of her later crimes. For many contemporary readers, Bárbara is both victim and monster: raped and rapist, innocent girl and guilty woman.

D. L. Shaw's comments on the editions of *Doña Bárbara* in his seminal 1982 article "Notes on the Presentation of Sexuality in the Modern Spanish-American Novel" substantiate the great distance between the ubiquitous sexual themes of recent years and the limited representation of the sexual act by women authors previously. Shaw places the New Novel, beginning in the late 1950s and 1960s, against the foil of the Latin American regional novel of between the World Wars, the *novela de la tierra*:

> The 1940s were a time when the *nueva novela* [New Novel] in Spanish America was still in gestation and certain affirmations of the period seem curious: Among these is Luis Alberto Sánchez's remark in his imprescient *América, novela sin novelistas* [America, a novel without novelists](1942) : "There are few men more preoccupied with sex than the South American or even more, the Indian American. However, his literature . . . is asexual. He flees from lecherous topics like an inexpert seminarian who was on a honeymoon with beatitude" ["Hay pocos hombres tan preocupados por el sexo como el sudamericano, o más todavía, el indoamericano. Sin embargo, su literatura . . . es asexual. Se huye de los tópicos lúbricos como lo haría un seminarista inexperto y en primeras nupcias con la beatitud" (29–30)]. To appreciate the basis for Sánchez's view it is perhaps enough to revert to the publication in 1928 of Gallegos's *Doña Bárbara*, probably the most popular of the old *criollista* genre. (275)

In 1942, Luis Alberto Sánchez could categorize the Latin American writer as avoiding sexual themes and as unable to handle them well. Then, and in 1982, Sánchez and Shaw could say the Latin American writer was overwhelmingly male.

Doña Bárbara's sexuality is "uncivilized" and repugnant to the patriarchal values of the novel, values which see female desires as loose cannon needing to be controlled. In his article, Shaw explains why this novel is particularly illustrative of Latin American writers' attitudes:

> If we compare the second, much altered, edition of *Doña Bárbara* (1929) with the first [from 1928], we notice an interesting detail. In the first edition Bárbara kills her husband, Apolinar, in circumstances which leave no doubt as to her sole responsibility for the crime. Later she takes a series of casual lovers from amongst the *peones* on her ranch. When Gallegos came to revise the novel just after its first appearance, he seems to have concluded that he had sacrificed Bárbara's character too much at this point. His reaction was twofold: on the one hand he suppressed the statement that Apolinar was Bárbara's husband, but left the murder itself unchanged; on the other hand he struck out the reference to Bárbara's peasant bedfellows. Bárbara could be a cold-blooded murderess and still be a heroine (indeed, as V. González Reboredo has recently argued, an archetypal heroine), but unchastity was quite unacceptable. (275)

Active female sexuality was unacceptable, more unacceptable than murder, certainly in part because criminality was suitable for a woman who was unmarried and had had a series of lovers. Perhaps most important of all, however, was the unpermittable alliance Bárbara formed with her workers, between herself as a landowner and ranch hands. She has power and authority, conferred on her by her riches in land. To preserve them, she needs to remain aloof, goes the narrative. In contrast, male landowners taking advantage of the wives and daughters of their workers has been an abuse frequently considered by prose fiction and history. One could say it was typical of portrayals of male evil within the hacienda milieu. In relation to the changing figure of the sexual woman protagonist other than the prostitute, Bárbara plays the similar role of lawless criminal. But Bárbara's story had to be edited because the time had not yet come for transgressive female sexuality to be popularly understood as significant— socially symbolic—if she was not a prostitute. Nevertheless, most sexual women characters in pre-1960s novels were outlaws, whether prostitutes or not, at least metaphorically, in that desiring active female sexuality was outside, beyond, off-limits, and punishable.

Carlos Fuentes's novella *Aura* (Mexico, 1962; tr. with same title, 1972) shows that this tradition of the "crime" of female sexuality continues into the contemporary period, even as the characterizations of the sexual woman begin to diversify. The story tells of a nubile, seductive "daughter" created/projected by an old, infecund, and dangerous witch, Consuelo. Like Santos Luzardo before him, the hero, Felipe Montero, prefers the daughter over the sexual "mother" who desires him. Trapped by Aura's sexual attractiveness, however, Montero is stripped of his identity and another personage is forced upon him. Montero's desire motivates the plot of *Aura,* which consists of his ineluctable, step-by-step fall into the seductive trap presented by Aura-Consuelo. Although female sexual pleasure in *Aura* does not show the kind of subjectification of female desire I am tracing here, the objectification and fear of female sexuality in *Aura* is instructive. Montero's tryst with Aura warns men of the dangers of women's sexual desires.

In this light, it is useful to contrast the horror stories of the dangers to society and to men of woman's sexuality, with a truly exceptional pre-1960s novel that attacks those who see female sexuality negatively. In *La mujer desnuda* [The nude woman](Uruguay, 1950), Armonía Somers's protagonist Rebeca Linke seeks to live naked of all social and material trappings, literally and metaphorically. As temerarious as Bombal's protagonist was timid, Linke can only pity those perturbed by her nudity and her sexuality. Rejecting obedience to convention, she wanders naked in the wilderness in search of love and freedom from hypocrisy. The story of this "Bárbara," this rejected sexual woman, is not a realist journey but a symbolic adventure. In the first chapter, tired of the conflicting messages coming from her body and her mind, Rebeca Linke decapitates herself. Later she grudgingly reattaches her head, remakes the link, despite the obvious advantages of being mindless. A modern parable of the radical nature of female sexuality, *La mujer desnuda* offers female sexual pleasure as socially disruptive and dangerous to the status quo and for that very reason a positive good. In its provocation of heterosexual men and their female partners, female sexual freedom in this novel causes rivalry among women and death to those who assume it actively, including Linke. But the fear and hatred of Linke, of women as sexual provocateurs, are not ineluctable forces in this novel. Instead they are contingent (and inferior) choices made by individuals suffering from the inertia of habit and a lack of depth of feeling. They fear the unknown and lack artistic sensitivity.

With its rebellion, *La mujer desnuda* from 1950 clearly sought to provoke in readers a strong reaction. Unlike Gamboa, Andrade, and Bombal, who also placed sexuality at the center of their thought, Somers (1914–1994) aligns herself definitively with the pro-sexuality camp. In this, she resembles authors after the 1960s. Perhaps for this reason also, she was until recently isolated as a writer and neglected by critics. But even

Somers's surreal novel represents female sexuality as a woman's "problem" that causes her suffering and marginalizes her, unless she represses,
denies, or controls it. At the same time, *Desnuda* makes Rebeca Linke a
(tragic) female hero for refusing to do any such thing. In this way, the
body-mind conflict in the novel—the episodes of self-decapitation and
rejoining of the head and torso—remains a dilemma whose resolution can
only come from radical social change, not individual adjustment.

In "Carta abierta desde Somersville" [An open letter from Somersville],
Somers asks herself whether she felt heroism was achieved in the novel,
merely by defying conventions: "I don't believe that it was heroism, but a
certain satisfying arrogance in irreverence before the myths in provocative
literature. And I believe that if a bird in flames flew out of fire, as I once
saw happen in a fire in this wooded place, and that in order to catch the
bird and try to save it, one had to burn oneself along with it, that is what
a writer with balls would try to do: burn himself [or herself] for a spectacular theme, sexists and antisexists aside."[30] In Somers's statement, she is
attracted to the dangerous nature of "a spectacular theme." Bravery is
needed by writers in order to face the public/critical condemnation for
having written irreverently, rebelliously. She speaks of her work with the
machismo of the vanguard writer, attacking the canon and social/literary
conventions.

The Newly Sexed Woman (Character)

As we have seen, twentieth-century Latin American novels before the
1960s have portrayed those female protagonists who desire or love men as
sufferers. Unlike the philandering males typical of the region's fiction
throughout the century, sexually active women characters have been depicted almost exclusively as prostitutes, adulteresses, and fallen
(mad)women who live marginal existences or die as a result of admitting
and acting on their desires. The exceptions to this literary formula have
been so rare that the figure of the sexual woman has come to evoke a
certain response in readers of Latin American fiction; she has been a
shared cultural icon for social as well as political dilemmas and has been
seen as characteristic of a segment of the population metonymically, coming either from the elite strata or the poorest underclasses, depending on
whom the author blames for the national crises.

Since the 1960s, however, the allegorical value of the sexual woman has
generally reversed from sufferer to harbinger of change. In general, the
desiring, sexual woman has become a hero, newly liberated from the pun-

ishing forces of childbirth, social stigmatization, and the power and venality of the old elites. She is no longer a victim or a perpetrator of the
"crime" of sex. Woman's desire is portrayed as dangerous, however, even
into the most recent period; this potential for harm is due not only to the
perceived loss of male prerogative in the sexual arena, but also because
women's sexuality in fiction has retained a symbolizing function for the
many other changes occurring in women's lives and affecting their families, workplaces, communities, and nations. The larger-than-life stature of
sexual women characters during these past three decades was reinforced
by the heightened recognition of women's contributions to the economy,
art, politics, and society brought about by feminist controversies, among
other things. Film, magazines and newspapers, stories and poems all reflect this changed and changing moment, but the novel—for its history,
length, and special readership—claims a public voice of great seriousness
and complexity.

Beginning in the 1960s, a new set of myths and symbols about women's
libidinous bodies became available to writers. The new narrative and
hermeneutic codes were not identical in all countries or for all writers, but
enough was shared so that a series of changing "truths about sex," as
Foucault ironically put it, can be discerned. For the pro-sexuality writers,
sex seemed the new truth, and literature the way to bring it to consciousness; the supposed inauthenticities of bourgeois modesty were to be wiped
away through the openness of confessional and pseudoconfessional writing which removed the masks of repression keeping individuals from personal sexual liberation. Radicals before Foucault talked about "living
freely" in their intimate sexuality—or failing to do so from societal resistance—because they envisioned merely writing uncensored sexual discourse as a political rupture with the past that would inevitably lead to
more free, open, and just societies. For its truth value, its attack on bourgeois morals, and its ability to pass the political censors, sexual fiction was
believed to possess revolutionary potential, while incurring much lighter
consequences for authors than explicit, direct volleys at political or economic injustice, corruption, or authoritarianism.

The most drastic and rapid transformations occurred between two
events, the commercial introduction of the birth-control pill and the mass
knowledge of AIDS. When the news wènt around the world in the early
1960s that an oral contraceptive for women would be marketed for the
first time, speculation came from many corners that if women were freed
from unwanted childbearing, rapid and drastic changes in the family—
and thus in the fabric of society—would result.[31] Adding fuel to the

anticlericalism of reformers and radicals was Pope Paul's 1968 *Humanae Vitae,* reasserting Catholicism's traditional stand against all new and most old methods of birth control. Many traditional Catholics were also upset by the pope's stand. Equally unacceptable to the pope were the ancient practice of coitus interruptus and coitus reservatus, the nineteenth-century version of condoms and IUDs, and the new hormonal contraception. Yet to many of the Catholic faithful, there did not seem to be a substantial difference between intercourse during a period of artificially induced lack of fertility with the pill, which the Catholic Church rejects, and timing intercourse to coincide with a woman's least-fertile days (the rhythm method, or its more sophisticated developments, like the Billings method), which the church recommends. By and large, Latin American women were not prevented from acquiring oral contraceptives by a personal decision to follow religious beliefs, however. For most women in Latin America, especially those outside urban centers, access to birth control remained and remains unavailable, difficult to obtain, or simply too expensive. Childbearing was and is an unavoidable eventuality of active heterosexuality.

No matter a writer's personal stand on oral contraception, the debate over its use reopened discussions about the intransigent problems it might help to ameliorate: women whose health has been damaged by excessive childbearing; countries whose industrial productivity has been hampered by women's lack of participation in the paid labor force; couples limited in their sexual activities by fear of another child they could not feed. It should be remembered that novels whose ideology was affected by debates over the pill need not mention birth control at all. In fact, it is often only in the representation of a scientific modernity that traces of this and other technological events remain in fictions.

Many of the social consequences predicted when the pill was first marketed have still not occurred, and may never happen in the ways first imagined, but certainly it can be said that for the first time, writers imagined in their fiction sexual women who were childless by choice. Whether or not birth control and easily accessible abortion were being practiced widely in Latin America during this period, the knowledge of their existence affected the way writers imagined sexuality for women characters. The mapping of a plot no longer needed to take into consideration the pregnancy of the young female lover as the most probable outcome, to be handled through a miscarriage or an abortion. There was a euphoria that utopian solutions were within reach and not utopian at all. Another reason that imaginations were set free is the circulation of ideas about woman's equality, feminist movements abroad, and women's importance within the family and society. Perhaps a more powerful reason, since many authors were not particularly feminist themselves, is the enabling power of increasing female education, which, combined with efforts to disseminate information about hygiene and sex, more prevalent during this period than ever before, has allowed many more women to avoid disease and to have more choices about childbearing.

Political events in the late 1960s and early 1970s, in contrast to those of the late 1950s and early 1960s, created a much more pessimistic political climate in many Latin American countries. In the Caribbean, the Cuban Revolution turned from a cause for elation into a divisive issue among intellectuals, as young writers like Gabriel García Márquez and Mario Vargas Llosa debated the Cuban government's actions regarding culture. In Mexico, student protests in the capital led to a 1968 massacre of hundreds in the Plaza de Tlaltelolco by military and paramilitary forces. In 1968, Peru experienced a "military revolution" that created an authoritarian regime, but one which did not use the systematic terror for which the countries of the Southern Cone became known. Chile's democratically elected Socialist president was toppled in 1973, and in Argentina the series of military coups was briefly interrupted by the disappointing return of Perón. Clearly, the sexual fiction written under such conditions of fear and disillusionment resulted as much from a desire to criticize the political scene in whatever discourse permitted it, as from a sense that women's issues were the most pressing. Sexual fiction about women could attack the status quo from a relatively disguised vantage point, speaking in a new way to new readers.

What is particularly Latin American—and I believe interesting to feminists everywhere—about the novels that use female sexuality seen from a woman's subjectivity is this phenomenon of disguise and displacement, a phenomenon that intensifies in the 1970s. The meaning of female sexuality is displaced from the gender/sex system, where it had indicated some truth or story about women, onto a different social grouping, perhaps the character's own race, class, or ethnicity (i.e., metonymically), or onto one entirely other to her (i.e., metaphorically). When the theme of female sexuality is deployed within a strategy of displacement, female sexuality is utilized to discuss women's lives as distinct from men's, but also, secondarily and on another level, in analogy to another element of identity. In this strategy female sexuality is employed to speak of one race or economic class in contrast to another; of sexual orientations or affective circumstance; of small differentials in ethnicity, region, and involvement with popular or traditional culture. For example, Brazilian and Caribbean novels may use a mulatto woman's sexuality first to generalize about women, then displace the distinction to address issues related to a strong African and African American presence in culture. In other novels, where female sexuality is synonymous with prostitution, the prostitution of women may first be generalized to women's economic subordination, then displaced to an attack on government corruption or the venality of elites. In other works exuberant female sexuality is displaced to signify heroic efforts by the poor to survive, transcend, or transform the world.

Displaced from representing women in general to representing other groups in a national landscape, "newly sexed women" characters in their demand for pleasure tend to represent groups that demand new, less repressive social structures. The title character in Miguel Angel Asturias's *Mulata* (1967; *Mulata de tal,* Guatemala, 1963) personifies the Indian gods' wrath when traditional subsistence farming practices and economies are sacrificed to the pursuit of wealth. Seen as a new, imported way of life, a way of life impelled by greed, capitalism destroys the balance of relations within the Indian communities, within couples, and between people and nature. The Mulata and her sexuality represent and foment the destruction of indigenous cultures. Because of the role of female sexuality as a cultural symbol, and for other reasons taken up later, I chose *Mulata de tal* as the first novel studied here in depth. It is the subject of chapter 2.

Other well-known novels that refer to racial or ethnic communities in the guise of the adventures of a sexual female protagonist are *Dona Flor and Her Two Husbands* (1969; *Dona Flor e seus dois maridos,* Brazil, 1966) by Jorge Amado and "From Cuba with a Song" (1972; *De donde son los cantantes,* Cuba, 1967) by Severo Sarduy. *No una, sino muchas muertes* by Enrique Congrains Martín, mentioned earlier, displaces the treatment of poverty and class conflict to that of an extremely poor, young girl's struggles to avoid rape and have sex. *La sombra donde sueña Camila O'Gorman* [The shade where Camila O'Gorman dreams] (Argentina, 1973) by Enrique Molina, rather than confront the authoritarianism of contemporary serial dictatorships, displaces the Argentine state's violent repression of liberals and innocents to the nineteenth century under the rule of dictator Manuel de Rosas. These novels question the distribution of values—ethical, economic, political, social, literary—along gender lines, but not only along them. Take for example the best-known to English-speaking readers, *Dona Flor,* which owes its fame to a popular movie based on it. Amado exploits women's class mobility through sexuality to broaden the novel's field of vision, to gain epic dimensions. Female sexuality is the theme bringing together the beginning and the ending of *Dona*

Flor; it is the motivating factor of the main plot and the realm-in-crisis which, when the crisis is resolved, brings the novel to a close. Nevertheless, hundreds of pages between the beginning and the ending have little to do with this theme. The intervening chapters weave a tapestry of micro-relations holding together a divided world: an underworld of gamblers, prostitutes, and poets contrasted with Flor's world of family, neighbors, cooking students, and church. Not only is Flor abandoned by the narrator for chapter after chapter, but also the partisanship of Jorge Amado's narrator for Vadinho and not for her living husband, Teodoro, distances the narrator from her, for she is truly torn between her two husbands until the very last pages. Despite Flor's acceptance of Vadinho's being so long postponed as to seem an afterthought, her pleasure throughout the novel is shown as a repressed force of great power. When finally released, the energy of Flor's pleasure joins with that of oppressed workers in a mythic and mythologizing resolution. Her pleasure foments revolutionary social and economic change, according to the narrator.

Severo Sarduy questions the significance of the image of the sexual mulatta as an icon of Cuban culture. Dolores Rondón, the mulatta lover of the "politician" Mortal Perez, occupies the central chapter of a racial and cultural triptych of the Chinese, African, and Spanish heritage of the island. Although the myth of the mulatta as the epitome of sexuality is nurtured in part by Rondón herself, she suffers from it. Sarduy's eulogistic form focuses reader attention on the sacrifice of the black, poor, and female to the blond, rich, and male. By drawing on an actual epitaph from a real tomb, Sarduy signals the historic reality that prostitution and concubinage were two of the very few roads for advancement in Cuban culture available to African Cuban women. Sarduy unsparingly attacks, parodies, and makes fun of cultural markers, including those which stereotypically celebrate the sexuality of the mulatta, while never pretending to provide an interpretation or a totalizing critique of Cuban society. Sarduy transforms the tragic (and typically Latin American) story of the sacrifice of a dark woman on the altar of race into a hedonistic word game about Cuban culture, thus submitting the myth of the hedonistic mulatta to inspection as a historic construct. Gender in "From Cuba with a Song" seems a spontaneous improvisation of the characters, cultural heritage is a matter of taste, and power and riches come within grasp only through political corruption. The surprising aspect of the Rondón chapter is the monumental and stable qualities the sexual woman manifests in a novel which, above all, consists of mutations, illusions, contradictions, and irony. She is exalted, while the racism from which she suffered is exposed as an element to be critiqued, although the critique itself is delayed until after the reading of the text.

Functioning similarly for the poor of the slums, the Peruvian novel by Congrains Martín portrays an exceptionally brave young Maruja who pursues her sexual desires despite physical risks. Familiar with the periphery of Lima (*las barriadas*), with its marginal communities of the extremely poor, Congrains created Maruja, a young girl who lives in shocking conditions on the garbage dump. An area of largely undocumented sociological character, at least in 1956–1957 when the novel was written, this "unknown" region of the real is a space in which women acted differently. Maruja has strength of character, a voracious sexuality, and an independence of spirit. These qualities save her from a gang rape similar to that suffered by the young doña Bárbara. Maruja's sexual daring allows her to survive in a violent world where nurturing, a more common female behavior, is practically nonexistent and if attempted would probably be suicidal. Ultimately, Maruja's intelligence, physical prowess, and willpower are (barely) a match for the sexism of the gang, allowing her to survive; Maruja's unscrupulous search for power over others, including those she desires sexually, makes for an aggressive sexuality, a "female machismo" that identifies defiance and force with success. Similarly, Argentine fiction writer Enrique Medina said he had feminist intentions when he wrote *Con el trapo en la boca* (1984) with an aggressively sexual, even murderous young female protagonist and narrator. Set around the time of the Malvinas War of 1982, the violence she suffers and promulgates, according to Fernando Reati, reflects the disappearances, torture, and murder perpetuated by the state during the "Dirty War": "the adolescent rebellion of the protagonist is doubly charged with political-sexual value, because the sexist structures that oppress woman and the political structures of authoritarianism are two sides of the same coin" ["la rebeldía adolescente de la protagonista cobra una doble valencia político-sexual, porque las estructuras sexistas que oprimen a la mujer y las estructuras políticas del autoritarismo son las dos caras de una misma moneda" (215)].

Another type of displacement occurred when the present situation could be read allegorically or metaphorically within a historical novel. One conspicuous example is Argentine Enrique Molina's *La sombra donde sueña Camila O'Gorman,* a hybrid of a historical essay about the nineteenth-century Rosas dictatorship, mixed with surrealist prose poetry in praise of sexual love between priests and virgins. For many readers, this work spoke to Argentina's 1970s political dilemmas as much as it recreated the past. A poetic text, *Sombra* includes historical detail subjected to imaginative manipulation and subordinated to the thesis that Camila O'Gorman's sexuality was a powerful life force in opposition to Rosas's pact with death. Female sexuality symbolizes resistance to the violence of the military and paramilitary groups that were terrorizing men and women, brutalizing culture, and killing normal human relations in both past and present periods of authoritarian rule in Argentina.

Before the 1960s, novels criticized sexual women for transgressing, but by the 1970s they criticize society for repressing women's transgressions. With the 1970s, legions of novels about female sexuality become either part of a new protest literature against women's condition, respond to the new sexual emancipation of women, or question the relevance of sexuality to a woman's condition. After the watershed decade of the 1960s, previous images of the sexual woman come under scrutiny (e.g., *La sombra donde sueña Camila O'Gorman*), and the figure of the sexually liberated single woman acquires a new prominence, as in Luisa Valenzuela's *El gato eficaz* [The efficient cat](Argentina, 1972). Lines in the sand have been drawn and novels tend to align themselves with one camp or another.

Chapter 3 is devoted to *An Apprenticeship, or The Book of Delights* (1986; *Uma aprendizagem, ou O livro dos prazeres*, 1969), by the Brazilian woman writer Clarice Lispector (1920–1977). In this work, a realistically portrayed urban schoolteacher who has had several lovers achieves greater spiritual and psychological wholeness through channeling her sexual energies into a single, worthy love object. In dialogue with philosophical, artistic, and moral works of wide international and historical range, Lispector's novel considers, then gives the lie to the (historical) idea that female sexuality creates a victim of either the man or the woman, whenever the female character is sexually aggressive or even merely active. These post-1960s novels assert secular characterizations instead of goddesses, heroes, or other utopian projections. Nevertheless, the figure of the sexual woman results in a frequent crisis of representation in these novels, a destabilization of assumptions, unlike the trends toward simplification of language and testimonial solidarity common in the post-Boom era, when other themes are treated. In the 1970s and 1980s, new narrative worlds are constituted by female sexual discourse through the languages of psychology, mythology, sexology, philosophy, or class struggle. In the process, texts redefine literary genres, rewrite women's history, and more often than in the '60s, poke fun at the seriousness of sex.

Manuel Puig's nightmarish vision of a futuristic society of forced prostitution for young women in *Pubis angelical* (1973; in English under the same title, 1986) is extraordinary for condemning an authoritarian state's technological intrusions into sexual life. In an interview in 1985, Puig said he wrote *Pubis angelical* as if it were two parallel lines. One "line" is the realistic narrative of Ana, an Argentine woman convalescing in a Mexican hospital, appearing in dialogue and in diary entries. The second "line" consists of Ana's dreams and is largely third-person indirect discourse. For readers, however, the novel does not have two kinds of discourse, but many: dramatic dialogue, an intimate diary, popular romance (*la novela rosa*), the spy thriller, and science fiction. The forms alternate to advance the stories or to repeat them with variations. Genres rarely mix within a single segment, although characters of one literary genre do appear in another. Thus the individual stories transcend the specific genre in which they first appear, for the reader. Except for the science fiction sequence telling of the angelical pubis of the title, woman's sexuality is the source of her victimization in the stories, much as it was in novels before the 1960s.[32] The angelical pubis, however, harks back to a 1960s utopian vision of female sexuality, capable of saving the world from itself by bringing about peace. This utopian vision has now become unfamiliar, abstracted, and inspected through the play of genre-switching, much like a bilingual's code-switching: in addition to literal meaning, the context or language also signifies. In Puig's novel, the contrast between the science fiction genre as the place for utopic speculation on female sexuality versus the romance section's pessimism about it draws the reader's attention and creates new meaning.

In another major example from the 1970s, Brazilian Nélida Piñón has freed her text, *A casa da paixão* [The house of passion](1972), from as much social realism as possible by stripping away descriptions of physical space, dress, and social banter, as if trying to accomplish the opposite of regionalists and folklorists, who dwell on such external matters for their own sake. The protagonist, Marta, is a cipher for the nubile virgin in the patriarchal family, following where her body leads—to seek the sun, to avoid the confinement of the house. Female sexuality in this novel becomes biological necessity made to conform to human culture. Father-daughter incest menaces Marta for the first half of the novella and only recedes from the foreground after the father becomes aware of his desire. He then brings in a rival to compete for Marta's affections. At first she rejects Jerônimo precisely because he was picked by her father: freedom from the father means freedom from everything connected to him. Eventually acquiescing to Jerônimo's pursuit, however, Marta then seeks sexual pleasure despite the pain of defloration in a brave act of physical self-assertion. Her desire for sexual pleasure results in giving up her control over her body and her self, by giving herself to the other. As a consequence, Piñón's omniscient narrator treats Marta's psychosexual growth as if it were a universal cultural myth of the female body. Furthermore, the book suggests that heterosexuality is for those women who consciously transfer love of their fathers to another man, and then are brave enough to face physical pain. Piñón's biologizing is decidedly monologic, narrating psychology as universal myth and ritual, and writing Marta's life as if history were merely the changing decorations of a single phenomenon of psychocorporal response unmediated by cultures.

By the 1980s, the thematization of female sexuality in many Latin American novels has by and large metamorphosed again, and appears less decidedly as either "good" (sexually active) or "bad" (repressed, repressing)—that is, as less symbolic of manichean moralities—and more a metonymy for barely imagined new realities and a metaphor for future transformations. By the late 1980s, female sexuality is a complex node of pleasure and pain in serious works of an intellectual bent, transcending binary oppositions through play, parody, and poetry. Authors sought to defamiliarize the dead schema of binaries or to abandon it altogether.[33]

If the historic 1960s marketing of the pill enabled a growing conceptualization of nonreproductive heterosexuality, in theory at least, then the news in the 1980s that intercourse could bring a frightening disease brought to a rapid halt most fictional speculation about utopian female sexuality. AIDS burst into public awareness in the 1980s and has shown diverse patterns of incidence and state response among the Latin American countries. The relatively high proportion of both heterosexual transmission of infection and of female cases, especially in the Caribbean, is unlike the transmission pattern in North America. It is an understatement to say that the news of AIDS has not been an instigation to write about women's sexual pleasure, but has instead led some to place disproportionate blame on women who are sexually active with many men, especially prostitutes, in fiction and in the media. Thus the trajectory of the sexual woman protagonist, which underwent a marked transformation if one compares before and after the dividing line of the 1960s and early 1970s, returns in the 1990s to many of the pre-1960s fears. A high incidence of AIDS in cities, among many other issues, continues to inspire novelists to represent sexually active women protagonists as playing with fire, adding this new disease to the past threats from venereal disease, unwanted pregnancies, and social ostracism.

For instance, Peruvian Vargas Llosa's erudite and interartistic novella, *In Praise of the Stepmother* (1990; *Elogio de la madrastra* 1988), uses the

stepmother-stepson quasi-incest theme to challenge the gains made in social respectability by "newly sexed woman" characters, by renaming the
woman with aspirations toward sexual liberation the new sexual predator
of our times. This short novel incorporates reproductions of famous and
lesser-known paintings into a mélange of sexual fantasies and realistic
dialogue. Interpreting both the paintings and the verbal text in chapter 4,
I argue the book's structure sets a trap for the sexual woman character
who believes the same moral rules apply to her sexuality as to her
husband's. But in a larger sense, female sexuality in this novel only matters
to the extent it helps or harms the male desire for satisfaction. Luckily, this
negativity is not ubiquitous in Latin American fiction, though it is pervasive among best-sellers and in the media.

At the same time, in the 1980s female sexuality becomes the signifier
par excellence of the doorway into a new world of writing for the small
but vocal group of (largely women) writers who see female sexuality as a
kind of discourse rather than its theme. In this new development, writers
organize their aesthetics, political opinions, and social critique around the
idea of female *jouissance,* as discussed by Jameson and referred to above:
a very different motivation for writing sexual fiction in Latin America
than those yet discussed. Tununa Mercado from Argentina, for instance,
conceives of writing and eroticism as deriving from the same source, "the
same libidinal energy" ("la misma energía libidinal"), such that each one
feeds the other. At a conference of women writers held in Argentina in
1988, the same year Vargas Llosa published *Praise,* Tununa Mercado explained the degree to which female sexuality guides her writing. This
excerpt is quite long but instructive:

> Writing would be, then, for me, a model of sexuality. But which
> writing? and which sexuality?
> *My Choice I.* A writing which does not think about the denoue-
> ment but instead in the intermediate zones; . . . a writing of free
> senses/meaning, with the goal of winning the space on the page
> . . . ; a writing that does not take the body as an abstraction and
> which knows how to let go, like a flow or a lymph, meaningful
> substances without fear of leaving holes in a reading through the
> corrosion of its advance. I believe that such writing, every time that
> I have turned myself over to it, like a secret seduction, is the height of
> eroticism. . . .
> *My Choice II.* A sexuality that does not conceive itself with an
> ending, as distant from consummation as the morning star that ends

the night of lovers; an ideal of meeting in which there are no arrivals, only continuities; an inaugural copulation in which there is no knowing, in which the text stutters; a punctuated meeting, with questionings that open and close, with periods and commas, with ellipses and exclamations, without the final period; a disobedient and irreverent sexuality.

"Masculine" writing surely must be like masculine sexuality over the female body: dominating, indiscriminating, without recognition of differences, placed inside a glove or a symbolic condom: the writing of representation and reflection more than of an indomitable desire, certainly it displaces over the text an idea of woman made ideological, an idea of narration made ideological, marked even by those fearful traits or traces of class, gender, race, color, marked by the terrible traits of crude realism that sticks the word onto the referent and does not allow even a tiny light in between them; that literature or that masculine writing eats women; that literature, in a certain way, is the comatose line that registers the slow disappearance of literature itself.[34]

Female sexuality for Mercado has become a freely floating signifier of excess, play, and imagination. Rather than follow the 1960s model of female sexuality as liberatory, "feminine writing" (*la escritura femenina*) serves as the escutcheon in a new heraldry of sexual *writing* as liberation.[35]

A reviewer put it this way: "In [Mercado's] *Canon de alcoba* [Canon of the bedroom], the body is one of the most important centers, and for that reason, Tununa Mercado's writing has been called erotic. But eroticism here is a point of departure and a point of dispersion throughout the book. The erotic is a sentence that desires another sentence, another body of sentences. More than writing about the body, it is a body of writing working on its own meanings and resonances, flowing with a particular rhythm that leads to a canon" (Domínguez 68).

Indeed, there are additional, more far-reaching aspects of Mercado's ideas in her critical writings and exemplified in her fiction. Jean Franco writes that Mercado (and Diamela Eltit from Chile) "attempt to make of 'the private' a kind of reserve energy from which the so-called public sphere can be destabilized, allowing for an 'eros' that is not simply tied to romantic love" ("Afterword" 231). The erotic always involves the greatest possible separation from the literal sex act, but in Mercado the sexgender system haunts the text as the power of resistance rather than being represented.

My requirement of a female subjectivity from which sex is experienced moves much of Mercado's fiction to the edge of my project in this book. Although I have selected for my chapters only works in which female sexuality is actually represented, my analysis will, of necessity and in fairness, consider such "discursive sexuality" when it is also present in the novels analyzed. But when sex is represented, we find, from the 1960s to the 1990s, a danger associated with female sexuality, even in texts when it is associated with freedom and/or feminism.

The Chapters

In order to describe the multifaceted phenomenon of a sexual woman character within her narrative context, much of the terminology from the fields of thematics and of characterization have seemed to me inadequate to express the ultimate inseparability of theme and character. Although at times I consider largely the theme of female sexuality and at others primarily the character of the "newly sexed woman," mostly I employ the concept of textual strategies to look at their seamless meld within the novel in question. Textual strategies are particularly useful for including the larger picture of characters in context. I call them *textual* rather than authorial strategies, since it is irrelevant whether the author consciously thought of them or not, whereas it is extremely important for the strategies to consist of a textual *presence*.

The question of "presence" has been much debated in contemporary theory, but after consideration I have largely weighed in on the side of presence, because my requirement of the representation of a sex scene has allowed me to limit a study that threatened to include most of contemporary literature. Nonetheless, there will be times when female sexuality is neither represented nor discursive, but signaled as extratextual. Not everything can be included in every text—some silences are inevitable and not worthy of mention. But the presences in a text may "draw" a conceptual (or dramatic or narrative or imagistic) circle such that a certain absence within is indicated; only silences thus indicated can be useful in interpretation. There is a tightrope to be traversed here, but as with any tightrope, the line must be taut or the walker will fall. If a silenced portion is to be noticed, there must be a tension created. I have sought the taut ropes, the ones that will bear the weight of critical analysis, before signaling any missing, silent, or silenced female sexuality.

I have made no attempt to identify "first" or "last" novels of any type and instead have chosen for closer examination those texts which both illuminate social issues related to female sexuality and speak to the history of the period from the 1960s to the 1990s, first encouraged by marketing of the pill and then shrunken considerably by the fear of AIDS. The novels by Miguel Angel Asturias, Clarice Lispector, and Mario Vargas Llosa examined in the next three chapters stand in for the three decades under consideration as the rise, apex, and fall of the liberatory stance of an indulgent, radical period in the portrayal of female sexuality. They also treat dilemmas of current criticism.

In Miguel Angel Asturias's novel, *Mulata* (1967; *Mulata de tal* 1963), a mythological sexual woman is literally dismembered and figuratively deconstructed as a cultural icon for transgression. In this fantastic, surrealist, and mythic tragicomedy, the Mulata de tal exudes allure and sadomasochistic violence: she destroys those who would make love to her. Though we read her subjectivity through her speech, we have little narrative focalization on her inner thoughts. We are not given the illusion that she is a full or real "person" realistically represented. Nevertheless, her sexual pleasure is concretely described, motivated at times by modern, human desires. Although oneiric, ludic, and didactic elements are common in the novel, her sexuality participates as sexual provocateur and social destabilizer in an allegorical critique of intersexual and intercultural relations in modern Guatemala. The main textual strategy is that of the game. With rules of its own, this novel creates a fascinating, imagined world in which the sexual woman has a revered, yet feared, role: part trickster, part destroyer.

In *Mulata* the sexual woman is not the prostitute typical of earlier novels from the region, or even of many later works from elsewhere, still trapped by clichés. In *Reading, Writing, and Rewriting the Prostitute Body,* for instance, Shannon Bell describes an "empowerment/victimization dichotomy" characteristic of discourse about whores, even feminist writings. Furthermore, an ambivalence about prostitutes is frequently found within texts as a tension.[36] In an unusual move, however, Asturias's sexual women, who are not mere walk-ons but major characters, either charge for sex, demand it, or freely offer it as the mood strikes them. Poverty may motivate a woman to sell her favors (e.g., the Mulata in her first appearance), but there is virtually no discourse of victimization. While some of his sexual women characters are recognizable because of their origins in myth and oral literature (e.g., the Llorona, or Weeping Woman), most are unpredictable actors in a satire. The unpredictable sexual women—the Mulata and others—indicate the view that allowing women free agency in the realm of sexuality will have unforeseeable (and perhaps uncontrollable) consequences. Sexual women clear the sociopolitical slate with their destructive powers, opening a space for change.

Sexual women characters have often been seen by Western society as fomenters of protest and resistance against domination, but those in *Mulata* uniquely represent an unco-opted outsider perspective, incarnate non-Western gods and spirits, and still retain their autonomy. In this, Asturias provides a very special staging of the Indian precapitalist way of life as seen through folklore, myths, and surrealism. His syncretic process of enunciation frames sexual woman characters in a manner not entirely Western and not truly Mayan. On the one hand, his characters provide damning testimony denouncing the destruction of contemporary Mayan societies; on the other, wearing the mask of ancient stories and folklore, the female figures find themselves in harmony with the (modern 1960s, urban) woman's newfound voice of unashamed desire which, according to all accounts, would be foreign to Guatemalan traditional (patriarchal) society. The Mulata et al. seem oddly out of place in a rural village when viewed with secular Western eyes, but they are not characters transplanted from modern cities either. His characters appear to hail from both places and from neither. Hybrid fruits of Asturias's fertile imagination, the female voices in this novel provide a fresh paradigm, and provoke all kinds of humor and ironies.

In addition to an exegesis of Asturias's hilarious and encyclopedic romp through Central American and personal myths, Latin American cultural assumptions, and international literary reference, I show that his Surrealist epic is an exposé of the threat posed by seductive international capitalism to modern Guatemalan Indians and their culture. The sexual woman, especially the Mulata of the title, symbolizes this threat. I argue that Asturias's novel, nevertheless, exhibits a delirious miscegenation of native and foreign cultures sympathetically represented. Both the material comforts brought by industrialization and most of the sexual pleasures the Mulata provides are attractive; the contradictions produce rich moral resonances and provide a Rabelaisian flavor to the highly ambivalent image of the demonic sex goddess at its center.

In contrast, the other two novels to which I devote chapters have realist settings in urban Latin America with sexual women protagonists facing sexual dilemmas that are first of all individual, and secondarily symbolical of moral, aesthetic, and political feminist questions.

Comfortably middle-class, the main character of Clarice Lispector's *An Apprenticeship, or the Book of Delights*, Lori, is an unmarried schoolteacher. Sex without emotional involvement has been easy for her. In the midst of her solitary sexual bliss, she contemplates what she will lose and gain by a monogamous attachment to a man. She is a thinker rather than a doer. Textual sexuality in this novel is withheld from the reader until the very last pages, because of the approach-flight pattern Lori adopts toward emotional commitment. Living with sex and seeking love, however, no longer present a woman with the risk of prostitution, rape, disease, pregnancy, a socially legislated subservience to a husband, the disintegration of one's traditional society, or financial dependency. The danger of sexuality for Lori comes from within: it consists of an overidealization of love that could crush her will. Lispector sings the praises of the body and pleasure, but describes them as emotional dangers to the sexual woman in ways they are not dangerous to sexual men. Even in today's liberal urban environments, it would seem that love, marriage, and children affect most women differently than men. Lori gradually learns that, when needed, she will have the tools to fight the onslaught of a cultural inheritance telling her to give up her identity in the name of love; she is "ready" for Ulysses when she feels strong enough to maintain herself as a thinking subject knowingly negotiating the ways in which they will act as a duo.

An Apprenticeship addresses writing itself, not so much in terms of production and authorship, as in Lispector's later work The Hour of the Star (1986; A hora de estrela 1977), but writing in terms of thinking and living. An Apprenticeship's primary activity is to situate a woman's sexuality within ideas of love. The protagonist Lori struggles for a new kind of engagement with her sexuality. Rather than the easy, uncomplicated, and insignificant physicality she had with her past lovers, Lori is seeking the profundity of erotic experience in the commitment of her whole being. She knows how to "make love," but she must learn how to love another. The superficial physicality of sex was the only shared experience accessible to Lori, but it eventually lost its attractions. Ascending from sex to love is a process of education, in Georges Bataille's words, of learning "to find a place for the disorders of lovemaking in an orderly pattern covering the whole of human life" (241). The textual strategy here is thus the reflection. There is a duality in the enunciation of Lori's apprenticeship: it is both her achievement and the handiwork of her teacher, Ulysses; a spiritual growth and the enhancement of her physical sexuality; religious continence and pagan sensuality; a solitary quest and a social liberation.

In the 1960s, the sexual myth par excellence was the idea that the satisfaction of sexuality would produce happiness, freedom, and radical social change in an uncomplicated way. Clarice Lispector configures Lori's relation with Ulysses as a restructuring of discourses and myths, particularly those about sexuality that see love and sex as placing in danger happiness, freedom, and radical social change. Instead, conceptions like Sartrian voluntary enslavement and Bataille's sovereignty are helpful for probing Lispector's representation of erotic love as involving the subjection or autonomy of the female lover. *An Apprenticeship* represents as impossible a stable equality among lovers. At the same time, it is a portrait of one couple's valiant efforts to destabilize the hierarchies that inevitably threaten all heterosexual love relationships, due to men's and women's inequality in society.

The third novel I treat separately in a chapter, *In Praise of the Stepmother*, by Mario Vargas Llosa, begins with premises that Lispector's Lori arduously achieves in conclusion, namely, that gendered roles exist a priori, but that one engages with such roles creatively. Inspired by a painting by the Peruvian painter and friend of the author, Fernando de Szyszlo, and originally planned as an interart project of the two men, *Praise* in its final form contains one Szyszlo reproduction and several paintings by others which the author considers his own personal obsessions. Published the year before the author's bid for the presidency of Peru, this experimental erotic novel with a sexual woman protagonist, the recently married middle-aged housewife Lucrecia, is the most sexually explicit of the three works to which whole chapters are devoted. In it, chapters of sexual fantasies alternate with chapters of the naturalistic and realistic types. The improvisation of sexual roles within the sex-gender system becomes a textual strategy of discovery and disclosure. For instance, the stepmother's actual orientation and opportunities contrast with the lesbian, exhibitionist, and pedophilic desires explored in "Diana at her Bath" ("Diana después de su baño"), the chapter in which a voice, Diana Lucrecia, narrates the scene in François Boucher's painting (1742) of the same title. Diana Lucrecia provokes a young boy voyeur. A goddess, she appears to have a limitless capacity for sexual pleasure and an ability to find pleasure in any circumstance. Although women at one time or another have probably had every fantasy imaginable, this narration is more a fantasy *about* women's desires than a fantasy a woman is likely to have. Within the main, realist plot, Diana Lucrecia's transgressions are contradicted or absent: Rigoberto is the focus of Lucrecia's sexual practice, not his son; Lucrecia's maid Justiniana makes no lesbian overtures; Justiniana disapproves of Fonchito's spying on Lucrecia's bathing. Similarly, the chapter "The Rosy Youth" [El joven rosado] gives voice to figures in the painting *The Annunciation* by Fra Angelico. The ekphrastic voice comes from a modest young virgin named María, selected among women to be the lover of a young man whose back shows the sign of the rainbow. Contrary to the story told by María from the painting, however, in the next chapter Justiniana rejects young Alfonsito's sexual advances.

Overall, Vargas Llosa's writing of female sexual pleasure places his fiction within an (anti)tradition of transgressive erotic writing, one which reinforces male desire and patriarchal dominance over women. Lucrecia and Justiniana act and fantasize within art's reified categories for women's provocative fantasies, rather than engage the social contradictions of the late 1980s to progress beyond them. With this novel, the conservative reaction against the association of female sexuality with freedom clearly has taken hold of a sector of sexual fiction. I deconstruct Vargas Llosa's indictment of the sexual stepmother to show the complexity of the aesthetic and ethical issues in his characterization of a modern Phaedra. In Otto Rank's chapter on the stepmother theme, he examines literary stepmothers in relation to the incest prohibition. He writes that the displacement of the mother to a stepmother changes the crime from that of literal incest: "Thus the stepmother is simultaneously the non-physical 'mother,' whose love for the son is no longer incestuous but nevertheless violates the father's claims and provides justification for the hatred between father and son, rivals for her affection" (92).

Interestingly, in *In Praise of the Stepmother* the relationship between Lucrecia and Justiniana is as close to a friendship as this employer-employee class division will allow, and this almost-friendship deepens in the sequel, *Los cuadernos de don Rigoberto* (1997; *The Notebooks of Don Rigoberto* 1998). If one reflects on the many novels I have mentioned, it is truly surprising the extent to which women's homosocial amity and mother-daughter affection has been marginalized in novels devoted to women's sexuality throughout the 1960s to 1990s. Peggy Job comments on this situation in Mexican woman's narratives from 1970 to 1987: "The celebration of feminine friendship/solidarity, which has been so much a theme in women's writing in Europe, the United States, and Australia, is absent from Mexican narrative, and so has the mother-daughter relation in search of a mutual comprehension by generations of women."[37] Although I suspect that relationships among women to be less markedly absent in Latin American narrative generally, when more female writers are considered, or when post-1987 works are included, Job's suspicion is worth noting.

Concerning novels of female sexuality, it may be the very fact of strong bonding between women in Latin American society that has led to a diminution of the representation of feminine friendship and solidarity in these novels focused on heterosexuality. Whatever the reasons—and I doubt there is a single cause for this phenomenon—the few women friends, the absent mother, and the infrequent solidarity with feminism among women in fictions about desire for men contradict social practices in Latin American societies, where nonsexual female bonding and political alliances along gender lines are common and significant.[38] Latin American novels about female heterosexuality greatly reduce the normal roles played by female friendship and women's support systems within the family and community. One explanation may be that sexual female protagonists are dangerously isolated from other female characters, not by a voluntary individualism or a hypocritical misogyny, but by the social ostracism and isolation caused by their lack of orthodoxy. Another possibility could be the focus of these heterosexual characters on the men in their lives.

A comment should be made about the norms for gender identity (the rules deciding who is female), and for gendered sexual practices (rules for woman's behavior in terms of openness, monogamy, and the gender of the object of sexual desire). Before the 1960s the norms are almost always oppositional (male versus female). But after the 1960s male-female oppositions tend to be transcended by making gender less definable, less rigid, or simply irrelevant. In *Mulata,* for instance, the Mulata is a (male) god-woman; In *An Apprenticeship* and *Praise,* the main characters question or reject the idea that a woman should be a virgin upon marriage. In "From Cuba with a Song," Dolores Rondón is possibly a transvestite and certainly a playful, imaginary creation that is more textual than referential. This gender slippage and the gender complexity become particularly interesting as times goes on. For this reason, male transvestites and (would-be) transsexuals, like Manuela in José Donoso's "Hell Has No Limits" (1972; *El lugar sin límites* 1966) and Molina from Manuel Puig's *Kiss of the Spider Woman* (1979; *El beso de la mujer araña* 1976), are closely related to the sexual women characters I discuss here. The situation of these gender-bending characters is more complex than a simple analogy to sexual women, but the sex-gender system limits the lives of both groups. One reason for the closeness is the experimental aesthetics and identity hybridization frequently seen in novels of the "newly sexed woman."[39] Gender ambiguity is a strategy for crossing borders and for changing the reified terms of discussion.

A further way to disturb traditional portrayals of sexuality very recently has been to circumvent the male-female dichotomy (and the polarization of gender) in heterosexual love by making lesbianism a central theme.[40] Lesbian love appears in the first commercially successful lesbian novels in Latin America in the late 1980s: Silvia Molloy's *Certificate of Absence* (1989; *En breve cárcel* 1981), Rosamaría Roffiel's *Amora* (1989; the title is the main character's name), and Sara Levi Calderón's *Dos mujeres* [Two women] (1990). Lesbian feelings, lesbian characters, and lesbian writing strategies were not absent from earlier novels; but they were (and still often are) encoded, marginalized, or silenced within a hegemony of heterosexual desire. Radically other in the representation of female sexuality, these works by Molloy, Roffiel, and Levi Calderón record, reflect upon, and project changes (and intransigencies) in their societies' attitudes toward women's dangerous desires.

2

Miguel Angel Asturias and the "Newly Sexed Woman"

In his classic novel *The President* (1963; *El señor Presidente* 1946), the Guatemalan author Miguel Angel Asturias fictionalizes the culture of authoritarian politics in Latin America through the figure of the dictator. Twenty years later, in *Mulata* (1967; *Mulata de tal* 1963), the figure of the sexual woman—similarly a character type, portrayed within a specific Latin American context—provides Asturias an opportunity to narrate the intimate culture of unequal gender relations. One of Asturias's last novels, *Mulata* was written many years after those for which he is best known today: *Leyendas de Guatemala* [Legends of Guatemala] (1930, augmented 1948) *The President*; and *Men of Maize* (1975; *Hombres de maíz* 1949). Appearing in 1963, just prior to the years of the great publishing boom in Latin American fiction, *Mulata* reflects the thinking of a politically committed writer already affected by the forces that in the 1960s bring about a discourse of female sexuality as liberation. His title character, the Mulata, is a sexual woman character who is complex and innovative enough to be worthy of extended examination. The Mulata carries forward into the 1960s some of the sexual woman's traditional associations with prostitution and corruption, yet in an entirely new way. The newness of his portrait of the sexual woman comes from three sources: an avant-garde, surrealist freedom from realism; an effort to represent an Indian point of view; and a nihilist, iconoclastic sense of humor.

Because of the novel's many ambiguities, *Mulata* has been difficult to understand for both critics and average readers. It contains a symphonic cast, allusions to myths and stories from marginalized cultures, and an anticonformist attitude toward Western reason and middle-class decorum. In the absence of an annotated edition, elements of the novel remain more than enigmatic, even to scholars.[1] The problem caused by the great effort required to understand *Mulata* is primarily one of audience, a dilemma in which Asturias sacrificed the impatient or casual reader for a chance to educate the patient reader willing to learn.[2] But these obstacles of complexity and obscurity must not prevent us from recognizing either the remarkably creative tour de force it is, or the contribution which *Mulata* makes to our understanding of feminist issues in Latin America during the 1960s.

The principal female characters, the Mulata de tal and Catarina Zabala, both sexual women to varying degrees, manifest some of the most interesting of the many ethical conundrums in the novel. The dilemmas of social justice they exemplify are not artificially organized to win against contrary opinions or resolved by a textual deus ex machina; Asturias's female characters are not lined up in service to ideas about gender, neither the idea that women are oppressed nor, the opposite, that women are inferior. This moral and political complexity allows the novel to express quite subtle points about female sexuality.[3] Whatever Asturias's own reasons may have been for his unconventional and untypical female characterization, he has produced a more versatile novel, one which can better appeal to readers today, than many dated, even predictable, cultural products of the 1960s, precisely because he created characters who dramatize still-debated cultural issues without either reducing them to opinions or flattening the characters to puppet stand-ins for them.

Like his unusual characterization, episodic strands in *Mulata* are culturally and ideologically heterogeneous. One consequence of this detailed mixing is a resulting fragmentation, a lack of the totalization one usually finds in Boom novels. This heterogeneous complexity opens the discussion of female characterization to a consideration of race, class, and ethnicity, making analysis more worthwhile. While the author's concern with gender was not minimal, neither was it a focus or a priority. During the 1960s, like today, sexism, if recognized, was considered less urgent and less important to criticize than capitalism or racism.

Asturias often repeated his desire to reproduce aspects of the Mayan worldview in his fiction. By trying to portray contemporary Indians and their changing environment from their own perspective, Asturias crossed many borders between languages, races, genders, and ethnicities. Realizing the extent of the political repression, economic domination, and cultural bigotry that indigenous peoples were experiencing in the 1950s in his homeland, Asturias uses his knowledge to create a fiction he hoped would reflect implicitly or explicitly the view of the Mayan peoples on the injustices they were undergoing. He considered the mimesis of certain characteristics of aboriginal thinking, especially those that freed him from Western ideas of realism or accuracy, to be his greatest positive challenge as a writer. His Neo-Indigenist fiction aimed at a "greater" realism through a poetic imitation of "deeper" cultural phenomena, eschewing both the superficial and what Western eyes consider exotic, native traits in favor of representations of what Mayans considered important. Amply documented in the biographies and interviews is Asturias's lifelong study of Mayan texts and ethnography. It was as a mature author, thirty years after his first Neo-Indigenist works, that he wrote *Mulata,* when his knowledge of Mayan ethnography, as presented in academic writings, was beyond question.[4] His direct contact with monolingual Mayans was limited, however.

A lifetime of reading the classical literature of the Quichés, the Cakchiquels, and other native American peoples contributed to Asturias's informed imagination, comfortable in the manipulation of linguistic and religious specifics of Mesoamerican Indian cultures, especially but not exclusively, those of the Mayan group. Humorously taught and aesthetically encoded, the Guatemalan's moral and economic lessons and his political critiques are imbricated in a poetry of stone sculptures, *huipils,* feather headdresses, and ritual sacrifice. Critic René Prieto correctly asserts that Asturias "was so profoundly impregnated with the generative grammar of indigenous manuscripts, such as the *Popol Vuh* and the *Annals of the Xahil,* that he was able to harness Western techniques with stylistic and thematic elements from Indian literature to create the first major break in the Western hemisphere with the mimetic tradition that typifies European literature" (*Archeology of Return* 12). Of *Mulata,* Harss writes that Asturias "says he thinks he has come close to fulfilling his lifelong ambition of achieving a satisfying synthesis of the material and mythical worlds of his people" (Harss and Dohmann 99).[5]

During the late 1950s and early 1960s, when he wrote *Mulata,* Asturias was not in Guatemala but Argentina. The author witnessed exciting intellectual debates in Buenos Aires and, after 1959, read about life in the newly revolutionary Cuba. At the same time, he was keenly aware that his Central American homeland was suffering from yet another rollback of Indian economic rights, democratic political reforms, and civil liberties. As a journalist, he was likely to pay attention to the paradoxical United States as well, in which the last of the witch hunts for Communists was occurring simultaneously with the formation of the New Left and the beginnings of student movements in many urban areas. These ambivalent times on the international stage and the way Asturias experienced them — as a professional journalist and outside his country — may help to explain why he does not actively promote in *Mulata* an emancipatory strategy for (sexual) women in a clearly discernible ideological stance. In contrast to his other fictions, in which he explicitly works out a political position advocating respect, justice, and freedom for a targeted social group (most often, Guatemalan Indians), in this novel Asturias seems poised to do the same for women, but does not. His novel's themes evince a readiness for the '60s debates, a squaring off on certain issues. His text signals where and how some of the arguments in favor of and against women's sexual liberation were coalescing internationally, as well as the fears that limited how such conversations took place. But feminism had not truly entered his field of vision and is not the issue around which the novel turns. This lack of focus regarding "the woman problem," as well as the exuberance of narrative serendipity in *Mulata,* place it on the earliest horizon of novels that ambivalently welcomed the "newly sexed woman" and yet still feared her. For these reasons, this study of the sexual woman character in recent Latin American fiction opens with *Mulata,* a novel that portrays her as a danger to traditional Mayan societies and to an all-important sense of community.

Miguel Angel Asturias was aware that forcing each and every woman into a traditional family and a woman's caretaker role was harmful and oppressive. In 1958, during the period of writing *Mulata,* he published an article in the Caracas newspaper *El Nacional* titled "La mujer: valor económico" [Woman: economic value] showing his interest in following and commenting on wives' new economic role and its effect on marriage. This article shows that he could accept, in theory, woman's economic equality with men in the family.[6] In addition, he could laugh at a backward morality only capable of polarized views of women (and wives) as either on a pedestal or undistinguished servants in relation to work. He makes this point in his typically image-laden language and repetitive style: "The semidivine or semidiabolical concept our ancestors had of women has gradually been put away with the old clothes and only once in a while does one still hear a reference to her as someone situated on a pedestal, far from daily life, outside the day-to-day struggle, isolated inside the four walls of her house."[7] Ideologically, he situates himself among those who understand that "woman's place is everyplace," as the feminist slogan goes.

Asturias writes that men should be pleased that their working wives/partners share in paying the bills. Furthermore, by working for salaries outside the home, women have become more serious individuals, having more in common with their spouses. Equally a wage earner, responsible, the "working woman" has a new awareness of herself in relation to man which may be called an incipient feminism.[8] In "La mujer: valor económico," Asturias laments the unjust refusal of husbands to contribute to housekeeping when the wife is employed outside the home. Unlike many other men of his generation, the Guatemalan writer gives voice to the unjust burden placed on women by the double workday, outside and inside the home. If the husband does not begin to participate more fully in the domestic chores at home, Asturias warns, married women—especially those with children—will suffer unduly when they try to maintain the house in addition to the new full day of work outside.

A sign that Asturias probably felt a certain discomfort with the pro-woman, modern stand he has taken, however, lies in his article's concluding irony. He is able to maintain, playfully, a phantom of the courtly attitude toward women that he has just rejected. Chivalry returns under the erasure of an exclamation of protest about his own remarks: "it must be repeated that today woman has become, on a higher level than ever before, an economic factor that is as important as, if not more important than, man, and this reservation is nothing more than a gallantry on my part, without which I couldn't say good-bye to you ladies who are also as beautiful, as graceful, as pleasant, and seductive, [as] when you weren't economic factors, but how horrible . . . I am returning to the past, when you were ours, but now, like the economic factors you are, you belong to yourselves, and you decide your own lives without taking us into account!"[9]

Though Asturias argues that the greater sex equality of the present age will bring improvements for all, he admits to feeling nostalgia for the lost "golden age" of women's subordination to men. He cannot quite leave behind the habit of complimenting women's beauty as if that were her most important feature, nor can he resist reminding her of her past in a sexist society. A doubling of pro-woman and anti-woman elements are present, inextricably joined in a historically new mix of qualities. A similar self-mocking gallantry, a joking reluctance to throw out old attitudes, in the midst of a conscious plan to promote greater justice, resurfaces with a vengeance in *Mulata*. Asturias's satiric romp through twentieth-century mythic worlds is overwhelmingly dystopian in *Mulata*. His women characters possess strength and intelligence yet are tinged with infernal shades and are violent in their personalities. The sexual woman characters engage in forceful, often successful, resistance to those who wish to control them. Since their desire is destructive of the status quo, they are dangerous to society. To the extent that they destroy oppressive institutions and patterns of thought, they bring about a wished-for change, but it would be misleading to call these dangerous female figures feminist or even protofeminist. Asturias uses the sexual woman type less to accomplish a pro-woman agenda than to criticize a money economy (capitalist agriculture) and Western culture (Catholicism, Hispanic American social practices), both of which were (and are) being forced upon the men and women of rural Native America. Abject poverty verging on starvation and a religious war surviving beyond the period of the Conquest underlie this comic tale of sexual women who become volcanoes and snakes. Nonetheless, the characterization of sexual women in *Mulata* coalesces around themes of gendered justice and social transformation important to the incipient feminism of the time.

A major impulse in *Mulata* is to entertain, even to dazzle the reader with poetic brilliance and the sheer magnitude of Asturias's capacity for invention. *Mulata* mingles the regional novelist's rural setting, the Boom novelist's modernist virtuosity, and a traditional storyteller's improvisational inconsistencies. In this imaginative exuberance, as in other ways, a mixing of many cultural elements can be seen. For instance, the text displays not only Modernist bravado, but also the Mayan love of wordplay, ornament, and spectacle. A typical example of this heterogeneous verbosity, which simultaneously can provide a sample of the novel's unusual representation of female sexuality, occurs when a minor character, the magician Juan Nojal, has noticed that the Mulata is missing her "sex," her "*lox*" in the language of the Quiché Maya.[10] When Nojal asks her how she has arrived at this sad state, he clarifies that he is referring "To that precious throat that is an object of love, to that box of red flints that the moon spreads out month by month, to the virgin offering, to the wrinkled sea shell, to the serpent-star, swallowing and sustaining, the one that orders a life worked out on axles of hope, that great butcher woman, a dream that hangs down from the heaven of the mouth of perverse people, a noose around the neck of a man who is alive, and bad and barren, like the flesh of flies, for those who take it in the place of pleasure, of pastime" (255T).[11] The processes of image accretion and making of lists in this speech reflect the powerful Juan Nojal's great reverence for the Mulata's sexual organs, and his sympathetic grief at her loss of them.

The same speech read in a humor unlike the character's, though, can have a comic effect. The solemnity of this ritualized, neoprimitive poetry about the pudenda exists for those who respect it, but for others it may provoke laughter, repulsion, or ironic derision, since the topic of Juan Nojal's rhapsody is, after all, the Mulata's sexual parts as *vagina dentata*. In this scene, a reader's attitude may derail what the character intends as serious; in other scenes, laughter is written into the reader's script and would not be ironic. For example, when the priest has a plan to defeat the Indian devils of the town of Tierrapaulita with contraband Catholic holy water smuggled into town inside coconuts, female sexes play a purely comic role. The devils foil the priest through the strategic placement of women's detached sexual organs on top of each coconut, so that when opened, each coconut appears to be a woman urinating. Asturias's burlesque of the iconography of Catholic-indigenous religious wars thus reveals some smuggling of his own: he has brought the contraband of farce into his serious attempt to make a neo-Mayan work. To say this another way, the omnipresent beauty of Asturias's language and his frequent recourse to obscene humor together provide screens hiding the extent to which the author laces the pleasure of his text with nodes of explicit social commentary. This authorial commentary usually revolves around the value of community and its imminent destruction by capitalism and the individualism it promotes. To complicate matters further, at other times the humor does not mask the serious intent, but rather explicitly derives from Asturias's serious project of providing a Mayan perspective on the modern world. Many of the chuckles in *Mulata* emanate from a pseudo-Mayan glimpse of Western culture and technology, the inscription of a clearly contemporary scene as a place of myth, magic, and legend.

In terms of the novel's humor, one of the best critical articles is Gerald Martin's "*Mulata de Tal*: The Novel as Animated Cartoon." Martin's comparison of the book with cartoons explains well its slapstick episodes and sheds light on the novel's tendency toward visualization. His comparison eventually breaks down, however, because his analogy does not suit other major aspects of the novel, particularly its language—richly poetic, sonorous, allusive as well as elusive. The plot does in fact consist of unreal violence and linear progressions of events that start, falter, and begin again, but on balance the novel contains little that is mechanistic like a cartoon. Rather than the cartoon, *Mulata* more closely mirrors oral works containing myths, legends, and tall tales featured in performances at social gatherings in many cultures. Like Walt Disney, Asturias did choose fairy tales and cultural myths as his subject matter, but a ludic strategy different from the cartoon is at work, one which employs myriad techniques and subgenres, and which occasionally approximates the simplistic, visual cartoon.

Mulata is a strenuous reading exercise that creates or re-creates complicated allegorical structures of meaning, then gleefully sabotages them in the name of art, of fun, or of the Latin American subaltern. Frustrated with the grand narratives of Modernism that had marginalized a majority of Guatemalans—the narrative of progress, the narratives of Freudianism, and the isms of the vanguard—Asturias shares an irreverence for cultural and historical boundaries with an anarchic, postmodern spirit. Simultaneously, however, unlike many postmoderns, this author retains his political commitment by attacking head-on the encroachment of international economic interests on rural, isolated cultures. He is able to achieve both a sabotage of overarching narratives and an engaged sense of writing by maintaining a creative tension between surrealist ideas of writing that fragment and wander, and a personal imperative to tell of the autochthonous (non-Western) emotional, religious, and spiritual reality, to which he had had a special, if limited, access.

The economically oppressed whom Asturias represents in his novel are largely, but not exclusively, contemporary *mestizos* (those of mixed Native American and European race and culture) or *ladinos* (Westernized Indians). Among the non-Mayan people represented, the most significant, however, is neither *mestizo* or *ladino*; the Mulata of the title is of mixed European (Hispanic) and African (black) background. The Mulata's racial name, repeated so often in the novel, refers the reader away from the author's home country, Guatemala, and away from his place of exile, Argentina, because neither had many African Americans.[12] By giving the Mulata African roots, Asturias makes the novel more broadly Latin American than Guatemalan, and more racially and ethnically inclusive than if all the characters had been Hispanic, Indian, or a mixture of the two.

In Asturias's interview with Luis Harss, the author gives some reasons for his racial designation of the Mulata. His decision to portray a multiracial world was a personal choice and an ideological point he wished to make, rather than an element deriving from textual necessities. He said: "The Mulata herself is a figment I invented. I called her Mulata in order not to use the word Mestiza, because it didn't seem to me the mixture of bloods was enough in Mestiza. I avoided Zamba, which would have given a combination of Indian and Negro bloods, because I didn't think the term would suggest that special grace of movement you find in the Mulata" (Harss and Dohmann 98). If the Harss interview is to be taken at face value, Asturias's stereotypical ideas about mulatto women as more graceful than *mestizas* or *zambas* led him to designate his title character "the Mulata." For this reason, he created a more geographically open story. This reason also suggests that the story is imbued with racist clichés about black and Indian women, unfortunately.[13] Clearly, though, the Mulata is Asturias's epitome of the sexy woman, and he portrays her as desired by all the men around her.[14] As Celestino Yumí's second wife, the one who marries him for his money, and whom Yumí bought as he would any other object, the Mulata's physical attractiveness predominates over all her other qualities. While men's sexual attractiveness to women is either grotesquely phallic or barely mentioned in *Mulata,* women's sexual attractiveness to men results in long lists of surreal, magical images.

The carnivalized sexual women in *Mulata* consist principally of the three wives of the poor woodcutter Celestino Yumí. His wives are: (1) Catarina (also called Catalina) Zabala, his wife of many years who becomes the dwarf Juana Puti, then the powerful witch Giroma; (2) the Mulata, a poor prostitute and a Moon Goddess whose true name is never known; and (3) the Huasanga, a ribald, raucous, demanding dwarf who has returned from the dead and enjoys stealing women's sexes.

In this novel, sexual women's power destroys rather than nourishes. Catarina Zabala learns from her husband Celestino Yumí to place herself before others and to calculate how to acquire wealth and power. The Mulata dances naked before her husband's farmworkers, creating a riot, while his cornfields burn unattended. The Huasanga robs women of their sexes and then carries around her booty like a string of garlic heads. There is no avoiding the fact that Asturias's lascivious females pose a threat to men and to the towns and cities in which they live. This destructiveness is the antithesis of the usual function of women in most traditional cultures, where they normally care for children and home, and, thus, pass on their group's knowledge, customs, and practices. The women in *Mulata,* however, teach no heritage to others. Abuela Já, the wise matriarch of the Salvajos, is the only exception to this rule; for her cultural and community roles predominate. But one can argue that a grotesque image of female power is perpetuated in Abuela Já's story as well, since she is not a human female, but a human inside a *jabalí* (boar) body.[15] Perhaps the reason she does not function as a destroyer is her animal part, or that she and all the Salvajos are a community apart, or because she is old and wise. The young women involved in themes of sexuality all incarnate at one point or another the destructive side of myths, legends, and folktales of autochthonous American cultures or of Asturias's personally surreal visions.

The destructive sexual women in *Mulata* pose particularly great danger during sex itself. Most violent of all, Yumí's sex with the Mulata is a bloody ritual. She frequently causes physical pain for Yumí and inflicts psychological damage. In addition, she finds masochistic pleasure in being cut, shot with arrows, and pierced with needles. René Prieto attributes the character's violent sexuality to a biographical (that is, a psychological) source in the novelist's life, but Asturias easily could have been presenting historically inspired images. The pre-Conquest Mayans had a warlike culture, one which was violently subjugated by the Spanish. The blood rituals and the customs surrounding self- and captive torture among the ancient Mesoamerican cultures, the brutality of the Spanish Conquest, and the cruelty of the Inquisition may be seen as antecedents to many, and perhaps most of the moments of violence in *Mulata*. In this chapter, I show that the origins of the mythic and magic dimensions of the Mulata and of Catalina/Giroma may be seen as metaphors for traditional Guatemalan culture in which female figures of power threaten economic, mythic, and matrimonial stasis.[16]

Within many pre-Columbian cultures, it was believed that life could only come from death; in the continuous cycle of life-death-life, destroyers were bringers of life because they advanced life to its next stage. On the function of death in Mayan cultures, most Mesoamerican experts agree: "There are, of course, many . . . manifestations of the belief that life is born from death. There is a scene on page 52 of the *Codex Borgia,* for example, showing the copulation of the god and goddess of death, a depiction of death in the act of creating life, a fitting image for a world that sees death as another phase of the cycle of life" (Markman and Markman 181). At a famous pre-Maya site in Chiapas, the Izapa Stela 50 connects a skeleton figure through an umbilical cord to another small creature; Markman and Markman interpret this as further evidence that "the belief that man and all other living things were 'born' from the bones of the dead is fundamental to the Mesoamerican view of life as a cyclical process" (211). Similarly, the bizarre image of the Mulata who has been split down the middle, and who then joins in a single dress with a "skeleton woman," points to such an image of cyclic transformation. The Mulata's union with death, in the form of the skeleton woman, foreshadows her future as a source of life.[17] In a sense, by causing death, female characters in *Mulata* create the conditions for new life. Indeed, both Catalina and the Mulata give birth: the former gives birth to a devil child, son of Tazol, and the latter gives birth to "herself," to another Mulata, the "Mulata daughter." The Mulata, a cruel hedonist, should also be read as a heroic, culture-saving figure because she destroys life. A paradox to Asturias's readers, but not to the Mesoamerican mind, the destruction achieved by the Mulata awards her religious status.

Dangerous Games

The inscription of the sexual woman in *Mulata* transpires as three textual strategies, or "games." For heuristic purposes, I am calling "games" certain embedded structures within the novel, each having its own rules and outcomes, in order to emphasize the sense of freedom and play in the novel. By speaking of discernible "games," I address larger literary elements than character, diegesis, or imagery alone. Each "game" has a specific place, the scene of its narrative sequences, where it is played best or most legitimately. Rules map the games further by defining permitted plays and players. Who can score, when the game can be played, and who or what decides questions of legitimacy and relevancy are part of each game.

The three "games" in which sexual women play significant roles in *Mulata* are the Money Game, the Mayan Game, and the Domination Game. The Rabelaisian carnival as described by Bakhtin could be considered an additional game, in the sense I am using the term. But I have not devoted a section to the carnival "game" owing to space considerations and because this game is already recognizable to most readers.[18] The playing of the three particular games that I do treat creates dangerous, destabilizing times for the represented world, when the status quo of woman and society are placed at risk in the hope of her and its transformation.

In the first of these subdivisions, the Money Game, the first part of the novel shows the moral devastation wrought by a cash economy on a rural village and its gender structure. When the novel begins, the poor woodcutter Celestino Yumí arrives at a local fair, where he will attend mass with his pants zipper down. From the frustrated pleading of his wife Catalina Zabala, we learn that he has gone to mass in other towns with his zipper open, and that he has become the target of local jokes and humor. He has earned the nickname, the Fly Wizard (*el Brujo Bragueta*). By soberly and repeatedly exposing himself in church, Yumí fulfills an arrangement he made with Tazol, a character invented by Asturias, at times called the Wind God, at times the Corn-Leaf Devil. Tazol's (and Yumí's) goal is to make women sin by thinking of sex during mass. In exchange, Tazol has promised Yumí great wealth. Before payment is rendered, however, Tazol convinces Yumí that Catalina Zabala has been unfaithful to him. Tazol offers to buy Zabala for even greater wealth, more than Yumí can imagine. Hurt and jealous, Yumí relinquishes his loving companion of many years to Tazol. Handing over Zabala sets in motion the events that destroy Yumí's enjoyment of his purchases, including his enjoyment of the seductive Mulata.

The author explains: "The starting point of the story is a legend popular in Guatemala: the poor man who comes into riches by selling his wife to the devil. It's a widespread legend in Guatemala. As to what the devil does with the woman, there are different versions. In one, he makes off with her, then he returns disguised as a woman to punish the man who sold him his wife. The man falls in love with the devil and the devil makes life impossible for him. Then the man yearns for the good little woman he used to have" (Harss and Dohmann 98). The miserably poor woodcutter Celestino Yumí has arranged such a Faustian contract with Tazol. The ill-gotten money from Tazol buys Yumí the seductive Mulata, and soon Yumí's desire for money has additional consequences beyond costing him the wife he loves. According to Asturias's interviews, one version of the legend would make the Mulata Tazol himself, disguised as a woman, in order to punish Yumí. But Asturias asserts there are other versions and thus leaves the Mulata's ultimate identity open. In the novel, the Mulata becomes "the mistress of a rich man" (52T) ["mujerón de hombre rico" (52)] who marries the newly rich, fabulously wealthy Celestino Yumí solely for his money.

The civil marriage of Yumí and the Mulata does not last long. Sorry for his previous greed, Yumí eventually retrieves Zabala from Tazol; she then helps him to seal the Mulata inside a sacred cave. Escaping from the trap, the Mulata returns as an erupting volcano, destroying his possessions and killing all found within the area of Yumí's mansions. Next comes a brief transitional period of renewed marital companionship, poverty, and humility, but Yumí and Zabala soon decide they want something more from life. They set off to become magicians by heading for the university city of wizards, Tierrapaulita. Before arriving, they have many adventures, including meeting the Salvajos mentioned above, and accomplishing Yumí's secret mission—to restore Zabala to full size. Since her time with Tazol, Zabala has been a dwarf. This period of wandering is their initiation into the fantastical world of devils and spirits as the story moves further and further away from a realistic setting. Once Yumí and Zabala arrive in Tierrapaulita, Catalina Zabala gains complete ascendancy through her liaison with Tazol. Yumí, now the mistreated and weaker member of the couple, once again falls for the Mulata's sexual attractions. She has returned to her seductive human shape and now works for Cashtoc (another indication she is not Tazol but a separate entity). Cashtoc is supreme lord of all the devils, including Tazol.

As in the Money Game, in the Mayan Game the Mulata is a main player. In the Mayan Game section, I discuss theories regarding the cultures of the ancient Mesoamerican peoples and their twentieth-century descendants to explain some hermetic facets of Asturias's representation of sexual women, especially the Mulata's hermaphroditic body, her violence, and the sequence of her incarnations.[19] Yumí's purchase of the treacherously alluring Mulata was the climax of the Money Game, in which greed is criticized, and the event that initiates full play in the Mayan Game, in which Mesoamerican beliefs are displayed explicitly. The Mayan Game largely pertains to the middle sections of the book, but helps to unite the whole by including scattered elements from the beginning and the end. In the novel's middle section, the meandering and complicated trials of Yumí and Zabala eventually take a back seat to the introduction of a new cast of characters in Tierrapaulita. The religious battles fought from this point onward relegate the apprentice wizard and witch to mere pawns in larger conflicts. It is important to remember that the novel's Mesoamerican cultural allusions greatly affect the meaning of female sexuality in the novel. Asturias told Harss: "Basically *Mulata* is a retelling of the myth of the sun and the moon" (97): "You have these two astral bodies orbiting without ever joining. The Mulata is the lunar principle" (Harss 98).

As the moon, the Mulata appears and disappears from the narrative as if in the full-moon or new-moon phases. In the novel's middle portions, Yumí's first wife, Catalina Zabala, gradually recaptures her place from the Mulata, then ascends to new levels of magical power, while the Mulata becomes eclipsed, once literally, and metaphorically in general. But what role does the moon play in Mesoamerican myth and religion? My section called the Mayan Game argues that the novel's Mesoamerican references to the moon, women, sex, and other matters coincide with anthropological ethnohistories from the first half of the twentieth century about Mayan peoples living in the Guatemalan region and to visual representations of pre-Columbian civilizations that Asturias may have seen. Although called here the Mayan Game for simplicity's sake, Asturias's strategy did not restrict itself to Mayan culture, and freely imitated Nahuatl (Aztec) and other autochthonous cultural elements. Among the ancient and contemporary allusions to Mesoamerican and Central American cultures, references to Mayan-related groups predominate whether or not from Guatemala, however.

With humor and poetry, Asturias's gradual strategic deployment of Mayan, Nahuatl, even occasionally Quechua allusions invests his narrative with a unique imagery, at the same time divesting the result of any documentary value. Asturias's mixing of many cultures in the novel comes from his outsider standpoint and desire for panoramic reach in his fiction, more than it reflects some observed reality. Having said this, however, I must add the corrective that, in this novel, one of the points made is that modernity has made Central American indigenous cultures more pervious to outside influences. There has been a certain degree of historic intermingling of pre-Columbian cultures, and modern technologies of communication and transportation have increased this for practically every culture on the planet.

The astronomical and astrological dimensions of the novel, displayed as mythological allusions and images, do not negate or otherwise limit the novel's themes of mastery and conquest that overshadow all other themes in the last chapters; instead the desire for power over others constitutes the third modulation of the novel's game strategy: the Domination Game. Asturias's economic critique (game one) and his mythologizing (game two) both feed into his concern with the historical in the Domination Game (game three). The Domination Game replays the religious, cultural, and economic struggles for hegemony between Euro-Americans and Indo-Americans with humor and revisionism. In the Domination Game, the act of buying the Mulata, previously interpreted within the Money Game and the Mayan Game, again requires reinterpretation from the perspective of the novel's final plot developments and themes. Within the Domination Game, buying the Mulata becomes ruthless trafficking in humanity. The main narrative segments in which this strategy appears occur after Yumí and Zabala have arrived in Tierrapaulita. In this part of the novel, the clashes are established. Next Catholic and indigenist conceptions are contrasted regarding religion, the afterlife, medicine, and—most important for our purposes—sexuality within marriage and sex in prostitution. All players become either winners or losers, conqueror or conquered, loved or betrayed. Asturias plays with the grand historical scheme of Christian supremacy, in order to knock it down, to show the flaws at its center. He who claims to have dominated, to have hegemony, is mad and delirious, hearing only what he tells himself. Prophetic of the new strength of the indigenous voice in Guatemala today and in the study of ancient Mesoamerica, Asturias ends his book by discounting the nonindigenous voice found in histories in Spanish that had claimed right, reason, and control.

The cataclysmic destruction at the end of the novel is told from the perspective of Indian consciousness, or at least how Asturias imagined Indian consciousness to be, in which gods and devils rule destinies. Asturias told Luis Harss: "In *Mulata* we have a priest surrounded by the forces of evil. Basically that is what the novel is all about. The Indian forces of evil: Cabracán, the god of earthquakes, and Huracán, the god of hurricanes, want to wipe man off the face of the earth. For them man is an intruder in the universe. They want to destroy him. That's what we might call the Indian viewpoint. But Catholicism has a different concept of evil. Satan does not want man destroyed. On the contrary, he wants man to multiply in order to increase the population of hell, if we can put it that way. So naturally the two conceptions clash" (Harss and Dohmann 98–99). This war has as its theater of operation the bewitched city of Tierrapaulita and environs, with the most frequent and bloodiest engagements inside the Catholic church presided over by the priest Mateo Chimalpín. In the middle sections of the novel, soon after Celestino Yumí and Catalina Zabala arrive, we read of occasional sparring between the priest and the Indian devils, as in the incident of the coconuts, mentioned before. But Chimalpín barely ruffles Cashtoc's dominance, until the Christian devil Candanga arrives. At that point, full-fledged war ensues in the church building, and the devils on both sides use the bodies of their minions in duels. If a movie were made of this novel, the special effects could be spectacular, as the dueling characters are possessed by the devil of the opposing religion, then one "morphs" into a human-sized spider (wearing a cassock) and the other into a human porcupine. After this battle, human once again, the priest seeks to hide his battle scars—pockmarks from the penetration of the porcupine's spines—but he survives the fight only in order to succumb to leprosy, elephantiasis, and madness. Tierrapaulita is destroyed by an earthquake, that is, by the Indian gods. Yumí and Catalina perish; the Mulata may die as well. Similar to the destruction brought on by the angry Mulata when she was an erupting volcano, the final catastrophe eliminates Asturias's other characters. Only the priest is barely alive on the last page. Taken to a hospital delirious, amidst orderlies and modern medicine, the priest's enchanted aboriginal world of Tierrapaulita has disappeared. The human winners and losers in the Domination Game forfeit everything when the forces of nature decide to play the endgame; the Indian conception, in which humanity should be destroyed, according to Asturias, wins out in the end.

Asturias's final chapters read as if they narrate a dream; the surrealist technique of automatic writing, vestigial in earlier chapters, here predominates. The closest approximation to the end of *Mulata* among well-known fictional works of Latin American literature would perhaps be the monologue of the dictator in *Autumn of the Patriarch* (1976; *El otoño del patriarca* 1975). But even Gabriel García Márquez's power-hungry dictator, whose breathless ravings unceasingly beat on the reader's attention without the benefit of paragraph organization or sentence periods, nonetheless maintains a psychological realism and an expressionism simpler to decode than *Mulata*'s final section. The associative technique of certain precursors, such as the elegiac dialogues of Juan Rulfo's *Pedro Paramo* (1994; *Pedro Páramo* 1955), is a great deal more tame and realist than the ending of *Mulata*. The plot, previously wandering but largely linear in its advance, in the final chapters submerges below a breakdown of over-arching structure, during which the reader is at pains to tell what is happening, and at what level of reality. Despite this apparent chaos, the narrator delivers sufficient information to discern the path to death (or other end) taken by the main characters.

The separation of my argument into three sections (or "games") should not hide the fact that the issues of any one section cannot be fully divorced—politically, aesthetically, or morally—from the issues of the others. The image of money in the Money Game relies at times on Mayan allusions and, more often than not, may be properly described as "power over others," just as the Mayan Game treats themes of both money and domination. This complex novel is like a large multiplex of arenas, with ball courts and stadiums for the simultaneous playing of many games. But the major events are staggered, at least in the brute sense, so that readers can better focus on one game at a time. The Money Game, where we will begin, is followed by the Mayan Game and then by the Domination Game. In order to comprehend the role female sexuality (and sexuality in general) plays in the scheme of the novel, the general rules for playing the Domination Game are set out at length in my final section, serving as a means to tie together the points brought out in the previous sections on the Money and Mayan games.

The Money Game

> Until the new spirit, the spirit of capitalism, displaces creations of the imagination that give meaning to life in the precapitalist world, until the new "rules of the game" are assimilated, the fabulations that the commodity engenders will be subject to quite different sorts of fantasy formation [from those emanating from the capitalist world]. In short, the meaning of capitalism will be subject to precapitalist meanings, and the conflict expressed in such a confrontation will be the one in which man is seen as the aim of production, and not production as the aim of man.
>
> Michael Taussig (11)

Asturias's Money Game opens a door through which the Western reader can glimpse a worldview in which spirits inhabit all things. In this conception, there is no mechanistic operation of natural forces, only willed actions by the spirits of mountains, corn leaves, or animals. Events may be the consequences of a divine master plan, but they are also caused by a complex interaction of the spirit and material realms. The particular way in which Asturias manifests this vast multitude of actors in his narrative has been called by Gerald Martin a "socialist surrealism" (Martin "Introduction" xiii). In contrast to socialist realism, "socialist surrealism" pursues goals of economic justice through the "greater realism" of an experimental writing based less on socialist conventions and more on psychological experiences: through imagining what would be psychologically *real* in an indigenist way of seeing things.

Asturias has fictionalized how someone unaccustomed to capitalist exchange might imagine the novel's initial circumstance of suddenly becoming rich. The rapid influx of cash results from a contract with a devil whose largesse appears marvelous, but which leads to death and mayhem. Despite the strangeness of the devil contract, the Money Game proves to be a realist element, or more accurately, a "found" cultural attitude placed within Asturias's artful collage of modern Guatemalan "reality" as seen from the Indian perspective. Understanding how and why a seemingly European devil contract can very possibly imitate an American reality provides one key to comprehension of the role of sexual women in the novel. But first, we need to understand the Money Game itself.

The Money Game in *Mulata* begins with woodcutter Celestino Yumí's sudden acquisition of incredible wealth through his pact with the devil. Yumí's deal with Tazol the Corn-Leaf Devil to trade his wife of many years for wealth impels the events of the first part of the novel. Loved for her loyalty, hard work, and willingness to share poverty with him, Catarina Zabala is turned over to the demon when Yumí is made to believe that she has betrayed him with their wealthy neighbor Timoteo Teo Timoteo, whom Yumí envies. When Yumí's wife disappears and tremendous amounts of money appear in his life (he finds treasure in a cave), his instigator and confidant Tazol calms the former's worries about being held accountable for a murder, with the advice that Yumí should buy everyone's complicity: "money is the best shield: against God, money; against the law, money; money for meat [flesh]; money for glory; money for everything, for everything, money" (43T) ["el dinero es el mejor escudo: contra Dios, dinero; contra justicia, dinero; dinero para la carne; dinero para la gloria; dinero para todo, para todo, dinero" (42)]. The mouthpiece for a cynical philosophy, Tazol establishes an equation between woman and the money to buy things. Yumí is a quick learner, turning around and using his ill-gotten funds from selling one wife to buy himself another. In the Money Game, sexual women are represented by the Mulata, a prostitute, and everyone is commodified as sexually desirable bodies or as workers, hands and hours of labor.

The explicit connection between riches and sexual women begins with the appearance of the Mulata. From the moment Yumí lays eyes on the Mulata, he treats her like a prostitute, asking her how much cash she charges: "He stopped and looked at her with the insolent security of a rich man who knows that the woman who can resist him does not exist, much less that one there, a paragon of misfortune, dressed in a yellow outfit that was in its dotage from age and use, her coltish body looking for someone to tame her" (48T) ["Se detuvo y la contempló con la insolente seguridad del rico que sabe que no hay mujer que se le resista, menos aquélla, tan planta de infeliz, vestida con un traje amarillo que era baba de tan viejo y usado, sobre su cuerpo de potranca, que estaría en busca de dueño" (48)]. The sudden, intense connection between the affluent Yumí and the rag-clad Mulata at the Fair is rife with their common obeisance to economic power. She is his "trophy" (49T) ["trofeo" (49)] and the symbol of his material success. Obviously poor, the Mulata sells herself to the insolent landowner for all the money he has on him and a civil marriage. Much later she laments: "I, who sold my flesh to the riches of the sun" (249T) ["Yo que vendía mi carne al sol de la riqueza" (253)]. Yumí had sold Zabala, but the Mulata sells herself to Yumí. The Mulata demands money and represents what you can buy with money. To further her symbolization of greed, readers are never told of the Mulata's life before she sells herself to Yumí. The mystery of her past makes the Mulata's exorbitant desire for Yumí's money, equally with her demand for sex, appear as Tazol's revenge rather than as the Mulata's independent action.

In the Money Game, Asturias is indeed associating prostitution with the modern capitalist desire for profit, but *Mulata* condemns the influence of a money economy on peasant farmers, rather than protesting against prostitution alone. As Alaíde Foppa wrote: "The Mulata . . . is an infernal character who causes the perdition of the ingenuous Yumí. But the real infernal symbol is money, that stains and corrupts everything" ["La Mulata . . . es un personaje infernal que causa la perdición del ingenuo Yumí. Pero el verdadero símbolo infernal es el dinero, que todo lo mancha y lo corrompe" (65)]. The author of *Mulata* censures the modern period in which he sees a "devilish" transformation from subsistence farming to cash crops in the region. Unlike *Men of Maize*, this novel focuses on individual and communal consequences of greed, rather than on factors that originate or exacerbate the love of wealth.[20] The narrator explains Yumí's need for money in this way: "Yumí kept his cribs full of dry corn leaves, *tazol* instead of ears, knowing that only in that way, transforming into bank notes those remains of the sacred plant, would he be able to confront the expenses and the demands of the Mulata" (55T) ["hojas secas de maíz, tazol en lugar de mazorcas, a sabiendas de que sólo así, transformando en billetes de banco aquellos restos de la planta sagrada, podía hacer frente a los gastos y exigencias de la mulata" (55)]. Not only does he acquire trash (the corn leaves and not the corn), he also defiles the sacred corn plant by his inordinate accumulation.

The theme of unworked-for wealth, especially when rapidly appearing as a windfall, and then associated with sexual women has, of course, a long history in European literary traditions whose basic characteristics are known to most readers and which I will not rehearse here. But Asturias claimed that the devil contract was "a widespread legend in Guatemala" (Harss and Dohmann 98, quoted above). The particular forms in Latin America that the Money Game assumes have found an able explicator in *The Devil and Commodity Fetishism in South America* (1980) by anthropologist Michael Taussig. When studying peasant farmers in Colombia and Bolivia, Taussig noticed that a sudden economic surplus by a man was seen by his community as the result of a pact with the devil, whereas the production of just enough goods to use, without excess exchange value, was interpreted as a merited gift of the fertile spirits of nature. In writing about his fieldwork, Taussig argues for a precapitalist logic he calls the "proletarian devil contract," because in it "is inscribed a culture's attempt to redeem its history by reconstituting the significance of the past in terms of the [capitalist] tensions of the present" (95). The peasant farmers explain capitalist acquisition in terms of the precapitalist spirit world.

The devil pacts contracted by men in Taussig's field studies happen only on plantations where the men work as wage laborers. This money needs to be salary or to come from outside the immediate physical and affective area of those who have "contracted with the devil" because eventually the arrangement produces a generalized sterility. Such a pact cannot be used for a man's home garden, whose products he needs to eat, or for raising his children, since it inevitably leads to the end of production (of food or children). For the same reason, the money gained from such contracts must be spent on nonessential expenses, such as liquor, tobacco, and women like the Mulata to avoid the resulting sterility being visited upon one's wife. According to Taussig, the subsistence farmers believe also that such a contract must be made in deepest secrecy with the aid of a sorcerer, who makes a small anthropomorphic doll and casts a spell (95).

The male version of the devil pacts Taussig uncovered among precapitalist Latin American societies where capitalism has made inroads thus parallels several aspects of the most explicit move in the Money Game. In just such a secret rendezvous with Tazol, Yumí arranges to exchange Zabala for money; she is transformed into a "tiny shepherdess" (54T) ["pastorcita minúscula" (54)] made of clay, and placed inside a box of toylike miniatures. Each time Yumí later desires an object for himself or for the Mulata, such as a horse or house, he removes a tiny clay figure of the item he wants from Tazol's box, and it magically appears. After removing all the other magic figurines, the heart-weary husband of the voracious Mulata removes the little clay replica of Zabala, breaking his word to the devil, and undoing the agreement to give up his wife in exchange for wealth. It is significant for *Mulata* that Taussig's findings reveal peasant farmer believers in the devil contract among both African Americans (mulattoes) of Colombia and mixed Hispanic–Native Americans (mestizos) of Bolivia.

Capital acquisition as seen through the peasant farmer Yumí's precapitalist worldview, that is, sudden wealth seen as magic, is mirrored in many smaller moves and countermoves in the Money Game. While not all magic in *Mulata* treats economic themes, a great deal of Tazol's sorcery can be read in this sense, as a translation of events into the epistemological figuration they would have had for the ancient or contemporary Mayan subsistence farmer. One humorous example of this translation occurs at an early moment when Tazol and Yumí are hatching plans for the latter's future riches. Tazol announces his plot to cause many accidental deaths among the greedy townspeople of Quiavicús, then to resell their bodies' essence to cannibals who will pay him gold tribute.[21] Surprised by Tazol's allusion to cannibals, Yumí asks, "Do cannibals still exist?" ["¿Todavía hay antropófagos?"], and Tazol replies: "They never stopped existing. They don't eat the corpse materially, but they stuff themselves on human flesh, people who exploit the working man, ranchers, coffee growers, plantation owners, those in whom the Christian and the wild beast are all woven up together" (45T) ["Jamás se han acabado. No es que se coman el cadáver, materialmente, pero se hartan de carne humana los que explotan al hombre de trabajo, hacendados, cafetaleros, dueños de ingenios, en los que se confunden los cristianos y las fieras" (45)]. Asturias's story has temporarily laid down its premodern mask revealing a critique of the economics of exploitation. Oppressors of the laborer are consumers of human flesh when seen from the Indian subsistence farmer's precapitalist perspective; cannibalism is a mask of—and a magic name for—labor exploitation within Asturias's Money Game. ✓

Women may also make contracts with the devil, Taussig writes, but the nature of such agreements is essentially different. The women's "redemptive sorcery is directed at the process of reproduction, not at material production as in the male proletarian's devil contract" (99). The woman's ritual is aimed most often at an unfaithful man, and specifically directed toward the destruction of the man's potency when it had extended to others than his partner: "This man can and must be kept within the bounds of *oeconomia,* providing for his spouse and children, and prevented from irresponsible multiplication. An exchange system between a man, a woman, and their offspring is threatened by his embarking on a vastly different system of exchange based on endless gain or yield. Faith in the magical rite [of the devil contract] is a manifestation of the virtue of the former system and the illegitimacy of the latter" (Taussig 100–1). In other words, a woman's contract comes into play when her lover's or spouse's actions are most akin to the investment of capital aimed at sheer increase. Within this precapitalist mind-set, the overextension of a man's potency, in infidelity, may motivate a woman's desire for magic "solutions" to prevent his "capitalist" sexuality based on a premise of expanding markets.

In the context of *Mulata,* the hypothesis of a further critique of capitalist production in the actions of Yumí's jealous wives provides a conceptual/thematic unity to later parts of the novel that otherwise may seem unconnected to its beginning.[22] Zabala comes to have her own devil contract with Tazol, one that provides her with the magical powers to control Yumí's profligacy. The conditions Taussig found in the field are mirrored in Zabala's meteoric rise in the magical world of Tierrapaulita during the central portion of the novel. As a clay statue in the box of riches Tazol gives Yumí, or in her dwarfed state as Juana Puti (the Mulata's plaything), Zabala has little recourse but to try to survive. This situation soon changes, however. Once the Mulata has taken her vengeance on Quiavicús as an erupting volcano, Zabala and Yumí embark on their journey to Tierrapaulita, "the shadowy realm of black magic" (111T) ["el tenebroso reino de la magia negra" (112)], where they will both learn to become magicians. On the way to Tierrapaulita, Zabala becomes pregnant by Tazol, and we may say that in that way she then "enters into negotiations" with him: "Women are heavily implicated in magic, it is said, in the use of sorcery against the lovers of their male consorts or, less commonly, against the unfaithful consorts themselves. In the majority of such cases the sorcery occurs when one of the women concerned is pregnant or giving birth" (Taussig 99).

After a series of magical adventures, including meeting the half-human Salvajos and Zabala's dangerous return to human size, Zabala gives birth (anally) to the son of Tazol, Tazolín or Tazolito, who renames his mother Giroma, "which means rich woman, powerful woman, mother of all magic" (133T) ["que quiere decir mujer rica, poderosa, madre de todas las magias" (136)]. Angry at Yumí's earlier betrayal of her with the Mulata, Zabala/Giroma asks Tazolín to turn Yumí into a dwarf. The dwarfed Yumí, now called Chiltic, is forced to perform for his meager bread, cheated of his earnings, and imprisoned when not at work, much as Zabala when a dwarf had been treated by the Mulata. But Yumí/Chiltic escapes from Zabala/Giroma and attempts to marry a third woman, the Huasanga, also a dwarf. Like man's "irresponsible multiplication," which Taussig says in his fieldwork was likely to provoke a woman to desire a devil contract, Yumí/Chiltic's attempt to marry for a third time provokes the newly powerful Zabala/Giroma into magical action against him. Overcome with jealousy when she discovers his marriage-in-progress, Zabala/Giroma changes Yumí/Chiltic from a dwarf into a giant to prevent the consummation of his marriage to the tiny Huasanga. Zabala/Giroma's actions meet the requirements of Taussig's description of the female version of the devil pact, employed not for money but to put a stop to Yumí's bigamy (or trigamy, if one believes the Mulata is still alive).

Prevented at the last moment, the marriage of Yumí/Chiltic to the otherworldly Huasanga stems from the Catholic priest's desire for profit. Upon discovering Yumí is a dwarf, Tierrapaulita's priest Chimalpín had been seized by the idea of marrying him to another dwarf, the Huasanga, for them to procreate. In his scheme, this unholy holy man could raise dwarfs and sell them to circuses and others. Treating Yumí/Chiltic and the Huasanga as commodities, the priest plans to sell their progeny as one would livestock, hence his invocation to multiply. During the marriage ceremony, the priest exhorts them to produce many dwarf children: "Pygmies, no addition: body to body, total pleasure! No chilling subtractions: contraceptives or abortions! Much less, long or short division! Multiplication—twins, triplets, quintuplets!" (148T) ["¡Pigmeos, nada de sumas: cuerpo más cuerpo, total placer! ¡Ni de escalofriantes restas: anticoncepcionales o abortos! ¡Menos división o separación! ¡Multiplicación . . . mellizos, trillizos, quintillizos!" (151)]. In this novel, Catholicism is associated with growth, capitalism, and conquest like the woodcutter's greed. For Chimalpín, the Huasanga's sexuality is a means to money, just as for

Yumí earlier selling his wife had been the key to riches. This time Yumí himself would have been exploited for another's cash. As is incumbent within the Money Game, though, the Huasanga and Yumí would be breeding not within a conception of production for use (to build a family), but rather one of reproduction for exchange (to sell the babies). The character of the priest who wishes to speculate for profit on the sale of dwarf children grotesquely points to the fact that capitalist practices often have made inroads alongside Christianity: the economic and religious transformations of indigenous cultures are inextricably entwined. Taussig's findings that economic behaviors are explained by theories of magic within communities experiencing this transition are one consequence of this multifaceted phenomenon.

As we have seen, in the Money Game the most important sexual woman character, the Mulata, enters the novel as a consequence of Yumí's demonic contract. Yumí sells Zabala to the devil, the Mulata is bought as sexual property, farmworkers are consumed by cannibals, and Yumí is (almost) bred with another dwarf as a money-making venture. His male contract is dissolved when he retrieves Zabala from Tazol's box of dolls, and her female version of the devil contract becomes the preeminent novelistic mode. Taking her revenge, Zabala turns Yumí into a dwarf, then into a giant, and eventually, in a jealous rage, sends the entire company of Cashtoc's devils after the Mulata, who has returned to human form after her earlier murderous rampage as an erupting volcano.

The fundamental link between literal economic activities (production), and figurative economic activities (reproduction), is established through Zabala's complicity with Tazol, though the female contract is implicit and commented upon by the narrator very little. While many exegetes of the novel have been quick to point out the devilish characterization of the cruel Mulata, Yumí and Zabala (the human couple at the center of the novel) also consort with Tazol. Each has access to economic and political power through a devil contract in his or her own name. Although everything ultimately derives from supernatural powers in a precapitalist conception of the spirit world in control, men and women are both susceptible to temptation and capable of wielding authority. Equal in capacity for evil, woman is characterized as less attracted to sex or wealth for its own sake than man, yet equally seduced by power. Furthermore, Zabala is clearly more powerful as a witch than Yumí ever was as a rich man.

For Western readers accustomed to capital accumulation, the patterns of gendered devil contracts appear to us as mere metaphors whose truth status relies on our imaginative comparison of it to other entities we do consider real. But for the Colombian mulattoes and Bolivian mestizos of whom Taussig writes, the proletarian devil contract is real. It explains the mystery of how some people acquire great quantities of goods and lovers. The closeness of Asturias's representation of the devil pact in *Mulata* to the Taussig model found in Latin American society strongly suggests that the novel's devil contracts are indeed, as the author said in the interviews quoted above, mimetic of beliefs among Guatemalan Indians and mestizos with whom the fiction writer had come into contact. If these moves within the Money Game are equally Mayan moves, that is, if these patterns are fictive representations of Mayan ways of viewing the world, then not only Yumí, but also Zabala, in parallel fashion, need to be understood by critics from within Asturias's conception of the Indian mind-set. The Mulata, Zabala, and the Huasanga play the Mayan Game in the novel because the threshold to the Mayan worldview has been crossed; all the characters play by its rules, even those who are not Maya themselves.

The novel represents an indigenous standpoint, one on the cusp of a transformation, where economic activities have changed but belief systems have not. From a precapitalist viewpoint, the war between the two devils, the Christian Candanga and the Indian Cashtoc, can be seen as a development of this theme of economic transformation, that is, of the transition from a subsistence economy to a capitalist one. For the Christian devil Candanga, on the one hand, representative of capitalist ideas of reproduction, more sex on the part of the populace is needed to produce more children. He wants his hell to be populated; the evil goal he imposes on the residents of Tierrapaulita is the (re)production of commodified humans. For the Indian devil Cashtoc, on the other hand, his evil plans are confined to the destruction of the living. He wants continuity in population levels, zero population growth. The capitalist, Christian conception requires growth; the precapitalist, indigenous worldview needs stability. Their war is the Domination Game.

In *Mulata*, the religious wars in the New World partake of a(n imagined) Mesoamerican perspective, and thereby dramatize the incursions of the new Western, rational system in terms of the previous magical, indigenist system of belief. By displacing the over-five-hundred-year-old religious conflict begun by the missionaries and conquistadores of the sixteenth century from its usual Western, rational enunciation, Asturias gains two things. First, a mythic version of the battle between Christianity and the Indian gods should remind readers of the Mayan culture as a radically different *logic* of understanding experience. Second, in replaying the image of a continuing, modern religious conquest, Asturias corroborates the precarious survival into the present of Mayan logic, experiences, and beliefs. He validates and valorizes the moral, religious, and political thought of the contemporary Guatemalan Indian, which since contact with the West cannot be the pure or separate culture from the European it was before contact, but which exists with its own hybrid distinctness and should be recognized.

The Mayan Game

For Mayans, the presence of a divine dimension in narratives of human affairs is not an imperfection but a necessity, and it is balanced by a necessary human dimension in narratives of divine affairs.

Dennis Tedlock, *Popul Vuh* (59)

The activities of production and reproduction, moves played in the Money Game, constitute a portion, and only a portion, of the themes and narratives encompassed by Asturias's Mayan Game. Some might assert that, when studied in detail, the whole novel is coextensive with the Mayan Game, and this would be only a slight exaggeration. The book's representation of female sexuality plays with Mayan imagery and ethics, not to the exclusion of other fields of meaning but in addition to our (much debated) Western, modern understanding. For example, Asturias's fictional "Dance of the Giants" ("Baile de los Gigantes") mimes a ritual drama of the same name performed by the Chorti Maya, documented in photographs and interpreted by anthropologist Rafael Girard in volume one of his multivolume *Los chortis ante el problema maya* (1949, vol. 1, 351–84; The Chorti in terms of the Maya problem). According to Girard, the biblical scenes enacted in the Chorti theatrical performance camouflage dramatizations of the *Popol Vuh,* prohibited by missionaries since the Conquest. Asturias's fiction thus alludes to nonfictional Catholic religious scenes which, for the Chorti, gain additional significance through their Mayan relevance.

Can we read references to the character of the Catholic priest in the novel in a similar way, that is, as having one meaning within Western, Christian systems of interpretation, and a second within the Mayan religious and cultural hermeneutic? What about the references to the Mulata? Are they also camouflaged Mayan allusions? Do the Catholic figures, and possibly others, dramatize both a cause and a sign of the disappearance of Mayan culture, as one might think within a wholly Western perspective, or are they instead a cause and a symbol of its masked existence? Or can they be something in between, or both? This section, called "The Mayan

Game," is devoted to highlighting and to evaluating the extent to which the characterization of the sexual women characters in *Mulata* is mimetic of some Mayan reality or, more frequently, mimetic of some discourse about Mayan culture. To reduce the huge amount of material, I confine myself in this section to the most significant allusions relevant to the portraits of Yumí's three wives almost exclusively, with only a brief discussion of other characters. Once the women's role as Mayan figures has been suggested, we can compare the Mayan allegorization to the Western, Catholic allegory to discern how they engage one another in dialogue. The specific question of the priest's and the sexton's significance and relevance to the question of the female characters' nature will thus be postponed until the section on the Domination Game, because in many ways it relies on the Mayan Game and can be discussed most efficiently afterward.

The Mayan Game is being played throughout the main narrative, in details and in major themes, as well as in the role of the sexual woman characters. Let's take a minor interpolated story as our first example. In Tierrapaulita, a character named Salomé recites poetry to the decapitated head of St. John the Baptist (171–73T; 175). The name of Salomé immediately brings to mind her biblical tale, but her speech in its form and content is actually a double symbolization. First, she alludes to the wars of early Christianity as her reason for bringing about John's death, but for the knowledgeable reader she also symbolizes a character from the *Popol Vuh*, a work that is often loosely called the "bible" of the Quiché Maya. Salomé is also the divine Ixbalanqué, the young princess of the underworld who is miraculously impregnated by the decapitated head of one of the hero twins. Salomé is present in *Mulata* because of her association with decapitation in *both* religious stories. While appearing directly and transparently a transplant from the New Testament, Salomé plays the Mayan Game in the same way that Girard found the "Dance of the Giants" to symbolize both Christian and Mayan stories.

Salomé's speech is the only text of any length in the novel typographically set as poetry; the dialogue between the mutilated Mulata and "the skeleton woman" ["*la mujer esqueleto*"], while not visually marked as poetry on the page, is nonetheless almost liturgical in its structure, its drama, its question-and-answer format, and its reliance on imagery. In this strange and fascinating ritualistic exchange between the two, the flexibility of the Mayan Game can be seen. In one part of their long exchange, the Mulata and the skeleton woman discuss the conditions under which the Mulata would accept the return of her sex, after Cashtoc's devils have stolen it:

"If they give you back your sex (blood of cacao its announcement, virginal blood its announcement, the child of your blood its announcement!), they give it back to you wrapped in soil, will you take it?" [asked the skeleton woman.]

"If they give it back to me wrapped in soil, I will take it," the Mulata answered; "I will wrap it in the soil that is the skin of the earth."

"If they give it back to you (it is fire, it is a serpent, it is a devourer of men!), if they give it back to you along the road of married couples, will you take it?"

"If they give it back to me along the road of married couples, I will take it. I will wrap it in the husband, who is the skin of the wife." (291T)[23]

Repetitive as well as ritualistic, this lengthy dialogue between the two women about female sexuality, only briefly excerpted here, comprises a series of images of Mayan life and sense of death, of pleasure and pain, in one of the novel's more serious moments. The union of death and life in a single process is crucial to the Mesoamerican worldview. The skeleton woman is also called "the woman who completed" the Mulata ["la mujer que la completaba"]: literally, the woman who joined with the Mulata in a dress to make her seem one complete woman when she was only half of one. Metaphorically, the skeleton woman is death; in joining with the Mulata (life), they create a whole and an unbeatable force.

This lengthy conversation between the Mulata and the skeleton female representing death may represent certain of the qualities contained in the formula used to close off story- or riddle-telling sessions in contemporary Mayan cultures. Like the discussion between the Mulata and the skeleton woman, one example of a "story-session epilogue" provided by anthropologist Allan Burns deals with a missing object. In the fiction, the women discuss the Mulata's missing sex, stolen by the Huasanga; Burns's real storyteller and his interlocutor from the Yucatán peninsula of Mexico speak about a series of objects. Among the modern Yucatec Maya, according to Burns, "The exchange is a dialogue. It is a formal conversation between a narrator and an interlocutor. The exchange exhibits several features of performance, including pauses which mark utterances, vocal qualities, and a penchant for brevity and understatement" (19). The session ends in this way:

Don Pas: "Let's hunt."
Don Felipe: "My rifle's broken."

Don Pas: "Where are the parts?"
Don Felipe: "I burned them."
Don Pas: "Where are the ashes?"
Don Felipe: "Eaten by a falcon."
Don Pas: "Where's the falcon?" . . .
Don Felipe: "Went in a well."
Don Pas: "Where's the well?"
Don Felipe: "Disappeared."
Don Pas: "Where'd it disappear?"
Don Felipe: "Into your belly button."
Don Pas: "True." (Burns 18)

If these similarities to the novel are meaningful, then the Mulata–skeleton-woman is mimetic of a still-existent storytelling formula. Eduardo Peñuela Cañizal has called Asturias's Neo-Indigenism a "semiotic action" (725), meaning by this term that the author preserves in his fiction the unique and unified forms of the system he is interpreting as well as the meanings that system has produced. According to Peñuela Cañizal, Asturias provides new modalities of enunciation, which become events for readers, and through which the latent ideology of the original speech act is performed, in addition to the speech's visible and apparent meanings. In the terms I am proposing, Asturias's imitation of modes of enunciation, as well as those things which Mayan culture has enunciated and given meaning, indicates that the Mayan Game may be played using form, content, or both.

For those knowledgeable of Mayan societies and myths, beyond the information provided by the text itself, there are at least two levels or kinds of semiosis within Asturias's Mayan Game. First, there are the narrations that imitate Mayan ways of interpreting events, the process or point of view in which every action means a deity is at work, and the use of formulas to tell stories. Second, there are the narrations that refer concretely to specifics of Mayan history or religion. On this level, or in this second kind of semiosis, the narrator, for example, explains that the Chewing Wizards have interpreters: "'Where are the great sorcerers?' They were probably at the foot of the cacao tree, . . . and in their hairy armpits, disguised as eagle owls, the interpreters with painted tongues, green the tongue of the one who spoke Quiché, indigo that of the one who spoke Zuhutil, red the one who spoke Cacchiquel, white the one who spoke Quekchí, yellow the one who spoke Mame, purple that of the one who spoke Pocomame, black that of the one who spoke Poconchí"

(294T).[24] These real languages of Central America, like the Cadejo and the Dance of the Giants, are allusions to content rather than to form (to the extent these can be separated).

The Mayan world consists of a large region in southern Mexico and northern Central America, of which Guatemala is clearly the center of Asturias's interest. Overall, Mesoamerica contains twenty-nine Mayan languages, and fully twenty-six of them are found in Guatemala. Unlike the centralized Aztec empire, the Mayan region shows great ethnic, religious, and political diversity over time and across the area (Barbara Tedlock 154, 168). The groups most pertinent to our analysis of his fiction are the Quiché Maya, in whose language the *Popol Vuh* is written, and the Chorti Maya of southeastern Guatemala (and near the ruins of Copán in neighboring Honduras). The *Popol Vuh* offers great literary interest and the Chorti have been favored by anthropologists for extensive ethnographic study because of their probable linguistic and cultural involvement in the development of Classic Mayan civilization.[25] Asturias read translations into Spanish of many of the surviving texts and saw artworks dating from the archaic to the modern.[26] The great synthesizing anthropologists of the first half of the twentieth century, those who sought commonalities within the multitude of cultures called Mayan, appear to predominate among his sources. Scholars like Sir J. Eric S. Thompson, who organized fragmentary, local, historical, and contradictory accounts into readable stories, attracted Asturias for instrumental and aesthetic reasons. There are many analogies in his novel that provide evidence that he knew of several works by Rafael Girard, the scholar of the modern Chorti Maya mentioned above, who wrote about the Dance of the Giants. Evidence from the novel I provide in this section indicates that Asturias was also likely to have known (directly or indirectly) Charles Wisdom's anthropological writings about modern Chorti communities.

Player 1: The Mulata

In "Algunos apuntes sobre *Mulata*" [Some notes about *Mulata*], a series of notes Asturias jotted down and sent to his friend the Italian critic Giuseppe Bellini, the novelist begins by emphasizing the absolute ordinariness of the Mulata: "Behind an ordinary woman, a married mulatto woman, a 'Mrs. Jane Doe,' is hidden a force belonging to the lunar woman, a woman who in her conjugal relations acts like the moon with the sun" ["Tras una mujer cualquiera, una 'mulata de tal,' una 'fulana' de tal, se oculta esta fuerza de la mujer lunar, mujer que en sus relaciones conyugales actúa como la luna con el sol" (19)]. This statement concurs

with the entirely (merely) human appearance of the Mulata at the beginning of the novel. Nevertheless, the Mulata soon leaves her human shape,
returning from her confinement in a cave, to wreak vengeance on Yumí,
Zabala, and the town of Quiavicús as an erupting volcano. In the novel's
later stories, as the human couple enters more and more deeply into a
magical world, the Mulata undergoes multiple transformations of her
body and her being. These changes are only possible if she is not a mere
human, but in fact combines human and divine qualities.

But what was/is the nature of the divine for Mayan culture? According
to the Markmans in *The Flayed God: The Mythology of Mesoamerica*
(1992), "Though frequently characterized as gods, that is to say, [as] inter-
mediaries between the essence of the life force and the countless living
things in the world of nature, in Mesoamerica they [the gods] seem to be
more precisely the spiritual components of the natural forces themselves.
The names of the gods are often no more than the names of those forces.
There is often no intermediate stage. And the same holds true for such
more abstract conceptions as the creative spirit and the patrons of
rulership" (60). The multiplicity of Maya gods, much more numerous
than the Greco-Roman deities, is another important characteristic to remember as we work to understand the caliber of and connection between
the Mulata's apparent humanity and her hidden lunar powers. Even more
significant is the fact that each of the many Mayan gods can appear in a
great number of forms, and that each god is difficult, if not impossible, to
distinguish from its purely human counterpart. In a fashion "comparable
only to the mythological tradition of India," Markman and Markman
further explain that "At the foundation of the mythology of the urban
cultures of Mesoamerica there is not, in the way of Greek mythology, for
example, a formal pantheon of gods who control the forces of nature and
of human destiny and who were thought to be agents of a higher divine
being. Nor was there any notion of a god who could have any 'real' relationship with mortal flesh. While they are often imaged forth anthropo-
morphically as ritual performers, sometimes 'disguised' in animal form
with animal features, Mesoamerican gods were imagined as invisible
forces of the realm of the spirit" (59–60). The intermingling of the human
and the divine in the characterization of the Mulata also relies on the
invisible spirit world as the element common to both the human Mulata of
the beginning and end of the novel, and the divine Mulata of the middle.

Among the diverse twentieth-century Maya, ethnographers have found
similar sets of beliefs in the multiple forms for each deity. Charles Wisdom
asserts: "Characteristic in varying degrees of all the supernatural beings

are (1) moral neutrality or duality, (2) sexual duality, (3) multiplicity, (4) bilocality in sky and earth, and (5) dual personality with native and Catholic counterparts. The concept of duality is so strong that the Indian will ascribe it with little hesitation to any being, even where duality would seem to serve no purpose, in such cases stating that the being in question 'must' be both male and female, good and bad, etc." (409–10T).[27] Markman and Markman phrase it this way: "Adding to the complexity of the Mesoamerican conception of the gods, most of the major gods were conceived within a structure that placed them simultaneously in oppositional and complementary positions in respect to each other, each defining their particular 'reality' in terms of the others. In addition, they often manifested opposing characteristics within themselves, being both masculine and feminine, having both benevolent and malevolent aspects, manifesting both youth and age, or having apparently opposed functions" (60). This complexity means that the spirit world manifests itself within the material world in exceedingly manifold forms.

This incredible variety gains a structure, or at least an order, by having an organization of opposing pairs of characteristics. In terms of the sex/gender division, Wisdom reports that "Sexual duality takes two forms: that in which a group of deities of one sex are related to a group of the opposite sex and that in which a single group is of dual sex, the male of the being affecting or dealing with women and the female affecting men. In the first type the male is placed in a relation of co-operation to a female, and the female is referred to as the 'woman' or 'companion' of her male consort. In the second the being is a single entity but can take on either sex at will, as the situation demands, and in some cases it has certain of the characteristics of both sexes in a single body. In either case the male form has relations with female people, and the female form, with male people" (410). Wisdom gives many examples of sexual duality among the deities and the evil spirits. The god of sleep, for example, "is of dual sex, the male sending sleep [dreams] to women, and the female, to men" (398T) ["es sexualmente dual: El varón lleva el sueño a las mujeres y la mujer a los varones" (450)].[28] The earth god (*dios de la tierra*) in Wisdom has both sexes: "He is both male and female, and it is the union of this pair which brings about the birth, or sprouting, of the cultivated plants, which are said to be their offspring" (402T) ["La deidad es masculina y femenina y es la unión de estos dos sexos la que hace que nazcan (o broten de la tierra al germinar) las plantas cultivadas, de las cuales se dice que son sus vástagos" (454)]. This earth god "is the native personification of the earth, the soil, plant growth, and riches and property in general" (402T) ["es la personificación nativa de la tierra, el suelo, el desarrollo de las plantas y la riqueza y la propiedad en general" (454)]. Corn has a male spirit, the passive form of the earth god; the bean has a female spirit.

Important for comprehending Asturias is the idea that most gods appear to be of the sex opposite to her or him who sees them. In this regard, Charles Wisdom includes several apparitions (apariciones) or ghosts (espantos) in Chorti belief who appear as minor characters in Mulata: the Sisimite, the Siguanaba, and the Cadejo. Only the guilty need fear the apariciones, Wisdom writes, because evil spirits leave the innocent alone, implying that Yumí, Zabala, and Chimalpín bear some guilt, since they see the apparitions so often and fear them so much. Taking a female (or male) form does not mean that the supernatural entity is limited to that sex, merely that it has temporarily taken that form. Translating this into literary terms, when Yumí and Zabala face the female Siguanaba, the Siguamonta, the Llorona de los Cabellos de Agua, and other such mythic figures (the Siguapate, etc.) in Tierrapaulita, the reader is seeing through the eyes of a male focalizer for the narration, either Yumí (127T ff.; 128ff.) or the priest Mateo Chimalpín (201T; 206). In Wisdom, the Sisimite, the guardian of hills with talons for feet, is usually male (but may be female), and is at times a giant and at times a dwarf. In Wisdom's description, when rocks are seen rolling down mountain paths at night—especially by drunks—the Sisimite is credited.[29] The Siguanaba, usually female but at times also male (to women), is female in Asturias. She drives insane anyone who sees her (him), and is a guardian of whirlpools in rivers. The Cadejo, multiple in Wisdom's description, has the form of a dog or a tiger in Mulata. Readers of Asturias will also remember the Cadejo as the male devil/seducer from his Leyendas de Guatemala. Like the female Moon and the male Sun who may appear in the other gender, the apparitions are not women only. If one follows the rules of the Mayan Game, it would be hard to make a case for negative images of women in Mulata based on these supernatural figures, since they are likely to have assumed female form simply because they are being seen by men.

Consequently, various questions arise. Should critics also consider the Mulata a female emanation of a sexually dual moon deity, a god/dess? If so, it is unavoidable to ask whether she is a woman character at all, as separate from the male ones. But if she is not a female character, what might be her male form? The Mulata is most closely associated with Tazol, Asturias's Corn-Leaf Devil. While the Mulata is clearly part of Tazol's plan to make Yumí suffer, there is no textual evidence, internal to the novel, that the Mulata and Tazol are two aspects of the same deity. But several intriguing possibilities as sources for the character of Tazol would indeed make the devil and the Mulata two emanations of a single divine force.

In "Caracteres demonológicos en *Mulata de tal*," Luis Pérez Botero believes Tazol to be a fictive rendition of the Huastec god/dess Tlazoltecoatl (usually spelled today as Tlazolteotl).[30] The critic cites Francisco Javier Clavijero, author of *Historia antigua de México,* as saying that Tlazoltecoatl is "the god of garbage, invoked to avoid the infamy that guilt could cause" ["el dios de la basura, invocado para evitar la infamia que pudieran ocasionar las culpas" (117)]. Recognizing the sexual duality of the deity, Pérez Botero also quotes Antonio Morales Gómez, translator of the *Tlilmatl, o Libro de los Dioses,* who describes the god as a "'shameless Venus' who presided over the life of Mexicans from noon until one-thirty in the afternoon because 'that was the time for *pulque*'" ["'Venus impúdica' que presidía la vida de los mexicanos desde las doce del día hasta la una y media de la tarde 'por ser ésta la hora del pulque'" (117)]. (*Pulque* is an alcoholic beverage.) Most intriguing is Pérez Botero's comment on the visual representation of Tlazoltecoatl in the Borgia Codex as "A naked woman who carries a child in front of her in a small cart and who seems to hold a snake in her hand at the height of her mouth" ["una mujer desnuda que lleva delante un niño en un carrito y parece sostener en la mano a la altura de le boca una serpiente" (Pérez Botero 117)]. The main advantage of Pérez Botero's hypothesis that the Mulata is the god of garbage *and* an immodest sex goddess is that it implies the essential unity-in-multiplicity of Tazol and the Mulata, for the former is the god of corn husks and the latter is a gorgeous, unashamed Venus-like creation.[31] Another purely practical advantage of this interpretation is that more is known about the Huastec Tlazolteotl than about her Classic Mayan equivalent, the moon goddess Ixchel.

Tlazolteotl is associated in colonial accounts with the serpent (Pérez Botero 117). The Mulata is also often generally associated with snakes; for instance, she is a "viper" ["víbora"] who requires its victim to participate in its own death (57T; 58), and she is "now dressed up in flesh, just as ready to be a snake as to be a woman" (49T) ["ahora vestida de carne, tan pronto era culebra como mujer" (49)]. To associate the Mulata with snakes is an important strategy within the Mayan Game, since the association of women with serpents, it should be remembered, recurs through Mesoamerica.[32] But the Mayan association with snakes is not unique to Tlazolteotl. This animal, associated more generally with women, is an important image for many episodes of *Mulata,* especially that of the "Virgin with a Rash" ["doncella con salpullido"], in which a spotted snake takes the place of a woman in bed in a brothel visited by the sexton Jerónimo.[33] The snake is indeed very important, but it is not proof that the Mulata is modeled on Tlazoltecoatl/Tlazolteotl. Indeed, there is insufficient evidence to map the Mulata onto Tlazoltecoatl and not onto the Moon Goddess Ix Chel, instead or in addition. Karen Bassie-Sweet explains that Ix Chel, from the Yucatán, means "Lady Rainbow," and that Chac Chel (or "Red Rainbow") from the Dresden Codex wore a snake headdress (54). Additionally, the snake features largely in Christian creation stories as well, of course.

In Eric Thompson's 1939 monograph "The Moon Goddess in Middle America, with Notes on Related Deities," the famous Mayanist dismisses "evidence of the former existence of a male lunar deity," deciding that "even the masculinity of this [previous] deity is questionable" (128). The debate about whether the moon goddess was always female or sometimes male continues today.[34] Thompson posits two moon goddesses in the Mexican traditions, Tlazoltecoatl-Toci and Xochiquetzal, both closely associated with weaving. In the Mexican tradition, Xochiquetzal was portrayed in the Codex Borbonicus as "the first woman to cohabit" (136), and "in her strongly sexual aspect" (134), according to Thompson. Celebrations in honor of this goddess consisted of a "drunken orgy" and "girls born on her day might become prostitutes if they were not careful" (136). Thompson mentions that prostitutes and homosexuals "were much in evidence" during the Tlaxcallan feast in her honor (136).[35] Whether or not the Huastec goddess Tlazoltecoatl-Toci, who presided over childbirth, was a source for the name Tazol, she manifested additional aspects analogous to Asturias's Mulata. Tlazoltecoatl-Toci "was said to cause earthquakes whenever she wished" (141) and was "the patroness of sexual licentiousness and prostitutes" (136).[36]

But there is ample reason to suppose that the final form of the name Tazol is an ambiguous hybrid, taking advantage of Colonial Mexican, Classic Mayan, and contemporary popular associations in Asturias's most syncretic mode. In addition to the Tlazolteotl, Tazol is likely to be related to the Quiché Mayan word *tz'aqol,* the common word for "maker" (Tedlock *Popol Vuh* 215). Asturias would have been familiar with the word from his experience in helping to translate the *Popol Vuh;* Tz'aqol was one of the two Maker Gods who (with Bitol) makes humanity from corn after several unsuccessful attempts with other materials. Perhaps most important of all is the fact that "in popular speech in Guatemala the corn leaves, the waste from corn, is called 'tazol'" ["en el habla popular de Guatemala se llama 'tazol' a las hojas de maíz, al desperdicio de la mazorca" (463)], according to Raúl Silva Cáceres. His etymological hypothesis provides such a simple and likely origin for the name Tazol that the probability Tazol and the Mulata were meant to be male and female forms of the same deity is greatly diminished. Additionally, I have less confidence in Pérez Botero's erudite proposal than in Silva Cáceres's popular one because the Mulata manifests her sexual duality in her simultaneously male and female body; there is no need for discrete male and female characters to reproduce the Mayan preference for sexually dual forms. Asturias represents divine sexuality in the Mulata's hermaphroditic body.[37]

Although Asturias leaves some ambiguity with regard to the meaning of the Mulata's "double sex" on several occasions, at least once there is little doubt that she is meant to have the vestiges of organs of both sexes. In a humorous exchange with Yumí, the dwarfed Catarina Zabala, having spied on the Mulata while she bathed, reveals to Yumí in her country slang some shocking news: "'Celestino,' the dwarf told him, 'this wife of yours, just so you should know, does not have the *prefections* of a woman, but neither does she have the *prefections* of a man. You have to know that I goed to spy on her, while she was taking a bath, and she isn't a woman, because she isn't a woman, I guarantee you, if I know my *prefections,* but she isn't a real man either, because she doesn't have your *prefections,* which I also know.' And having said that she rubbed up against Yumí. 'You mean to tell me that she's a . . .' Celestino swallowed the word. 'I don't know what she is, but she isn't a man and she isn't a woman either. She doesn't have enough inky-dinky for a man and she has too much dinky-inky for a woman'" (66T).[38] Though modified by adjectives in the feminine throughout, the Mulata does not have a typical set of female sex organs ("she has too much dinky-inky"). In this very conversation, Zabala calls the Mulata "your wife" ["ésta tu mujer"], nevertheless.

In the conversation where Yumí learns of the Mulata's hermaphroditism, he remembers that there is "a gender that's neither rooster nor hen, the neuter gender" (67T) ["existe un género que no es ni gallo ni gallina, el género neutro" (67)], which he learned in school. Not used to formal reasoning, he attempts to explain the Mulata's body in terms of such a neuter gender. His hypothesis that the Mulata has a "neuter" human body lends weight to the idea that the events in the book should always be read as story, since only language has a neuter case. In other words, even when Asturias's surreal narrative imitates a Mayan concept such as the sexual duality of the divine, that is, when the novel performs a speech act which translates a Mayan modality, this Spanish inscription always remains first and foremost a creative invention, a move in the game, and secondarily a mimesis of some existent.

The Mulata's sexual indefinition makes her disturbing to characters and readers alike. Yumí defends himself from his embarrassment at Zabala's news of the Mulata's hermaphroditism by quoting the Mulata on the necessity of giving her back during sex: "She explains to me that the moon also does it that way with the sun, that because of that the moon always has her back turned, we never see her face, because if she were to turn around the sun would take her from the front and they would breed monsters" (66T) ["—Ella explica que la luna también lo hace así con el sol, que por eso, la luna está siempre de espalda, jamás se le ve la cara, porque si se volteara, el sol la tomaría por delante y engendrían monstruos" (67)]. To which Zabala responds: "That may be so. But the moon, from back or front, we know is a woman, and this Mulata of yours . . ." (66T) ["—Tal vez que sea eso. Pero la luna, por la espalda o por delante, sabemos que es mujer, y ésta tu mulata . . ." (67)].

For feminist criticism, the Mulata is a most interesting kind of female character—one for which even biology is questioned as an absolute definer of sex, and through which the binary sex/gender system is shown to be insufficient to describe the true variety of the forms of the human body. In Judith Butler's philosophical attack on the idea that sex is a precultural category, *Gender Trouble,* she articulates particularly well the post-structuralist theory that biological definitions of male and female have changed historically and culturally, and that any differentiation of human bodies into the two sexes relies on specific values and decisions that are not universal. Thomas Laquer's book *Making Sex* has provided further evidence from the history of biology for the constructivist theory that definitions of biological sex, like those of social gender, are ideas; as such, the defining qualities of one's sex depend on one's culture and not on the "realities" of the physical body.

In Asturias's *Mulata,* the novelist makes hilarious the ease with which in Mayan culture gods are goddesses, too; in so doing, he plays with the modern obsession (both feminist and antifeminist) with the fixed-sex/gender binary of male and female. Discomfort with muddled sexualities becomes in this novel the butt of a joke. In Elizabeth Grosz's 1991 article "Freaks," the author of *Volatile Bodies* reminds us that the deformities that have attracted the most attention in ancient and modern cultures have been "monsters of excess, with two or more heads, bodies or limbs; duplicated sexual organs" (36). Hermaphrodites, especially of Yumí's neuter kind, are not "monsters" of excess but rather of ambiguity: "In popular nonmedical discourses, there seems to be something intolerable, not about sexual profusion, a biological bisexuality (which is fascinating and considered worth paying for by audiences), but sexual indeterminancy: the subject who has clear-cut male *and* female parts seems more acceptable than the subject whose genitalia is *neither* male nor female. These subjects imperil the very constitution of subjectivity according to sexual categories" (31). The voyeurism in the modern media's attention to "freaks" attests to the pleasure and identification involved, Grosz adds. But "there is a counterbalancing horror at the blurring of identities (sexual, corporeal, personal) which witnesses our own chaotic and insecure identities" (35–36).

In interviews Asturias said he was relying on ancient Mayan texts when he has the Mulata refuse sex with Yumí from the front, but he adds that these writings are ambiguous.[39] We do not know whether they condemn anal sex or vaginal sex from the rear. This ambiguity is maintained in the novel's portrayal of the sexual act between the Mulata and Yumí, but not when the naked Mulata runs through the burning cornfields and would accept sex with the crazed workers chasing her. In the latter case, Asturias clearly portrays her as desiring anal sex: "It was madness when the most daring of them pointed at her sex, her double sex, without love, with hatred, and the bestial and moonlike Mulata turned her back to await the penetrating, virile, compulsive attack from the side opposite the face, through the lead-red and tightest ring of Saturn" (57T) ["Fue la locura, cuando los más atrevidos apuntaron hacia su sexo, su sexo doble, sin amor, con inquina, y la mulata, lunar y bestia, volvióse de espaldas a esperar el ataque penetrante, viril, compulsivo, por el otro lado de la faz, por el anillo, bermejo plomo, más cerrado de Saturno" (57)]. The workers chasing the Mulata reject her backside, uttering, "Gold is better" (57T) ["Mejor oro" (57)]. Turning from the Mulata, the poor laborers seek to grab the ingots appearing magically in place of the burning *tazol* or corn husks. Like Yumí, the peons who work for him are attracted to her perfect body as if to a magnet, but they, too, are repelled by her sexual unorthodoxy.[40]

Additionally, in contrast to her hedonism, the Mulata's cruelty in bed with Yumí is represented as a frustration with her sexuality from the rear, and, in a larger sense, as a gnawing unhappiness that nothing—not riches, sex, cruelty, or self-mutilation—could assuage. She had bowmen shoot arrows at her, barely tearing the flesh: "until she would fall out of time into a vague and gnawing eternity, her immensely wide pupils were two moons of tar, two solitary coagulants in the midst of absolute terror, fear, fright, doubt, a weeping in shouts, the weeping of someone without an owner, without a handle, and right there, the suicidal terror, the wish to do away with her present image, beating her face against the impassable, and right there, the howl, that most anguished howl as she found herself once more with her lunar, vertebrate, pierced-through, passive, climacteric self" (58T).[41] Asturias's insistence on anal sexuality in this scene of the burning fields may be (as some critics have written) an indication that Asturias meant us to read the Mulata as shockingly depraved and diabolical. Alternatively, Asturias may be making moves with the Money Game, showing the workers involved in the same choice between a sexual woman and money that Yumí had made. But a more nuanced approach, it seems to me, would be to see how one strategy interacts with another in this scene: a move within the Mayan Game—the Mulata's double sexuality—is placed in check by the move within the Money Game, namely, the appearance of unearned gold. Rather than attributing the worker's actions to an authorial episode of women-hating, or fear of unconditional, female, or anal sexuality, the cause is his protest against greed and its destruction of Mayan culture. Dangerous and destructive as she is, the Mulata is condemned more for her greed and cruelty than for her lust or self-torture. Additionally, pervasive as the Mayan Game is, we must be careful not to see the novel as a faithful representation of Mayan culture in every aspect, or as something other than invented stories whose import comes from the interaction of Mayan and non-Mayan allusions.

Returning to Mayan sources for the Mulata, there was another name mentioned above for the Moon God/dess: Ix Chel. Based on the study of Mayan hieroglyphs and on collation of ancient archeological evidence with living informants, researchers Schele and Miller describe the typical sculptures of the two aspects of the moon goddess Ix Chel:

Among the pantheon of Maya gods, two females are particularly associated with the activities of daily life; although these women are divinities, their behavior resembles that of human women. The most important female divinity is Ixchel, the moon goddess, known from the codices and the widespread devotion to her at the time of the Conquest. She has two aspects in Classic Maya depictions, both associated with making cloth. At times she appears as a demure, young weaver; at other times, she is a sexy, comely courtesan associated with spinning. . . .

A second female type is the courtesan [aspect of Ixchel] who wears unspun cotton in her headdress. . . . In spite of the association with spinning, we never see this woman at work, in contrast to the industrious weaver. She sometimes wears a cape, but generally she is depicted wearing no garment over her breasts, which is the custom of many Maya women today when they are at home. Like the erratic moon, this woman is not a model of constancy. In paintings and clay sculptures she is paired with old men, deities, and even large rabbits, as if she wandered from one to the other. In one notable example from the Detroit Institute of Arts . . . , she embraces a leering old man, who lifts her skirt to feel her thigh. In similar figurines, her companions hug her or fondle her breasts. These figurines, produced with a keen eye for human behavior, comprise much of the erotic art known for the Maya. (Schele and Miller 143–44)

Schele and Miller not only confirm Thompson's assertion of the lunar goddess's association with licentiousness; they also emphasize this quality's coexistence with her other aspect as a virtuous woman. Coe reports that Ix Chel means "Lady Rainbow" and that she was the "goddess of weaving, medicine, and childbirth; she was also the old Moon Goddess, and the snakes in her hair and the claws with which her feet and hands are tipped prove her the equivalent of Coatlicue, the Aztec mother of gods and men" (*The Maya* 166).

Without comprehending the moon's dual nature as both licentious and virtuous, it is difficult to make sense of the symbolic role the moon plays for the Chorti Maya of the first half of this century in the anthropological literature with which Asturias was most likely to be familiar. Her virtuous aspect carried great moral exemplarity. According to Rafael Girard, "In the cosmic order the sun and the moon are the prototypes, and at the same time, the models/patrons, of man and woman; they represent the ideal couple whose conduct should be imitated" ["En el orden cósmico el sol y la luna son los prototipos, y a la vez los patrones, del hombre y la mujer; representan la pareja ideal cuya conducta debe ser imitada" (*Chorti* 1:202)]. This scholar of the Maya, Girard, whose work was known to Asturias, stresses that the homology of the sun and moon to the human heterosexual couple had its greatest impact on attitudes regarding agricultural practices. A woman could best cultivate planted seeds when she was pregnant (202–3). As a result, the moon is the patron of pregnant women, "who, like plants, operate under its influence" ["quienes, como las plantas, operan bajo su influencia" (203)]. Wisdom agrees with Girard that the moon "deity is the patroness of childbirth and also has some connection with plant growth" (400) ["patrocina los partos y tiene cierta relación con el desarrollo de las plantas" (452)] for the Chorti Indians.

Wisdom adds: "In a vague way she [the moon goddess] is considered the female consort of the sun god, and she lights the world at night 'while her companion sleeps'" (400) ["Se considera, aunque en una forma poco precisa, que la diosa luna es consorte del dios sol, y que alumbra el mundo de noche, 'mientras su compañero duerme'" (452)]. In *Mulata*, the raising of corn and the issue of subsistence versus capitalist farming plays an important role in the literal and figural meanings of the narrative, as we saw in the Money Game.

In Girard's chapter on marriage practices among the Chorti Indians, he quotes a native informant, Ciriaco Hernández from the village of Catacamas, on a related practice used to assure the maximum fertility of the crops via the maximum fertilization of women by men: "A special town crier with a musical instrument passed through the streets of the town announcing the fixed date had arrived for the fulfillment of marital obligations, yelling in a loud voice: 'It is breeding time.' The Indians devotedly obeyed the ordinance" ["Un funcionario especial con su tamborilero pregonaba por las calles de la población que había llegado el plazo fijado para cumplir con el deber conyugal, gritando en voz alta: 'Ya es hora del engendro.' Los indios acataban devotamente el reglamento" (*Chorti* 1:203)]. Either this section of Girard, or some other informant on the practice, may have been the source for Asturias's fictional portrait of the Christian devil Candanga and his nightly call to mate— "Breeding tiiime!" (213T) ["¡Al engendroooo!" (215)]. If so, this refrain would be an important example of attributing Mayan characteristics to the Christian devil. The call to propagate the species in *Mulata* is transformed from an extratextual anthropological report revealing rarefied, ritualized sexual activity among the Chorti, into Candanga's capitalistic plan to populate hell through the forced breeding of humanity, which Asturias criticizes in the Money Game. Candanga takes the priest's plan for the production of dwarfs to a divine level, exhorting all humanity to breed every night.

Girard also recounts that after sex, the Chorti men were only able to return to work twenty-four hours later, after careful vigilance and rest to recuperate after their exertions. This comment may help to explain why the Mulata's sexuality was portrayed as so dangerous, even life threatening, to Yumí. Thompson includes a report from a native informant that "his grandfather had told him that in the old days a man had intercourse with a woman only between full moon and its disappearance" (135; see also Girard, *Chorti* 1:192). Since the moon reigned at night, the sexual act should occur then also, during the most propitious time for development of the seed, so that it would not incur undue risk for the man. Among the contemporary Maya, the sexual act is considered particularly debilitating to men, according to Wisdom, and excesses were to be avoided, as with other pleasures and vices. Even without torturing him, the Mulata was dangerous to Yumí because the frequency of their sex would have been excessive in Mayan belief.

Similarly, in the *Popol Vuh,* two young, beautiful women represent dangerous sex; they are used as a trap in the hopes of destroying the Quiché Maya gods. In Tedlock's recent English translation, their names are Lust Woman and Wailing Woman. In Asturias's translation of the *Popol Vuh,* the members of the pair are called Deseable (Desirable) and Agradable (Agreeable). At the point where the two women play a role, the Mayan gods Tohil, Auilix, and Hacauitz have been killing the "tribes," that is, any foreigners who do not claim to descend from these three gods.[42] The powerful Mayan gods frequently went bathing at the river, but whenever the tribes caught sight of the powerful ones, the gods would disappear. So the tribes hatched a plan to send their rulers' beautiful young daughters to bring about the Gods' destruction through sex. (How the gods were to be brought low is not entirely clear from the text.) Of superior intelligence, the three gods do not lay with the women as expected, and instead they destroy the tribes through the unknowing embassy of the princesses, by sending back with them deadly gifts that kill the leaders of the tribes. Like the historic figure of the Malinche in Mexico, these mythic characters betray their own community, though they had no choice in the matter. Lust Woman and Wailing Woman could not choose whether to wait for the gods at their bath, nor did they know that the beautiful robes the gods gave them for their fathers contained the power to kill the wearers. According to Asturias's translation, the leaders are defeated, and the young women insulted as tricksters or deceivers ["engañadoras" (118–20)]. Tedlock's translation adds that the profession of Lust Woman and Wailing Woman became prostitution as a result (Tedlock 167–69, 310–12). In the *Popol Vuh,* and in Mayan culture in general, astute intelligence, especially the ability to trick one's adversary, or to avoid being tricked oneself, is highly valued. If you are fooled by impostors, you have lost the game.

Hidden names in the *Popol Vuh* also are a sign of strength.[43] The Mayan Game Asturias was playing thus justifies in part the fact that the Mulata's name is never revealed. By having an unrevealed name, she has an advantage over others, a shield the like of which not even the gods Tazol and Cashtoc can boast. At her weakest moment, the Mulata equates her sex with her name, as if she had had a name (albeit unknown to others) when she possessed her sex, but which she loses when her sex is stolen. She calls her sex "my name as a woman, my occult name, because without it, without my sex, I'm nameless, I have no name!" (289T) ["gracia de mujer, mi nombre oculto, que sin él, sin sexo, soy innominada, no tengo gracia!" (295)]. The translator has rendered "gracia" as "name," but literally it could also be "gracefulness" or "attractions." Thus "gracia de mujer" could be "feminine attractions."

The Mulata's relation to Mayan religious modalities, especially her analogy to the Moon Goddess, is helpful for understanding not only the danger she posed as Yumí's sexual partner, but also the violence, bloodletting, cruelty, and body fragmentation with which she lives. As a seductive Venus, she is Yumí's bittersweet reward from the devil for making the money pact, but as a divine spirit of nature, the Mulata becomes Tazol's instrument of demonic revenge, tormenting Yumí during their time together, during "explosions of fury that coincided with the phases of the moon" (54T) ["explosiones de furor coincidentes con las fases de la luna" (55)]. Yumí's desired life of wealth and plenty is transformed through her cruelties into unspeakable physical torture, unimaginable mental suffering, and illimitable mental depravation and corruption. For instance, crazed by the beatings he receives from the Mulata and by lack of sleep, missing his beloved Niniloj (Catarina Zabala), Yumí begins personally beating his workers and allows his incipient greed to become all encompassing, which leads him to treat his workers as mere objects, as we saw in the Money Game. Finally, he can stand it no longer and he breaks his contract with Tazol. The penitent woodcutter-turned-landowner retrieves his first wife Catarina, tries (unsuccessfully) to kill the Mulata, then, with Zabala's help, walls her up in the cave where the moon sleeps. As mentioned earlier, the Mulata escapes and is transformed into destructive lava as the Moon Goddess's volcano aspect. Before a sadistic woman, now cruel nature, the Mulata destroys Yumí's devil-bought possessions, burning to the ground and burying the town of Quiavicús at the same time.

The Mayans of the Classic Period (A.D. 250–950) believed that ritual bloodletting and torture were necessary to keep the world alive. In Mesoamerica, ritual killing was "the most sacred form of sacrifice," but "symbolic bloodletting and animal sacrifice and autosacrifice" were frequent, sometimes daily occurrences: "The classic élite were obsessed with blood, both their own and that spilled by high-ranking captives. . . . This was drawn at calendrically important intervals by men from the penis, and from the tongue by their wives" (Coe The Maya 173). Coe further explains that Classic Mayan practice involved ritual punctures, cutting, and child-murder: "Self-mutilation was carried out by jabbing needles and sting-ray spines through ears, cheeks, lips, tongue, and the penis, the blood being spattered on paper or used to anoint the idols. . . . Human sacrifice was perpetrated on prisoners, slaves, and above all on children (bastards or orphans bought for the occasion)" (170–71). The authors of *The Flayed God* emphasize that such autosacrifice was frequent and that: "Sacrifice was necessary to maintain the ongoing process of creation, since in this world life, like the corn that comes from the 'dead' seed, can only be born from death" (Markman and Markman 96).[44]

In an analogous manner, during the time after Yumí has retrieved Zabala, but before he has rid himself of the Mulata, she asks her servant Zabala/Juana Puti to pierce her with needles. It is as if the Mulata knows that Yumí and Zabala are attempting to do away with her and that she accepts her new role as a captive about to be sacrificed. As if participating in a Mayan sacred ritual, the Mulata is tormented with arrows: "She sang, laughed, danced, she would have herself chased by archers who were so good that they would shoot their arrows at her and aim for just the slightest scratch, a feeling of multiple wounds in which she would twist around" (58T) ["Cantaba, reía, bailaba, se hacía perseguir por arqueros tan hábiles que disparaban contra ella sus flechas calculadas para el levísimo rasguño, sensación de múltiples heridas en que se retorcía" (58)]. These ancient cultural practices are most vividly rendered by Asturias in the figure of the Sacrificer (Sacrificador), the double of the medicine man, or *curandero,* whom the priest Chimalpín consults. The Sacrificer is described as if in a surrealist version of the paintings, codices, and stelae of the Classic Maya: "wearing a tunic made from pieces of human skin, a heart painted on his chest with blood . . . On his fingers, hundreds of hearts were palpitating in agony like wounded birds" (308T) ["vestía una túnica de pedazos de piel humana, en el pecho un corazón pintado con sangre. . . . En sus dedos cientos de corazones palpitaban agónicas, como pájaros heridos" (313)].

Less ominous than the Sacrificer, the Mulata performs religious self-sacrifice. Later, interested in seeing the moon's cave, the Mulata at first hesitates, worrying that the moon will find her insignificant, "an insect." Encouraging Mulata as part of a plan to free Yumí, Zabala replies in local vernacular that the moon will "think that you be sacred" (70T) ["Va a creer que sos sagrada" (71)]. Fascinated, the Mulata accepts Zabala's offer to guide her to the moon's cave. Her body heavy from marihuana, the Mulata arrives at the miraculous spot "dressed in an interminable laugh, the pins stuck in her ears, her hands, her arms, her legs, wounds from which a red laugh also felt like bursting out, laughter made from drops of blood" (71T) ["vestida de risa interminable, los alfileres clavados en las orejas, en las manos, en los brazos, en las piernas, heridas de las que también antojaba brotar una risa roja, un reír de salpicaduras de sangre" (71)].

The Mulata's pierced ears and piercing arrows may well be a mixture of Mayan with Christian martyrdom, to be sure; the image of early Christians going happily to their deaths is also appropriate to my argument for the allegorization of the Mulata as a religious figure. Later in the novel, the statues of saints in Chimalpín's church in Tierrapaulita are magically given animal heads in a syncretic visual representation of the two religions. This religious mixing is discussed further in the Domination Game.

The Mulata's sexual desire for Yumí, which in the Quiavicús segment of the narrative surfaces as bloody, ritual violence— "her raging need to destroy" (55T) ["su rabiosa necesidad de destruir" (55)]—in Tierrapaulita impels the Mulata to make a crucial mistake, and thus brings about her demise. She disobeys her lord Cashtoc, himself a "king" of destruction, when she desists from his mandate to possess the sexton Jerónimo's body in the battle between Cashtoc and Candanga, the Indian and Christian devils, respectively. A rebellious Eve contradicting the god's orders, the Mulata, in this inning of the Mayan Game, next attempts to (re)marry Yumí, already her husband, in a black mass, blaspheming against Christianity. In so doing, she aids and abets Candanga against her lord Cashtoc. The Mulata's punishment for disobeying Cashtoc is first to be "castrated" by the dwarf Huasanga (who robs the Mulata's sex); then the Mulata is tortured and cut in half (vertically) by the Chewing Wizards. Afterward, the Mulata laments that in their cruelty they have left her heart whole so that she can suffer the more from her subjection: "Why did they leave me with a whole heart?" (246T) ["¡Me dejaron el corazón entero!" (250)]. Given the Mulata's cruelty in Quiavicús, the reader may be surprised to learn that the Mulata has a heart which makes her suffer; indeed, her image in Tierrapaulita has become "humanized" by her continued lovelust for Yumí, and in comparison to the true and powerful devils inhabiting this town. Though never a rounded character, the Mulata has evolved from torturer, to self-tortured, and now to victim.

In Tierrapaulita, an infernal battleground where Christian and Indian devils wage war, the humanized but divine Mulata has a new role to play and evinces a different range of behaviors from those of the ritual torturer and regal self-sacrifice when she lived in Quiavicús. She now complains and begs. Additionally, she experiences no sexual desire. We can infer from this that the Mulata's desire for men emanated from the physical part that the Huasanga detached from the Mulata's body, her sex, or *lox*. Her demonic power over others and aggressive aptitude for destruction have been removed with her body parts. The Mulata has become weak and passive. She poses no danger to the Huasanga, to Zabala/Giroma, or to Cashtoc, and is ignored when, in order to plead for her body's reintegration, she wants entrance to Zabala/Giroma's lonely mansion Casasola, where Yumí is imprisoned and the Mulata's stolen sex floats in a cooking pot.

Even this wandering, abject half of the Mulata, with a heart but without a sex, is attractive to men and devils. In the chapter "A Woman Cut in Pieces Keeps on Moving, Like a Snake" [La mujer, como las culebras, partida en pedazos, sigue andando (258)], the Tipumal, "a devil of corrosive and rapid lust" (254T) ["el diablo de lascivia corrosiva y pronta" (258)], practically kills his wife, the devil Tipumalona, in the hopes of having sex with the half of the Mulata still walking about. But when the Mulata shows him that her mutilated half-body has no sex, they part, uninterested in each other (255T; 259). In contrast to her unsexed half-body, the amputated sex of the Mulata in the cooking pot, even without other body parts attached to it, attracts Yumí sexually. Left paralyzed by day in Zabala/Giroma's revenge for his attempt to (re)marry the Mulata, Yumí is obsessed with the Mulata's severed body parts, as they lie in a pot—dissociated, detached, beautiful, and alluring. When he makes love to the giant Zabala, she uses the detached sex of the Mulata to attract him, and he has orgasms there (290T; 295).

During the narrative segment set in Tierrapaulita, the Mulata de tal becomes first a wandering penitent and then a petitioner at Casasola, as mentioned. Once again, the Mulata is Zabala's antagonist and is in competition for Yumí's body; the Mulata still has divine attributes and powers, since she survives being cut in pieces, but this time she is a rebel and a minor mythic figure, subordinate to a powerful devil, Cashtoc, instead of a symbol for the power of money in the real world. The story has left behind a focus on the personal tragedy of Yumí's devil contract to follow a group of pawns in a panoramic chessboard of myth. Consequently, the story of the human couple Yumí and Zabala has changed. While the narrative focus rarely leaves Yumí, Zabala has become the active one of the husband-wife pair and he the reactive. Zabala/Giroma now has a functioning devil contract for the acquisition of magic knowledge, whereas Yumí's now-defunct devil contract had been to acquire material wealth.

Despite her punishment for disobedience, the Mulata retains her duality as both human and divine even while possessing only half a body. Owing to her desire for Yumí, however, she progressively loses what is left of her strength and powers until, in the holocaust at the end of the novel, she has none. The Mulata in the last pages explains: "I lost my magic . . . my occult powers . . . my power of enchantment" (340T) ["yo perdí mi magia . . . mis poderes ocultos . . . mi poder de encantamiento" (345)]. In the final pages, the narrator describes the Mulata's condition as daughter of herself in terms of a fall from her sacred state, which had been so evident in earlier sections: "her lips without blood, her eyes without glow, what she could have done with the flesh of those lips, and the mirror of those eyes, if they had not deprived her of her power as intermediary between the real and the unreal" (342T) ["los labios sin sangre, los ojos sin brillo, qué va la carne de aquellos labios, y el espejo de aquellos ojos cuando no la habían privado de su poder de medianera entre lo real y lo irreal" (347)]. Jerónimo, alias Sheet, opines: "she was the same certain Mulata, except without her magic, there was trickery, slyness, left-handedness" (341T) ["era la misma Mulata de Tal, sólo que sin su magia, había embustería, taimería, zurdez" (346)].

√ The images of the Mulata first as victimizer in Quiavicús then as victim in Tierrapaulita, unfortunately have been read by most critics only as her sadomasochism. But the label of sadomasochist can be better applied to characters when they are realistically portrayed, as images of people from Western culture. It hardly seems an appropriate term for the religious, ritual violence perpetuated by an entire culture. It is true that the Mulata bites, scratches, and pummels Celestino Yumí until his blood flows during √ the sexual act (see, for example, 54T; 54). But his blood alludes to her sacred nature and to the ritual function of sacrifice in classic Mayan culture where blood flows from captives, and from priests, kings, and queens. Finding the label sadomasochistic inappropriate does not negate the cruelty and violence she meted out and received, but rather the psychological and individual turn given to them by this term. Extracting blood from Yumí is an event of importance to a group; it reflects religious beliefs held √ by a culture. I am not justifying, mystifying, or accepting cruelty; I am explicating an unusual ideology in a novel that plays with Mayan homologies. To miss the Mayan conception of her violence is to lose the meaning √ given to destruction in the novel as a whole.

During the final earthquake destroying Tierrapaulita in the last chapter, "It's Quaking on the Moon" ("Está temblando en la luna"), several events and images associated with the Mulata can be clarified in light of the

Mayan Game. First, the Mulata, who has recovered her sex and the other half of her body, achieves a new transformation and gives birth to herself: "I'm my daughter . . . I'm my mother" (340T) ["soy hija mía . . . mi madre soy yo" (344)]. Pérez Botero's hypothesis that the Mulata was based on the myths surrounding Tlazolteotl, at least in the deity's female form, is relevant here. According to Markman and Markman, the Great Goddess "is a fertility goddess, a life giver, and as such seems to have represented the Mother Goddess in her totality, including both her negative and positive aspects. To complicate matters, she had many aspects, each known by a different name. . . . As the great conceiver, she is portrayed in the *Codex Borbonicus* giving birth to a child that resembles herself, suggestive of [the Huastec] Tlazolteotl's generative and regenerative powers. In addition, she was a moon goddess, and as Ixcuina was the wife of Mictlantecuhtli, lord of the underworld" (187). In the Mayan Game, when the Mulata, after being made whole again by recovering her sex, gives birth to herself, she does so as the mythical act of a divine being, as a Moon Goddess entering a new phase.

Additionally, the forms of Mayan narration may have been imitated by Asturias, at least in one or two aspects, as we saw in the ritualized dialogue of the Mulata with the skeleton woman. In a concise description of Mayan narrative visual art, Schele and Miller suggest how differently point of view is rendered in the Mesoamerican archeological sites than in Western visual art. Schele and Miller list four main "compositional formats" for the narrative component in Mayan visual art: "a single moment characteristic of the entire sequence of action"; "a continuous series of moments"; "contrasting episodes from different parts of the action sequence"; and "simultaneous narrative" (38).[45] The first three are easy to comprehend merely by their descriptive names; the fourth may be descriptive of the Mulata as her own daughter. The fourth category of compositional format is the one most different from Western art: simultaneous narrative "presents a single moment, but it uses the features of several different stages in a sequence. For example, a captive shown at the instant of his capture could be dressed in the uniform of a sacrificial victim, which in the real episode, he would not wear for hours or days after his capture" (Schele and Miller 38). The Mulata portrayed as her own daughter could be imitative of the temporal simultaneity Schele and Miller have described, since she is both childless and her own grown child. The distortions of cubism are another possible kind of stylization Asturias may have sought. In fact, what is most likely is that Asturias mixed the aesthetics of modern avant-garde movements and that of Mayan narrative to form a hybrid allowing him to imitate his beloved Mayans and still reflect the experimentalism of the new.

A second mystery in the chaotic final chapters which the Mayan Game can help to gloss is the two distinct versions of the Mulata's ultimate fate. The narrator tells the story that the Mulata was ripped apart by the Chewing Wizards (los Brujos Masticadores), and that after a series of adventures and humiliations in "The Magic Broom" chapter, she recovers her missing body parts before Zabala/Giroma can stop her. She is victorious and whole once again (294T; 300). However, the Mulata daughter says that the Mulata, her mother, was torn to pieces by coyotes: "'And what became of your mother?' Sheet ventured, shooing away a cloud of black flies, sticky from the moon. 'Didn't you know? Coyotes tore her to pieces.' 'But you were left. . . .' Sheet made his voice roguish, almost amorous . . . but she gave no sign that she knew she was the object of his veiled flirtation. . . . [N]ow he has me outside, the Mulata was thinking, a Mulata of unbaked clay, but just the same as when he had me inside, because we are in the same tremor" (340T).[46] The Mulata daughter contradicts not only the narrator's tale of the recovered unity of the Mulata's body, but also the reader's information from the narrator that the speaker is the Mulata reborn. She gives this new explanation to someone who was present and should know what happened, as the Mulata's thoughts about her possession of Jerónimo/Sheet reminds us.

In the very final moments of the novel, in the midst of general chaos and widespread magical occurrences, it is as if certain magic elements, which express an indigenous standpoint on events we readers would see differently, were being retranslated back into realistic events, although using Mayan logic to do so. The story of the Mulata's *sparagmos* by coyotes has been told to the sexton Jerónimo/Sheet in a way in which he as a (rational) Christian can understand. In other words, the Mulata's punishment is first told by a third-person narrator when the text is focalized in Yumí, then told again by the Mulata daughter as a "realist" event when the focalization has moved to the sexton.

Both versions of the Mulata's punishment are true; their differences reflect disparate hermeneutic systems. In the final chapter, as elsewhere, the Christian overlay (the sexton's point of view) does not negate a Mayan interpretation of the catastrophe. We readers who have reached the final chapter have a greater knowledge and understanding of the magical events than at the outset; we can accept she was killed by coyotes, but we know the coyotes are the Wizards who punished her. Also in the final chapter, the narrator comments that the Christian devil Candanga wants to punish the Mulata for having abandoned Jerónimo's body, "where she was in the service of arcane plots" (244T) ["en que estaba al servicio de arcanos designios" (248)], because "she had revealed herself, the way a photograph is revealed by exposure to light" (244T) ["se había velado ella misma, al exponerse a la luz, como se vela una fotografía" (248)], but the Chewing Wizards, in the service of Candanga's enemy Cashtoc, pay no heed and take her away. We readers have also learned that she survives as herself *and* in the daughter telling the tale. From this, we deduce that in this novel realistic explanations are mere coverups for, or better yet, partial explanations of, what happens on the mythological level. We can tell the score in the Mayan Game. If coyotes ripped the Mulata mother into half of her former self, then they would be the animal equivalents, the *nahuales*, of the Chewing Wizards.[47] Furthermore, through the information supplied by the narrator, the reader knows more than Jerónimo/Sheet does, as in dramatic irony. This irony has a critical edge and a political purpose.

This training given by the narrator prepares the actual reader to doubt that rational explanations contain the whole truth and to see such explanations as ironic. Readers' suspicions are corroborated in the final pages by astronomical events that signal there is more to the story than the Mulata's death from a coyote attack. Once the Mulata's aspect appears diminished, once she has lost her powers, her planetary form grows correspondingly. The sexton protests against what he cannot believe, but he sees that as the Mulata weakens: "The moon was shining more and more strongly" (339T) ["La luna brillaba cada vez más fuerte" (344)]. Despite Zabala/Giroma being called "the mother witch" (344T) ["la bruja madre" (349)] in this chapter, the Mulata and not Giroma has a celestial counterpart, the moon, and perhaps a happy exit into the sky. Thus three things are confirmed: that the Mulata recovers and survives; that the Mulata is killed by coyotes; that as the Mulata wanes on earth, she waxes powerful in the sky. The reader's task is to make sense of these versions of her story.

A third baffling and critically debated mystery occurs when the Mulata daughter attempts to open the parcel of Yumí's supposedly golden bones tied on the back of a snake. Remembering her demonic marriage to Yumí "for the rest of my [her] death" ["para toda la muerte"], the Mulata "untied Yumí's golden bones from on top of the snake, her back to the moon to cover the theft with her shadow, but in a luminous trickle of brightness, in storms of light, the lunar rays passed through her transparent body and *lit things* [*burned her*] up as she leaned over the snake and untied the bundle" (344T, emphasis and alternative translation added) ["desató de sobre la culebra los huesos de oro de Yumí, de espaldas a la luna, para cubrir el robo con su sombra, pero el luminoso reguero de fulgores, en tormentas de luz, los rayos lunares pasaron a través de su cuerpo transparente y *la incendiaron* inclinada sobre la culebra, desatando el atadijo" (349; emphasis added)]. Previously the Mulata mother had been "velado," "developed" by light like a photograph (244T; 248), the Mulata daughter's body now becomes transparent and lunar rays pass through it (344T; 349). Whereas the night Yumí's corn plantation burned, fire and light added to the Mulata mother's dangerous glory, greed causes the Mulata daughter to disappear. But does the moon's "fire" *kill* the daughter, when it did not kill the mother before, as some critics have assumed? Perhaps. The daughter has lost the occult powers of the mother, it is true. But moonbeams do not normally kill; I prefer to see this polysemia or ambiguity of light and fire (*incendiaron*) as a transformation.

The text does not settle this final question as to her fate, so we must rely on inference. If the Mayan death-brings-life worldview is to be maintained in this scene, as I believe it should, then even if a character, any character, is said to die in the final earthquake, her or his death merely marks one more in a long series of transitions. Basically, death is one kind of body transformation among many in the novel: the Mulata changes into a volcano; Zabala into a dwarf, then returns to full size, then becomes an enormous witch; and Yumí, from old to young, into a dwarf and then into a giant, in addition to his murder by Tazolín, his paralysis by Zabala's spell, and his transformation into a porcupine. In *The Flayed God*, the Markmans comment that "Once we understand that this wondrous display of seemingly separate gods is really a depiction of the process through which the world of the spirit continuously manifests itself, we can begin to understand and appreciate the beauty and profundity of the Mesoamerican mythic vision. The vast complexity becomes profound simplicity when we realize that for the seers of Mesoamerica who elaborated this marvelous system, all observed reality, all the gods and spiritual forces, are finally manifestations on various planes of 'reality' of the unitary essence of all being that is complete in and of itself" (Markman and Markman 61–62).

The religious idea that Mayans were made from maize, and that one is reincarnated in his or her seed, has long been seen by anthropologists as a wish to overcome individual death in the survival of the species. In this "vegetation metaphor," as it is known, death is extremely important for the community, a requirement of its perpetuation, in fact; one must die (or be "cut down"—sacrificed) in order to grow again. Indeed, the destruction of the lives at the end of the novel can be seen to facilitate the future birth of the unborn. This cyclic view may explain the unusual image of the snails who ask for life in the midst of the fiction's grand catastrophe. The novel's deaths, disappearances, transformations, and revelations have other common elements, but most importantly, there is a general refusal to accept biological death as an end to either an individual or a community. Both the Catholic and the indigenist conceptions of the afterlife come into play in this denial, such that any "deaths" described—including the Mulata's—are never true finalities.

The belief that the dead are merely transformed has previously been featured by Asturias in *Men of Maize* as the survival of Gaspar Ilóm. In that novel, as in Alejo Carpentier's *The Kingdom of This World* (1973; *El reino de este mundo* 1949) with Mackandal's death, the plot features popular resistance through a leader's transcendence of death. In these two examples, large popular communities—of aboriginal communities in Guatemala in the former and African slaves in Haiti in the latter—believe that the death of their revolt's leader means that henceforth his actions can be more effective than ever, not that he is lost to the rebellion. In both books, the dead leader has been freed from the bounds of the human body, from the limits of time and space incumbent on the living. The Westernized characters who think rationally in *Men of Maize* and *The Kingdom of This World* are blind to this negation of death, but readers, in contrast, are gradually trained during the reading of both novels to perceive the transcendence of death escaping the field of vision of the white, upper-class characters. By showing Gaspar Ilóm's and Mackandal's persistence beyond life, the novels contradict both Western historiography and traditional realism in fiction. In history and realist fiction, to narrate the death of a rebel leader is to represent the literal end of his life and the metaphorical end of his cause. In contrast, in *Men of Maize* and in *The Kingdom of This World,* these deaths confer magical powers and increase the dead leader's influence. Similarly, Asturias's writing in *Mulata* denies that physical death puts an end to a character's actions.

As we have seen, in the final apocalypse the Mulata first becomes a mere human and dies, then she becomes her own daughter, and finally her spirit wanes on earth as the moon waxes. Next her daughter becomes transparent, as the moon's rays reach the bundle of Yumí's bones. As an image of her fate, this transparency is at least as important as whether or not she dies. A divine or semidivine figure, the Mulata possesses a spirit form capable of many incarnations, and she is also fiction—an "intermediary between the real and the unreal." If one does not read the Mulata *only* as a human being, or her actions as mimetic of a *purely* Western idea of reality, the novel gains a divine dimension, and ultimately makes more sense, as a historical-mythic version of the end of an age, though not the death of a culture. "Transparency" symbolizes her body in Western history, a corporeality which to those around her has become invisible, a part of the landscape. By recognizing her transition from seen to unseen, and from human to spirit in the sky, we, too, play Asturias's Mayan Game.

The transformations of the Mulata largely play by Mayan rules. But the main narration, the epic stage of Tierrapaulita, undergoes a significant ideological shift with the arrival of Candanga, which signals the beginning of the Domination Game. The narration slowly (re)turns, in great uneven jerks, from an Indian conception of what is happening to a Western view of things. Catholic accounts of the conquest represent Indian culture and religion according to Catholic lights; pre-Columbian gods become devils, and the religious peoples of the Americas lost souls. In the Domination Game section, we shall see that playing the Mayan Game at the very end of the novel means showing how the surviving peoples and civilizations were erased partially or completely from history by those who kept the record. Asturias aimed to bring such erasures to the awareness of his readers, even if he could not provide us with the erased information. The Mulata remains transparent; we cannot fully "see" her. But before we can turn to the issue of power-over-others in discourse, I need to comment on the novel's other sexual women within the Mayan Game.

Player 2: Catalina Zabala

Yumí's first wife Zabala alternates with the Mulata for the dominant position of power and sex: when Zabala is in the ascendant, the Mulata is not; when the Mulata sleeps with Yumí, Zabala has suffered an eclipsed fate. They are the two women Yumí exchanges in the Tazol contract. The simple woodcutter surrendered his industrious, kind companion-in-poverty, and bought with the money the profligate, sexual, hermaphroditic "woman" with no name. Zabala's name changes with her status: Catalina (or Catarina), his respected wife; Niniloj, his dear beloved; Juana Puch or Juana Puti, a dwarf returned to life after having been in Tazol's box of miniatures; and Giroma, a powerful witch and devil consort, the mother of Tazol's son Tazolito (or Tazolín).

In color imagery also, the Mulata and Catalina are oppositional: the black eyes and brown-black skin of the former contrasts with the constant reference to white in Yumí's mourning for his lost treasure, his Niniloj, on the white hills—or "white mountain" (37–38T) ["cerro blanco" (37–38)]—after he has given her to Tazol. Within Mayan myth and art, colors are not gratuitous or merely decorative. Black was the color of the road to Xibalbá, the Place of Fear, the underworld or hell, which was filled with disease and pestilence (not flames as in Christian belief). In "The War between the Wives" chapter, after the dwarf Huasanga has weakened the Mulata by stealing her sex, the Chewing Wizards of the jaguar god Cashtoc easily finish off the Mulata by taking her off to the West, whose color was black (Coe *The Maya* 164). Once there, as we have seen, they split her in half vertically, and diminish her powers to those of a pitiful penitent. According to Asturias's translation of the *Popol Vuh*, "white earth" ["blanca tierra"] is "the dust with which a victim was painted; to be covered with it, or to eat what was covered with it, was equivalent to being sacrificed" ["es el polvo con el cual se pintaba a la víctima; estar untado con ella o comer lo que estaba untado con ella, equivalía a sacrificarse" (159)]. In the ancient civilization, "young men painted themselves black until marriage (and warriors did so at all times)" (Coe *The Maya* 144). When the novel begins, the Mulata is a warrior and Zabala a sacrificial victim.

When Yumí makes his contract for riches with Tazol and gives Zabala in exchange, she is diminished to a minuscule clay figure. When he wants to have her with him again, and removes her from Tazol's box, she grows back only to the stature of a dwarf. She hides her identity and protects Yumí by assuming the name Juana Puti, but is mistreated as a plaything by the Mulata. This image of the Mulata playing with Zabala/Juana Puti could be another of the many allusions in *Mulata* to Classic Mayan art. Schele and Miller note that moon goddesses and dwarfs often appear together in terracotta sculpture (150). Perhaps the reason the Mulata never becomes a dwarf is that she is the aspect of the moon goddess who plays *with* dwarfs. Art historian John Scott's commentary on a dwarf figurine from Campeche, Mexico, states that "Although many dwarf figurines are from the [Mexican] island of Jaina [where the erotic statuary of Ix Chel is found], they are not restricted to that locale" (Scott n.p.). Schele and Miller add that "At the Maya court, just as at the court of the Aztec ruler Motecuhzoma [Moctezuma], dwarfs were special courtiers who entertained the royal family"(150).

All the dwarfs Coe, Schele and Miller, Scott, and other critics mention are male; Asturias's innovation seems to be his invention in *Mulata* of two female dwarfs—Zabala/Juana Puti and the Huasanga—who are more important for longer times than the principal male dwarf: Yumí, when he is called Chiltic, during the time of Zabala's greatest power. The Sombrerón, "a dwarf with a square for a hat" (208T) ["enano con la plaza como sombrero" (212)], a figure from folktales, also appears briefly.

While Zabala is a dwarf, she and Yumí leave Quiavicús to find a cure for her short stature and to become magicians. Wisdom notes that, among the Chorti, dancers and musicians are religious "specialists," having a single or limited function, in contrast to the more profound and general esoteric knowledge and sacred activities of the sorcerer/ess (i.e., the *brujo/a, hechicero/a, adivino/a*, etc.; 424–30). Since dancing, singing, or playing a musical instrument requires less magical expertise and power than that needed by a "professional" magician, Yumí and Zabala embark *as performers* when they leave Quiavicús in their quest to become "great magicians" ["grandes brujos"]. The reunited couple are also reminiscent of the trickster Hero Twins of the *Popol Vuh*, who dance and perform for the Lords of the Underworld. As Markman and Markman point out, ritual performers were an anthropomorphized form of the invisible spirit gods. But the converse is also true: human access to the spirit world could be had through dance, music, and theatrical performances, as well as through bloodletting and ritual death. As a performer, Zabala has begun her transformation into the witch Giroma.

These dwarf-giant transformations of Zabala and Yumí allegorize the value placed on an individual by others. For example, when the wealthy Yumí renews his love for Catalina, he is able to find the strength to break his contract with Tazol and the knowhow to trick the Mulata into leaving them. But it takes the desire of two men fighting over the dwarfed Catalina—Felicito Piedrasanta against Celestino Yumí—to force her body, violently, back to its original size. Similarly, Zabala/Giroma's jealousy of the dwarf Huasanga magically changes Yumí from his dwarfed stature as Chiltic to that of a giant. In the Mayan Game, Asturias also plays with the size of his characters metaliterarily. Chapter titles state that size transformations are measures of affection: "The Great Fly Wizard Is Turned into a Dwarf by His Wife's Vengeance" ("Gran Brujo Bragueta convertido en enano por venganza de su mujer") and "A Woman's Jealousy Turns a Dwarf into a Giant" ("Celos de mujer hacen de un enano un gigante").

The Mulata-Zabala opposition in imagery, roles, and symbolism may result from the fundamental duality within the multiple aspects of the lunar deity, each wife representing one pole in the polarization of her qualities. The forms of the Moon Goddess in art may provide some clues as to whether or not there is a homology between these novelistic and mythologic characterizations. Coe has written about some beautifully haunting female images among the barely understood Jaina ceramic funerary sculptures from Mexico. This scholar believes, as do Schele and Miller (discussed above), that the two common Jaina representations of women are both forms of the Moon/Mother Goddess, Ix Chel: "of two common, rather Freudian motifs, one depicts a mature woman sheltering a grown man as though he were her child, and might well be Ix Chel, the Mother Goddess; while the other, an ugly old man making advances to a handsome female, must be an aged underworld divinity and his consort, Ix Chel, who is also the Moon Goddess" (Coe *The Maya* 122). In *Mulata*, the former of these Moon Goddess images compares to Catalina Zabala, the sheltering, maternal wife of Yumí's youth and middle age (childless by him, but hardworking and good) and Giroma, the "mother witch" ["bruja madre"] of the final chapter. The second image of the Moon Goddess, the "handsome female," is like the Mulata, an attractive woman desired for her youthful sexuality. Playing the Mayan Game meshes the two figures into one, understanding Zabala and the Mulata as dual aspects of the same divine force, whereas a simple reading would give Yumí two separate and antagonistic wives.

Player 3: The Huasanga

One mark of the Huasanga's indigenist conception is her trickster personality: impish and astute. The name of the Huasanga, and her peculiar function as thief of women's sexes, however, does not appear to come from a written or sculptural source of Mayan myth or folklore. Her name perhaps derives from "guasanga," which, in Central America and other Caribbean regions, means "noise, bustle; cry of applause; confusion" ["Bulla, algazara, barahúnda"] (*Diccionario de la lengua española* 685). Luis Pérez notes that, like Candanga, a name of African origin, "Huasanga" may bring to mind, through the *-anga* ending, the Mulata's African heritage (783). The Huasanga has only a small role to play and is a flat rather than a multifaceted character. She symbolizes female competitiveness in a heterosexual woman who will stop at nothing to satisfy her dangerous desires. Few images of female desire are more bizarre or infantile than this dwarf's piercing cry, "I want to try a giant" (149T) ["Quiero probar gigante" (152)], meaning that she wants to have sex with Yumí, who has been suddenly transformed into a giant by Zabala, precisely in order to make such sex impossible.[48]

In contrast to Zabala's and Yumí's temporary dwarf stature, the Huasanga begins as a dwarf and remains one. If stature in this magical novel is a visual representation of desirability to others, then the Huasanga follows the rule. Her permanently small size, like the temporary dwarf states of the main couple Zabala and Yumí, is emblematic of her lack of attractiveness to others, of the minimal desire (or outright repulsion) the Huasanga arouses. She is always without a loving partner and without anyone who desires her sexually. A ribald inversion of the Mulata's somber sexual attractiveness, the Huasanga suffers from dissatisfaction and solitude as much as the Mulata herself.

The Huasanga is described as a fantastical dandy: "Huasanga [was] mounted on Cadejo, wearing Giroma's sex in the buttonhole of her riding jacket like a flower" (245T).[49] As mentioned above, the Cadejo is a devil from folktales to whom Asturias dedicates a chapter of his *Leyendas de Guatemala*. The Huasanga's thefts of sexes are her key to success with her companions, especially the Cadejo, a devil fond of forcing himself on others. The Huasanga steals women's sexes for no other reason than to show them off as prizes, that is, to improve her own rank with the male crowd around Cashtoc. Furthermore, she steals Zabala/Giroma's sex, but then gives it back to her with little motivation; she steals the Mulata's sex, then secretly informs the rebel how to recover it before Giroma can make it truly her own. To complete the picture, the Huasanga is disloyal to everyone, except perhaps to herself or to Cashtoc. Her alliances are strategic and not lasting; although on the Indian side in the War of the Religions, she is a greedy individualist who collects sexes instead of money.

The Huasanga never steals men's sexes, only those of women; she steals them from both Zabala/Giroma and the Mulata. Because these sexes are from Yumí's other wives, the Huasanga prizes them the most, of all her gory booty. The devil dwarf keeps the Mulata's sex "like an ocarina" (245T) ["como una ocarina" (248)]. But the Huasanga also purloins sexes from other, unnamed women; when the thief arrives at a council of Cashtoc's devils, "She was carrying the female sex organs like a string of onions" (165T) ["Traía los sexos femeninos como cabezas de cebollas" (168)]. The Huasanga's activity of stealing sexes reveals her aggression and her victimization of other women. Since she alone has a propensity for stealing such an item, the Huasanga always keeps her own sex. She always feels exorbitant desire, yet never is satisfied by anyone. In this way, sexual play within the Mayan Game is similar to the Money Game: the active impulse for sex, versus the passive desire for it, comes from the activity of the male, whether the woman is a prostitute, a moon goddess, or a devil dwarf. In her lack of satisfaction, the Huasanga symbolizes lust and desire in women, as do the Mulata and Zabala/Giroma.

Perhaps this recognition of female sexuality in all sorts of bodies can be recuperated by a feminist reading. Scenes of the Huasanga in *Mulata* have been seen as an insult to women, by some who consider the graphic description of female sexual organs an aggression against what is secret and private. But Asturias's "vulgar" and "obscene" work can also be seen as the reverse, as a text in which female sex organs enter into Spanish not as an insult, but as a long-overdue (tragicomic) representation. Personally, I find it difficult to see the mere mention of a body part objectionable, and having gone through feminist consciousness-raising and body-awareness sessions with a speculum and mirror, I even see it as a positive development. Western society's prohibitions have inhibited some women, more in the past than today, from looking at themselves without clothes or mentioning their "female complaints" to doctors, with sad consequences. Asturias—though undeniably humorous and irreverent—speaks the words Western culture normally keeps silent. Can he be compared to certain feminist visual artists of the 1960s, whose paintings, sculptures, and photographs sought to recuperate female sexual organs from the cultural realm of the unspoken and the invisible? In Judy Chicago's *The Dinner Party*, to mention a well-known and monumental work, the triangle shape of the table that dominates the piece is an abstract symbol for woman's sex; the plates have raised sculptural emblems to signal the labia. One person's pornography may be another person's erotica, or, as I want to suggest for Asturias, one critic's pornography can be another person's joke—to be laughed at by feminists and nonfeminists alike. For if one objects to Asturias's playful and ironic tale of stealing women's sexes, then a major element of his experiment in Neo-Indigenist revisionism of Western culture, the Mayan Game he is playing, will have been missed. Without understanding his main conceptual strategy of having fun while seeking a redress of the Mayan Indian's situation through the mimesis of a non-Western hermeneutic, then not only this element of female sexes, but also the plot and imagery, lose their pedagogical import and are relegated to mere frivolity. In other words, the physicality of female sex organs in the novel is a move in the Mayan Game.

Another important question needs to be posed regarding the Huasanga's penchant for stealing sexes. What does it mean to the novel that a woman's sex is detachable? While the Huasanga's small size seems a fairly simple objective correlative to her negligible attractiveness to the opposite sex, her action of robbing sexes from other women seems more than a representation of greed, though that is indeed significant. It is not the same for Judy Chicago to make huge ceramic plates that look like giant, multicolored labia for exhibit in a museum and for Asturias to create a character who wears a vulva in her lapel, carries one around like a whistle, and steals so many she strings them together like onions, even when the sculpture and the novel share a pedagogical effect on the Western reader and viewer. But are the Huasanga's robberies also Mayan moves? How can we understand them? And are the separable sexes similar to, in another narrative thread, the sexton's arm, which disappears into thin air? At the moment Jerónimo attacks the coconuts topped with women's sexes, angry that the Indian devils have spoiled the priest's plan to bring holy water into Tierrapaulita, the sexton dares to attempt to fight against the great Cashtoc. The sexton's arm is powerless against the supreme god of Tierrapaulita and disappears. Later, it is returned to him with added magical powers that he uses to rescue the priest from Cashtoc's conflagration. Like women's sexes, the sexton's arm is detachable and reattachable. Another example of missing body parts, to which I return later, results from the leprosy of priest Mateo Chimalpín, which causes his body to fall apart and certain parts to grow huge in life-threatening, delirium-producing, mind-mystifying ways.

Yes, the removal and replacement of half of the Mulata's body, the theft of her sex, the frequent letting of her blood, Zambala's magical transformation from a normal stature to a dwarf and so forth are Mayan technologies of the body in which a divine or spirit world intervenes. Thus they are enabled by the Mayan Game. Neither accidents nor human actions alone, these events produce "Mayan" forms of body-knowledge, ones that exhibit for readers microrelations of power, and thus also are strategies of the Domination Game. Asturias's hybrid, inventive incursion into Classic and contemporary Mayan cultures in *Mulata* entails deployment of several such technologies of the body. Among them, many common elements and attitudes are Mayan, mixed in with the non-Mayan (both from other indigenist groups and from the Occident).

A conversation between Tazol and Tazolín/Tazolito, his young son by Catarina Zabala/Giroma, is enlightening on this question of the ideological import of detachable body parts. The young devil has just recounted to his father that the Huasanga has stolen his mother's sex. She is now "despoiled of [her] sacred fire, of her sex, by the turbulent dwarf" (165T) ["Desposeída de su fuego sagrado, de su sexo, por la turbulenta enana" (168)]. Unconcerned, Tazol responds to his upset son with the grand vegetable metaphor that underlies Mayan culture and religion, in which humanity comes from corn: "Mr. Everything-at-Once, it's easy to see that you're young, but with the years, with the centuries, you'll see how they go about cutting off [amputating] our souls and our bodies, making fire-wood of us! That's why you have to renew yourself! And happy are humans, who are cut off by death when they get old, and are sown into the ground to come back to life again!" (165T; alternative translation added) [" —¡Don completito, bien se ve que es usted joven, pero a través de los años, de los siglos, verá cómo nos van amputando el alma y el cuerpo, haciendo leña de nosotros! ¡Por eso hay que renovarse! ¡Y felices los humanos, que son cortados por la muerte, cuando ya están añosos, y sembrados en la tierra, para volver a la vida de nuevo!" (168)]. On the one hand, Tazol is referring to his own figural amputation, that is, the reduction in the numbers of people who believe in gods like him, brought about by the work of Christian missionaries and by modernization; on the other hand, he envies, or says he envies, the human ability to die and be reborn, like corn that is cut down and grows again annually. Death, like the loss of limbs and sexes, is not the product of a blind nature, but a harvesting, a definite action by a certain spirit. The gods feed from the human community, as humans do from the animals and plants on our farms.

If we can further imagine a conception of the body in which each separate (and separable) part can have a soul, in which each part of the body can independently take part in life, we come close to Asturias's vision of divine-human, life-death, and body part–person relationships in the Mayan Game. In addition, there is a Mayan notion of the individual as a grain of corn on the cob that is the community; in the novel this notion is reversible. Imagine each community as a single body, and each person within it as either an arm or a sex, a detachable part within the whole. Individuals are given and taken away by the gods, but the community survives. In this way, sexes can be stolen, arms can disappear, and the character survives.

At this point, it is important to remember that the Money Game playfully rewrites existing folktales that use precapitalist logic to interpret the sudden acquisition of wealth as a (male) devil contract. The acquisition of magical powers is the female version of the human-god relation. This sport is played by Asturias through a refiguring of the gendered devil-contract story in such a way as to preserve its moral kernel regarding the corruption caused by cash economies. At the same time, Asturias wields the devil contract as a discursive weapon to criticize the enslavement and poverty of Indian workers (cannibalism). Similarly, in the Mayan Game, Asturias transforms into hybrid fictions many myths, legends, and tales, both ancient and modern, and once again mimics indigenous modes of conception, at least to the extent they were understood by the non-Indian and written down. But he uses humor and shock tactics to prevent anyone from being fooled, even temporarily, into confusing the fictional *Mulata* with what he would have believed were authentic Mayan philosophies, religious beliefs, or poetic techniques about which he read or heard.[50]

The third of the major strategies that Asturias employs, the Domination Game, has more to do with his interpretation of history and of historical documents, and less to do with individual struggles within an economic context (the Money Game) or with the Guatemalan Indian's collective beliefs within a mythic-religious context (the Mayan Game). The author's dual concerns in the Domination Game are the weight of history on the present and the ideology of historical discourse. Even such abstract concepts as these affect the novel's serious and tongue-in-cheek technologies of the body; for example, when the priest wakes to discover that he is covered with pockmarks, he instructs Jerónimo to tell the doctor that he has been bitten, not by smallpox, but "by the moths of proto-history" (285T) ["no lo picó la viruela, sino la polilla de la protohistoria" (291)]. The ending of the novel, interpreted in the Domination Game section, continues to combine a purposeful selection of varied cultural artifacts and allusions, to intermingle them seamlessly, while maintaining a ludic disrespect for all sacred cows. As we now trace the basic rules of this third game, the challenge is to measure its impact on the image of sexual women, particularly on the Mulata de tal.

The Domination Game

I do not know if the comparison is too daring. But it is necessary. The use of destructive forces, the secret which Alfred Nobel extracted from nature, made possible in our America the most colossal enterprises. Among them, the Panama Canal. A magic of catastrophe . . . could be compared to the thrust of our novels, called upon to destroy unjust structures in order to make way for a new life. The secret mines of the people, buried under tons of misunderstanding, prejudices, and taboos, bring to light in our narrative—between fables and myths—with blows of protest, testimony, and enunciation, dikes of letters which, like sands, contain reality to let the dream flow free or, on the contrary, contain the dream to let reality escape.

Cataclysms that engendered a geography of madness, terrifying traumas, such as the conquest: these cannot be the antecedents of a literature of cheap compromise; and thus, our novels appear to Europeans as illogical or aberrant. They are not shocking for the sake of shock effects. It is just that what happened to us was shocking.

Miguel Angel Asturias, Nobel Prize acceptance speech

The Domination Game, like the Money Game and the Mayan Game, consists of new and unique recombinations of many discourses: in this case, discourses about the conquest of the Americas and about the establishment of colonial and postcolonial dominions. My exposition of this strategy in *Mulata* could be accomplished by narrating Asturias's possible historical sources and evaluating the way in which the received information becomes the strawman for the indigenous perspective, much as I did above with the contrasts among proposed sources for Tazol in the Mayan Game. This method would certainly demonstrate how *Mulata* succeeds in debunking the illusion of reality in the historical record of the Spanish Conquest, a discursive equivalent of "unjust structures" which must themselves be destroyed, according to Asturias in his acceptance speech for the Nobel Prize. However, to demonstrate fully the way in which Asturias brings about the novel's apocalypse, to explain the poetic justice of the novel's ending and his use of perspectivism to elucidate the Mayan versus the Catholic versions of the historical record—to do all this would require a more far-ranging essay than the limited topic of my discussion, the sexual woman, allows. Instead of such a complete rendering, this section treats a selection of certain types of "game moves" not covered previously. These moves are neither wholly about greed nor entirely from the Indian point of view. They trace in broad strokes certain outcomes of the Domination Game, if not its entire ideological score.

As explained above in the Dangerous Games section, each of these three games is a means through which form and content, plot and character, imagery and discourse work in combination to accomplish communication, to speak on a subject. The Money Game admonishes against capitalism and greed, while at the same time representing contemporary realities without recourse to a traditional Western realism. The Mayan Game takes advantage of this opening toward the "Indian viewpoint" and compounds the mythological elements, leaving behind all pretense of a realist setting in the novel's middle section. But the Domination Game, with its goal of an Indian and a mythological perspective on the historical conquest of Mesoamerica, presents a particular challenge to simple explanations. The historical documents by which we understand the wars between Native Americans and Spaniards were largely written by the conquerors—the priests and soldiers who had a stake in how the narrative was judged. Asturias's literary strategy in the Domination Game transmits a mythologizing and invented version of the history of Indian resistance and survival, intended to remind us that there is another side of the story.

Asturias appears not to stray from the facts of the Conquest—the massacres, the epidemics, the explicit goal of subjugation—but to represent how these actions were felt and understood by the indigenist survivors. We hypothesize this from the strong evidence of the Mayan Game which he continues to play in the episodes we discuss in this section. But during the parts of the book where Asturias plays with themes of domination, subjugation, and repression, simply inventing or imitating a voice or a hermeneutic system for the dominated is not sufficient. Links to existing historical discourse must be forged as well. If his goal is to reach out to those who may not yet see the Amerindian legacy as he does, if Asturias wished to guide and to educate his readers, he must provide guideposts from familiar territory to the unfamiliar and teach how to read the new map of the past with examples and explanations.

Speaking very generally, Western history sees the winners in the War of the Religions as the Catholics, and the believers of the Indian religions as the obvious losers. But *Mulata* topples this top-down view in a series of deconstructive moves. The history of the colonial and pre-Columbian period is sketchy, and Asturias could find many places in the historical record where the Western, conquering perspective was already perturbed. If our knowledge is muddy on a certain point, the missing information provides a place of possible contention with history. If the autochthonous belief system disagrees with Catholicism on the morality of a certain historical act, that act is a possible breach in the wall of power. If a historical personage had mixed allegiances, then his other Mayan voice had not been completely silenced. In this section, my procedure is to bring to mind those whom history has presumed to be the winners and losers—the dominating and the dominated—and then I show how this scheme is regrounded, reversed, from the Indian standpoint in the novel. In the reversal, losers do not lose, at least not as completely or as often as had first appeared. Before we can see how female sexuality fares in the Domination Game, we must briefly follow the double-plays of this strategy.

The novel's last chapter can be compared to a long frieze in which a reckoning is made of the characters. There are many events in this section, events that largely serve to (re)situate figures, moving them from one ideological or hermeneutical form to another, like the church statues given animal heads by the Christian devil, or like the final jostling made by members of a large group about to be photographed, in which everyone positions themselves so that their image can be fixed for posterity. These final concatenations make impossible simple discussions of the truly Catholic, the authentic Maya, the entirely human, and the purely divine. One would not expect a further multiplication of levels and identities to occur as late as in a novel's conclusion, but that is what we find: even more complications in the ways of ethnic, national, religious, and gender identities are to be understood. Beyond our current ideas of hybridity, *mestizaje,* transculturation, heterogeneity, gender crossing, and racial passing, the novel's final chapters celebrate a human complexity reaching cultural indecidability.

In the Mayan Game, we saw how *Mulata* recasts mythological elements appearing in Classic Mayan art, Aztec conquest catalogs of the gods, and twentieth-century ethnographies into an imaginary Mayan perspective. In his pioneering essays on indigenist literature, Peruvian critic Antonio Cornejo Polar argues that "the indigenist novel should, to put it one way, historicize myths. Clearly this process cannot help but transform, in turn, in a reverse direction beginning with myth, the conception of history" ["la novela indigenista debe, por así decirlo, historificar el mito. Como es claro, este proceso no deja de transformar a su vez, en sentido inverso, partiendo del mito, la concepción de la historia" (76)]. Asturias's Neo-Indigenist novel does in fact mythify history, representing how specific moments of the past (history) might appear in the Mayan Game (as myth). The historic actions Asturias transforms into what the West calls myth are not the recorded events of named leaders by and large; names easily recognized by readers, such as Hernán Cortés or Moctezuma, La Malinche or Sor Juana Inés de la Cruz, do not appear in the novel. The history that is retold in surreal fiction, within an Indian point of view, tells of the missionary work of a marginal, invented Catholic priest. But for the non-Christian population, the significance of missionary work over the centuries cannot be overestimated. The story of priests in America has been repeated thousands of times in a thousand variations; they are histories in a minor key which have transpired in 1596, in 1996, and in every year in between.

At the same time, Asturias uses mythological elements within a narrative that largely retains a recognizable historical frame of the twentieth century. The resulting fictive strands are clearly products of the process of mythologizing temporal, modern events. By imagining the Mayan point of view in this recognizable historical moment, the recorded history of missionary work is revealed as a one-sided discourse, an interpretation of multicultural scripts from a Christian hermeneutic alone. Historical discourse previously masquerading as transparent truth gains the opacity of its cultural bias. To put it another way, the Christian lens through which the history was seen, itself becomes visible, through a contrast with the same object examined through the non-Christian lens. Viewing history

through Mayan eyes highlights the possibility of alternative ways of seeing, and questions the received interpretations, by reconstructing them
within a different value system.

For example, the Domination Game, played in economic terms when
the novel opens (the Money Game), gains mythic content and form when
in the middle section Cashtoc calls together his servants, the Giants. They
come quickly, as always when summoned to him, but they are startled by
his call, "Because they had dominated Christianity" (197T) ["Dominada
como tenían la cristianidad" (202)]. Cashtoc announces to them in a crucial speech that the Christian devil Candanga has arrived, and that they
must destroy Tierrapaulita and then abandon the city. In one of the major
jumps from a Mayan perspective on Mayan gods' activities to a Mayan
perspective on divine beings in Christian belief, Cashtoc explains: "This
crafty foreigner [Candanga] conceives of man as the flesh of hell and tries,
when he does not demand, for the multiplication of human beings, who
are isolated like him, devilishly religious like him, to fill up his hell! That
is why he undid the mirror vapor that the heart of Heaven had poured over
the sexes, a mirror vapor in which man and woman, in the magic instant
of giving life, left a copy of their images mixed in with the new being,
whose navel they offered to the community, meaning by it that this one
would not be alien to the existence of all, but part of their existences,
which at the same time are part of the existence of the gods!" (199T).[51] In
other words, Candanga promotes individualism and anticommunity feelings through his attitude toward sexuality. After his speech, the great
Cashtoc takes his "earth-born devils" and abandons Tierrapaulita, but the
religious fight does not end. A group of his cortege jump off the comet's
tail on which Cashtoc is ferrying them to the mountaintop, and return to
Tierrapaulita to continue the fight against the heaven-born devil Candanga. Though much reduced in number and power, the Mayan deities
continue to act upon humanity and Tierrapaulita after the arrival of Christianity. The Mulata also plays a greatly diminished, though still significant, role in the games of domination after Cashtoc leaves town.

Sexuality, and specifically the individual pursuit of pleasure, becomes
paramount where Candanga rules. Whereas Asturias's *Men of Maize* emphasized the fertility of men and women for the resistance and survival of
the native peoples, *Mulata* concentrates on the themes of sexual desire.
The Christian devil scorns the values of community and the importance of
restraint, because his only concern is to increase the population of hell. As
one of the priests around the Archbishop warns, original sin is even more
difficult to wipe out than the Indian religion: "'What makes it difficult,'

sighed the curial as he spoke, 'is doing battle with the Lucifer who has become involved in human progress, marvelously adapting himself to modern customs like all of us, and partly because, as I see it, the Devil, by means of original sin, enters into the natural formation of man, sixty or seventy per cent, and I'm being conservative!'" (204T).[52]

Interestingly, the Catholic priests agree with Cashtoc that the Mulata's sexual desire for Yumí merits condemnation, even damnation. A defector from the Indian community, disobedient to Cashtoc, the Mulata is left less than human—half a human—and without her *lox*, her sex, her center. She has promoted destruction and thus attained a certain divinity, but her Indian allegiance has become vitiated by her constant response to Candanga's call for sex. Her defection and punishment mark how far the historical tide has turned against the Indian devils in favor of Candanga, so much so that the hand-to-hand combat to take place shortly after Candanga's arrival is between the Christian devil and the Christian priest, rather than between Christian and non-Christian devils. Cashtoc has left Tierrapaulita for the Christians to squabble over.

Early on, after Yumí reneges on his devil contract, the Mulata shows herself as not merely a poor prostitute and insatiable sex partner in the Money Game, but also a goddess and sacred victim in the Mayan Game, as discussed above. In the web of power relations defining the Domination Game, she is next described as a vassal of the devil who has subdued even Tazol: Cashtoc. As these additional meanings accrue to her character, she remains first and foremost a mixture: a mulatto woman more involved in Native American cultures than in residual African American ones, though she is never *merely* a woman nor *entirely* a woman either. A crucial moment for her and for the novel is when the Mulata's divine spirit, under Cashtoc's command, enters the body of a non-Indian (white?) man, the church sexton, whose complete name is Jerónimo de la Degollación de los Santos Inocentes (Jerónimo of the Slaughter of the Innocents by Herod). At first a heterosexual woman (and a hermaphrodite), in this twist of the plot late in the novel, the Mulata "becomes" a man.

The Mulata's desire for Yumí has not abated since he betrayed her by retrieving Zabala, but rather seems to have increased. When she faces Yumí as the Mulata-in-the-sexton's body, s/he is thus at that moment paradoxically homosexual: "Jerónimo . . . felt more and more feminoid, more and more of a sodomite, the certain Mulata was already in possession of all of his parts" (230T) ["Jerónimo . . . se sentía cada vez más feminoide, más sodomita, la Mulata de Tal alumbraba ya todas sus partes" (233)]. The novel's matter-of-factness regarding a man's desire for another man is possibly another move in the Mayan Game. Homosexuality as a practice, at least among some of the elite, has been documented in archeological discourse.[53] Be that as it may, Asturias follows a long line of literary classics and Hollywood clichés from Western culture also, in rendering men's hand-to-hand combat as only a gesture or an intuition away from a homosexual embrace. This homosexuality of the female Mulata seems related to her anal sexuality, but not explicitly.[54]

In the religious war, the Mulata has temporarily taken possession of Jerónimo's body to do battle against Candanga; later, in the same way that multiple versions are given about the Mulata's death, the Mulata tells the sexton another version of what happened to her/them. She laments: "My role was to fight against the evil spirit lodged in the body of Yumí, who was the Infernal Christian Prince, and against the latter I fought to the utmost, he tried to ruin me with the dirty story of his smallpox, but I opposed him with the vain but historical tale of the Chamber-Potters, and there we were" (341T) ["Mi papel era luchar contra el espíritu maligno alojado en el cuerpo de Yumí, que era el Príncipe Infernal Cristiano, y contra éste me batí a fondo, trató de perderme con la historia sucia de sus viruelas, pero yo le opuse el fantaseoso como histórico relato de los Bacinicarios, y allí estábamos" (346)]. As in the *Popol Vuh*, ingenuity, wordplay, and trickster stories are the arms of war wielded by the warrior. The conflict between the two sides at first is entirely verbal, of wits and of sexual desire, in which religious and ethnic hegemony is at risk. Although the Mulata gains the upper hand at first as an obscene storyteller with her tale of the Chamber-Potters from a bygone colonial period, when Yumí transforms into a porcupine, her desire overwhelms her and she returns to her own body to experience penetration by Yumí's porcupine spines.[55] She is punished by Cashtoc for her disobedience, cut up by the wizards, and robbed of her sex. The Chewing Wizards "would take away her magic, her magic clothes with their symbols and colors" (245T) ["debían desposeerla de la magia, de sus vestidos mágicos por los símbolos y colores" (248)]. Her sexuality causes her demise, within the version seen from an indigenous vantage point that credits with reality such things as magic, Wizards, and the ability of one spirit to possess another. Her sexual desires bring on the punishment of body fragmentation, as they had previously made her anguished and the destroyer of the village of Quiavicús.[56] Her death, transformation, or ascension to the moon leaves a legacy of sexual energy to repopulate the decimated world; the snails can be born once she is gone.[57]

The verbal duel between the Mulata-as-sexton-for-Cashtoc and Yumí-as-Candanga abruptly ends once the physical attack commences. The Mulata advances in an attempt to castrate Yumí— "to despoil him of his male attributes" (240T) ["de despojarlo de sus atributos varoniles" (244)]—then Yumí "grew quills out of each of his pockmarks, turning into a ferocious hedgehog [porcupine]" (240T) ["soltó una espina por cada picadura de viruela transformándose en un puercoespín feroz" (244)]. Leaving Jerónimo behind almost dead from his puncture wounds, with the Mulata out of Jerónimo's body and looking on, Yumí-porcupine-Candanga attacks Father Chimalpín, who in self-defense has transformed into a "giant cassocked spider with eleven thousand hairy legs" (241T) ["una araña gigante, ensotanada, de oncemil patas peludas" (244)]. Upon discovering that the porcupine is Yumí, the Mulata endeavors to protect him and ends the duel between him and the priest by covering the scene with a blinding mist, which paralyzes them (241T; 245). The priest, still a spider, begins to preside over a black mass in celebration of the third wedding between the Mulata and Yumí, while the townspeople obey Candanga's command to breed.

What does this incredible physical battle sequence in the church mean in the Domination Game's War of the Religions? Who are the participants, and who the winners and losers? Transformed into a porcupine and possessed by the Christian devil, having almost killed the sexton Jerónimo, Yumí turns and attacks Father Chimalpín. This is the moment when the Christian devil duels with the Christian priest, a significant loss of participation for the novel's indigenous contingent. Cashtoc and the Mulata-possessing-Jerónimo no longer are contenders for victory against Candanga-Yumí. This fundamental shift from Cashtoc in control of everything (because the priest had failed to outwit him with the coconuts), to when the priest confronts not Cashtoc but Lucifer (Candanga) in an Indian's body, and again fails to win a victory, may reflect the initial invasion of Christianity into authochthonous comprehension of spiritual life. Indian conversions to Christianity began with the Conquest and continue today. The porcupine attacking the spider may be a Mayan Game version of this religious fight, in which the Mayan standpoint colors events which with effort become comprehensible within a Christian hermeneutic as well.

But textual evidence points to an additional game being played, the Domination Game, rather than a mere inversion or revision of the Mayan Game in which an Indian viewpoint alludes to purely Christian referents.

Other details, especially a change in narrative focalization, lend weight to a second hypothesis: the opening of the major moves in the Domination Game, a game in which the contenders pretend to no less than a control of knowledge. In an earlier interlude outside Tierrapaulita at the end of part 1, the novel suggests that the events up to this point, or at least the latter portion of them, have been the report given by the priest to a superior. Perhaps part 1 of the novel is Father Chimalpín's rendition of the narrative to his superior, or perhaps only the latter parts of it that occur in Tierrapaulita. In any case, in part 2, Christianity overtakes or attempts to overtake all other conceptualizations. In its domination of interpretation, devils are, and must be, the Devil, the one and only Devil, just as there is only one true God. The crowd around Cashtoc cannot be credited with any activities, good or evil. Candanga is responsible for all that is not God.

The transition from a non-Christian viewpoint back to a Christian one occurs first in the skeptical reception given to Chimalpín's opinions: "His grace, a man with worn-out patience, folded his hands, twisted his mouth, frowned, bored by the detailed account that old rheumatic parish priest, deformed, with one leg longer than the other, was giving him of his fight with the most primitive forms of the devil in Tierrapaulita, the most pestilent witchcraft, the fiercest hatred of God, the worst superstition. . . . In the curia no one listened to the tales of the priest from Tierrapaulita" (202T).[58] When Chimalpín informs the Catholic priests in the capital city about the siege of Tierrapaulita by Cashtoc and the debacle of the urinating coconuts, they scoff at his fears: "If the Devil were the way that old priest paints him, it would be easy to reduce him to impotence. Against the demon of earthquakes, reinforced concrete, and against hurricanes, the planting of high-crowned trees to break the violence of the winds" (203–4T) ["Si el demonio fuera como lo pinta ese cura viejo, fácil sería reducirlo a la impotencia. Contra el demonio de los terremotos, el cemento armado, y contra los huracanes, la siembra de árboles de copa alta, para romper la violencia de los vientos" (208)].

Returning to Tierrapaulita from his foray to the capital to ask the Archbishop for help against Cashtoc, Chimalpín finds that Candanga is the new enemy against whom he must wage war to win the souls of the citizens of Tierrapaulita. On this return trip by mule, "coinciding with the diabolic changing of the guard, the millennial moment of the abandonment of a town by the earth demons in favor of the Christian devil" (204–5T) ["coincidiendo con el cambio de guardia demonial, el momento en mil años del abandono de una ciudad por los diablos terráqueos al demonio cristiano" (209)], the priest arms himself with a small library. Calling them the "heavy artillery he would use against Satan," the books are "the complete works of Saint Thomas Aquinas, a *History of the Church in the Indies*, by Fray Diego de Mendieta; the *Criticón* of Baltasar Gracián; the *Apologetics* of Bishop Las Casas; a book of sermons by various preachers, Bossuet foremost; the *Compendium of Moral Theology*, by Father Larraga; and, to the Greater Glory of God, books on cataclysms, hurricanes, predestination, devil worship, not to mention the *Manual for Exorcists* of Fray Luis de la Concepción, the Holy Bible, and, for light reading, the Apocalypse."[59] Allusions to these books, providing humor and irony to the narrative, are sprinkled about, but for our purposes here, the mention of Bishop Las Casas may be the most important to explain for the Domination Game.

In Asturias's historical drama devoted to Bartolomé de Las Casas, *La audiencia de los confines* [Audience at the edges of the world] (1957), published during the time between his two major Neo-Indigenist novels, *Men of Maize* and *Mulata*, the massacres and persecutions of the Indian and the early attack by European missionaries on Native American cultures feature largely. In Asturias's play, the dignified, tragic reformer Las Casas feels great guilt upon realizing that his recommendation to import African slaves rather than to employ Native Americans for heavy labor in the Spanish colonies has permitted a continuation of human suffering rather than a diminution of it. Set at the moment of Las Casas's return to America from Spain, Asturias's play foregrounds the reform Las Casas has fought for and won from the king for the Indians as much less of a victory than the priest had previously thought. Although in Asturias's portrayal his protests against the servitude of the Indians appear heartfelt—"No more whipped Indians! . . . No more chained Indians!" ["¡No más indios azotados! . . . ¡No más indios encadenados! . . ." (*"La audiencia"* 234)]— Las Casas is confronted with his moral failure when he is mobbed by the poor blacks who will continue to be enslaved under his new laws:

VOICES: What a black fate is that of blacks! . . . What a black fate is that of blacks! . . .

FRAY BARTOLOMÉ (*he doesn't know what to do so he falls to his knees*): Forgive me! Forgive me! Don't accuse me without hearing me out! I advised bringing blacks to the New Indies, but the infamous commerce already existed! The suffering of the Indians blinded me into proposing that those helpers of color, also slaves, also slaves, should with the cross of the conquest come to help my poor little beasts of mud, who, due to their physical makeup, could not tolerate any more![60]

Asturias shows Las Casas essentializing the races, attributing different characteristics, especially physical tolerances in work, to Africans and Native Americans.

In the final act of *La audiencia de los confines*, the reformer priest must watch while the Christianized Indians he wants to save poison themselves with their venomous arrows rather than be subjugated as slaves. The priest Las Casas desperately attempts to stop them and then absolves them of their sins. The governor takes his sword and cuts the cross used in the absolution, saying: "Here no one absolves anybody! Let us feed hell!" ["¡Aquí nadie absuelve a nadie! ¡Dejad que alimentemos el infierno!" (248–49)]. In *Mulata*, feeding hell with souls is the task of devils, especially Candanga the Christian devil. Candanga sees procreation as an investment toward a future increase in his capital, that is, in damned human souls. At the very end of Asturias's play, the governor is stripped of his power and Las Casas is rescued from him, but the author's interest clearly lies more with the bishop's internal debate and his sad self-justification of a sullied reform program.

In *Mulata*, Asturias shows himself as having meditated on Las Casas's mistaken hierarchy of races. He seems determined to confuse the racial composition of his characters and not to pit one race against another. Whereas in interviews Asturias still flirts with racial stereotypes and admits it, in his textual strategies in *Mulata*, he allows no single race or culture as absolute victor in the Domination Game. Most important, no single race or culture even monopolizes the "play." Observers (i.e., readers) lose the ability to discern the character's team. When blacks (like the Mulata) are also Indians, the poor (like Yumí) become rich, the women (like the Mulata) have men's sex organs, and the devils of the contending religions each possess the bodies of representatives of the other, it is very hard to see race, class, sex, ethnicity, or religion as defining your team in the games of domination or being dominated. Additionally, members of teams (i.e., ethnic groups, economic classes, genders) constantly switch sides; the opposing devils, Yumí, his wives, even the sexton Jerónimo and the priest Chimalpín come to experience the loss of the self and the end of identity.[61]

Jerónimo has been the means by which the Battle between the Gods — at first waged by the Indian Devil (Cashtoc-Mulata in Jerónimo's body) versus the Catholic Devil (Candanga in Yumí's body)—is converted into a duel between two Christian religious figures, the devil Candanga (Yumí) and the priest (Chimalpín). In the final cataclysm, Jerónimo again plays an important helper-transitional role. The sexton attempts to help his boss Chimalpín seek a cure for the pockmarks left from the porcupine's (Yumí's) piercings. The most efficient cure recommended by the shaman, the Male Umil (Varón Umil), is for the priest to make love to a virgin with a rash, "so that in the jingling of love his bites would fall off, and her rash would go away in blood" (308T) ["a fin de que en el zangoloteo del amor, se le cayeran las picaduras a él, y a ella se le fuera el salpullido en sangre" (313)]. Somehow parallel, the virgin's rash and the priest's pockmarks (the signs of present and past disease perhaps) would disappear in sex, according to the shaman. Upon hearing of this solution, the sexton decides that the virgin is one cure he would be happy to test for the priest. He acts only in the interest of the priest's safety, of course! Discovering that the Virgin with a Rash is a spotted snake, Jerónimo grabs a sheet to cover his nakedness and flees the brothel in the midst of a terrible earthquake. In this process, Jerónimo gains the name Sheet (Sábana). Neither priest nor virgin loses the outer marks of their disease, and the priest is forced to more desperate measures: to ride the Meat-Eating Mule (la Mula Carnívora).[62] As the priest's surrogate in the search for a cure, Jerónimo connects Chimalpín to disease a second time, in the form of Sheet.

According to Wisdom, the death god Chamer among the living Chorti "is a skeleton, dressed in a white robe like the one used to cover cadavers during the funeral ceremony" (398) ["es un esqueleto vestido con una sábana blanca como la que se usa para cubrir los cadáveres en la ceremonia funeraria" (449T)].[63] The sexton's renaming is thus another move within the Mayan Game. To see Sheet/Jerónimo, the death god Chamer wrapped in a mortuary sheet, is to be close to death.

Furthermore, when astride the Meat-Eating Mule, the priest's face is "so pale that it looked more like a skull" (328T) ["tan pálida la cara que más parecía una calavera" (334)]. His cadaverlike appearance underlines his analogy with Jerónimo/Sheet, and brings to mind the role of disease in the encounter between the Native American peoples and the Europeans who arrived here. As is well known, European diseases devastated the Native Americans. Even today, if one of the few still extremely isolated tribes in the Amazon are approached by outsiders, most members of the tribe are likely to die a slow, agonizing death brought on by the diseases which the outsider carries and against which the tribe has little or no immunity. Unfortunately, missionaries were often a tribe's first contact with European illnesses. Unknowingly at first, later at times knowingly, religious fanatics have brought about the physical death of those whose souls they sought to save for Christ. Perhaps the priest's and the sexton's association with death announces not only their impending demise but also this dark historic role of the Church as a bringer of disease to indigenous peoples. In the Domination Game, causing the death of an adversary is a winning move.

For its part, America may have contributed syphilis to Europe—at least this theory was widely believed in Asturias's time, although archeological evidence has suggested otherwise in the last twenty years (Brody). Additionally, until the fifteenth century, syphilis in Europe was often confused with leprosy. The hypothesis should be considered that the priest's leprosy on the final page may be a veiled allusion to syphilis. Certainly one can make the case for at least an analogy between the priest's leprosy and syphilis, owing to their historical confusion. An additional reason to read his leprosy as a metaphor for syphilis is the shaman's otherwise bizarre association of the priest's pockmarks with the brothel and sex in the cure of the Virgin with a Rash. If indeed Chimalpín has syphilis, then America has wreaked its vengeance on him in the novel's conclusion.

Asturias's strategies for deconstructing the seemingly impenetrable wall of ethnic, racial, religious, and gender domination of the Indian are mixed and varied in *Mulata*. Although the most extreme example of cultural heterogeneity in the text must be the spirit possession of the Christian sexton Jerónimo by the Mulata in the name of the Indian devil Cashtoc, there is a highly effective example from early in the adventure that heralds neither from Mayan nor Westernizing, modernizing Latin American sources. I would like to consider it briefly at this juncture because my analysis up to this point has not taken it into account, except by analogy. Added to the mythological, cultural, and religious allusions from these two main contexts of Mesoamerican myth and the history of the conquest is an unexpected reference from the world of entertainment during Asturias's lifetime. As with the joke about cannibals in the Money Game, an allusion survives from the modern world in which Asturias moved, rather than from an indigenous world he read about or invented. We need to understand this foray into other fields of reference to see the degree to which heterogeneity reigns and sabotages the given discursive representation of complete historical and social domination.

During the Mulata's first marriage to Yumí, when she brought him both vast riches and great physical suffering, one night suddenly Yumí's vast farmland catches fire, as mentioned earlier. The Mulata de tal is sexually excited by the destruction and leaves their bed to watch the flames. The narrator describes her from the point of view of the farmworkers who are mesmerized by her physical beauty: "She was dancing with her neck encircled by a necklace of small golden bananas, from which a plantain hung that beat at her breasts while she danced. That was how the peons were looking at her. The foreman. The young men. Around her waist and her forearms, golden bananas and purple bananas, moving in time to her hips, her buttocks, her feet, her ankles" (57T).[64] In this novel about the colder Central American highlands where corn is planted, the mention of bananas—a plant from the warm coast—is surprising. Bananas are out of place in upper altitudes. For an educated, Western reader, however, the incongruity of the Mulata dressed in bananas is all the greater for being the trademark costume of the early film star Josephine Baker. A famous mulatto woman whom Asturias may very well have seen in Paris, Josephine Baker was North American, an exile most of her adult life, and an exuberant dancer. Asturias's early visit to the French capital coincided with the time of Baker's first years there. Le Revue Nègre and Baker were much discussed among the surrealists whom Asturias knew. Her most famous dance was performed in a costume of bananas painted gold which has been preserved in photographs and films.[65] A further confirmation that the early characterization of the Mulata's physicality is at times inspired by Baker comes from another playful detail. Celestino Yumí and his first wife Catarina Zabala, unable to kill the Mulata after several attempts, finally lure her away from town and wall her inside a cave. What story do they give out to the curious who wonder where Yumí's second wife has gone? That she traveled to "Europeland" (75–76T) ["se fue de viaje por las Europas" (76)].

While the allusion to Baker is both masked and brief, it is emblematic of the freedom with which the novel is composed and the subtlety with which Asturias promotes a political agenda through images. The Guatemalan author serves his political ends by managing to remind readers of North American racism—the reason Baker made her career in Europe—at the same time he supplements his primary setting (the corn-growing agricultural zone where the dance occurs) by bringing to mind Josephine Baker's banana costume. Through the brief image of the Mulata wearing bananas, Asturias recuperates for his novel a distinctly Guatemalan and Central American agricultural component. To the limited extent that the novel takes place in a realist setting, it occurs among cornfields and the mountainous highlands, not in the coastal areas, where most bananas are produced. This other Central American agricultural product, the banana, should remind readers of the activities of the United Fruit Company and of Asturias's searing treatment of the subject in his aptly named "banana trilogy."

The novel's ironic accretion of identities, such as Josephine Baker for the Mulata, creates a stereotype-obliterating, multiple composition for the main antagonist and focalizer, Yumí, as well as for the Mulata herself. In these middle and late sections of the novel, Yumí has no money to reign as he once did over a retinue of servants and an army of farm laborers, having lost all his possessions gained via the devil contract. He set off with Zabala on the road to become a magician and then was physically transformed into a dwarf and a giant, he died and was resuscitated. By the time the Mulata-as-Jerónimo tries to seduce Yumí, the latter has also been possessed by Candanga, the Christian devil. The battle between the two devils is thus fought by two substitutes: the bodies of Catholic Jerónimo and Mayan Yumí, invaded by the spirits of the Cashtoc emissary (the Mulata), and by Candanga, respectively. The Christian devil invades the Indian's body and the Indian god/dess invades the Christian's body. To explain this multiformity in another way, each body fights the devil of its own religion/ culture: Yumí's body is pitted against Cashtoc's spirit and Jerónimo's body against the spirit of the Christian devil, Candanga. Importantly for themes of domination, whichever devil wins, the other side has the appearance of winning, because the devil was inhabiting the body of the worshiper of the other religion. If Cashtoc wins, it will appear that Jerónimo has gained the day; but if Candanga defeats his opponent, Yumí will be the victor. Despite the priest's desire for a Christian conception of the world in which only God and the His fallen angel spar, things remain much more complex than that, even in a world from which Cashtoc has largely retired.

Through the two spirit possessions, differences between the believers of the pre-Columbian religion and the Christians become infinitely less relevant, since no matter the outcome, both sides in the religious war can claim a semblance of victory and defeat. Asturias said of the novel that "The parts of the book having to do with the Catholic Church are interesting, and typical. Because these are the Catholic churches in our countries. It's a type of Catholicism very much mixed with local beliefs, where the Indian officiators often wield more authority than the priest in his own church" (Harss and Dohmann 98–99). Within the fictional world, one cannot tell by "looking" who are the Indians and who the non-Indians. In other words, the way Asturias plays the Domination Game gives the lie to an easy tagging of race or skin color to religious identifications. At the very least, the outcome of the War of the Religions has now become difficult to calculate in racial or ethnic terms. Nearly every border established by society has been crossed—in the alternative technologies of the body offered by other religions, in the coastal interpolations of bananas, in the story of the cosmic insurance salesman and the allusion to Josephine Baker, and in serendipitous yet pointed associations between the mythic and the objectively real.

Ethnic and racial identifications are not some absolute evil that Asturias wishes to discredit entirely, however. On the contrary, his artistic project relies on the idea that specific cultures have distinct points of view. But he favors a communitarian ethics over a Christian or capitalist individualism. Cashtoc explains to his devils:

> Creation was dust and dust will be all that is left of the cities we destroy! . . . Real men, the ones made out of corn, have stopped existing in reality and have become fictitious creatures, since they did not live for the community, and that is why they should have been suppressed. That is why I annihilated them with my Major Giants, and just as long as they do not reform, I will annihilate all of those who forget, deny, or reject their condition as kernels of corn, parts of an ear, and become self-centered, egotistical, individualists.
> . . .
>   Plants, animals, stars—they all exist together, all together as they were created! It has occurred to none of them to make a separate existence, to take life for his exclusive use, only man, who must be destroyed because of his presumption of existing in isolation, alien to the millions of destinies that are being woven and unwoven around him! (198–99T)[66]

Like the scientific theory of Gaia, according to which our planet is a lifeform needing all its parts to live in coexistence, Cashtoc's message urges appreciation of the natural world and of human groups. Ultimately, Asturias seeks to promote the validity of this autochthonous worldview within modernity. To do this, his strategy is to show the moral superiority of those cultures which eschew increase for its own sake and which understand their villages as extended families. Cashtoc's speech, only excerpted here, lashes out against greed and egotism, as have many moves already analyzed within the Money Game. The change in these latter portions of the novel, and one difference between the specific Money Game and the general Domination Game, is that Cashtoc has reached the point of leaving his people to fend for themselves because they have surrendered to the new individualist morality. Asturias does not paint twentieth-century

Guatemalan Indians as angels untempted by a cash economy, or unaffected by their contacts with modernizing influences, whether large or small. His interest lies in seeing their economic and political hardships relieved, and in recognizing their cultural autonomy and personal dignity.

To his credit, Asturias's indigenism has not been bedazzled by the outer trappings of autochthonous culture, by the tourist's interest in exotic clothing or comfortable performances of rituals no longer believed in. To deconstruct moves toward cultural and religious hegemony of Christian modernity, he chose the idea of a spirit possession—as he had done previously in *Men of Maize*—whereby the significant battles of culture could occur inside people, rather than only as outward aspects or only as confrontations between people. His point is that wherever there are struggles for domination of one culture over another, wars of allegiance are also being waged within those people whose strategic or historic alliances conflict with their sympathies, or within those forced to betray some of their beliefs in order to be faithful to the rest. Fiction is adept at this internal dialogism, as Bakhtin has shown. Within each individual character, disaccord manifests itself. Moreover, the high stakes of the religious conflict Asturias so humorously represents are reduced in their significance, perhaps to inconsequence, if the teams are not racially and culturally determined but at each instant infinitely reconfigurable.

The indigenous conceptualization whose recognition Asturias promotes can even undermine or attenuate the importance of class, at least to the extent that individuals or groups have oversimplistically been considered members of one, and only one, economic class, rather than to have multiple ways in which they fit into power structures through economic relations. Feminism has reminded us that a wealthy white woman may belong to the bourgeoisie and still have no money of her own; among the indigenous fictional figures in Asturias's novel, an extremely poor woman with magical powers (Catalina Zabala) can gain fabulous wealth and absolute control over others. The novel also denies the loss of a Mayan presence in Central America, because that presence has not been lost. It has merely been transmuted, mixed and diluted, but it exists—even within the sectors of Latin American society not normally considered indigenous. *Mulata* requires the reader to recognize the brutality and grotesqueness of the domination of the Indians, as well as the insidious effects of modernization on such a disenfranchised sector of the population.

Like the spirit possessions in the church, the transcendence of death in the novel further problematizes conceptions of race, religion, class, and culture, because it reinforces mutability and change. Overcoming death surfaces early in the book in the form of the Mulata's invincibility, then returns in the middle sections as Yumí's resuscitation from death. The death of individuals, even many of them, is only a seeming stability, a fixed endpoint in the constant movement of the universe. The repeated defeat of death in the novel teaches that Mayan culture and the Mayan people are not lost, since they have survived in heterogeneity, despite calls for authenticity and the like that would prematurely label them moribund or extinct. The Spanish Conquest is thus incomplete and the plans for domination of the native peoples have not been accomplished.

But a culture can die in ways other than the physical death of its members. Nonsurvival of a culture occurs when its existence is denied or is not positively and explicitly recognized by any discourse. This erasure is not the same as the disavowal of those practices and institutions which may constitute a culture. If, for example, those who wear Western clothes and speak Spanish have maintained their parents' indigenous religiosity yet do not realize that they have retained this part of Mayan culture, then that culture has been forgotten by them and has effectively died, despite the continuance of its practices. Asturias's writing protests against the violent cultural clashes of past and present, but not against only them; he also satirizes the idea that Catholic priests should have the last word on autochthonous cultures, during the Conquest or today. In the later portions of the novel, when Jerónimo is Sheet, Chamer is unrecognized by the characters. Christians may in the end destroy Mayan beliefs by not recognizing the heterogeneity of those forms of Christianity influenced by local practices. In another way, the culture has been erased; Asturias seeks to retrace its outlines for his readers to see.

As we have seen in the Mayan Game, for most of the novel Yumí has been the focalization point for a bemused narrator, who at times—as in the tales of the cannibals and the coconuts, for example—has a definite personality showing in authorial comment, but who at other times can be an epic poet of strangely syncretic dignity, as in the story of Salomé. Nevertheless, the attribution of the narration in the latter portions of the novel to another source—the demented, dying priest, attuned only to his own inner voices—goes a long way toward explaining the combative nature of the cultural encounters in parts 2 and 3. Because of the priest's insistence that everyone worship *his* religion and practice *his* culture, the characters he defines as Others are obliged to fight to the death for their very survival. Chimalpín employs the us-them morality of the proselytizer, a voice that condemns all other religions. Yet he succumbs to contagion through frequent, prolonged contact, both literal and metaphoric. In the Mayan

Game, the priest's pockmarks are the visible marks of his penetration by Yumí's porcupine spines, the near victory of an indigenous *nahual*. In the Domination Game, Chimalpín's scars signal his sin, his alienation from God, and his distance from the truth. The novel's holocaust ending is narrated as Chimalpín and Jerónimo see it, and neither understand what is occurring in Mayan terms. We see through the priest's eyes or the sexton's eyes, but the reader is not fooled into gullible acceptance of their versions. Instead we have been prepared by the earlier sections to resist and to read otherwise. Both the text's complexity of focus and the sympathetic reader's constant need to translate events from one allegorical level to another together speak to a dynamic perspectivism. This complexity is not gratuitous but an arduously achieved multiplicity of point of view.

Raúl Silva Cáceres dubbed Asturias's style in this novel an "obsessive discourse," in which "the plot and the development of the events . . . appear strung together in a capricious and abstruse manner, and many times contradict each other and are strung together in a way similar to the speech of a madman or a child or, simply, with the spontaneity and lack of causality with which popular fables and legends are told. That does not prevent the novelistic world from being structured to perfection."[67] In Silva Cáceres's designation of Asturias's style as "obsessive," he collapses into a single characteristic what I am suggesting is a multifaceted and complex phenomenon of focalization and point of view, as well as of levels of allegorization and gaming.

Specifically, the final chapter, "It is Quaking on the Moon" ["Está temblando en la luna"], does not have Yumí as narrative focalizer. Within this chapter, first the sexton Jerónimo/Sheet and then the priest Mateo Chimalpín function in Yumí's stead. The priest is the focalizer during the last pages of the novel, told in the third person. While it is difficult to state any more concretely when the mobile point of focalization comes to rest in a prolonged fashion on Jerónimo, then on Chimalpín, it is clear that the last chapter raises the complexity of the narrative voices and focalizers exponentially. The authorial narrator is little help and is present at the end largely in the ordering of the telling, with much less comment than before. The Mulata and Zabala are participant narrators for all of the final chapter except the last page and a half.

One reason for the changes in narrative point of view and voice, especially the transition from the simple peasant (Yumí) to that of the would-be religious authorities of the village (Jerónimo and Chimalpín), may lie in the tragic historiography—the tragic history of the history—of the Mesoamerican peoples, as I suggested above. The fact is that their past can be discerned today primarily from glimmers of information reconstructed from the texts of the conquerors, missionaries, and other would-be destroyers of the Mayan world(view). The repetitive and contradictory nature of *Mulata* could be an extreme stylization of semiotic patterns Asturias found in historical discourse about the Conquest even into the twentieth century. In Asturias's day, additionally, the Mayan hieroglyphs were still undecipherable; hence access to the Classic Mayan meanings was denied to him more than to us. Thus Asturias gives us the priest and his assistant, voice and countervoice of the errors and distortions that omit the Indian religious conception.

During this chapter's apocalypse and afterward, when Jerónimo/Sheet has lost his comic, dissenting voice, the dizzying velocity of the textual dynamism prevents easy answers to the questions of what remains to be fought over, who should fight, and what it all means. The reader can understand very little as literal. We see the events through the Christianizing, moralizing eyes of Jerónimo and Chimalpín, whose corrupt standpoint is symbolized by the leprosy[68] of the delirious Father Chimalpín on the last page. A critique of their hegemonic view would indeed be expected to arise from a resistance within the novelistic world; elements such as disease from a Mayan perspective are not gratuitous or natural but spirit-sent. Explicit authorial commentary would have been too heavy-handed in the context of this delicate representation of the subtleties of historical discourse, but readers did need some guidance coming from the text as to how to understand the ending. Indeed the totalizing conception of the two Christians is made to appear absurd or false in several ways. The representatives of Western religion moralize against indigenous culture as the product of a single Christian devil, for instance, whereas a whole legion of Indian devils has been sporting with them. In addition, Jerónimo and Chimalpín see sexual women as representatives of Candanga, yet the Mulata is a warrior for Cashtoc.

First of all, Jerónimo ridicules the priest, and echoes one of the Archbishop's chamberlains when he says the priest is "old-fashioned! . . . thinking that natural forces, earthquakes and hurricanes, were the work of the Devil . . . and talking about giants, as if we were in the age of Enoch!" (333T) ["atrasado! . . . considerar las fuerzas naturales, sismos y huracanes, obra del demonio . . . y hablar de gigantes, como si estuviéramos en la época de Enoc!" (338)]. The priest had played the Mayan Game at first, but Jerónimo mistrusts Chimalpín, whom he finds "crazy, crazy like the fellow from Assisi with the wolf" (334T) ["loco, loco, como el de Asís con el lobo" (339)]. Second, the priest's zeal to condemn and find fault seems excessive, when in the end, his value judgments come down to the same thing: the spotted snake who was the Virgin with a Rash was supposedly a woman transformed: "the evil girl became a snake" (330T) ["la mujer mala se volvió serpiente" (335)]. Most important, the duo's demonizing versions of what happens are comically undercut by the existence of other versions previously recounted. Another example in addition to the Mulata's death, discussed earlier, is the remarriage of Yumí to the Mulata in the black mass presided over by the priest. It is first told in the voice of an authorial or objective narrator (242–43T; 246), then recounted by the sexton to a seemingly amnesiac priest (288T; 293–94), and then is retold by the Cleaning Woman to Jerónimo himself as he waits to "test" the Virgin with a Rash as a favor to the priest (322T; 328–29).

The final apocalypse of the novel has, at one level, a participant-narrator (Jerónimo/Sheet) to whom events are revealed by scenification or in dialogues, yet on another level, all can be seen as occurring in the progressively sicker consciousness of the priest, who wishes to condemn all gods as devils and all native peoples as devil worshipers. The sexton's perspective, while Christian, is less polarized as to moral and religious values; Jerónimo's more comic characterization functions always as the porous membrane between the extremely heterogeneous world of the Mulata, Yumí, and Zabala, and the more rarefied though still mixed world of Catholic, historical modernity. The viewpoints of the sexton and the priest, essential for understanding the final disposition of the characters, are overlays on Mayan gaming. Thus it is clear that before the priest's disease blinds him, it (and all it symbolizes) provokes distortions in his sight. Prior to the priest entertaining himself with the memory of the children he prepared for Communion back in Tierrapaulita, the reader is entertained with the narrative of certain events told repeatedly with variations. Lost to the present moment, Chimalpín remembers only his own versions of the past. The hypothesis that major portions of the novel, including the last chapter, occur in Chimalpín's mind may be impossible to prove, but I have been convinced by the following points, among others.

The character of Chimalpín, about whom we know almost nothing other than his name, brings to mind the chronicler Chimalpahin, as was suggested by Luis A. Pérez. Author of *Los anales de Chimalpahin* [The annals of Chimalpahin], this chronicler wrote about the Quiché Indians during the period 1258 to 1612 (Pérez 762). His full name was Domingo Francisco de San Antón Muñón Chimalpahin Cuauhtlehuanitzin and, according to Miguel León-Portilla, he "typifies in his own person the educated Indian of colonial Mexico who wanted to make his own all that was good of his indigenous legacy and all those contributions that came as a consequence of the encounter between the two worlds" of European and autochthonous peoples ["tipifica en su propia persona al indígena ilustrado del México colonial que quiso hacer suyo lo que tuvo por bueno de su propio legado indígena y de las aportaciones provenientes, como consecuencia, del encuentro de dos mundos" (301)]. Schroeder writes that Chimalpahin declared himself a Christian, but preferred to do his writing in Nahuatl, the Aztec language.[69] The church on the outskirts of Mexico City in which the author Chimalpahin worked most of his life (1579–1660?) was devoted to the care of lepers after 1628 (Schroeder 11).

Mexican historian and critic León-Portilla is particularly enthusiastic about this native historian because so much of his work has been corroborated by others. This critic waxes especially eulogistic about Chimalpahin for a poem he collected, which is also to be found in the *Colección de cantares mexicanos* [Collection of Mexican songs]. This doubly documented poem, the "Song of the Women of Chalco" ("In chalca cihuacuícatl" or "Canto de las mujeres de Chalco"), is also one of the few compositions of the period with a named author: Aquiauhtzin of Ayapanco. For our purposes, however, what is most important about the poem with which Chimalpahin is associated is that in the song, the women of Chalco "invite the master of Tenochtitlan to a fight in which only he who was well endowed sexually could triumph. War is transformed into an erotic siege, the approach of opposites, a sexual act with all its preambles; and the song finishes with the victory of the little woman of Chalco who, with all her enchantments, manages to make hers the powerful Axayacátl" (León-Portilla).[70] Whether or not Asturias intended his character Chimalpín to be modeled after the collector of this poem, similarities abound in the sexual battle in the church between the Mulata (the little woman of Chalco?) and Yumí (Axayacátl?). Significantly, Chimalpín is the only one to survive the destruction of Tierrapaulita and thus becomes the repository of their story, just as Chimalpahin rescued the poem.

In this scheme of things, the Mulata and Catalina Zabala have become emblems of a narrative progression toward the grand conflagration in the priest's mind, rather than representatives of the Indian peoples or of good/ bad women. At first, Yumí's wives had symbolized the stakes for which each side was playing this violent and sardonically hysterical game. By the end, the remaining sexual women characters are the Cleaning Woman (la Tintorera) and the Virgin with a Rash (la doncella con salpullido): that is, a brothel madam and her prostitute (snake). Under these new names, as picaresque characters from a sexual fringe, sexual women are again bought for money, and live among the working poor. Sexual women lose out in the Domination Game, fought in Chimalpín's mind.

Conclusion

> In perfect (although inverted) symmetry to the action at the beginning of the allegory, Catalina-Giroma rises to power through her dealings with the corn-leaf devil. She loses no time in punishing (or further debasing) her husband. . . . In other words, the ex-king is reduced to being a dwarf, while the ex-dwarf becomes a giantess.
>
> René Prieto, *Miguel Angel Asturias's Archaeology of Return* (220)

Asturias's profoundly difficult and ambiguous novel merits the reconsideration it is currently receiving by critics of all persuasions. In this work, Asturias takes readers on a wild roller-coaster ride of magic with hundreds of characters of diverse ethnicities. The characterization of sexual women in *Mulata* exuberantly, poetically, humorously, and satirically is a colloquy of many female voices, orchestrated by an authorial sympathizer. There are recognizable Western-style images of both women-hating and female empowerment, but we also find non-Western, Mesoamerican-inspired images of female lustfulness and power. Asturias's complex patterning of multiple voices, variegated narrative strands, and ambiguous meanings leaves a welcome place for widely diverse interpretations. Yet some discriminations should be made.

Overly reductive interpretations, especially, are not helpful. Regarding the characterization of sexual women in this novel, it has been difficult for critics to resist the idea of the Mulata, Catalina Zabala, and other sexual women as having been invented by an author who hated women. A biography might allege such a hypothesis, but analysis of the novel itself can only establish that Asturias rarely showed women other than in a male gaze. The sick priest, the slapstick sexton, and the Indian everyman Yumí are his focalizers. More important, however, is Asturias's Mesoamerican "translation" of present and past culture wars in which the sexual women are involved. In this light, the figure of the Mulata, with her insatiable sexual appetite and greed, incarnates forces that bring an era to an end. Her activities, seen today as evil or cruel, are analogous to the work of predators in the natural world. Hers is not an ethic to emulate, but a function to comprehend. As René Prieto summarizes in "El papel político del erotismo en *Mulata de tal*": "If *Men of Maize* is a song of life and hope, *Mulata* is a celebration of death, an ode to disenchantment" ["Si *Hombres de maíz* es un canto de vida y esperanza, *Mulata* es una celebración de la muerte, una oda al desencanto" (83)].

Mulata does not represent a rejection of women. Powerful male figures dominate the more realistic first half of the novel, but strong female ones play a greater role in the more magical second half. If one were to weigh the characters' actions solely in terms of rewards and punishments, men would be portrayed more negatively than women. In balance, women (especially Catarina Zabala at first) are accorded more favorable representations, morally and aesthetically. Throughout, since they are less instigators than indefatigable castigators of unfaithfulness and greed, women fare well. They do commit crimes, but they are punished for them. Paramount is the fact that there are very few positive images of anyone—woman or man. In addition, Asturias's characters in *Mulata* are polyvalent and ambiguously gendered, his narrative structure and poetic imagery accuse men and women equally of bringing about the destruction of themselves, of Yumí's hometown Quiavicús, and of the city of magicians, Tierrapaulita.

The poetic beauty—even the ribald humor—of Asturias's descriptions of female pudenda may indeed be carnivalesque in the sense Mikhail Bakhtin described in *Rabelais and His World*. In this view, as in the feminist one, the humorous explicitness in the Guatemalan's representation of female sex organs is a positive reclaiming of them in language; through his writing Asturias provides readers with the idea of female sex organs as presence, unlike novels that univocally imitate the male-dominated world in which the female body is characterized by absence (the missing phallus). Can Asturias be recuperated for a postmodern feminism for this act of giving women material bodies, with sexual organs, in his writing? Indeed, women's sexual organs attain the status of actants, if not actors, in the magical narrative. Sickness, especially sickness resulting from an inner corruption in a conception of justice more mythic than legal, is another way in which sexuality and the body are emphasized.[71]

In terms of female sexuality, while both Catholic and native religions have provided spiritual comfort and ethnic cohesion to their believers, both have restricted "good" women to the home and expelled "bad" (read: sexual) women from the local community. In contrast to this moralizing attitude, Asturias appears interested in liberated female sexuality as a symptom of the cultural problems he is addressing, but unaware that his narrative focus on the male indigenist perspective on modernization might not speak to a female Indian's experience. In his conception of modern racism and economic exploitation in Latin America as structural (and not merely as consequences of ignorance and intolerance), Asturias probably realized that Native American women were oppressed in their poverty as women *and* as indigenous peoples. However, it is unlikely that he fully understood that the gender hierarchy made the effect of modernization on women not only different, but also harsher than on men. A later or more postmodern thinker would perhaps have voiced a separate female standpoint and placed it in dialogue with the many male focalizations he does use, in recognition of this difference. Catarina Zabala, Yumí's wife and companion, might have been the best candidate for such narrative mediation, but only occasionally does she speak from a gendered position different from Yumí's. Nevertheless, Asturias's accomplishment of extreme heterogeneity in characterization remains unassailed by most other writers to this day.

The image of sexual women as dangerous certainly prevails in the Money Game, because in the context of capitalist gain and commodification, sexual women are commensurate with prostitutes. Epitomized by the Mulata at the Fair, their supposed goal is to strip men of their cash. The danger posed to men by female sexuality in the Mayan Game lies in the Mulata's destructive power as a lunar goddess and force of nature. She reflects a fundamental life-death connection, as a result of which, causing death in appropriate ritual circumstances promotes life. In the Domination Game, there is a great deal of continuity with the other games and reliance on their stratagems. The moves in this game lay on top of—rely on—Mayan gaming, which sees the sexual woman as destructive. In the Domination Game, the most anti-woman versions of Catholic myth, history, and theology blame women (and female sexuality in particular) for the expulsion from paradise. The danger posed by sexual women—allies of devils in the eyes of Jerónimo and Chimalpín—is the loss of one's soul. But this most virulent anti-sex and anti-women stance is satirized, not presented directly or without irony. The priest wishes to "save face" and remove his scars, signs of his battle with a human porcupine (Yumí-as-Candanga). Rather than sleep with a woman, he risks his life on the Meat-Eating Mule.

The sexual woman's danger to man exists under all the systems and in all the forms presented. As a prostitute, a volcano, or a snake, the sexual woman helps Cashtoc to destroy modernized Indians who have become individualists and serves Candanga in his campaign to promote population growth in hell. Like the destruction caused by the Mulata herself, the termination of the magical world is furthered by her actions. Only distorted voices from the past survive into the contemporary, technological present to give explanations and distribute blame.

Nevertheless, the death and destruction she causes, while feared by Yumí, Jerónimo, and the priest Chimalpín, were sacred in Mayan culture and thus are respected in Asturias's text. In Asturias's writings as far back as his legal thesis in 1923, *Guatemalan Sociology: The Social Problem of the Indian* (1977; *Sociología guatemalteca: El problema social del indio*), he found the Indian's poverty and lack of political rights unacceptable. The author's attitudes on the subject do not change between the time of his education and *Mulata* of forty years later. Regarding Indian culture, however, he does an about-face during his years as a writer, diplomat, and frequently, an exile. Whereas in his thesis Asturias evinces few regrets that the Indians of his time should lose their language and cultural practices in the interest of improved hygiene and political consciousness, the author's late works, including *Mulata,* favor popular resistance to such a devastating loss of cultural identity imposed from without. This later, more subtle and sympathetic attitude, that Mayan culture must be saved to the extent possible and not jettisoned merely because it might retard modernization, may have been one of many motivating factors in writing *Mulata.* Especially the ending of the novel, in which the culture Asturias has come to love fights for a chance to survive against moves by Christianity and capitalism to dominate it, reads as if calculated to vindicate an endangered culture on the brink of extinction.

I have been inspired by the Mesoamerican ball game to speak of his book in terms of closed times and spaces with their own rules of play, in order to address Asturias's ideological strategies in *Mulata* as life-and-death games with religious significance. The Money Game section speaks to his Marxian sense of economic conflict within macrosystems of class. The Mayan Game section reminds that Asturias's invention was, as often as not, a selection from the whole wealth of native materials with which he was familiar. The Domination Game section elucidates the narrative, historical, and religious rules regulating the novel's ultimate conflagration, which I have explained insofar as they concern the image of sexual women.

As we have seen, the Mulata character provides a bridge to this magical work from his banana trilogy, three committed Marxist works about the United Fruit Company, Central America's coastal laborers, and neocolonial economic policies. As Josephine Baker, the Mulata briefly reminds us of the author's Paris period. But for this reader, the Mulata is most of all a heterogeneous construction based on diverse cultural, historical, and personal materials; she represents a certain indefatigable quality, whether or not she dies in the end. Because focalization remains for most of the novel with Yumí (until we see things through the eyes of Jerónimo/Sheet and then Chimalpín), the Mulata is most often positively imbued with energy, an irrepressible energy, as a resistance against domination in the forms of money, men, religion, culture, propriety, even heterosexuality and definitions of normal gender. Her sexuality—admittedly impossible to extricate from her destructive function—is more utopian than dystopian. It lives in the open, feeds her spirit, keeps her powerful, and, when stolen from her, continues to live and to seduce Yumí. Without her sexuality, the Mulata has barely enough presence to cast a shadow; when she has it, it provides her relief from the inexorability of time.

Although not a feminist project of empowerment, *Mulata* nonetheless names the supposedly unnamable parts of the female body, ironically and humorously clouding the mirror—to imitate a Mayan expression—which fetishizes female body parts in patriarchal discourse. As a work that refuses to reduce cultures and genders to mere stereotypes, perhaps it can contribute in some small way to clearing out some essentializing conceptions. Begun in Argentina in 1956 when events in Guatemala had sent its author into the most pessimistic of spirits, and finished in 1962 before the great rifts over the Cuban Revolution had begun to appear among Latin American intellectuals, *Mulata* contains within it both utopian aspirations for freedom and dystopian skepticism. It reflects conflicts typical of the time, tensions which, even at the beginning of the twenty-first century, are still productive of discourse intending to disrupt patriarchal power. Asturias's huge range of infernal voices and demonic characters is such that *Mulata* satirizes consumerism, greed, and rampant individualism; it exposes corruption, ignorance, and prejudice; it decants hatred on the oppressors of the weak and the repressors of culture; and ultimately it blames just about everyone involved for the hellish state of Guatemala in this period. But he does not particularly blame these malignant states of affairs on women's liberation, on sexual women, or on women in general.[72] He names women dangerous accomplices with men in the crime of repudiating the ancient past and oppressing the native peoples of Guatemala.

Life and Death sculpture (vertically split skull). Mayan. Photo courtesy of the Museo Nacional de Antropología, Mexico City. Reprinted by permission of the Instituto Nacional de Antropología e Historia, CONACULTA-NAH-MEX.

The Young Moon Goddess, Ix Chel,
with her name glyph. After the
Dresden Codex by Michael D. Coe.
From *The Maya* by Michael D. Coe.
Drawing copyright 1999, Michael D.
Coe. Reprinted by permission of
Thames and Hudson.

The Old Moon Goddess, Ix Chel,
with her name glyph. After the
Dresden Codex by Michael D.
Coe. From *The Maya* by Michael
D. Coe. Drawing copyright 1999,
Michael D. Coe. Reprinted by per-
mission of Thames and Hudson.

Embracing couple: Young Moon Goddess with an old man. Mayan ceramic, 24.8 cm., A.D. 700–800. Courtesy of Founders Society Purchase, Katherine Margaret Kay Bequest Fund and the New Endowment Fund. Photo copyright 1990, the Detroit Institute of Arts.

The Giants preparing for a *convite*, a danced procession the night before the religious procession of Holy Week. Guatemala City. Photo: Sara Facio.

Tlazolteotl, Moon Goddess, female god of sensuality. Detail. After the *Codex Borgia* by Gisele Diaz and Alan Rodgers. From *The Codex Borgia: A Full-Color Restoration of the Ancient Mexican Manuscript*, art copyright 1993 Gisele Díaz and Alan Rodgers. Reprinted by permission of Alan Rodgers.

the goddess

moon sign

rabbit

Young Moon Goddess sitting in the crescent moon, holding a rabbit. Line drawing: Linda Schele. From *The Blood of Kings* by Linda Schele and Mary Ellen Miller, copyright 1986. Reproduced by permission of Linda Schele.

The Moon Goddess

Josephine Baker in banana-skirt costume. Photo: Studio Waléry, Paris, for a scene in the Folies Bergère revue "La Folie du Jour," 1926. Courtesy Bryan Hammond, private collection.

3

Clarice Lispector and the Promise of Freedom

> And we might wonder how it is possible that the lyricism and re-
> ligiosity that long accompanied the revolutionary project have, in
> Western industrial societies, been largely carried over to sex.
> Michel Foucault, *The History of Sexuality,* vol. 1 (8)

At first glance, *An Apprenticeship, or the Book of Delights* (*Uma aprendizagem, ou O livro dos prazeres* 1969) must seem an odd choice to represent the novels which take as their principal subject the sexuality of female characters during the period of full-fledged liberatory sexual politics in Latin American literature. First of all, the Clarice Lispector work does not come from the 1970s, the decade when the effect of the events of the 1960s would have had time to percolate into literature. Second, concepts of race, indigenous culture, and miscegenation, the themes of Miguel Angel Asturias's *Mulata de tal,* are not major issues and are barely mentioned. How can one sustain a comparison to Asturias? Third, Lispector lyrically tells a woman's story of learning to love a man, with a happy ending of their grand coming together in bed. Where lies the danger there, the danger still associated with female sexuality in the post-1960s period? Fourth, this novel is written by an author who admitted, long after *An Apprenticeship* appeared, that she had not been able to write about social issues before *Hour of the Star* (1986; *A hora da estrela* 1977). How can her earlier novel be seen as representative of a new era of a full-blown sexual liberation movement?

Regarding the first objection, that *An Apprenticeship* from 1969 is not a novel of the 1970s, I must remind readers of the arbitrariness of the idea of a decade and that "the '60s" as a period of social and cultural history does not appear or disappear on any strict calendar demarcation. A more important reason that one should discount the objection *An Apprenticeship* follows too quickly on the heels of *Mulata* is the difference between the histories of Brazil and Spanish America. Brazil experienced an earlier onset and thus has had a longer history with literary eroticism and sexual fiction by 1969. Furthermore, the year 1968, held as the watershed year by Fredric Jameson and other theorists of the 1960s, does not hold for Latin America as a universally significant date. The literatures of Mexico were greatly affected by the 1968 massacre in Tlaltelolco, it is true; but those of Chile and Argentina were more radicalized by their own military coups and repressive dictatorships of the 1970s. The resistance and liberation movements in the Southern Cone tend to be fictionalized en masse later than in Mexico, later than 1968. Brazil's main galvanizing event, its military coup, on the other hand, occurred in 1964. The manipulation of sexual and intimist fiction for social critique thus became visible earlier on the Brazilian literary scene. In fact, I was pleased to find this early Brazilian work in order to address through its example the lack of synchrony within the diverse Latin American experience. As with many other groupings within Latin American literature, Brazilian literature's sexual fiction has had its own rhythms, and by 1969 a book like *An Apprenticeship*, even by a woman, was fashionable and not an oddity.

A second objection to my choice of Lispector's novel might be the thematic discontinuity between Asturias's Rabelaisian, Neo-Indigenist satire of race and history and the realistic and amorous themes that preoccupy the Brazilian work. In *An Apprenticeship*, the protagonist, Lori, works as an elementary school teacher in a metropolitan area, Rio de Janeiro. There is no literal or symbolic concern for agricultural practices, cultural miscegenation, or macroeconomic structures and policies; historical discourse plays no explicit role. The optic of this Brazilian fiction obsessively focuses on the nearby and the present—the microevents of a realistically portrayed daily life. The characters are middle-class educators, far from the illiterate, culturally rich mestizos and criollos of the Guatemalan work. Indeed, just about the only ideas and activities shared by these two texts fall under the rubric of themes of female sexuality.

Unlike Asturias's *Mulata*, *An Apprenticeship* does not thematize the role of the sacred predatory sexual woman in a divine scheme, but rather the role of sexuality in the life and loves of a philosophically inclined, meditative, articulate, and sexually active woman. Near the end of the novel, Ulysses asks her about her past: "'How did you used to enjoy sex?' 'It was the only thing,' she said, 'that I did right'" (110T) ["Como é que você se dava com sexo?—Era a única coisa, disse ela, em que eu dava certo" (163)]. As a consequence of the shift from Asturias's epic saga of vast numbers of characters to that of Lispector's close-up on one individual, I am sure the danger Lori's sexuality poses appears greatly attenuated compared to the Mulata's threat of death, torture, and the end of indigenous cultures. But a woman's practice of sexual liberation, that is, of sex without love and without guilt, is undoubtedly the problem posed by Lispector's novel. In *An Apprenticeship* Lori is an experienced, sexual woman. Her antagonist in the plot and her teacher in the apprenticeship, Ulysses, is Lori's new love interest. The imagery associates her with prostitutes, sacred and otherwise, and the climax and resolution of the plot involves putting into practice the lessons of her apprenticeship in living and loving.

Most important, Lori conforms to the new fictional stereotype of the sexually liberated woman because she is able to have sex without pregnancy, disease, or social ostracism; she supports herself financially, and is sophisticated culturally, educated, young, pretty, and alone. When Ulysses asks Lori why she moved to Rio from Campos, she answers with brutal honesty, typical of this type of female hero: "I didn't want to . . . get married. I wanted a certain type of freedom which wouldn't be possible there without causing a scandal, beginning with my own family. There everyone knows everyone else's business" (29–30T) ["É que eu não queria. . . não queria me casar, queria certo tipo de liberdade que lá não seria possível sem escândalo, a começar pela minha família, lá tudo se sabe" (51)]. Lori's sexual experience, in combination with her fear of losing her newly acquired freedoms, qualify her as a "newly sexed woman." "Newly sexed women" believe in the liberationist power of sexuality; the novels in which they are found either show them enjoying this garden of earthly delights and the world being a better place for their having done so, or their mistake and the world's loss. During the period of the prevalence of this ideology among Latin American liberal writers and intellectuals, this character may be subtly parodied, ridiculed, or made to seem overly idealistic or naive to readers—as is Lori—but the general concept of sexuality as liberatory, as freedom from unjust repression or domination, goes largely unquestioned.

So what are the other characteristics of the theme of female sexuality in *An Apprenticeship*? How can we understand this particular novel's image of the sexual woman? With Asturias, the danger of female sexuality threatened the world more than the character herself, although the Mulata did not emerge unscathed from her pursuit of her sexual desires. With Lispector, the dangers the period associates with female sexuality threaten Lori more than they threaten her world. She wants to learn new, unknown meanings for her sexuality in an apprenticeship, but she is frightened: "Almost running, she said goodbye to Ulysses: he was the danger" (48T)

["Ela se despediu de Ulisses quase correndo: ele era o perigo" (78)]. In Asturias, sexuality required change because it brought destruction to the world; in Lispector, Lori cannot remain the same; she must allow parts of herself to undergo transformations from the way she is at present, if she is to have sex and love together with Ulysses. Ulysses wants to wait to have sex until love can develop, or at least until she can enjoy sex within a love relationship. A series of casual lovers in the past had not touched her emotionally. She must weigh carefully whether to proceed in her affair with the professor (Ulysses);[1] she wonders if she should act as she has with her lovers in the past, or strive to integrate her sexuality into her life differently, in unforeseen ways. The ideas of progress and learning are both affirmed and questioned; the problem for Lori is that the unequal gender hierarchy shows all too clearly that love between men and women as equals is an (impossible) ideal that jeopardizes the (also impossible) ideal of female sexuality as freedom. Lori's internalization of sex-gender roles blocks her possibilities for being as equally powerful as a man when she falls in love.

That the character of the woman-in-love finds herself in peril from the dangers of female sexuality in a female-authored book should not surprise. Those women who have experienced (or identified with those who have experienced) the dangers of an active sexuality to personal safety, reputation, or well-being are simply more likely to focus on this aspect when writing realistically of female characters. As we saw in the introduction, however, women writing about female sexuality entered Latin America's canon of fiction very late, in fact, mainly during the post-1960s period, when there were larger numbers of women being published than before. Women writers could afford to take greater risks once the genre gained a certain transgressive acceptance in criticism and unmitigated popularity in the marketplace. This historical phenomenon of women's greater contribution to sexual fiction is represented here by Lispector. There have always been women writers addressing these topics, of course. But the early women who did so were exceptions, whereas soon after the foment of liberation politics became massive, women were published as never before on all topics, including female sexuality.

In Lispector, the danger to Lori is conveyed through frightening imagery and through dialogue, more than through narrative events. For most of *An Apprenticeship*, little happens except on an inner stage, in part, because Lori is paralyzed by the opposing, equally threatening alternatives. The great variety of the ways in which the equation "female sexuality = danger" occurs in Latin American literature can be well demonstrated by this lyrical work, so untypical of stereotypes of Latin American fiction in the English-language media. But poetic prose is not so uncommon among bourgeois women's fiction of this period, internationally or in Latin America, or among the feminist fictions today that explore the ethics of living. The region's prose exists as a tremendously and irreducibly diverse set of discourses, and it should not be reduced to so-called magical fictions, political works, or some inevitable combination of the two. I hope the profound incommensurableness of Asturias and Lispector in almost every aspect of theme and style, except sexuality, serves to remind the reader of the heterogeneity of Latin American (sexual) fiction. Additionally, the many contrasts should remind readers of my intention not to *describe* the whole field, but to focus on three particularly rich examples in terms of feminist issues.

In a third objection to the Lispector novel's exemplifying the fiction imbued by the sexual liberation movement in its Latin American apogee, the hypothesis could be advanced that although female sexuality in *An Apprenticeship* may predominate thematically, and although it may threaten Lori's self-image and her relationship to Ulysses, nevertheless the treatment given these themes and characters is unrelated to the new social movements of the 1960s. According to this objection, Lispector's book continues Brazil's erotic tradition, but it does not gesture toward the condition of women in general or toward feminism in particular. But such a hypothesis would overly restrict feminism to the (unreflective) strategic activism prominent at the beginnings of social movements.

To understand the sociopolitical relevance of Lispector's novel, it is essential to think in terms of philosophical and literary feminism, so much more frequent in the United States than in Latin America, but which existed there and flourishes today as never before. Latin American feminist movements have most often called themselves "women's movements," which are not quite the same as "women's liberation movements." These women's groups and individual thinkers/writers/activists struggled much more on explicitly political and economic fronts than their North American and European equivalents. For Latin American activists, the importance of envisioning a domestic and personal politics consistent with ideals of justice and equality for women was just as imperative. In this aspect, Lispector's novel, while not early as sexual fiction in Brazil, appeared before many women's groups had articulated the feminist issues that I examine in her novel. Conscious feminist micropolitics existed, but became *frequent* only about a decade later in much of Latin America.

Like Asturias, Lispector, in her fiction, promotes ideas of women's equality in sexual relations from a unique, individual perspective rather than as part of a movement. Unlike *Mulata*, in which female sexuality was debated as a moral question, *An Apprenticeship* assumes a woman's sexuality was ready for liberation. In addition to answering my quest for a newly sexed woman protagonist in a post-1959 novel in which the idea of "sexual liberation" manifests itself fully as a social and political liberation, *An Apprenticeship* also presents interpersonal dilemmas that still interest feminists today. Lispector's originality in this regard has not always been appreciated, even within Brazil. Outside Brazil critics have remarked how the type of writing Lispector produced was followed by others, marking a new trend. Judith A. Payne and Earl E. Fitz compare the Spanish American and Brazilian New Novel generally and remark: "What was new, however, was the degree of gender consciousness that infused the Brazilian new novel and that . . . distinguished it from its far better known Spanish American counterparts. . . . Only the Brazilian model offered an alternative vision of such issues as gender, narrative voice, and identity" (2). These two critics add another important difference between the two traditions to their list a few pages later: "Amidst the many similarities between the new novels of Brazil and Spanish America, one clear difference emerged: women writers in Brazil attained greater critical recognition than did their counterparts in Spanish America" (4). (This difference affected my selection of texts to examine in detail here, since I wanted to reflect this historical situation.) By analyzing *An Apprenticeship*, therefore, I recognize Brazilian literature's leadership in publishing sexual fiction and women writers.

In Brazil as in much of the rest of Latin America, prose is expected to comment on society and to provide insight into ethical dilemmas. Lispector's novels of interiority have been taken by some critics to be synonymous with political disengagement, even as an immoral neglect of social issues. This reading comes, in part, from the near invisibility of traditional political issues in her work and, in part, from the contrast between Lispector's topics and those of the Marxists and populists—Brazilians like Jorge Amado, Graciliano Ramos, and Rachel de Queiroz—who were popular during Lispector's lifetime. From her first novel, *Near to the Wild Heart* (1990, hereinafter referred to as *Wild Heart; Perto de coração selvagem* 1943), her writings have provoked controversy in Brazil because of the novelty of their lyrical treatment and their subject matter of middle-class life (see Fitz, *Clarice Lispector*).

Nonetheless, it is certainly true that momentous political events such as the military takeover in Brazil in 1964 are not directly reflected in

Lispector. Critic Marta Peixoto wrote: "Her work does not thematize the literal, political violence of war and torture or other overt forms of state brutality. . . . There are crimes in Lispector, but they are used mainly for their symbolic value, as vehicles and correlatives of guilt and inner conflicts" (*Passionate Fictions* 102). Nor should one forget that when *An Apprenticeship* was being finished and published (1967–1969), military repression in Rio de Janeiro, where the author lived, was at its fiercest. Direct protest would not have been permitted, especially if Lispector had wanted to write specifically about the military dictatorship (which is doubtful). Only *Hour of the Star,* Lispector's final novel, makes writing the site of less than ambiguous narratorial commentary on poverty, social class, and brutal, physical social violence. The representation of social concerns in *An Apprenticeship,* in contrast, is largely performed within interior monologues which examine interpersonal and personal events, often from an ethical perspective, which the narrator then comments upon and contextualizes. Intersubjectivity enters as a condition of existence that informs, forms, and deforms subjectivity.

The psychosocial nature of the theme of female sexuality in *An Apprenticeship* manifests itself first in the educational leitmotiv emphasized in the novel's title. One of the first of many fine critics of Lispector, the Brazilian Benedito Nunes, wrote of *An Apprenticeship:* "For the first time, although in an awkward, abstract, and pedantic way, life in society as a theme enters Clarice Lispector's novels, at the same time that the dialogue, preceding and following the act of love, brings consciousnesses together instead of separating them" ["Pela primeira vez, ainda que maneira canhestra, abstrata e pedante, a vida social como tema ingressa no romance de Clarice Lispector, ao mesmo tempo que o diálogo, precedendo e sucedendo o ato de amor, aproxima as consciências em vez de separá-las" (77)]. In *A tessitura dissimulada: o social em Clarice Lispector,*[2] Neiva Pitta Kadota writes that the novel's title "*An Apprenticeship, or The Book of Delights* . . . reminds one of a manual of sexual initiation, but in truth, it is a criticism of romantic language and almost a philosophic essay on pleasure, but the pleasure of self-knowledge. . . . The pleasures of *The Book of Delights* are conditioned on the acquisition of knowledge and the slow evolution of being in relation to the capacity to love. It is a journey crossed by a mutational language that avoids set phrases in favor of didactic discourse and masks itself in the romantic."[3] In an apprenticeship there must be a master from whom the apprentice learns, a profession to enter, skills to acquire, and a social context for all of these. The profession here is that of lover; and the skills to be acquired are those which further commitment to the love relation, without any coercion by the state, religion, or family, and without clear social norms or the precedents of a tradition: in other words, commitment without marriage or other external constraints keep the lovers together. The social context for Lori's apprenticeship is the urban anomie of apartments and casual liaisons. Lori learns the insufficiency of casual sex for a fully lived life, and "frees" herself from past habits to enter the brave new world of reciprocal commitment. Lori's apprenticeship teaches her to become a "master in loving" in a new way: self-defined, spiritual, romantic, and in mutual relationship. √

Most important for understanding the social element in this novel, Lori sees Ulysses as her teacher often when the would-be lovers are together. Ulysses admits having undergone an apprenticeship before gaining the mastery he feels he has now: "What I am actually doing, Lori, is telling you about part of the road that I've already traveled" (67T) ["Lóri, a verdade é que estou contando a você parte do meu caminho já percorrido" (106)]. Though he is at times overcome by desire, speechless and anguished, an apprentice, he always wants control and has authority: "You are the right woman for me. Because in my apprenticeship there has been no one to tell me the obvious" (62T) ["Você é a verdadeira mulher para mim. Porque na minha aprendizagem falta alguém que me diga o óbvio" (98)]. Ulysses molds Lori into the woman he wants. Lori teaches herself much of the knowledge she gains in her apprenticeship, but he guides her, counsels her. She says to Ulysses: "You have transformed me into the woman that I am" (113T) ["Você me transformou na mulher que sou" (169)]. While emphasizing the biblical language of An Apprenticeship, Olga de Sá writes that in this novel we find "a directed apprenticeship, this time by a man, Ulysses, who despite being a little affected, as a professor of philosophy, is Lori's guide; she, like the female Samaritan of the gospels, had already had five husbands (lovers) and had not learned to love" ["Uma aprendizagem orientada, desta vez por um homem, Ulisses, que embora um pouco afetado, como professor de filosofia, é o guia de Lóri; esta, como a samaritana do Evangelho, já tivera cinco maridos [amantes] e não aprendera a amar" (A escritura de Clarice Lispector 204)].

In the New Testament, whose language is sprinkled throughout in An Apprenticeship, Mary Magdalene provides a precedent of a sexual woman who could teach Christians how to be humble in order to learn (the) love (of Christ). In other words, Christian love can be learned and could be an antecedent for Lori's schooling. In Plato also, love (eros) helped the lover to ascend on a ladder of values in order to learn to love the divine. While closer to biblical heterogeneous narrative than to Platonic dialogue, Lispector's story captures more of the Greek themes and ideas when it emphasizes the educational power of love in that a philosophy professor teaches the questioning novitiate why and how to love. Self-knowledge becomes the key to climbing a ladder of eros, though in the Brazilian fiction we do not find the rungs of the Platonic ladder leading to God. It is relevant that in *The Symposium*, the voice explaining the apprenticeship of love to Socrates belonged to Diotima, a woman philosopher-prostitute. Plato's work describes an ascension from a desire for beautiful bodies to a desire for the whole person, from serial lovers to a single, worthy one. But the higher rungs of the Platonic ladder, those that lead one to leave behind the desire for a person in order to seek higher values (ideas), and from there to a higher being (the divine), are less explicit. Greek imagery and allusion, in Ulysses' name and elsewhere, are significant not only because love and education are thoroughly integrated but additionally because the didactic, essayistic quality of the novel defines it generically and makes it more social than if it had been more purely lyrical. This didacticism is ruthlessly ironic, however, especially in the silencing of Lori at the end, when she had only just learned to speak. Truncated dialogue, almost a reverse Socratic *elenchus,* becomes crucial to the later portions of the novel.

If *An Apprenticeship* contained more humor, it would qualify as a "theoretical fable," Alicia Borinsky's term for Spanish American fictions which "are written and received as post-theological and post-philosophical discourses, in which simulacra of philosophy, religion, theology, and history rehearse their elements [of self-reflexivity] as a joke in danger of reinscription" (x). In Lispector, the various "simulacra" "in danger of reinscription" include the discourses Borinsky mentions, plus popular conceptions of psychology, spirituality, and romantic love. With little comedy but a great deal of irony, these social conceptions are paraded in order to be debunked.

In addition to the factor of the social nature of education, the second reason *An Apprenticeship* is social and related to liberation movements results from its association of sexuality with religious belief. In answer to Lori's question to Ulysses about whether he would still love her after having made love, Ulysses replies: "The truth is, Lori, that deep inside I've searched my whole life for divine rapture. I had never thought that, instead, I would discover the divinity of the body" (111T) ["no fundo andei toda a minha vida em busca da embriaguez da santidade. Nunca havia pensado que o que eu iria atingir era a santidade de corpo" (165)]. The philosopher and historian Michel Foucault similarly wrote of a new twentieth-century religion of sex: "the essential thing . . . is the existence in our era of a discourse in which sex, the revelation of truth, the overturning of global laws, the proclamation of a new day to come, and the promise of a certain felicity are linked together. Today it is sex that serves as a support for the ancient form—so familiar and important in the West—of preaching. A great sexual sermon—which has had its subtle theologians and its popular voices—has swept through our societies over the last decades; it has chastised the old order, denounced hypocrisy, and praised the rights of the immediate and the real; it has made people dream of a New City. The Franciscans are called to mind" (7–8). Similarly, Lispector disrupts and recombines the patterns usually found in discourses of women-in-love and of religion, to produce subtle, ambiguous new textuality that deconstructs as much as it confirms the religious claims for sexuality. From Ulysses, Lori learns "how to learn" about human love by contemplating God's love for creation. In one long sequence, for instance, she knows God loves Ulysses, since He loves all living things; she wants to love Ulysses, so she imagines herself imitating God. In this way, the novel inscribes an uplifting consecration of Lori's person and station via her apprenticeship in the new "sexual sermon," whose rules tell her how to fit sexual love into a romantic love relationship. Despite the fact that myths, religions, and cultures have most often portrayed the woman-in-love as self-destructive, self-sacrificing, and abject, Lori represents a negation of those representations through dignified homologies to the spiritual quest.

The intertwining of religious feeling and erotic love in *An Apprenticeship*, as well as in Lispector's preceding novel, *The Passion According to G.H.* (1988, hereinafter referred to as *Passion; A paixão segundo G.H.* 1964), has, with reason, led some critics to call her works "mystical." Writing before *An Apprenticeship* was published, Luíz Costa Lima asserted that *Passion* problematized religion in a "reverse mysticism" ["a mística ao revés" (125)]. By mysticism in reverse, Costa Lima means a progressive interiorization and meditation on the sacred that leads to finding God in the things of the world, rather than a communion of the soul with God. Similarly, Mazzara and Parris call Lori's apprenticeship a "practical mysticism." They assert that Lori's quest for love parallels a mystic journey; it is "practical" because it is human, not divine.[4] In other words, the "mysticism" of these critics links her to (an)other human being(s), not God; it pertains to the realm of society and social psychology. While the divine exists according to Lori's belief system, *An Apprenticeship* rarely addresses literal religion, while speaking constantly of the "religion" of love and sex.

There are parallels between Lori's trajectory and the road Christian mystics travel. *An Apprenticeship* recognizes the mystical path as one that may be chosen (it is the road taken by G.H. in *Passion*), but Lori elects to follow Ulysses's lead and go in another direction—that of sensual, erotic participation in human affairs. In other religions, like Tantrism, mystics need not be continent but can choose sexuality as a path to the mystical experience. But Lori does not begin to seek a higher love and change her direction to pursue human love, nor does she choose sex as a way to reach God. Lori decides *not* to have sex, temporarily, as a path to find *human* love-with-sex. Her inner conflict revolves around her self-definitions, her opinions, pleasures, and actions touching on her affair with Ulysses, and not her ideas about God, to which she self-confidently and rebelliously adheres throughout.

The idea of an apprenticeship would seem to require the illusion of a simple, unified, organically developing self. Interestingly, however, Lori is represented as a volatile mixture of multiple, antithetical desires and ideas. In constant inner movement, her consciousness has chosen to identify as significant select parts of her world, and Lori's particular choices until now have left her without love. After Lori's move from Campos to gain a measure of freedom from the scandal of her sexuality, she wants to change, to break free once again, this time from her own entrenched ways of thinking and acting. Sadness and fear of intimacy plague Lori, but these feelings are not represented as natural states or the bedrock of her personality. She does allow herself to redefine what is important; happiness and the courage to love become hers at the end of the apprenticeship.

The linking of liberty to love and sex for women—for Lori—is the third way, after educational models and religious associations, that *An Apprenticeship* treats social themes. The theme of freedom is intimately related to the construction of female sexuality in *An Apprenticeship*. An envelope of discussions about Lori's freedom in society at the beginning and end of the novel encases a long middle section treating the period of her learning while alone. Lispector's expressive use of punctuation contributes to this particular thematic development.

In the preliminary and most experimental section of the novel, Lori characterizes herself as an animal breaking free from invisible bonds through a blind, hysterical thrashing. Phrase after phrase in the beginning section join thoughts and activities in a flow punctuated rhythmically with commas and divided into paragraphs. Only after three pages do we find the novel's first period; it coincides with the freedom of Lori's inner animal from its cage. Lori's comprehension of the meaning of sexual love furnishes her an escape from the cage in which she finds herself. The first long sentence ends: "She was tired with the effort of a freed animal" (3T—note that the translation omits the period) ["Estava cansada do esforço de animal libertado." (14)]. The freed animal rests, and Lori rests: full stop. Then the rhythmic prose begins again; Lori needs to decide whether to keep seeing Ulysses. Then comes the second full stop. When she comes to think about him, seeking to free herself from her bonds of habit and idea, she need thrash about no longer.

An Apprenticeship begins with a comma, as if the novel were a continuation from some previous writing after a pause.[5] It ends with a colon, indicating a pause and incompletion. The novel lies "in between," similar to Lori's apprenticeship, an in-between time, after she has gained sexual experience and before she loves, during which she makes the transformation from one stage (casual sex) to another (sex with love). Because the text falls between a comma and a colon, in a sense An Apprenticeship begins before the text itself—in the peritexts—and ends after it. The final incomplete fragment makes for an unusually marked openness to the ending. The novel's main concepts, such as the apprenticeship and time, emphasize process and the intermediate; in parallel fashion, it "begins" after a suppressed beginning and "ends" before a suppressed ending.

The main reason the novel's treatment of female sexuality is related to feminism is precisely this important subtheme of female freedom within a newly sexed love relation that Lispector has indicated through her experimental open beginning and expressive open ending. At first Lori considers it unfair to need to give up her sexual freedoms for love; she does not want love for Ulysses to require a sacrifice, but rather to enjoy her sexual desires when moved by them. In Lispector's first novel, Wild Heart, the protagonist Joana wonders: "How was she to tie herself to a man without permitting him to imprison her?" (29T) ["Como ligar-se a um homem senão permitindo que ele a aprisione?" (32)]. Lispector parodies herself by revisiting Joana's question in similar terms in An Apprenticeship, but with a different result. Lori asks God to make her believe that giving herself to a man is not dying, because until this point she had equated love with death. Lori prays "make me feel that to love is not to die, that giving one's self doesn't mean death" (34T) ["faz com que eu sinta que amar é não morrer, que a entrega de si mesmo não significa a morte" (58)].[6] Lispector accomplishes the linkage of sex and freedom in An Apprenticeship, not only through the punctuation and interior monologues, but also through uncommon philosophical and religious overtones, as well as the ironic resonances and deconstructive representations for which Lispector has gained worldwide renown. One element of this sentiment/presentiment of death from love is the danger to Lori from her ideas of heterosexual romantic love. Her fear of "death" is a fear of self-sacrifice: the idea that she must give up herself, and her freedoms, in order to love a man. The self-immolation she fears exceeds a relinquishment of some small personal freedoms in order to act out a pas de deux; the death-from-love Lori fears includes participation in schemes of power/knowledge that include male domination and female subjection.

A practice of reworking concepts and contexts in several separate volumes is habitual in Lispector and not confined to Joana's and Lori's questions in *Wild Heart* and *An Apprenticeship*, respectively. Any study of the Brazilian's work must consider that her individual texts acquire added meanings from the echoes they contain from the rest of her oeuvre. Significant pieces of the author's earlier novels *Wild Heart* and *Apple in the Dark* (1967; *A maçã no escuro* 1961), for example, reappear in *An Apprenticeship*. Uprooted from the earlier fictions, the images, names, and situations gain parodic resonances and new connotations. Ideas and images in the short stories and other prose contained in *The Foreign Legion* (1986; *A legião estrangeira*[7] 1964), published the same year as *Passion,* are also signaled by the nostalgic gesture toward antecedents in *An Apprenticeship*—first indicated by the opening comma—and serve the latter novel as an important source.[8]

Although I shall discuss several relevant stories and chronicles from *The Foreign Legion* in detail, *Passion* is clearly the most generally relevant of Lispector's other texts for understanding *An Apprenticeship*. The novels work as a matched pair exploring opposite faces of love. The first-person narrator in *Passion,* G.H., lives in a penthouse apartment and meditates on the nature of divinity; Lori lives on the ground floor and contemplates the divinity of nature. Additionally, G.H. transcends the "desert" of her racism toward Janair, her behavior toward lovers, and her feelings of repulsion toward the ugly, to enter the depersonalized, neutral world of God's love; Lori plunges into the rain to transcend her misanthropy and timidity, joining the personalized, sensual world of erotic love. The act of tasting the oozing whiteness of a cockroach smashed in a closet door provokes G.H.'s prolonged, intense meditation on the nature of God, love, and consciousness; Lori eats appetizing apples and pears and is blessed with a "state of grace."[9] *An Apprenticeship* shares with *Passion* the partition of love into its two main forms, agape and eros. The opposites of life and death, suffering and joy, love and hatred, absence and presence, and paradise and hell are frequently transcended through paradox in both books. Love is inhibited by fear and rewarded by gifts greater than itself in *An Apprenticeship*, as it is in *Passion*.

To a certain extent the closeness-in-opposition of these two novels explains the preference in Lispector criticism given to *Passion* over *An Apprenticeship*. *Passion* came first, which makes *An Apprenticeship* seem derivative, as if a foil or sequel, which it is not. *An Apprenticeship* has also suffered neglect because it is denser in Lispector's own images and less accessible on a first reading. This later novel has greater self-referentiality and a more chaotic structure. *An Apprenticeship* is written in a highly codified system of images and topoi which become more visible and more comprehensible, if *Passion* is considered relevant to it. But Lispector did not reduce *An Apprenticeship* to a (mere) entelechy of the concepts traced out in *Passion*. In fact, *An Apprenticeship* marks a turn in characters and themes away from those in *Passion* which will grow more and more marked with time. Unlike G.H., who sought to transcend her body, or Lori, who learns to live through her body, many characters after *An Apprenticeship* are only body or merely text. Lispector's subsequent narrators also portray characters more ironically than in these two works of her middle period.

Most important for my purposes here are the closely paired opposite valences given to love and sex for women in the 1964 and 1969 fictions. The wealthy protagonist of the earlier novel, G.H., is dismissive of sexuality in a love relation: "Oh, people attach the idea of sin to sex. But how innocent and infantile a sin that is. The real Hell is the Hell of love. Love is the experiencing of a greater danger in sin—it is the experiencing of the dirt and degradation and the worst of happiness. Sex is the startling of a child" (*Passion* 126T) ["Ah, as pessoas põem a idéia de pecado em sexo. Mas como é inocente e infantil esse pecado. O inferno mesmo é o do amor. Amor é a experiência de um perigo de pecado maior—é a experiência da lama e da degradação e da alegria pior. Sexo é o susto de uma criança" (*Paixão* 128)]. In contrast, Lori identifies with her sexuality: "'It was the only thing,' she said, 'that I did right'" (110T; 163). In *Passion* the narrator interrupts serious meditations laughingly saying that she wants to go dancing; in *An Apprenticeship*, the nightclubs and parties where pleasure can be had without commitment or love concern Lori, but she finds them sad, even tragic: the club was "dry water" (73T) ["era a água seca" (115)], and she breaks her habit of going there to continue her journey seeking self-understanding.

The strategy Lispector uses to tell Lori's story is that of the reflection. In contrast to Asturias's strategy of the game, the reflection is brief and lyrical, a moment of inspiration or insight, an image or a statement, rather than an epic confrontation of antagonists. Unlike a game, which requires an opponent—even if one plays against oneself—the reflection tends toward solitary actions of a single character. When there is another character, as in the case of Ulysses, this second character functions as a "reflection": more foil than antagonist, more double than partner, more a second self than an other. Another characteristic of the reflection is focalization in close-up, so to speak: what is reflected is only visible within a certain limited range, as when one is seated directly in front of a mirror. To see one's reflection in a mirror, one must be directly before the glass; turn the glass even slightly and the image disappears to the side. Lispector's strategy does not debate ideas, intuitions, emotions, and actions as much as it displays them; these constituent aspects are reflected, and reflected upon, in *An Apprenticeship*.

Many have commented on the philosophical tendencies of Lispector's work; critics speak of "reflections" in the sense of meditation or commentary. For instance, Kadota has recently made it her task to show how this quality in Lispector has social repercussions: "This is what I intend to show about Clarice Lispector: a conscious posture, of continuous *reflection,* although many times concealed in her representations as signs, consolidated in the poetic and/or paradoxical language in the flow of consciousness, which confuses/constrains the reader who is unused to a fragmented narrative which continually gets in the way, accustomed as s/he may be to the linear and factual story" (emphasis added).[10] Like most critics, Kadota barely mentions *An Apprenticeship,* even in her chapter on the erotic in Lispector, and Kadota does so, following the lead of Olga de Sá, only to say she sees the novel as parodic (113–14). My intention, in contrast to that of Kadota and other previous critics, is to begin with the literal reflection as a literary strategy and then look to its meaning as meditation. In this way, I am able to point to the crucial light imagery within the novel's main section, "Luminescence" ("Luminescência"), which entails a full hundred pages of the 116-page book in translation (and 140 of 174 pages of the original). Additionally, the scenes in which Lori considers her image in the mirror can be given the special attention they merit.

"Reflection" in science is "the return of a wave from a surface that it strikes into the medium through which it has traveled" (*Columbia Encyclopedia* 2292). Thus the elements required for a reflection are three: the "incident ray," the reflecting object, and the reflected ray. The "incident ray" names the light (sound, etc.) coming into a medium (air, water) or striking an object; on its way back into the air or water the light becomes the "reflected ray." Unless the angle at which the incident ray strikes is a right angle, the direction of the reflected ray will be reversed in its return to the seer. The law of reflection states that the angle of hitting the object and leaving the object are always equal. But there may be refraction instead of reflection. "Refraction" is the "deflection of a wave in passing obliquely from one transparent medium into a second medium in which its speed is different" (2295). Refraction refers to changes in speeds of light which create curves, whereas reflection treats trajectories in straight lines where only angles and directionality change.

✓As a narrative strategy, the reflection is a return of an image. In this concept of return, I am not assuming some sort of extratextual original image, but rather a doubling of images always within the plot, imagery, structure, and so forth. Lori's reflection in her mirror is the return of the light her body has reflected into the mirror; her subsequent meditation on her visual image, or on the image of others, is another kind of return, a return in a different form, a return and a transformation of the visible image into a mental one. In philosophy, psychology, and common parlance, a "reflection" can have the further meaning of a memory. In one sense, it may appear unfortunate that English does not have two different spellings, as Spanish and Portuguese do, to represent in writing the distinction between visual reflections (Port., *reflexo;* Sp., *reflejo*) and mental reflections (Port., *reflexão,* Sp., *reflexión*) for this chapter on Lispector's complicated and nuanced use of light and repetition. Since my purpose, however, is usually *not* to separate the returned visual and mental images, but to draw attention to the ways they blur together in the novel, to the blurring which makes the term *reflection* so important, I generally welcome this English double meaning. The Portuguese is always given in case the distinction may be relevant.

Lori's search for love is a desire to find herself in her facticity, as others see her, as Ulysses sees her, as an object known, and not only a subject, because she is lost and unhappy in her social relations. Mystified by connections between inner and outer, Lori studies her outer self in a mirror, in the novel's first section, "The Origin of Spring or The Necessary Death in Daytime" ("A Origem da Primavera ou A Morte Necessária em Pleno Dia"). She succeeds in "finding [in] one's outer self the echoes of one's inner self—'ah, then it's true, I didn't imagine it: I do exist'" (62T) ["Encontrar na figura exterior os ecos da figura interna: ah, então é verdade que eu não imaginei: eu existo" (19)]. In the epistemology of Jean-Paul Sartre, consciousness is "verified" by the gaze. Lori's learning about her social self, her being-for-others, is the Sartrian "body-seen," which precedes the "body-lived," a later stage in her apprenticeship which involves an understanding of herself to herself.

Lori gives salience to certain events in her past and ways of understanding them, rapidly forgetting others. For instance, after Lori summarizes her trips to Europe as a frightening evening in Paris and a silent night in Berne, Ulysses points out that these memories are emblems of the way she sees herself in the world: timid, depressed, introspective, cautious, and cut off from intimate social contact. She must have seen "orange trees, sunshine, and bees in the flowers" ["laranjeiras, sol e abelhas nas flores"], he asserts, but she has never learned to "have" these things, to make them her own (30T; 53–54).[11] To the extent her past did include the moments she remembers, the trajectories of this light are "reflexive." But to the extent they are distorted by the process of forgetting the happy moments, they are refracted as memories.

The overriding strategies in *An Apprenticeship* are the return and the transformed return, the reflection and the refraction of external images. Reflections and refractions may be simple or complex, single or reiterated, direct or aslant. Whether literal mirrors, mental images, memories, or her love object (Ulysses), the return of (literal or symbolic) light symbolizes a specific kind of knowledge gained by the lack of transparency of objects: reflection is the examination of self-knowledge as a means of continually renewing the commitment to living in the world.

Dangerous Reflections

Eroticism is a sterile principle representing Evil and the diabolic.
Georges Bataille, *Erotism* (230)

The danger Lori's sexuality poses occurs primarily as imagery. Lori looks in her mirror and the image returned to her is not that of a neutral or beautiful being, but rather of a dangerous one. These mirror reflections upset Lori, but they also spur her on, especially at the beginning of her apprenticeship, to modify her understanding and her behavior. Three examples of moments when Lori's image is reflected back to her should suffice to suggest the variety of these images as well as their complicity in portraying Lori as dangerous. The first example begins with the images Lori sees in the literal mirror. The second treats Ulysses' efforts to bring to Lori's attention her dangerous image, even as she pursues sending different signals to those around her. In the third, the narrator employs images of Lori as seemingly dangerous, but denies the danger is real. Lori's dangerous reflections teach her about herself, her surroundings, and her society.

Example 1: The Mirror

In the opening section of the novel, we find the first example of Lori's literal mirror. The mirror is an instrument for her to try to see herself as others, particularly Ulysses, see her. Lori's early way of understanding herself during her apprenticeship, the literal mirror, reflects back in her direction and for her benefit the image she projects through her clothes, the decoration of her apartment, her makeup, how she wears her hair— markers which she can choose, indeed must choose, for signaling about herself to others.

Trying to decide whether to wear earrings as she readies herself to meet Ulysses, Lori sees herself in the mirror as a sphinx: "and there was also something in her painted eyes that said sadly: 'decipher me, my love, or I will be forced to destroy you'" (5T) ["e havia também algo em seus olhos pintados que dizia com melancolia: decifra-me, meu amor, ou serei obrigada a devorar" (16)].[12] This jump between an absolutely casual, daily event (deciding earrings) and an unusual self-image (a sphinx) is typical of Lispector's strategies in this novel. The cultured reference, that is, the allusion to classical mythology, distinguishes the imagery here from that of other Lispector works. In Lispector, imagery corresponds closely to characterization. While Lispector's imagery contributes to themes, as does most imagery, this writer augments her imagery's overall thematic impact with pointed, striking homologies to her protagonists.

In Egypt sphinxes were often male and may have represented the pharaohs, but in Greek myth the Sphinx was a female monster with the body of a lion whose name meant "the strangler." In Sophocles' *Oedipus Tyrannus*, for instance, the story is told of the Sphinx's terrorizing the Thebans, killing all those who fail to answer her riddle. In the Greek play, once Oedipus (and not Ulysses/Odysseus) solves the Sphinx's riddle with the answer, "Man," the monster kills herself. Hence, the danger called forth by the mirror image of the sphinx is either that she will kill those around her, or that she will bring about her own death.

The Sphinx in Greek myth and in Sophocles' play threatens death. But what might "death" mean in *An Apprenticeship*? Death has a contested value, at least at first. Before making significant progress in her apprenticeship, Lori is depressed and desires literal death as a chance to end a horrible existence: "Being human was to her like an unending death without the final relief of death" (9T) ["A humanidade lhe era como morte eterna que no entanto não tivesse o alívio de enfim morrer" (22–23)]. In contrast, Ulysses finds death and pleasure inextricable, telling her: "Dying has to be a natural pleasure. After dying a person doesn't go to heaven. Dying is what paradise is" (38T) ["Morrer debe ser um gozo natural. Depois de morrer não se vai ao paraíso, morrer é que é o paraíso" (64)].[13] Later, far along in her learning, Lori agrees with Ulysses that death in itself is a promise: "Dying would have the same absolute poignancy of something good" (83T) ["Morrer teria a mesma pungência indivisível do bom" (128)]. By this, Lori and Ulysses mean that literal, physical death provides the promise of a release from the travails of life; the contemplation of one's future death grants the perspective to take the good things of life as gratuitous gifts and the strength that comes from knowing that the bad things of life have an end.

The first and foremost element in the Sphinx reflection, however, is the general association of Lori's visual image with a mysterious and monstrous danger. It is part of Lori's early negative view of death and life. But who is the victim and who is the perpetrator? Second, what does the danger consist of? Third, what riddle does she ask, and what answer(s) may save her or them? This third question underlines the importance of knowledge and education, already announced in the title *An Apprenticeship*, repeated in Ulysses's didactic role, and related to Lori's quest for a different way to be and to love. The relatively simple scenes involving literal mirrors refuse to divulge clear, unequivocal answers to these questions, but through them we learn useful information regarding the perils facing the characters from female sexuality.

To attribute the phrase "decipher me" to Lori's mirror image implies that she is pleading for understanding and for help. Lost and confused, Lori examines possible sources of guidance and help. The hazards suggested by the image of the Sphinx include that of mental fragmentation, her lack of a sense of a unified self. The diversity of the outward manifestations of herself does unsettle Lori; in what way should she live if her mirror images have no common element? The Sphinx's riddle in Greek myth similarly poses questions of identity: "What walks first on four legs, then two, then three?" In the succession of changes in time, how can one be a continuity? Lori as the Sphinx wants the illusion to persist that the many different systems of power/knowledge in which she is entangled make sense as a whole rather than compete with and contradict one another. She wants to feel they can be negotiated in a simultaneous, or homogeneous, and conscious manner. For this reason, repetitions of a mirror reflection she has seen provide her some comfort through an impression of the stability or at least of another return, of the same image. Ulysses provides her with such a repetition when he says: "'Your face, Lori, has the mystery of the sphinx: Decipher me or I'll [devour you].' She was surprised that he had also noticed what she saw when she looked in the mirror" (62T, trans. modified) ["'Teu rosto, Lóri, tem um mistério de esfinge: decifra-me ou te devoro.' Ela se surpreendeu de que também ele tivesse notado o que ela via de si mesma no espelho" (97)]. She takes great consolation from the repetition, but dislikes the allusion.

At another moment in which Lori contemplates herself in the mirror, she discovers that she "looked like a dressed-up monkey" (59T) ["parecia um macaco enfeitado (93)"], a mirror scene to which we shall return several times in this chapter. The reader had been told earlier that the ape symbolizes what Lori has surpassed in her "training." The ape is an animal reflection beyond which she has grown: it was "as if she were evolving from an early primate into Pithecanthropus erectus" (49T) ["como se passasse do homem-macaco ao pitecantropus erectus" (79)]. This second mirror scene occurs after a cocktail party that Lori attended wearing too much makeup. She had hoped to pick up a man and to forget Ulysses. But since she had already evolved beyond the monkey image, the mirror shows her that her trip to the party had been a regression in her apprenticeship. The danger posed by her monkey reflection is more subtle than that of the Sphinx, but also more intrinsic to many of the scenes in An Apprenticeship; it appears conjoined with the leitmotiv of the mask. Lori "painted her eyes and mouth so heavily that her face, whitened with powder, looked like a mask. She was applying someone else's face to her own, a someone who was terribly uninhibited and who was proud of herself to the point of vanity. That someone was exactly what she was not" (57T) ["pintou demais os olhos e demais a boca até que seu rosto branco de pó parecia uma máscara: ela estava pondo sobre si mesma alguém outro: esse alguém era fantasticamente disinibido, era vaidoso, tinha orgulho de si mesmo. Esse alguém era exatamente o que ela não era" (89–90)]. Despite freely choosing what to wear, Lori had used makeup to become a desired object, rather than to express herself or her own desires, and thus was condemned to falsity and deception.

Clearly, though, "wearing a mask" in An Apprenticeship transcends the mere putting on of makeup and clothes: "Youngsters whose faces were honest," thought Lori, "created their own masks as they grew up. And it was very painful, for the realization that henceforth one would play a role came as a frightening surprise" (58T) ["Inclusive os adolescentes, que

eram de rosto puro, à medida que iam vivendo fabricavam a própria máscara. E com muita dor. Porque saber que de então em diante se vai passar
a representar um papel que era de uma surpresa amedrontadora"(92)].
One danger imbricated in the topos of masks, then, is the very need to have
one, the imperative of the imposition of a fixed, outer image, because the
option of not wearing a mask is even more risky.

The narrator comments on Lori's realization, still before the bathroom
mirror, that her mask was false and that she feared being without a mask,
in this way: "Lori also was wearing the heavily painted mask of the clown.
The same one that youngsters chose in passing through adolescence so as
not to remain naked during the rest of the struggle. No, not that it was
wrong to leave one's face exposed to the world. But that face, if left exposed, could when attacked suddenly become a terrible, involuntary
mask. It was less *dangerous,* then, to choose to be a persona for oneself.
Choosing one's own mask was the first voluntary act of a human being.
And a lonely one" (59T, emphasis added).[14]

The voluntary mask is "the horrible freedom of non-being" (58T)
["Era a liberdade horrível de não-ser" (92)]. Deciding the mask one's mirror will reflect back converts into a choice an ineluctable necessity—the
other's appropriation of the body as an object (Sartre's "For-itself-for-
others"). To refuse a designation one has been given by others, and to
choose a voluntary mask, is to gain oneself as For-itself, as a "person."
The narrator finds the voluntary mask, chosen by an adolescent, to be a
positive choice for living: "But when he finally attached the mask of what
he had chosen to represent himself to the world, his body took on a new
firmness, his head could sometimes be held high like that of one who had
overcome an obstacle: the person existed" (59T)[15] ["Mas quando enfim se
afivelava a máscara daquilo que se escolhera para representar o mundo, o
corpo ganhava uma nova firmeza, a cabeça podia às vezes se manter altiva
como a de quem superou um obstáculo: a pessoa era" (93)]. Lori's mon-
key-mask and her clown-mask are not voluntary in this sense, but merely
her attempt to satisfy others, especially men.

Lori learns in the apprenticeship to put on or take off masks as she
chooses, and in the process of approaching the end of her time as an
apprentice, she learns how to decide whether and by what means to be
seductive to others. Significantly, Lori discovers the mask of her makeup
to be contingent and therefore susceptible to manipulation. Though attracted by the idea of masked actors going on stage in ancient Greco-
Roman theater with their faces hidden (58T; 92), she can choose to live
without the mask of her makeup, which she does two weeks later for the

first time (60T; 94). The mask, the false exterior, has not disappeared; when she goes out without makeup, Lori has courageously accepted her face itself as the voluntary exterior she wants to project. In the novel's finale, when she runs to Ulysses' house in the downpour, she goes without makeup and in her nightclothes.

Example 2: Ulysses

Names, too, are masks by which one is known to others; they are reflections returned by the outside world, though not by glass mirrors. Parents give names to children, but one can choose a new one to express something about oneself, to show oneself more clearly, or to hide more deeply. Ulysses "had told her once that when people asked her her name not to reply 'Lori,' but that she might answer instead, 'My name is I,' for your name, he had said, is 'I'" (2T) ["dissera uma vez que queria que ela, ao lhe perguntarem seu nome, não respondesse 'Lóri' mas que pudesse responder 'meu nome é eu,' pois teu nome, dissera ele, é um 'eu'"(11–12)]. Like the voluntary mask, choosing a voluntary name that pinpoints its inner source—the deictic, the I—is a "horrible freedom": "horrible" because it objectifies, reifies, but a "freedom" because it is chosen rather than given. Until Lori transcends her given name, she cannot live her consciousness as an viewpoint, a *choice* of standpoint from which to know the world, according to Ulysses' idea.[16]

For Lori, to take off her makeup and metaphysical mask, to stop acting a part in a script, is to acquiesce in the hypothesis "if I were I" (93T) ["se eu fosse eu" (140)], that is, to rename herself. Her questions about "if I were I" concern the ideas of interior and exterior, about what is mental or subjective versus real or objective.[17] Namelessness is a gesture toward a prebirth, pre-Oedipal time and toward existence without masks. Losing one's name is a reverse baptism which signals the shedding of the self's clothes.[18] After her epiphany, her "state of grace," Lori asks herself: "Who am I?" (106T) ["Quem sou eu?" (157)], because she is learning a "gentler, more silent way of existing" (106T) ["um modo mais leve e mais silencioso de existir" (157)]. The night Lori crosses town in the rain to enter Ulysses' home for the first time, her state of emotional readiness is called "that point of mature wheat" ("this mature relationship" 106T) ["esse ponto de trigo maduro" (158)].[19] Like wheat, she can stand in the rain and let herself feel without the protection of a mask. For Hélène Cixous, the "point of mature wheat" is the culmination of a "de-personalization," and "the great objectification of oneself" which is "the getting rid of the name" (Cixous, "Reaching" 52).[20]

In a second kind of name-reflection of Lori's image back to her, Ulysses explains to Lori that, although her name really is "I," the name she goes by—Lori—is a short form of Lorelei, the name of the mermaid who entices men to their death in Heinrich Heine's *Songs of Homecoming* (*Heimkehr*). This reflection surprises, not only because of his allusion to another dangerous woman-animal monster like the Sphinx, but also because Ulysses changes the symbolism, refracting the image. He tells Lori: "Lorelei is the name of a legendary character in German folklore celebrated by Heine in a beautiful lyric poem. According to the legend Lorelei seduced fishermen with her singing and they ended up dying in the ocean. I don't remember the details anymore. No, don't look at me with those guilty eyes. In the first place, I'm the one seducing you. I know, I know that you get yourself up for me but that's because I am already seducing you" (67T).[21]

In "Loreley," the second poem in Heine's lyric cycle, a beautiful blond woman sings to a sailor, who, in his passion for her, does not see the reefs before him and drowns.[22] Lorelei was a siren who lured boatmen to their death; speculation is that her name evolved from that of a treacherous rock in the Rhine. Like Homer's sirens, Heine's Lorelei symbolizes dangerous (female) seduction of an adventurous, wandering male. Thus Lori is hurt when Ulysses compares her to Lorelei, a destroyer of men, but he quickly rescinds the comparison, explaining that she does not fit the role. In other words, first Ulysses shows Lori the meaning of her name "Lorelei": he "reflects" her name back to her. In so doing, he implies she has attempted to seduce him, to destroy him. But when he sees reflected in her face her unhappiness, he then tries to adjust the Lorelei image to his vision of the reality of their relationship. He wants to convert the involuntary "mask" of her given name into a story she can accept about their relationship, a voluntary mask.

Ulysses does "survive" the encounter with Lori/Lorelei, so his assessment that she has been seduced and is not the seducer is accurate. Lori has not "killed" Ulysses the sailor; instead, it is Lori who is brought to a "pseudodeath" on the rocks by Ulysses' siren song. Not he, but Lori "felt lost, like a survivor from some shipwreck who had been tossed up on a dark, cold, deserted beach" (27T) ["eu me senti perdida, salva de algum naufrágio e jogada numa praia escura, fria, deserta" (47)]. After her swim at dawn, "her dripping hair is that of a shipwrecked person" (54T) ["seus cabelos escorridos são de náufrago" (86)]. Lori muses: "Who knows, she thought as her mind digressed, she might belong to a line of Loreleis for whom the sea and the fishermen were the hymn of life and death" (69T)

["Quem sabe, divagou, ela vinha de uma linha de Loreleys para as quais o mar e os pescadores eram o cântico da vida e da morte" (109)]. He seduces; she suffers and struggles to learn the skills to survive the shipwreck of seduction.

Nevertheless, Ulysses tells Lori that upon hearing about Lorelei her eyes look "guilty" (67T) ["culpados" (106)]. In the continuation of his commentary on the name Lorelei, he denies that he is a fisherman, but not that he is a sailor (67T; 106). Of course, Ulysses translates into Latin the name of Homer's wily sailor Odysseus, who survives the sirens to return to Ithaca and to his wife Penelope, who has waited for him while besieged by disrespectful suitors.[23] Lori's concept of herself as unfaithful and dangerous, the opposite of the faithful Penelope, has again returned to her. It is easy to see that, though Lori may think of herself as a Circe, a seducer of men, she does not possess the strength over Ulysses to imprison him against his will on an island of love. He waits in his apartment for her unannounced arrival because he wants to. So what kind of role is left for her if she is neither a true-wife-in-danger nor a dangerous, seductive witch? Thus far Lori has eliminated traditional images for her life-voyage but has not yet constructed her own.

Never quite free of the image of herself as possessing the dangerous ambivalence of the Sphinx, Lori is more often victim than victimizer. The violence in the novel is often directed toward Lori, and her wishes are that the threats, both physical and metaphysical, against her person cease. In the most obvious instance, Lori is afraid of rape during the "night of terror" (16T) ["a noite de terror" (32)], an episode in which a "half-crazy man, with long arms like a monkey's arms" (16T) ["um homem meio doido, com braços compridos de macaco" (32)], follows Lori home and hangs around outside. This fear of male violence brings Lori to ask Ulysses for protection. He responds quickly to her telephone call of alarm, and he convinces the stranger to leave. Despite the danger to others with which her mirror images and her name seem impregnated, the reality is otherwise. Women, even a femme fatale or a liberated woman such as Lori purports to be, are vulnerable in modern cities, as they were/are in rural societies. The newly sexed woman, no less than the prostitute in previous literature, has fewer safeguards against male violence and runs more risks than the good woman who never leaves home unaccompanied. Alternatives to the protective boyfriend, husband, or father, such as male and female friends or organized activities in groups, do not interest Lori.

In an important article in this regard, "Rape and Textual Violence in Clarice Lispector," expanded in her book *Passionate Fictions*, Marta

Peixoto wrote: "Lispector became an acute and unsparing observer of even the subtlest and least conspicuous forms that violence can take, and, as her work progressed, [she became an] increasingly aware witness to the interconnection between private and public kinds of violence, including the complex ways in which they implicate writers and readers" (103). Neither Peixoto's article nor her book deals directly with *An Apprenticeship*, but they explain well the understated and textual nature of violence found throughout Lispector. As we shall see in the next section, "Lessons of Love," Ulysses' lessons about violence are resisted by Lori, unlike his lessons in love. But where does the narrator stand on the issue of who is victim and who victimizer in *An Apprenticeship*?

Example 3: The Narrator

The glass mirror and the metaphorical "name-mirror" of Ulysses' opinion both show Lori that her outward image is mysterious, monstrous, and threatening: a sphinx and a dangerous mermaid. Similarly, the narrator declares that Lori "felt like" ["se sentia"] a dangerous feline. In this reflection reported by the narrator, we perceive the closeness of the character and the narrator. These third-person reports provide "mirror" images, that is, images of Lori, but exclusively for the reader, rather than for the protagonist herself (or other characters) to meditate upon. They compare to mirrors for Lori only in the sense and to the extent that Lori is conscious of these images. Conscious thought about consciousness, or about oneself, is a reflection. Therefore, when the narrator's obsessive focalization on Lori becomes free indirect discourse about Lori's image, a reflection in the sense of a narrative strategy is produced.

Lori constantly looks within to attempt to understand herself, and the narrator imperceptively moves from the (rather rare) outside observation of Lori to the frequent reporting in the third person of Lori's observations about herself. An extended, repeated example of this type is a highly significant one in which the danger to those around her is only apparent, though she is a predator:

> Lori felt like a dangerous jaguar with an arrow imbedded [*sic*] in its flesh which was slowly circling about some frightened people to determine who would take the pain away.[24] And then a man, Ulysses, had sensed that a wounded jaguar is not dangerous. And approaching the beast, unafraid to touch it, he had carefully pulled out the arrow.

And the jaguar? No, there were certain things that neither humans nor animals could be grateful for. Then she, the jaguar, had taken a few slow turns in front of the man, hesitated, licked a paw and then, as if neither word nor sound was important, had quietly moved away. Lori would never forget the help that she received when all she could manage to do was stammer in fear. (88T)[25]

As with the sphinx reflection, the wounded-jaguar image repeats soon afterward when, in a telephone conversation, Ulysses helps her to understand what she is feeling and soothes her spirit. Once again this imagery is delivered by the narrator, however, in contrast to the sphinx icon and to the Lorelei name, as if the narrator were confirming for the reader that the high stakes that the supersensitive characters place on minimal events were appropriate. The narrator describes Ulysses' actions in this way: "Once again he had no fear of the wounded jaguar and had removed the arrow imbedded [sic] in her flesh. . . . Her love for Ulysses came over her like a wave" (94T) ["De novo, pois ele não tivera medo do tigre ferido e lhe tirara a flecha fincada no corpo. . . . O amor por Ulisses veio como una onda" (142)]. Wise and not in danger, Ulysses helps the wounded, dangerous-looking Lori. Such knowledge and kindness has the reward of her gratitude and love.

Lori's identification with dangerous animals remains strong throughout. For instance, the narrator summarizes Lori's coming to conscious of the meaning of her visual image when she sees herself with excessive makeup as a "dressed-up monkey," discussed above, then comments: "And she knew that she was as ferocious as the rest of humanity, we who are mere reflections of our ancestor the ape [monkey]. We would never find the true human within us. And whoever did was truly blessed because giving up one's ferocity was a sacrifice" (95T) ["E sabia que era uma feroz entre os ferozes seres humanos, nós, os macacos de nós mesmos. Nunca atingia em nós o ser humano. E quem atingia era com justiça santificado. Porque desistir da ferocidade era um sacrifício" (144)]. Lori wants to be, and at times is described as, an animal that has given up its violence. The sacrifice of her violence—Lori as harmless, wounded jaguar—and Ulysses' recognition of that sacrifice, his knowledge that she is harmless, brings on her feelings of love for him because for Lori, humanity consists of sacrificing one's ferocity.

In *An Apprenticeship* the animal world, full of light, glows with the luminescence of feelings: "What had saved Lori also was that she felt that, if her private world were not human, there would still be a place of great beauty for her. She would be a diffuse mass of instinct, tenderness and ferocity, a trembling radiation of peace and strife as if she were in human form, but it would be more permanent because if her world were not human she would be an animal" (24–25T).[26] For Lori, the key to opening the door to the divine, and hence the door to love, is through the animal aspect of humanity: "Humans encountered obstacles like reasoning, logic, comprehension that did not complicate the lives of animals, while animals were blessed by a sense of what is right and with the ability to follow it" (99T) ["Os humanos tinham obstáculos que não dificultavam a vida dos animais, como raciocínio, lógica, compreensão. Enquanto que os animais tinham esplendidez daquilo que é direto e se dirige direto" (148)]. While the predatory feline metaphor is overcome in the plot (Ulysses knows Lori is not dangerous; Lori gratefully feels love), the comparison of the protagonist to such an animal bears closer scrutiny.

As I argued in "Clarice Lispector's (Post) Modernity and the Adolescence of the Girl-Colt" regarding other Lispector works, the female voice in this author often achieves a union or simultaneity with an animal, predatory or not. Lispector's first-person chronicle (crônica), "An Image of Pleasure" (Legion 131–32T; "Uma imagem de prazer" Para não esquecer 30, 32), can help us understand Lori's commentaries on the animal state in An Apprenticeship. Appearing before the novel, this short prose fragment not only has the emphasis on animal and light imagery, but also the title word "Pleasure" ("prazer"), so important in The Book of Delights (O livro do prazer). In "An Image of Pleasure," in a clearing in the woods, with many butterflies and a lion, a woman is knitting in the semidarkness. The female narrator identifies with the tranquil lion and gains great pleasure from having the calm lion at her side. Though not the biblical story of the lion and the lamb, the image of feline violence transcended pleases the woman in the chronicle, much as Lori (the wounded jaguar) is pleased when Ulysses senses she is harmless in An Apprenticeship. In terms of light imagery, in the chronicle, the animals see the woman covered with "cosmic spots" ["manchas cósmicas"] of blue and green, which are there "to show that she is not blue or green." Similarly, Lori sees "cosmic spots": "Meanwhile, sometimes she just guessed. There were cosmic masses that took the place of understanding" (25T) ["No entanto às vezes adivinhava. Eram manchas cósmicas que substituíam entender" (45)]. I suspect these colors in the semidarkness correlate to Lori's praise for an animal awareness, which is synonymous with pleasure and uninhibited by moral values.

In addition to Lori's image as feline predator whose violence is transcended, the narrator at times reports Lori's subjectivity as gender. In an odd distancing, the narrator no longer refers to Lori by her name. In her sensual, sexual swim at dawn, for instance, the narrator speaks of Lori repeatedly as "the woman" (53T) ["a mulher" (84)]. The odd phrasing is not a Portuguese linguistic feature but rather Lispector's signaling of Lori's (awareness of her) femininity.[27] The night she decides to give herself to Ulysses, she is again inscribed as from one gender and not the other: "Lori was a woman, [a person, an attention, an inhabited] body, watching the heavy rain fall" (106T, translation modified) ["Lóri era uma mulher, era uma pessoa, era uma atenção, era um corpo habitado olhando a chuva grossa cair" (159)]. Put into the language of *An Apprenticeship,* gender would be considered a mask (femininity) and a name (woman). Cultures define "being a woman" differently, of course, according to their particular values. Additionally, some individuals defined within their culture as biologically female never identify with "being a woman"; "femininity" is a label or image they resist. Significantly, the novel sees as progress the moment Lori actively opts for her "destiny as a woman" when she "recognizes" Ulysses: "And then the day finally came when she learned that she was no longer alone. She recognized Ulysses, she had found her destiny as a woman" (84T) ["E então veio finalmente o dia em que ela soube que não era mais solitária, reconheceu Ulisses, tinha encontrado o seu destino de mulher" (130)]. The narrator assures the reader of Lori's choice of gender. These words illuminate Ulysses' (mirror) role in reflecting Lori's image back to her as a woman, not a man. From these narratorial reports, we learn that both characters choose to maintain gendered differences in love, to follow the gendered scripts offered them by their society.

The Consequences of Mirrors

In separate incidents, one in Paris and told to Ulysses (27T; 47–48) and one dramatized (58–59T; 91–93)—Lori's moment before the mirror when she saw herself as a "made-up monkey," leading to the commentary on masks—Lori thinks she projects the image of a prostitute. Both times, she is wearing excessive makeup and travels alone by taxi. In the narrated episode, we read: "The way the taxi driver looked at her made her realize something: she was wearing so much makeup that he had probably taken her for a prostitute" (58T) ["O modo que o chofer olhou-a fê-la adivinhar: ela estava tão pintada que ele provavelmente tomara-a como uma prostituta" (91)]. Not a prostitute, Lori is the modern, urban "newly sexed" woman of sexual fiction.

In Lori's alienation, however, she unknowingly facilitates the other's process of objectifying her, by turning herself into a painted object. Her excessive makeup prevents others from seeing her naked face, prevents their gaze from finding her revealed self. They see in her "someone she is not":

> So something humiliating could happen as was happening now in the taxi to Lori. It was simply that, after years of relative success with the mask, suddenly—even faster than that because of a glance or a word overheard from the driver—suddenly the [mask of life's war] cracked like dried mud and the uneven pieces fell to the ground with a hollow sound. And her face was now bare, mature and sensitive, as it was no longer prepared for existence. And the face with the cracked mask wept silently so as not to die.
>
> She went into the house as though fleeing from the world. It was useless to hide. The truth was that she simply did not know how to live. She felt better indoors [, she looked at herself in the mirror] as she washed her hands and saw the persona attached to her face. (59T; trans. modified)[28]

Lori's mask falls to the ground when she perceives the taxi driver's opinion of her, but her makeup remains. The loss of this first mask, her war mask, leaves her face bare until she again looks in a mirror, and she finds her "persona." But *persona* is Latin for "mask," so Lori sees the mask, but now its connection to her face is revealed. On the one hand, normally in society we think of eyeliner, mascara, powder, and rouge as a social mask designed to do one of three things: either to enhance one's looks and make the person more alluring; to separate a person from the quotidian or the human—as in a clown or death mask; or to gain the physical appearance of another, as with theatrical makeup. On the other hand, in common parlance, to have a persona can refer to an exterior image different from the reality, as in the media persona of a celebrity. In literary criticism we tend to speak of the persona as aspects of an author seen through the fictional mask of a character, that is, the autobiographical elements that inevitably play a role in the construction of even nonautobiographical fictional subjects. Furthermore, to speak of a "persona" in criticism indi-cates a certain mythic or psychological approach to a text. But whether in its general usages or in its specific application to literature, the persona cannot be seen in a mirror, as Lori does here. One can only see the makeup that may aid in achieving the construction of a persona. But Lori contemplates her image in the mirror, then washes her hands, though after recognizing that the mask and face are linked, she "was relieved to find her soul bare again" (59T) ["e com alívio estava de novo de alma nua" (93)]. The makeup creates the mask, which leads to the formulation of the persona. Consequently, her persona is visible to her and to others.

There is one more point to be made about this mirror scene. Before Lori washes her face, she looks prehuman: "Her eyes under the heavy makeup were very small and dull as if intelligence had not yet manifested itself in man" (59T) ["Seus olhos, sob a grossa pintura, estavam miúdos e neutros, como se no homem ainda não se tivesse manifestado a Inteligência" (93)]. This visible lack of intelligence, and the separation of an animal past from the thinking humanity of the present, indicate Lori's lack of progress in her apprenticeship, her early stage in learning from Ulysses about life and love. At the end of the whole episode, Lori resolves never again to go out "without protection" (59T) ["sem proteção" (93)], and takes a sleeping pill. These two actions confirm her continuing timidity, especially her avoidance of emotional pain, which insulates her from experiencing life's pleasures. While Lori makes progress—she understands the role of the mask now—she still cannot bear to wear the voluntary mask she has chosen. Accepting the consequences of the impression a chosen persona would make on others is still too difficult. It is as if she had more to lose than merely being taken for a prostitute by taxi drivers.

In another conversation, Ulysses suggests that Lori has acted like a streetwalker. Verbalizing the taxi drivers' opinions that Lori had suspected, Ulysses tells Lori that her actions parallel her exterior facade, the makeup that makes her look like a prostitute: "Listen, Lori. You know perfectly well how I met you, but I want to remind you for a reason. You were waiting for a taxi and, after looking at you for a long time because you were physically attractive, I approached you and began to talk to you with the pretext of how difficult it was to find a taxi at that time. I offered to take you wherever you wanted to go in my car, and after five minutes of driving, I invited you out for a drink and you accepted without the slightest hesitation. Did all your lovers pick you up in the street?" (30T).[29]

Lori learns through this repetition how she appears to others, but Ulysses' reflection is too much, offending her. She replies: "Of course not. I don't want to talk about them" (30T) ["Claro que não. Eu não quero falar neles" (53)]. The narrator comments: "They both fell silent, he perhaps worried that this was the first time that jealousy had appeared on the scene, she happy that it was the first time" (30T) ["Ficaram calados. Ele talvez pensando com cautela que era a primeira cena de ciúmes. Ela feliz, pensando que essa era a sua primeira cena de ciúmes"(53)]. Lori reflects upon their disagreement and is encouraged by the feelings it produced in them; he wishes for another outcome to the same scene.

In "A Special Type of Choice of Object Made by Men (Contributions to the Psychology of Love, I)," Freud examines the kind of man who prefers a woman in a relationship with another man, particularly a woman with a reputation for sexual experience or who works as a prostitute and whom the man wants to save from the life she lives. Ulysses asks Lori about her past lovers as if her sexual past were crucial to his excitement while around her. Freud reasons that a man with a "need for feeling jealousy" has a libido "attached to mother for so long, even after the onset of puberty, that the maternal characteristics (of being attached to another man and being overvalued) remain stamped on the love-objects that are chosen later, and all these turn into easily recognizable mother-surrogates" (9:169). In the case of Lori and Ulysses, they both are attracted by the gendered script of prostitute and john, but Ulysses does not like the jealousy he feels to rise to the surface. Lori interprets his jealousy as a sign of love, but is less pleased by being mistaken for a prostitute.

In her apprenticeship, Lori discovers the meaning of being a body-in-the-world early on through the feedback given her by life's many reflections of her image. She learns that to others she is an object to be known (a mask, a name, a possible prostitute), and that her face and body, at the same time they send messages to the world, provide her an orientation on the world. By changing or choosing her mask, by living fully her body, she also alters her ability to comprehend (*inteligência*). Through seeing and being seen, she and her world interact and interreact. Before this discovery, when not aware of her outer image and her body's role in defining her awareness, Lori used herself as a mere instrument: "Because with her previous lovers it was as if she had lent her body to herself for pleasure, it was only that and nothing else."[30] In the past, physical sex had not been an adequate or an important means to self-consciousness; her body had been negated as a passageway or medium, and the senses had become closed doors, blocking her from herself. Ulysses sees this insulated, fearful sexuality as insufficient; he wants a fuller eroticism of not only her body but her "body-soul" (28T) ["corpo-alma" (49)]. To achieve this, he guides her through ceremonies which work on her awareness of her body, her mind, and her relations with him, teaching her lessons of love.

Lessons of Love

Civilised order is not to be founded on the deepest sexuality, on
disorder, that is; limits are to be set to this disorder by connecting
it to order, by merging the path of disorder with that of order
and by trying to subordinate the former to the latter.

Georges Bataille, *Erotism* (241)

The enunciation of Lori's learning occurs in stages, during which Lori becomes aware of the divisions between interior—her attention—and exterior: the mask, the name, and the persona. I prefer to use these terms from the novel to discuss what may indeed be close to the idea of the subject, in order to suggest a Lispectorian middle road between a philosophical position that accepts the idea of individual will (self-resistance, agency) and one that rejects everything except a subject's place in networks of power/knowledge, as in certain interpretations of Foucault. I can make clear the relation between Lispector's images and standard terms in existentialism and phenomenology by speaking of the self at times, but I wish to maintain a critical distance from the illusion that the divisions and contradictions which Lori finds troubling can in some way be overcome once and for all. As we shall see, the novel's marking of its story as an intermediate writing, a middle term by the beginning comma and ending colon, makes the education themes particularly open. Between an acceptance of humanist ideals of autonomy and sovereignty and a nonacceptance of them through antihumanist, ironic, and poststructuralist strategic deconstructions of these ideals lies Lispector's ambivalent irony of both success (progress) and failure (regression).

The first phase of Lori's apprenticeship is to "touch the self" ["tocar em si"];[31] the second is to "touch the world" ["tocar no mundo"]; and the third is to "reach others" ["chegar aos outros"]. The narrator's heuristic separation of Lori's apprenticeship into three steps proceeds cumulatively; each new stage in learning interprets the learning gained in the previous one, which remains in force. The phases of her apprenticeship cannot be skipped or interchanged, since the first enables the second, and the second enables the third. She can regress, but that is possible only because the order has been definitely established. In the novel's biblical imagery, the fruit of life can be eaten only after the Apocalypse, after death and rebirth. By completing all three phases, Lori evolves from an "I" to a "We," from an alienated observer to an emotionally involved participant in life. The apprenticeship proceeds unevenly, though, with learning taking place in one sphere of her life at one moment, in another sphere the next.

In the first stage of learning, when Lori wants to "touch the self," the self that here is composed of disparate, even conflicting, "parts" preparing for a union. This divided or fragmented state that Lori experiences is different from a mind-body split; she has a "mind-mind split"—a consciousness haunted by repressed elements that return to her as if from the outside. From these pseudoexterior images, these "incident-ray" reflections, Lori learns what she has forgotten or repressed about herself. The dangers of the sphinx, the name Lorelei, and the wounded jaguar are all disarmed by her coming into authentic contact with herself. In this first stage, they become harmless masks that she can wear voluntarily or take off at will.

The relation between this stage of her learning and her sexuality may be seen in her perception of Ulysses' virile beauty the day they decide to meet by the swimming pool. The sparkling light reflected off the water makes him seem unreal. Weeks later in a bar, he still impresses her as imbued with the pool's sparkling lights (61T; 95). Lori's discovery of her love for Ulysses is represented by this "luminescence," the title of the novel's main section. A glow and a reflection from the pool, his luminescence grows in crescendo as her feelings expand and intensify from desire to erotic love. Her imagination is crucial to the maturation of her desire: in the bar the water's reflections are in her mind, a fiction of love, and this is a sea change in her way of desiring a man. In addition, his gaze in the searing light and after dark tells her who she is; his gaze confirms her as desire, as a fact of her identity in her comprehension of herself. Since she is aware of the light and its reflection, the narrator calls this "progress." Lori has become open to Ulysses in a new way.

In Sartrian phenomenological psychology, love is how we assimilate the other's freedom to see us as an object. Lispector's brief chronicle "Who She Was" ["Quem ela era"] in *The Foreign Legion* might be said to translate into dramatic form the Sartrian idea that the lover reflects back to the beloved an image of self. Her chronicle is a brief dialogue, with each speech in parenthesis, as if the words were thoughts as much as spoken:

—(I love you)
—(Is that what I am then?)
—(You are the love which I have for you)
—(I feel that I am about to recognize myself. . . . I can almost see myself. I am almost there.)
—(I love you)
—(Ah, that's better. I can see myself. So this is me. Which I portray full-length.) (*The Foreign Legion* 125T)[32]

Love is how the complex back-and-forth of the gaze can be understood symbolically: "I am the one who desires, and desire is a particular mode of my subjectivity" (Sartre, *Being and Nothingness* 362). By loving Lori, Ulysses "mirrors" her to herself. He provides verbal confirmation for her sphinx-reflection and Lorelei refraction, and his nonverbal love is the single most important force to shape her understanding of her being-for-others. He is her exterior mirror and echo, her Sartrian "concrete other." His love furthers her education, perhaps even more than the verbal lessons he proffers.

Once Lori has progressed in her recognition of her self, Ulysses must occasionally adapt to her and not the other way around. In a scene comparable to the one in which he explains the name Loreley in Heine, Ulysses characterizes Lori and their relation to each other as a fantasy in which he is a painter and she a blank canvas (31T; 54–55), which he now realizes is fantasy, and thus false. Ulysses imagined himself imposing figures and colors on her canvas where before there were none. But he has come to learn Lori's "canvas" has forms already; it is not a blank awaiting his brush. He also believed that her canvas had been "darkened by a layer of smoke from some bad fire and that it wouldn't be easy to clean" (31T) ["enegrecida por uma fumaça densa, vinda de algum fogo ruim, e que não seria fácil limpá-la" (54–55)], but the narrator informs the reader that Lori thinks clearly at this moment and "almost" with light, brilliance. Her canvas is clean: "Yes, everything became clear and she rose up from inside herself almost with splendor" (32T) ["Sim, tudo se esclarecia e ela surgia de dentro de si mesma quase com esplendor" (56)]. Ulysses originates the painterly comparison of creation, inspiration, and pleasure to describe his Adamic attitude toward himself, before whom Eve (Lori) is derivative, but the narrator turns the tables, gradually reversing Ulysses' image of himself and of her. The world becomes Lori's canvas. Her visual delectation of the open air market ("a feira de frutas e legumes e peixes e flores") is described as a recuperation of her powers of self-definition: "As if she were a painter just coming out of an abstract phase she had, without becoming representational, now entered a new realism" (90T) ["Como se ela fosse um pintor que acabasse de ter saído de uma fase abstracionista, agora, sem ser figurativista, entrara num realismo novo" (137)]. Abstractionism in painting allows the maximum freedom to the spectator. Earlier, Lori as painter had given others—like Ulysses—free rein to find what they would in the canvas of her self. Once she paints the forms of "new realism" there, however, spectators have their freedom to interpret (her) bounded by limits she has established.

Ulysses' conscious goal in educating Lori is not to convert her into an object for his fantasies, which she already is, but to prepare her for her own. Lori does acquire a limited autonomy that allows her to act, at the same time that Ulysses acquires a limited object-quality so that her "fiction" may have free play. Her apprenticeship is, in part, the distancing of the would-be lovers until the moment when she is ready to act as an autonomous woman, and, in part, a new mental and emotional coming together in which they will begin to alternate as subject and object. As we saw above in the chronicle "Who She Was," the Lispectorian woman-in-love alternates with a man in seeing and being seen, speaking about and being spoken about, which contributes to her identity formation. He teaches her to treat him as an erotic object that she can use as a mirror to multiply her desire. Additionally, he teaches her the importance of being a transgressor. Ulysses teaches Lori how to eat the forbidden apple, in addition to that which she knows how to do, to be "eaten," that is, to be desired by others.

A most important lesson of love, paradoxically, is that she should resist him: first literally, in that she should postpone the fulfillment of desire; then metaphorically, in that she should accept only those lessons that suit her. There is at least one extended example of this latter kind of resistance, reflecting her new inner strength and freedom. Ulysses wants to take Lori to the forest of Tijuca to eat "chicken in blood sauce" ["galinha a molho pardo"], a common Brazilian dish. To prepare the meal, the chicken is bought alive. Its throat is cut, the flowing blood is collected to make the gravy, and then the animal is killed and carcass dressed and cooked. He wants her to join in a feast that, to his understanding, forges links between our human, animal, and divine selves, like Christian Communion, which celebrates Christ's humanity. Fearful, Lori would prefer something else, but Ulysses will have none of it:

> Of course we must eat it and not forget or lose respect for the violence we all have in us. The small acts of violence keep us from the big ones. Who knows, if we didn't eat animals, we would probably eat people blood and all. Our life is cruel, Lorelei. Blood is shed when we are born and it is shed when we sever forever the possibility of perfect union that the umbilical cord represents. And many bleed to death internally or externally. We must believe in blood as an important part of life. Cruelty is love, too. (68T)[33]

This dinner in Tijuca is Ulysses' ceremony or ritual, just as Lori's ritual, announced as such and repeatedly emphasized, is her early-morning swim in the ocean. Hers involves the incorporation of seawater as a holy sexual intercourse; his, the incorporation of blood as a sacred banquet offered to violent humanity. This "animal sacrifice" is associated with love, in his view. According to Ulysses' teaching, the eating of meat reminds us of our primitive savagery, of which lovemaking also forms part. Lori enjoys the taste but attempts to balance or mitigate the violence in her world, despite Ulysses' insistence that she receive inoculations of controlled violence to prevent a full outbreak. The novel thus opposes her consecration of sensual pleasure to Ulysses' consecration of the violence of everyday life.

His positive association of living one's sexuality with ritualized violence parallels Georges Bataille's theory of the correlation between religious feeling, transgression, and eroticism. Ulysses wants to teach Lori about accepting violence, but after her brief objection, she teaches herself about pleasure and pain. Lori's responses to Ulysses' ritual of symbolic violence show her developing personal strength and power of imagination as well as a new, more mutual student-teacher relation, but she is still not very strong and cannot tolerate the death that bombards her senses at the fish market: "Again she breathed in the poignant, violently perfumed death of the silvery blue fish, but the sensation was stronger than she could bear. And, at the same time that she was feeling an extraordinarily pleasant sensation of growing faint because of her love, she felt also as though she were escaping from herself in self-defense" (69T).[34] Lori has learned from Ulysses that the sensual experiences of taste and smell, even the taste of blood and the smell of death, can be utilized for erotic excitement and an incitement to love. Her lover's choices of the animals for his lessons—fish and chickens—are particularly significant for Lori, for the novel, and for Lispector's work as a whole. For Lori, the dead fish at the market remind her of her swim in the ocean and her nonviolent, erotic epiphany there. For the novel, the return to maritime images underlines Lori's thought that smelling the fish was the only way "to feel the great anguish to live more profoundly which that smell provoked in her" (69T, trans. modified) ["sentir a grande ânsia de viver mais profundamente que esse cheiro provocava nela" (109)]. Lori recognizes her predatory nature, but she has renounced it.

In terms of Lispector's work, chickens are more significant. Lori loves chickens and for that reason protests against Ulysses' plans to have one killed: "Even though I couldn't kill a chicken because I have so much fun seeing them alive, bobbing their ugly heads up and down looking for worms" (68T) ["Logo eu seria incapaz de matar uma galinha, tanto gosto delas vivas, mexendo o pescoço feio e procurando minhocas" (107)]. The chicken is an animal that Lispector returns to again and again in her stories and chronicles. Once again, intertexuality adds nuance and valence to what may have appeared straightforward or transparent.

In Lispector's famous story "The Foreign Legion" ("A legião estrangeira"), appearing in the collection of the same title, young Ofélia, made mature by her family before her time (like young Lori), wants to play with a chick that she hears peeping in the kitchen of the neighbor who is telling the story. Ofélia feels "the humiliation of such intense desire" (98T) ["á humilhação de querer tanto" (108)], but her pride keeps her from admitting or acting upon it until the narrator, a gentle educator "with the extreme harshness of someone who is saving the other" (98T) ["com a extrema dureza de quem salva" (109)], reminds Ofélia to choose pleasure. Ofélia loves the chick and in her rapture soon forgets the presence of the neighbor. But the fragile baby chick dies, and Ofélia is left with grief as the memory of her love. The narrator feels remorse for not having prepared the girl for the risks of pleasure, which greatly exceed the safety of living without it. The narrator of "The Foreign Legion" explains to the absent Ofélia: "Oh, do not be so frightened! Sometimes people kill for love, but I promise you that one day you will forget everything, I promise you! People do not know how to love, do you hear me, I repeated as if I might reach her before, in refusing to serve the truth, she should proudly serve nothingness. I who had not remembered to warn her that without fear there was the world" (101T).[35] The idea is that *with* fear, the world disappears, becomes nothingness, death in a pejorative sense, like death for Lori at the beginning of *An Apprenticeship*, like Lori who takes sleeping pills to avoid remembering the incident with the taxi driver. The narrator in "The Foreign Legion," clearly a character and not omniscient, speaks like Lori of the end of the novel, in favor of taking risks for love.

In another famous essay/story from the same Lispector collection, "The Egg and the Chicken" ["O ovo e a galinha"], the chicken has a consciousness of itself as a chicken and possesses an interior life. Though the narrator can see the chicken as something-to-eat, an object which serves a human purpose, the chicken is described as having a (reduced) being-for-itself. In other words, "chickenness" is linked with self-consciousness. Additionally, "chickenness" means femaleness; mothers and creative people who give the world their "eggs" are "chickens," too, according to this story. Perhaps most important for the comparison to Lori's sexual learning, however, is that understanding the egg and the chicken differs absolutely from eating the egg. Lori need not eat the chicken to recognize the violence, the war, of daily life. Furthermore, the story's narrator aligns herself with chickens as victims: "I belong to the freemasonry of those who have seen the egg once and then deny it as a means of ensuring its protection. We are those who refrain from destroying, only to be destroyed ourselves" (*Legion* 52T) ["Faço parte da maçonaria dos que viram uma vez o ovo e o renegam como forma de protegê-lo. Somos os que se abstêm de destruir, e nisso se consomem" (*Legião* 54)]. The sacrifice of a chicken in blood sauce during dinner with Ulysses thus suggests a consecration of violence toward the feminine, the maternal, and the creative. Though enigmatic and paradoxical, this story seems to support the notion that Lori's resistance to Ulysses' blood ritual is a positive move, even if an action taken out of fear.

As Lori's teacher, Ulysses impresses on her the importance of "respecting" one's own violence, of not rejecting its attractions. He warns Lori of the need to accept death (the fish at the market), seduction (inherent in her name Lorelei, who lures sailors to their death), and violence in the meal of chicken in blood gravy. She should acquiesce, even welcome, these elements of "real life," he tells her, despite her negative feelings toward them. In the middle of the night after the meal with Ulysses in Tijuca, Lori muses: "The world is a party that ends in death" (77T) ["O mundo é uma festa que termina em morte"(119)]. She has learned that she can gain strength from having imagined the worst that could happen: her own death. The pseudodeaths of the body in orgasm and of the ego in love henceforth lose their ability to frighten her because she has imagined her own death from (male) violence and survived psychologically. She has learned to take risks. In general, she cooperates with Ulysses and struggles to acquire the lessons he would give her, unless she knows them already. But her new willingness to learn and acceptance of death does not mean she has accepted the need for blood rituals: she understands the egg but "refrains from destroying."

Nonetheless, in every other way Lori is a good pupil of Ulysses' eroticism. Lori's first resistance to Ulysses' ideas of love, that is, her initial resistance to his menu is overcome in her apprenticeship because the violence of chicken in blood sauce is only symbolic of violence to women. After her initial resistance, she eats the chicken and enjoys it. In her gendered script, she can partake of chicken, understand what she is doing, and still refrain from the male role. The eating is refracted to an experience of sensuality. When the narrator discusses the later moments of confusion that bring Lori's new self into being, the context of symbolic violence has been replaced by a "hunger for life" (105T) ["fome de viver" (157)]. Lori now wants to eat the best and the heaviest meats; she wants to have all the mixtures, the spirit and the flesh (184T; 128). In the concatenation of her feelings, however, she next feels "the ultimate pain" (106T) ["a grande dor" (157)]: "There was the opposite of numbness—a gentler [lighter], more silent way of existing" (106T) ["o contrário de um entorpecimento: era um modo mais leve e mais silencioso de existir" (157)]. Not tempted to avoid the pain, she watches herself experience it and seeks to understand. She no longer fears and insulates herself. Lori's easy willingness to wait, courage to transgress, and deep religious feeling have been encouraged by Ulysses in the same meal.

With the frequent buying of food, the eating, drinking, and planning to go to restaurants and bars in the novel, each experience signifies different things, but each also foreshadows the final object taken into her body: Ulysses' sexual organ. She eats the apple, the pear, and the chicken in brown sauce. In Brazilian slang, "to eat someone" is to be dominant in sex, the putative male role. Roberto Reis explains the usage succinctly, for another purpose:

> Brazilians conceive of [hetero]sexuality, writes [Roberto] Da Matta [in *O que faz o Brasil, Brasil?* 60], not as the encountering of opposite and equal individuals (a man and a woman who can be their own persons), but as a way for one to absorb the other, which does away with a sense of equality symbolically consented to by society. Sexual acts, therefore, establish a difference and a radical heterogeneity by just changing the individual into either the "eater" or the "eaten," Portuguese metaphors that . . . resemble the English duality top/bottom. . . .
>
> [A]ccording to the patriarchal and male-oriented values still held in the Brazilian imagination to date [1996], the woman must "give herself" and be "eaten," but not the man. The man who is "eaten" is thought of as effeminate (if not queer), which contradicts the manly image he is supposed to put forth. (Reis 105–6)

Reis adds that, in Brazil, "So-called activity and passivity acquire the sense of dominance and submission" (107). In this sense, the fact that Lori eats the apple, and yet learns not to fear that the apple has been eaten, gains a further resonance as a suggestion that, on the register of power between the sexes, there can be alternation of sexual roles, an equality over time if not at every moment, in an activity previously conceived of in Brazilian slang as inherently and stereotypically hierarchical.

Lori has learned to delight in the lights and colors of the world. Her progress continues when, as if in a religious vision, she is moved to taste an apple. A single bite provokes her epiphanic "state of grace."[36] Later she dreams of retaining the sensuous visual pleasure of seeing the apple even while tasting it; then she both tastes the apple and continues to see the fruit in its pristine entirety: "The fruit of the World was hers. Or if it was not, that she had just touched it. It was an enormous fruit, scarlet and heavy, suspended in dark space, shining almost as if it were gold. And it was in midair that she placed her mouth on the fruit and managed to bite into it, yet leave it intact gleaming in space" (112T).[37] She has lost her fear of biting the apple; she can love sexually (eating) and still love spiritually (seeing). After being awakened to the divine order, she "touches the world," that is, she enters the second stage of her sexual apprenticeship. It is as if the divine and human worlds denoted the same thing, or were two languages translatable into each other. The narrator speaks of Lori's epiphanic state upon eating the apple as the moment when she understands differently the relations between humanity and divinity: "She had experienced something that seemed to redeem the human condition, although at the same time the narrow limits of that condition were marked" (99T) ["Havia experimentado alguma coisa que parecia redimir a condição humana, embora ao mesmo tempo ficassem acentuados os estreitos limites dessa condição" (150)].

Lori's desire for Ulysses is like a hunger, as if she could "feed on Ulysses' presence" (86T) ["comesse a presença de Ulisses" (133)], but unlike a hunger that could be satisfied by food, his presence would not simply satisfy her, but confirms and prolongs her desire. Sartre also compares sexual desire to hunger; he writes that they are different relations between consciousness and facticity, but both happen to begin in physiological responses of the body. With hunger, consciousness responds in a flight toward its possibilities, "thus hunger is a pure surpassing of corporal facticity" (*Being and Nothingness* 363). With desire, however, the body is not surpassed: "The being which desires is consciousness *making itself body*" (365, Sartre's emphasis). The philosopher adds: "desire is consent to desire" (364). Desire is thus an appetite which does not have disappearance of desire as its motive. Desire instead aims to become flesh (to become the object of desire) for the appropriation of the other's flesh (in order to continue to desire).

Despite being "in between," making progress without having arrived at her full potential, Lori begins to reap in images the "fruits" of her apprenticeship. Lori speaks to Ulysses in the middle of their night of love: "I feel as if with no sadness or remorse, I have finally bitten into the flesh of the fruit that I thought was forbidden" (113T) ["Sem tristeza nem arrependimento, eu sinto como se tivesse enfim mordido a polpa do fruto que eu pensava ser proibido" (169)]. In addition, the forbidden fruit of the Tree of Knowledge is supplemented by another fruit in *An Apprenticeship*, the fruit of the Tree of Life promised to the resurrected after the Apocalypse: "He who has an ear, let him hear what the Spirit says to the churches. To him who conquers I will grant to eat of the tree of life, which is in the paradise of God" (Revelation 2:7). Lori, "Unlike Eve, when she bit into the apple she entered paradise" (97T) ["Ao contrário de Eva, ao morder a maçã [Lóri] entrava no paraíso" (146)].[38]

In her apple epiphany, Lori is like one of the resurrected, a believer in Christ, a servant of God. The first of *An Apprenticeship*'s epigraphs comes from Revelation 4:1, the biblical annunciation that the trumpet of God will reveal to St. John His plan for the end of the world.[39] Each horse of the biblical Apocalypse unleashes a specific type of disaster on the world dominated by Satan. The Black Horse of Famine is released from the third seal opened by the Lamb of God, Jesus Christ; its rider carries a scale to measure wheat (Revelation 6:5–6).[40] After the righteous have died and Satan has ruled on earth, after the Black Horse of the Apocalypse sets hunger on the living, then the righteous will be brought back to life and will eat the fruit of everlasting life. This fruit does not give knowledge, which God forbids to Adam and Eve, but gives life after death. Indeed, life after metaphorical death is Lori's achievement, more than love or understanding; she learns to survive the dangers of life rather than to hide from them: she has entered the fray of experience.

Reflections on the Sexual and the Sacred

> In order for my flesh to exist and for the Other's flesh to exist, consciousness must necessarily be shaped in the mould of desire. This desire is a primitive mode of our relations with the Other which constitutes the Other as desirable flesh on the ground of a world of desire.
>
> Jean-Paul Sartre, *Being and Nothingness* (369)

Lispector's strategy of reflections to construct Lori's apprenticeship in sexuality separates out moments in which the protagonist sees herself differently, in a new way. Another set of new insights related to Lori's sexuality are those framed with religious auras. The association between the sexually liberated woman and danger seems far afield from the realm of the sacred, but there are many ways in which cultures have indeed connected sex with religious prohibitions. Being sexual thus becomes a religious transgression.

Simple forms of the novel's "consecrations" or "spiritual reflections" flash by quickly throughout, as in the phrase Ulysses "transformed her from child to Pietà, the mother of men" (109T) ["a transformava menina em Pietà, a mãe dos homens"(162)]. This Madonna image is placed where it is the most ironic: at the moment when Lori arrives at Ulysses' apartment ready for sexual love. This consecration stresses, for instance, Lori's paradoxical innocence at the moment she is ready to love the man she desires. In other examples of consecrating images, Lori's perfume associates her with ancient, obscure religious rituals: "perfuming herself was for Lori a secret, almost religious act" (5T) ["Já para Lóri perfumar-se era um ato secreto e quase religioso" (16)]. Ulysses asks if she is a "priestess" (68T) ["sacerdotisa" (108)], and she considers herself "the chosen one of the leaves" (79T) ["a escolhida das folhas" (122–23)]. Lori realizes her teacher and friend wants her to become an initiate—"novice" (67T) ["uma iniciada" (105)]—in life, and when later she discovers she loves the perfume of flowers, the narrator confirms that "She had been initiated into the world" (79T) ["era uma iniciada no mundo" (122, 128)]. After her long prayer to God, and phone call to Ulysses, she learns that "Living was like having a veil over her hair" (81T) ["viver era ter um véu nos cabelos" (125–26)].[41]

In the final episode, certain images reflect Lori in the role of divine creator. In the dark she reaches out and with "her hand touched the bare chest of the sleeping man [Ulysses]. In this way, she created him with her own hand and made sure that its [her hand's] skin would forever carry the imprint of living" (112T) ["sua mão tocou no peito nu do homem adormecido: ela assim o criava pela sua própria mão e fazia com que esta para sempre guardasse na pele a gravação de viver" (167)].[42] Lori's inspired creation of Ulysses occurs in the imagination of a "free" human being, at the beginning of a developing, newly sexual relationship for which her apprenticeship has prepared her. Similarly, during her early-morning swim, Lori had parted in two "the waters of the world" (53T) ["as águas do mundo" (85)].[43] Inside her is the world and she is inside the world. This apparent paradox may be understood as homology to consciousness, able to reflect on the world and to reflect on the ability to reflect (on the world). It is also a parallel to seeing the whole apple after one has taken a bite from it.

In her ocean consecration, Lori finds the union of male and female. For Lori, the ocean, o mar, is masculine and holds her in an explicitly sexual embrace. Lori feels "the sea inside like the thick liquid of a man" (53T) ["o mar dentro como o líquido espesso de um homem" (85)]. The male ocean has a distinctive smell (cheiro) signified by the feminine word maresia. The pleonasm *o cheiro maresia* conjoins two nouns, "smell" and "smell of the sea," which retain their male- and female-gender endings. In this sense, Lispector reflects in her writing the union the narrator says Lori found.

The two major consecrations for Lori consist of her swim in the ocean and her "state of grace," or epiphany, after eating the apple. In comparison to the simple reflections making Lori an initiate on her way to priestess and then Madonna, extended consecrations in *An Apprenticeship* are reflections/meditations on Lori's image that import systems of myth, ritual, ceremony, or belief into the images and epiphanies of Lori's learning. Extended consecrations are Lori's incarnations of religious or spiritual stories reflected back to her. In the process of importing religious systems, these narratives of consecration link the dualities of body and spirit, male and female, sex and love, human and divine. The dualities gain concrete form as unbalanced hierarchies: body and spirit are united, male and female mingle, sex occurs within a love relationship, and a mere human glimpses the nature of divinity. This obliteration of the separation of dualities may be accomplished through the positing of a third term—such as the animal for the human/divine contrast—or through the collapsing of the two halves of a binary into a unity, such as, for instance, that sex and love can temporarily be the same thing. Announced by the narrator, understood by Lori, these two extended religious reflections of the swim and the apple contrast with Ulysses' principal consecration, the meal of chicken in blood sauce, which the narrator does not comment upon and which frightens then pleases Lori. In contrast to the consecration of Lori's utopian dreams of peace, creation, and plenitude, Ulysses' ritual exalts the violence and the strife which humanity must control in itself if it wishes to overcome its animality. Lori's and especially Ulysses' consecrations loosely coordinate the animal imagery with the religious themes so that it has an allegorical impact.

Unlike the other birds in *An Apprenticeship*—sparrows, swallows, mockingbirds (*pardais, andorinhas, sabiás*)—the chicken is domesticated and docile and cannot fly away. Lori, too, is associated with nonflying winged creatures; in one of the final images, Lori transforms into a chrysalis, or *pupa,* where she will sleep until she becomes a mature butterfly with wings. After making love with Ulysses, Lori observes: "'I have never known myself as I do now,' Lori thought. . . . And it was a synthesis also, as it encompassed at the same time everything great and small. 'I know myself as the larva does that is transformed in [to] a chrysalis: my life is between plant and animal stages'" (110T) ["'Nunca me sei como agora,' sentia Lóri. . . . E era também o mínimo, pois tratava-se, ao mesmo tempo de um macrocosmo e de um microcosmo. 'Eu me sei assim como a larva se transmuta em crisálida: esta é minha vida entre vegetal e animal'" (63–64)]. The lessons of love Lori learns first provision her with self-knowledge so that she can choose tests of growth, moments to grow stronger, at an appropriate level and pace. Ulysses no longer needs to warn her she is attempting too much or going too fast; she can judge for herself. And the pupil may decide she can try more than her teacher suggests for her. But by the end of the novel she has not yet become a butterfly; her wings have not fully developed. The operative word in Lori's reflection in the final pages is "between": "my life is between plant and animal stages" (110T) ["esta é minha vida entre vegetal e animal"(164)].

Interestingly, Georges Bataille's explicit argumentation on the sacred and the sexual comes very close to Ulysses' teachings. Bataille's two qualifications for eroticism are met in *An Apprenticeship*: the sexual act should be resolute and premeditated, and it should be a profanation of the divine. It is Ulysses who establishes these two conditions: that they not fall into sex, but decide to prepare themselves for it; and that they transgress against deeply felt Judeo-Christian marriage rules. In comparing the French writer's ideas to those of Ulysses, I do not wish to claim that Lispector sought to portray (Lori's) sexuality in religious terms because she was aware of, or responding to, Bataille's ideas.[44] Though Lispector read French, Bataille was not widely known until later in his life, or more accurately, until after his death. My intent here is to clarify the Brazilian text's ideology with regard to female sexuality, not to comment on authorial intention or possible intertextuality.

Georges Bataille argues that sexual taboos originate in a community's efforts to control sexual violence, especially rape and incest, through religion. Religions, he argues, then establish further sexual prohibitions supplementing those against rape and incest alone. The additional taboos become quite complicated marriage rules, dictating with whom, when, and how sexual intercourse is permitted, according to each culture's values and rituals. Eroticism is defiance of these religious prohibitions surrounding sexuality. For the French writer, eroticism is an "organized" activity, neither spontaneous nor calculated to obtain a specific end, which runs along tracks of the prohibited but within restrictions designed to maintain a social order. In addition, eroticism connects sex to freedom: "Without transgression, we lose the feeling of freedom that the full accomplishment of the sexual act demands" (Bataille 107). In this theory, humanity accepts "animal" sexual desires, at the same time it refuses to be overpowered by them, which provokes escalating echoes of desire. The inner experience of eroticism demands a sensitiveness to the need for a sexual taboo no less great than the desire which leads a person to infringe it. This sensitivity to taboo is religious sensibility, according to Bataille, because the origin of law is a religious prohibition. The respect for the taboo against which one transgresses links desire closely with terror, intense pleasure, and anguish (Bataille 38). By recognizing our animal nature, latent beneath a thin veneer of respect for taboos, *and* recognizing the sacredness of transgressions performed under conditions of ritual and mystery, we prepare consciousness for the echoing, escalating pleasures of body-and-mind eroticism.

When Lori goes to Ulysses' house, her intent is conscious and transgressive in this way; beforehand she is rocked by an unexpected epiphany, like Ana in Lispector's story "Love" ("Amor").[45] The disarticulation is felt as another act of violence against her, another threat, however, rather than an acceptance of her feelings of violence toward others: "She had lost her bearings a little as if her heart had been removed" (105T) ["Ficou um pouco desnorteada como se um coração lhe tivesse sido tirado" (157)]. Then: "Her heart began to beat harder and she felt pale as all her blood left her face because quite suddenly she felt Ulysses' desire and her own. She remained standing for a moment, for a moment caught off balance. Then her heart beat even faster and louder because she realized that she would not postpone it any longer. It would be tonight" (107T).[46] Fully aware she is not only defying her old habits, but also flaunting social mores, Lori faces squarely the community's prohibitions against her actions. An internal transformation has transpired in which her fear of intimacy has changed to a willingness to risk breaking with her deeply internalized taboos. In Bataille, nausea reinforces the taboos as the internal opposition to erotic transgression; Lori's experience with nausea—no less an existential anguish than a moral one—comes from her fears. For Lori, pleasure was on the edge of anguish (87T; 134).

To understand fully the events that occur once Lori arrives at Ulysses' house in the novel's conclusion, we need to understand his ritual in which together they eat and solemnly enjoy the chicken in blood sauce. As Ulysses' consecration continues after dinner, she resists engaging in those activities she has learned are male in order to keep her female possibilities. Voluntarily she has assumed the mask of gender and does not relinquish it: "Because he was a man, he busied himself with stoking the fire. She could not remember ever doing that. It was not her role because she had her man to do that. As she was no longer a virgin it was fitting that the man accomplish his mission. . . . It was not an order on her part, for she had a man now and she would lose her status if she gave him an order" (73T) ["Ele, o homem, se ocupava atiçando o fogo. Ela nem se lembrava de fazer o mesmo: não era o seu papel, pois tinha o seu homem para isso. Não sendo donzela, que o homem então cumprisse a sua missão. . . . Não a comando seu que era mulher de um homem e que perderia o seu estado se lhe desse uma ordem" (114–15)]. Stoking the fire is a ritual of sorts, Ulysses' other ritual, during which Lori sorts out a new understanding: she seeks an order in the chaos of sexuality by making a "contract" between them that allocates along gender lines the roles they are to fulfill.[47] Even in her hunger to live, Lori is willing never "to stoke the fire" in order to retain her mask of gender. Gender is both externally imposed and internalized, Catharine MacKinnon reminds us, "so that feminity is identity to women as well as desirability to men" (6). In Sartrian terms, Lori feels that if she stops her being-for-itself-for-others, that is, stops the willing enslavement of her freedom in order to love, she will lose the object quality that makes her attractive to him erotically.

Not only is being a woman intrinsic to her identity; it also increases Lori's desire. As the flames slowly die in the fireplace in Tijuca, she burns with desire: "She seized the moment, then, and her inner fire *consumed her*" (74T) ["Encarniçou-se então sobre o momento, *comia*-lhe o fogo interno"(115, emphasis added)].[48] She wants to reach out and take Ulysses' hand but does not, because doing so would be like searching for pleasure in a nightclub instead of waiting for it to arrive by itself. By denying herself, she desires more. As she "burns brighter" herself, Lori acts out *in her mind* her desire: "Then, as everything was going to end, in her vivid imagination she grabbed the man's free hand. And still in her imagination, as she took that hand in hers, she burned gently all over, she burned and blazed" (74T) ["Então, como tudo ia acabar, em imaginação vivida, pegou a mão livre do homem, e em imaginação ainda, ao prender essa mão entre as suas, ela toda doce ardia, ardia, flamejava" (116)]. Obedience to social roles limits Lori's actions, but her imagination has been set free to transgress against her internalized rules and to follow her desire. An action taken in the imagination has an unlimitedness that the actual action cannot match. Paradoxically, her renunciation of action behind the mask of gender eroticizes by being purely a voluntary, mental prohibition.

Similarly, after the "night of terror," Ulysses had earlier refused Lori's invitation to come in for coffee: "she asked as a pretext to make him come in. He stayed on the doorstep. . . . with his lips pressed tight, he looked her up and down. Finally he said: I'll call you during the day" (17) ["perguntou ela como pretexto para fazê-lo entrar. Ele ficou no limiar. . . . com os lábios apertados, e olhou-a de alto a baixo. A final disse:—De dia telefono para você" (33)]. Lori's reaction is to try to understand his refusal by using her most frequent tool: "She looked at herself full-length in the mirror in order to judge what Ulysses had seen. And she found herself attractive; yet he had not wanted to come in" (17) ["Olhou-se de corpo inteiro ao espelho para calcular o que Ulisses vira. E achou-se atraente. No entanto ele não quisera entrar" (33)]. Presumably, if what we learn from Lori works for Ulysses, his postponement of sex with her increased his desire for her in his imagination.

Bataille insists that women are the privileged objects of desire, after first admitting that women and men can equally have access to eroticism as subjects. In *Erotism*, Bataille appeals to sheer numbers to shore up his proposition: "Theoretically a man may be just as much the object of a woman's desire as a woman of men's desire. The first step towards sexual intercourse, however, is usually the pursuit of a woman by a man" (130). Suzanne Guerlac sees in Bataille the philosophical need for recognition by the Other, satisfied for the man in heterosexual eroticism by a woman. Guerlac highlights the importance of "a heterosexual eroticism *à deux*, a gendered scenario of relation to an erotic object" (91): "The woman—the erotic object—is essential in eroticism in order to render it *saissable*, in order to figure it or present it to consciousness through the mediation of visual form. . . . Its appearance requires the presence of the 'paradoxical object'—the beautiful woman prostitute—an object which signifies the absence of any object" (Guerlac 104). In Guerlac's discussion of Bataille, "the dialectic of the erotic object is necessary to Bataille's theory of eroticism as the support of figuration or fiction—the fiction of death in particular" (103).

The ideal sex object for men, according to Bataille, is a woman who is either objectlike (a prostitute) or, interestingly, autonomous and authentic. Lori's lesson from Ulysses is this one, in which she tries to learn the woman's role. At the moment when Ulysses first offers Lori a ride the day they meet, Lori has the appearance of Bataille's beautiful woman prostitute. Although there is only a metonymical connection between prostitution and Lori's talking to a man on the street, Ulysses associates her behavior with that of a "streetwalker" (30T; 52–53). Lori's excessive makeup and her fears of being mistaken for a prostitute further associate her with Bataille's ideal erotic object for a man, despite merely being loose, a "liberated woman" who does not take money for sex. Ulysses' home is located in the red-light district of Rio, but he protests that no prostitute has ever entered his house, which Lori has not visited either (72T; 114). Clearly, Ulysses has been attracted to Lori before she began to develop under his tutelage; will he desire her after she has abandoned her fears, when she is an active subject rather than mere object?

The new problem for Lispector's lovers, then, in Lori's late stages of learning, would seem to be the effect of an active, authentic, and still liberated female sexuality on Ulysses' feelings toward her. Would he still be attracted erotically if the prohibitions against sex with her were no longer strong? Ulysses is attracted to the passive, empty cipher of the beautiful woman he saw on the street, yet his idea is to reform her, to change her so that she can actively pursue him and fantasize with him as an object: imagining him to be a passive, empty cipher of the handsome man. Although Ulysses never plays the (feminine) role of prostitute for Lori, he does gain a glow, or luminescence, which appears to have the function of inscribing her desire for him. Several difficulties still stand in the way of his teachings, however. First, Lori's eroticism differs from his in its principles, especially its utopian nonviolence, its masks, and its rituals. Second, in gendered scripts, male and female roles are not simply reversible.

Liberations: The Freedom to Enslave Yourself

[In love] one does not demand the abolition of the Other's freedom but rather his enslavement as freedom; that is, freedom's self-enslavement.
Jean-Paul Sartre, *Being and Nothingness* (379)

Before the comma that opens the main text, before the epigraphs, *An Apprenticeship* has a note from "C.L.," about freedom: "This book asked for a greater liberty than I could give without fear. It is much above me. Humbly I tried to write it. I am much stronger than myself"[49] ["Este livro se pediu uma liberdade maior que tive medo de dar. Ele está muito acima de mim. Humildemente tentei escrevê-lo. Eu sou mais forte do que eu" ("Nota" 5)]. This prefatory note refers to a transcendence, a surpassing, an excess, or in the novel's vocabulary, a "progress" beyond reflections of the self: "I am much stronger than myself." Freedom is usually constrained by a fear of consequences; perhaps Lispector, like her character, wishes to go beyond herself, beyond what readers have come to expect from her. In this case, the freedom to write according to the needs of the writing rather than thinking of the reader required unusual strength. What Clarice may have meant about her creative process is a matter of speculation; the inclusion of such a statement in the peritextual materials, however, signals early on the opposing poles of freedom versus fear that characterize Lori's apprenticeship.

Like "C.L.," Lori becomes more free by changing, that is, moving or removing, her internal barriers barring the manifestation of her liberty. Lori's anxieties prevent her from using the license she could have for the taking: "so much so that it would be useless to have more freedom; her insignificant condition would not allow her to make use of freedom. . . . Ulysses' human condition was greater than hers" (6T) ["a ponto de que seria inútil ter mais liberdade: sua condição pequena não a deixaria fazer uso da liberdade. . . . A condição humana de Ulisses era maior que a dela" (19)]. In Sartrian existentialism, freedom cannot be given or taken away, but instead manifests itself or not according to concrete circumstances. Foucault's conceptions of power similarly see power everywhere, and freedom as the coincidence of personal desire with the resources to act successfully on it. Fears limit our actions in this later philosophy as well, but there is the added problem in Foucault that our conscious desires may in fact be a response to power as much as those things we wish to repress. Removing her internal barriers would not be sufficient if Lori suffered overt political repression, physical violence, or economic oppression, but making her more fearless by changing her attitudes has a snowballing effect in terms of the freedom she accords herself to act on her sexual desires. Once she tastes the freedom she had denied herself, she begins to hunger for that which others deny her as well. Reaching a greater freedom by going beyond one's previous conceptions of oneself may also mean reaching out to others, including society as a part of self. "I" is transcended in the "We" of love for Ulysses, and in another sense, transcended in her new love for other people, for her students, for her community. But revisiting this freedom from the perspective of Foucault's theory, we see how her sexuality is encouraged by the people around her. She is incited, instructed, and corrected in the proper ways to live and love. The liberationist model is paradoxically based on male dominance and expert advice rather than on an expression of her liberty. She is occasionally silenced, but only as a means to teach her how to produce a (different) discourse of sexuality.

Significantly, Lori's fears are explained as a limited stage of growth through which she passes on her way to being capable of love, from vegetal to animal phases, from larva to pupa, as we have seen. Similar to Lispector's image of the chrysalis for Lori's transformation under Ulysses' guidance, Bataille's image of the chrysalis for man's erotic feelings toward woman is complex: "Man achieves his inner experience [of eroticism] at the instant when bursting out of the chrysalis he feels that he is tearing himself, not tearing something outside that resists him. He goes beyond the objective awareness bounded by the walls of the chrysalis and this process, too, is linked with the turning topsy-turvy of this original mode of being" (Bataille 39). An internal violence, the anguish or nausea that can bring about eroticism, according to Bataille, results from an epiphanic experience that he calls plethora, the momentary feeling of plenitude which brings in its wake the death (of the individual) and the surpassing of death in the union of individuals. This surpassing of death is the perpetuation of the species.

According to Suzanne Guerlac, the chrysalis or nymph in Bataille's "L'Histoire de l'erotisme" explains the "dual operation of interdiction/transgression." The chrysalis in Bataille is man transgressing against culture, which itself came into being as an attempt to deny nature. In denying sexual intercourse its reproductive aspect, eroticism affirms death. It is thus a denial of human culture, which came into existence through denying animal nature. By denying death, culture celebrates life. Through the denial of culture, that is, through the premeditated, conscious denial of the denial of nature, the larva transforms itself, and man's consciousness is prepared for the erotic moment.

Whereas Bataille sees in the transformation of larva to chrysalis the internal violence from conflict of conscience, Lori stresses her enriched consciousness, her silent, slow maturation according to "natural" processes in order to become the chrysalis. Lispector's dense passage on the chrysalis reorganizes the various themes (learning/knowledge, names/self, world/individual, plants/animals), already represented in images, into a new image from the insect world for developmental change. At the same time, if Bataille's theory coincides with Ulysses' teaching of eroticism, as it would appear to do, then another gender reversal has occurred. According to Guerlac, Bataille's theory calls for man's Hegelian recognition in a woman, and his tearing himself free of the chrysalis to emerge a mature butterfly; in Lispector's novel a woman finds her Hegelian recognition in a man, and secretes around herself a protective chrysalis as she changes from larva to pupa. This "recognition" of Ulysses and of Lori's destiny is the reflection of the self in the mirror of the loved one. "And then the day finally came when she learned that she was no longer alone. She recognized Ulysses, she had found her destiny as a woman" (84T) ["E então veio finalmente o dia em que ela soube que não era mais solitária, reconheceu Ulisses, tinha encontrado o seu destino de mulher"(130)]. In

Sartre, this recognition is the decision to give up certain choices, to enslave oneself willingly. If one interprets according to Foucault, Lori inserts herself into the discourse of gendered sexuality.

For Bataille, eroticism is the bursting forth from the chrysalis, the liberation of the butterfly from its binding. In Lispector, the larva changes to chrysalis, that is, Lori enters the confining, hard chrysalis rather than liberate herself from it: "Lori thought . . . 'I know myself as the larva does that is transformed in a chrysalis'" (110T) ["sentia Lori . . . 'Eu me sei assim como a larva se transmuta em crisálida'" (164)]. Moving with nature, Lori had been a larva and progresses in the direction of beauty and identity.[50] If all goes well, she will undergo a maturation process and emerge from her protective case. But some nymphs die from disease or are eaten by predators. Biological metaphors carry the possibility of death, or to put it another way, express the fragility of life. That Lispector concentrates the finale in an image of Lori's (voluntary) confinement means her apprenticeship was not so much liberating in itself, but could, possibly, lead to freedom later. The nymph inside the paper chrysalis has the first visible indications of wings, but they are not yet capable of flight.

The violence Lori has accepted, the way she learned to live with danger, is the mimicry of her own death, of life within the chrysalis stage which, from the outside, appears still and unchanging. *Larva* comes from Latin for a ghost or a mask, and Lori has both elements: the figuration of death and the wearing of the mask in the final scenes. As readers, we have followed her slow, wormlike crawl and then hectic production of a chrysalis/home where her development can continue. Inside, drastic mutations hurry her toward a future time when she will perhaps burst forth a butterfly. The book traces a process, but the book's end marks only another point of transition, another beginning in her life. Before Ulysses' teaching, Lori's definition of freedom had been merely that of being free to have affairs without scandal in the anonymity of the metropolis (29–30T; 51). When she tells him about her move to Rio, she says she gained freedom (65T; 102). In the final scenes, he believes that teaching her to love him made her free: "[Lori:] 'Do you think that I offend my social structure with my enormous freedom?' [Ulysses:] 'Of course, happily. Because you have just come out of prison as a free being, and no one pardons that. Sex and love are not forbidden to you. You have finally learned how to exist. And that provokes the unlocking of many other freedoms, which is a risk for your society.'"[51] To transgress against sexual prohibitions, he adds, is to gain consciousness of the possibility of breaking other rules. Lori's socialist teacher, Ulysses calls his newfound happiness "revolutionary" (66T) ["revolucionária" (103)]. The Repressive Hypothesis is the name given by Michel Foucault to the theory that power seeks to repress our sexual practices, and that practicing our sexuality "freely" not only provokes self-knowledge but also revolution. Foucault has extensively argued the error of the Repressive Hypothesis and the idea that power organizes the entire domain of sexuality, that power "has tirelessly coaxed and forced its [sexuality's] articulation, making of it the truth of our being that knowledge must try to discover" (Woodhull 168). Foucault's conception contradicts the lessons of Ulysses.

Under his tutelage, Lori does grow to a new social awareness: "Everyone was fighting for freedom—that was what she read in the newspapers—and she was glad that finally she no longer tolerated injustice" (84T) ["Todos lutavam pela liberdade—assim via pelos jornais, e alegrava-se de que enfim não suportasse mais as injustiças" (130)]. However, she does not envision great social changes. In her new consciousness, she sees only her (previously unrecognized) social responsibility and a need for charity to others. Having fomented her desires, Ulysses has made her more aware of the people around her. Lori wants to help her students with clothes they normally cannot afford: "And I want to be busier, too. I'm becoming very fond of teaching. I want to clothe, teach and love my students and prepare them for a way of life that I was never prepared for" (114T) ["E mesmo quero ficar mais ocupada: o ensino está me apaixonando, quero vestir, e ensinar, e amar meus alunos, e prepará-los para um modo como eu nunca fui preparada" (170)]. When Ulysses realizes that she has developed a new social conscience, he awards her a new status as a conscious subject, so he pronounces the apprenticeship over. Though she does not feel ready, he gives her instructions about how and where their sexual meeting will take place. Then the narrator adds: "He was offering her a kind of freedom" (102T) ["Era uma liberdade que êle lhe oferecia" (153)]. However, Lori gains only the freedom to choose when the meeting will be, not other aspects of their sexual encounter. Even so, she would have preferred that he decide the date and the time, too. No longer does she hide from risk and the freedom that accompanies it, but she does not seek freedom out either or look to define her life herself.

Ulysses' invitation to sex typifies the conversations of the couple throughout the novel. This is true even at the very end, where the pronouncements about Lori's new freedom are frequent and where she manifests the maximum freedom ascribed to her—when she goes to his house as he told her to—unannounced. Ulysses speaks and Lori listens, Ulysses decides and Lori obeys. In this way, the novel develops an implicit message of power imbalance in their love relationship ironically undercutting the explicit message and belief of the characters. While Ulysses seems consciously intent on having an equal partner in transgressive eroticism, he also wants to keep Lori as his fantasy-object à la Bataille. He is controlling and orders her about—so that she can be free? There can be little doubt that sexual desire moves Lori to action, primarily positively, toward a self-definition and social consciousness. She decides: I like the smell, I want the apple, I can take risks; as a sexual being, I should. He asserts "Lori, you are now a superwoman in the same sense that I am a superman, only because we have the courage to walk through the open door. It will be our responsibility to struggle to become what we really are" (113T).[52] She has crossed his threshold, literally, but the rest of her superwomanly powers remain a promise. At the same time, gender holds her back from acting and especially from rebelling against Ulysses. Gender is primarily a negative limit, a prohibition (women can't, women wouldn't, women don't, I as a woman should not), whereas sexuality is portrayed as a positive force inciting her to speak and act as a desiring subject.

The narrator asserts that Lori feels equal to Ulysses in the final pages: "Lori could finally talk to him as an equal" (113T) ["Lóri pode enfim falar com êle de igual para igual" (168)]. But what she tells him is the nature of the remaining taboos that are obstacles in her path: "'I've always had to struggle against my tendency to become some man's slave,' Lori said, 'because I've always admired men compared with women. In men I sense the courage to be alive. While I, as a woman, am slightly more delicate and therefore weaker, you are primitive and basic'" (113T) ["Eu sempre tive que lutar contra a minha tendência a ser a serva de um homem, disse Lóri, tanto eu admirava o homem em contraste com a mulher. No homem eu sinto a coragem de se estar vivo. Enquanto eu, sou um pouco mais requintada e por isso mesmo mais fraca—você primitivo é direto" (168)]. Because she still identifies with the category "woman," Lori treats herself as an entrapped object (of desire). Concurrently, through the lens of gender she glimpses freedom because men appear to live more freely. Lori grew up in a masculine world of a father and four brothers; her mother died when she was young. By watching Ulysses, she learns about the freedom she could have. But she has not lost the habit of obeying him and of obeying the idea of being a woman.

The extent to which she engages with Ulysses over her own voice and life is limited to silent protest. In the final pages we find Ulysses' uncontested commandments, lists of his desires, and his speech. She is reflecting out loud about who she is, and he says: "But that you don't ask. And the question should be answered differently. One doesn't make oneself very strong by asking the worst question for a human being. I, who am stronger than you, I can't ask myself who I am without being lost" (115–16T) [" — Mas isso não se pergunta. E a pergunta deve ter outra resposta. Não se faça de tão forte perguntando a pior pergunta de um ser humano. Eu, que sou mais forte que você, nâo posso me perguntar quem eu sou sem ficar perdido" (172–73)]. Another example of Ulysses' hegemony, in addition to the dictatorial quality of his speeches in general, is the tiny dialogue on the final page: "'My woman,' he said" (116T) ["Mulher minha, disse êle" (173)]. Instead of responding, "My man" ("Homem meu"), she says, "Yes, I'm your woman" (116T) ["Sim, sou mulher tua" (173)]. Although they are now lovers, the patriarchal context has not been modified, despite affirmations of Lori's greater freedom.

It is important that in these final lines Ulysses does not permit Lori to speak about what interests her—having a child. When she says she would like to get pregnant that night, he silences her in his typical censuring fashion: "Be patient. Besides, the next time you'll have to take precautions because we're going to wait for the right moment to have a baby. In fact, to make it easier for that reason too, the best thing really is to get married" (115T) ["Seja paciente. Aliás, da próxima vez, você tem que tomar cuidado porque vamos esperar pelo momento certo de ter um filho. Antes para facilitar, inclusive, o certo será mesmo nos casarmos" (172)]. In rejecting out of hand Lori's desire to become pregnant that night, Ulysses is confirming the eroticism of this first sexual encounter. Ever the teacher of male theories of sexual pleasure, that night at least he does not want either the biblical imperative to multiply or the animal "sex without desire" (10T) ["cio sem desejo" (23)] to return.

As we have seen, freedom is Lori's supreme concern in the first section, "The Origin of Spring or a Necessary Death in Broad Daylight" ("A Origem da Primavera Ou a Morte Necessária em Pleno Dia"), and in the final dialogue of the postcoital denouement. At one early moment, "freedom" ["liberdade"] or words derived from the same root occur six times on a single page (3–4T; 14). Lori's pain is described as the movement of a hysterical animal that wants to be free. Unaware of the exact movements that will break its bonds, the animal that panics in chaotic "lack of control" (3T) ["des-controle" (14)], which finally, blindly, liberates it. Lori rips the "net" holding her and rests, mimicked in the text by expressive punctuation (a period). Her freedom from captivity brings a moment of decision: whether to continue seeing Ulysses—that is, whether to learn what he has to teach and wants to teach her. In these first pages, Lori is still unsure about him; he may be a trap that could return her to her "cage" of fear. The ending does not return her to her cage, but sends her, certain of her desire, to the protective chrysalis of Ulysses' home amidst a return of the discourse of freedom.

Homologous to the broad deployment of sexuality traced by Foucault, the characters believe in the Repressive Hypothesis that sex can set you free. In *An Apprenticeship* the theme of the relative power of men and women does not progress in phases, culminating in an equality between master and apprentice, as did Lori's progress in love. Instead, the theme of enslavement versus freedom occurs in an alternating series of affirmations and negations. Her self-image may be powerful and empowering (like the black horse) at one moment, or frightening and frightful (like the prostitute) at another. However, the discourse shows that, though sexuality works to produce speech and action, it does not free the speaker. Indeed, her consecrations of her own body in holy communion with the ocean and the apple, which do empower her, are solitary. Ulysses' final act is to interrupt her and expostulate; the last words in the novel are his: "You think that:" (116T) ["Você pensa que:" (174)], ending the novel with a colon. Lori listens and patiently waits her turn.

Conclusions

Though Lori's sexual apprenticeship produces a discourse of her erotic self and brings her to her third stage, "reaching others," announced as a new state of affairs ushering in greater freedom for her in society, these changes remain extratextual. She may no longer be fooled by superficial or self-damaging freedoms, such as the freedom from feeling emotions, but she is beguiled by Ulysses' words, which contradict his actions.

The unequal power between Ulysses and Lori, as man and woman, does not appear explicitly among Ulysses' ideas. Nevertheless, his domineering style replicates the surrounding social structures of gender domination. Although their love may be untraditional, and they would be "liberated people" living a sexuality which is tame but sexually transgressive, Ulysses makes the decisions for the two of them. The text verbally promises a general freedom for Lori while it delivers a diegetic domination of Lori by her lover and a continuation of her submissiveness. The announcements of Lori's freedom in society are utopic, and with regard to Ulysses, they are negated. The characters believe that together they have created a new liberated woman, whose freedoms are more than sexual; the novel represents their beliefs as premature, if not delusional, wishful thinking.

The last sign of her possible rebellion is Lori's attempt to resist Ulysses' control of her speech. Ulysses says: "Know when to keep quiet so that you don't lose yourself in words" (114T) ["Saiba também calar-se para não se perder em palavras" (169)]. Lori resists only momentarily: "No. I've kept quiet all my life. But very well, I'll talk less" (114T) ["Não. Eu me calei a vida toda. Mas está bem, falarei menos" (169)]. Voluntarily she will speak less, she will obey him. By speaking less, she interacts less, and thus she agrees to regress from the greatest point she had reached in her learning. The two believers in the promise that sex delivers one from oppression, that sex is liberating, contradict their words with their actions. After all Lori's struggles to adjust her dangerous reflections to a voluntary image she can accept, and the narrator's strategies for deconstructing the meaning of her struggles as taught rather than self-taught, her sexuality is nonetheless still constituted imaginatively as a gendered and hierarchical relation. *An Apprenticeship* as a whole, by displaying sex but delaying until after the novel's end the freedom that was supposed to accompany it, inscribes the great difficulty, perhaps the impossibility, of reaching freedom through sexual "liberation" as conceived here.

One of the earliest writers to comment on Lispector in Spanish, the Mexican feminist novelist and poet Rosario Castellanos has attacked the simplistic assumptions surrounding the liberation of women-in-love elsewhere. Castellanos's brief review of *Passion* is interesting because it corroborates the early international feminist interest in Lispector. However, I want to discuss a different Castellanos essay, one which treats the ideological implications for women of gender and sexuality in the 1960s. In "The Liberation of Love" ("La liberación del amor"), a brief article published in 1972, Castellanos speaks to the "self-effacing little Mexican woman" ["abnegada mujercita mexicana"] who wishes to do something to improve the lot of woman, but only inside the strictures of Mexican culture, without the "aggressivity" of United States women's liberation, and without altering the power arrangements of gender.[53] Upper-class, educated, comfortable women, like those Castellanos addresses, often found the feminist movement suspiciously female and intellectual, unladylike and foreign. Castellanos ironically and comically proposes "The Movement of Women's Love" ["El Movimiento de women's love"], to such readers, as a deforming mirror which can teach them how this desire to maintain traditional Mexican culture perpetuates male privilege and female subjugation. In this (fictitious) women's movement, the 1960s rhetoric of liberation is transferred to values traditionally (and negatively) called feminine.

The Movement of Women's Love promotes the cynical proposal that if women are beautiful and manipulative enough, they can have power over their lives and over their men, without any outright organized struggle for social change. Today, decades later, the principle underlined in Castellanos's sarcastic article is well understood: feminine wiles are the weapons of those who do not have equality, who have no other way to affirm themselves. The unevenness and instability of patriarchy allows for many configurations of power between individual men and women. Under continual negotiation, the struggle for self-definition and autonomy on the part of women (and men) in relationships (both heterosexual and homosexual) is never "won" once and for all. But Castellanos's so-called Movement of Women's Love leaves the gender hierarchy intact even when these manipulative women gain power behind the scenes. In Lispector, similarly, if one supposes hypothetically that Lori has indeed achieved an equality with Ulysses in their love, which she has not, then those women who have not been equally lucky in their individual negotiations will be in a worse position than if she had overtly struggled for changes for all women. In this hypothetical situation, Lori's newfound equality and happiness would be a positive good. The drawback would be that she must depend on Ulysses' largesse for her new situation to continue; he may choose to be bossy, dogmatic, and controlling at any time, since the unequal roles have not changed.

Lori's characterization, not surprisingly, lies somewhere between the neoconservatism of Castellanos's fictional Movement of Women's Love and a collective feminism. Lori progresses to a point of intermediacy. Before her apprenticeship, she was thoroughly disengaged, even from love. She did not think of freedom except as having lovers free from scandal; additionally, she did not seek equality in her new love relationship. But she does change. Instead of avoiding contact with people, now she will "mother" and "father" her students, caring for them emotionally and physically. She will object to social injustice. As Lori lives her new "freedom," choosing with less fear among the options presented by her circumstance, she simultaneously becomes a woman-in-love. That is, she actively takes a partner in the complicated dance of gender relations in a society which asks for passivity from women-in-love-with-men. Voluntarily she puts on the mask of gender, but she can take it off at will. The dangerous reflections that the mirror and other people have shown her about herself she accepts, in fact hungrily solicits, rather than shuns. Seeing without blinking, acting with hesitation, endeavoring to understand how she who does not contribute to society hurts others, Lori nonetheless does not appear to have learned to imitate Ulysses' blind security that he knows what is best for others. Still humble, still questioning, Lori's luminescence has only just begun to glow.

Clarice Lispector in a protest march, 1966. Reprinted by permission of Paulo Gurgel Valente. Photo courtesy of *Revista Manchete*.

Clarice Lispector in Rio de Janeiro with Ulisses, her dog. Reprinted by permission of Paulo Gurgel Valente. Photo courtesy of *Revista Manchete*.

4

Mario Vargas Llosa and the End(s) of Sexual Freedom

I am not a person who is in favor of promiscuity, for example—
because I believe that it cheapens sex and debases the sexual
experience; instead I am for the intransigent defense of desire.

No soy una persona que esté a favor de la promiscuidad, por
ejemplo—porque creo que ella abarata el sexo y envilece la
experiencia sexual; en cambio estoy por la defensa
intransigente del deseo.

Mario Vargas Llosa, *Sobre la vida* (115)

In terms of the "newly sexed woman," the 1980s were a time of reaction: reacting to the threat of AIDS, reacting to the new popularity of sexual fiction, reacting to the new marketability of the woman writer. To a continued positive image of the sexual woman character, many writers reacted by beginning to explore the ways sexuality for women was not freeing or indicative of social change. In the eighties and after, for the first time, a large group of those writers who used to believe in the 1960s goals of liberation, including the goal of a sexual revolution in literature, are beset by disenchantment with the sexual-liberation movement, leading them to rethink its presuppositions or reject its promises. Other writers, those primarily seeking radical social change, reconceptualize sexuality in nonheterosexual terms or turn from sexual fiction to other fictional topics. *In Praise of the Stepmother* (1991, hereinafter *Praise*; *Elogio de la madrastra* 1988) by Mario Vargas Llosa furnishes fruitful ground for study because of its *mise en abîme* of this response to the 1960s. It opens with a portrayal of a liberated sexual woman, Lucrecia, who is adored by her husband, Rigoberto; she learns that her sexuality can provide her with feelings of autonomy and power. Regarding the social character of the female eroticism in *Praise*, one critic wrote: "Upon transgressing against the taboo of incest, in the mind of doña Lucrecia suggestive images reminiscent of a libertarian political terminology get stirred up, which indicates the eminently political character which prohibition has in the novel: 'I have won *sovereignty.*' . . . She felt fortunate and emancipated'" (Reati "Erotisme e historia"; emphasis Reati's).[1] In contrast, Rigoberto has lost all hope in collective ideals: "In his youth he had been a fervent militant in Catholic Action and dreamed of changing the world. He soon realized that, like all collective ideals, that particular one was an impossible dream, doomed to failure" (54T) ["De joven había sido militante entusiasta de Acción Católica y soñado con cambiar el mundo. Pronto comprendió que, como todos los ideales colectivos, aquél era un sueño imposible, condenado al fracaso" (80)]. But the novel ends treating her like the sexual woman protagonists of the past, such as the Doña Bárbaras, whose mere presence defiles her surroundings and whose ethics eventually destroy her.

Another reason *Praise* is a good novel with which to close this study is that it exemplifies the erotic Latin American literature called for by Julio Cortázar in the 1960s. By the end of the 1980s, critics can no longer say that the region lacks a strong vein of erotic fiction, as well as an important body of political fiction that finds sexuality useful for illustrating power relations in Latin American society. Cortázar, I dare say, would be pleased; but he might also be scandalized, however, by the anti-woman finale to the Vargas Llosa fiction that belongs to this example of the sexual fiction. With an ending that excludes female sexuality and parodies Christianity's anti-sexual tendencies, *Praise* signals the historical endpoint to the popularity of the 1960s liberationist sexuality, especially female sexuality as a carrier of a symbolic charge of social freedom.

The turnabout in attitudes toward the sexual woman character, in which the social changes wrought by the sexual woman character are portrayed as pernicious rather than beneficial, and exemplified by *Praise,* has been growing in popularity. As we have seen, in the 1960s model writers seeking radical social changes employed the sexual woman character in one of two ways, both of which were considered positive: as threatening to the status quo because she brought radical changes to it; or as a harbinger of positive future changes who was herself threatened by an unjust world not ready or willing to accept the transformations she represents. But in the 1980s, an increasing number of writers took up (hetero)sexual fiction in order to write cautionary tales warning that the dangerous sexual woman might, if given the chance, wreck the fragile ship of society. This group maintains a belief in her importance, but the danger she threatens is thought to have negative effects, not positive ones.

Before the 1960s idea of the revolutionary potential of sexual women disappears, it lingers, reduced to personal pleasure: an individual hedonism without potential for social change, a "culinary" amusement, in Jameson's term. Rigoberto in *Praise* exemplifies this individualistic or parodic idealism when he rejects the social activism of his youth in favor of a solipsism of individual pleasure: "He then conjectured that as an ideal, perfection was perhaps possible for the isolated individual, if restricted to a limited sphere in space (cleanliness or corporeal sanctity, for example, or the practice of eroticism) and in time (ablutions and nocturnal emissions before going to sleep)" (54T).[2] He prefers to perfect himself, to have the most perfect bowel movements, rather than better the world: "Ever since, in the most secret decision of his life—so secret that probably not even Lucrecia would ever be privy to it in its entirety—he had resolved to be perfect for a brief fragment of each day" (54–55T) ["Desde que, en la más secreta decisión de su vida—tanto que probablemente ni Lucrecia llegaría a conocerla a cabalidad—decidió, por un breve fragmento de cada jornada, ser perfecto" (80–81)].

Rigoberto's love for Lucrecia is a fetishization of her body parts, a worship and an objectification of her physical persona. This way of looking at love and people and women considers them property; rather than primarily enjoying her body as part of her, he loves her as an assemblage of body parts: "For thanks to his unyielding perseverance, he had managed to fall in love with the whole and with each one of the parts of his wife, to love, separately and together, all the components of that cellular universe" (27T) ["Pues gracias a su perseverante obstinación, había conseguido enamorarse del todo y de cada una de las partes de su mujer, amar por separado y en conjunto todos los componentes de ese universo celular" (45–46)]. He loves her *because* everything in her body was or could be erogenous (27T; 45).[3] Similarly, Rigoberto likes the idea of equal treatment, equal love, given to each of the parts of his own body; this is not to say that any part is equal to "him," but that among the lesser parts under "his" dominion, they are all equally dominated and equally favored: "With each individual organ and area the master of his labors for one day, perfect impartiality with regard to the care of the whole was assured: there were no favoritisms, no postponements, no odious hierarchies with respect to the overall treatment and detailed consideration of part and whole. He thought: 'My body is that impossibility: an egalitarian society'" (60T) ["Dueño cada órgano y sector por un día de sus afanes, quedaba garantizada la perfecta equidad en el cuidado del conjunto: no había favoritismos, postergaciones, nada de odiosas jerarquías en el trato y consideración de la parte y del todo. Pensó: 'Mi cuerpo es aquel imposible: la sociedad igualitaria'"(86)]. But even this personal redoubt of ✓ male sexuality as a libertarian space of perfection eventually surrenders. He sacrifices sexuality itself in the end in favor of abstinence.

The choice of Vargas Llosa's novel as indicative of 1980s trends may still seem controversial at first, despite its dramatization in miniature of the period for two reasons. First, Mario Vargas Llosa continues this novel with a sequel, *The Notebooks of Don Rigoberto* (1998; *Los cuadernos de don Rigoberto* 1997), an even more liberationist book than its predecessor. In fact, *The Notebooks* reverses the protagonist Rigoberto's stand regarding his and his wife's sexuality taken at the end of *Praise*. In the first novel, Rigoberto expels his wife from their house and praises asexual chastity in the novel's climax. In theory he had believed sexuality outside marriage was advantageous for the individual; this opinion he had shared and even inculcated in his new spouse Lucrecia. But in practice he had ✓ been unable to accept her having an extramarital affair, or that she had betrayed him with his own young son. Rigoberto's feelings of loss and the affront to his morality were too much for him to be able to live his sexual philosophy in action. In the 1997 sequel, Rigoberto forgives ex-wife Lucrecia and they reconcile, largely because he belatedly realizes that he had applied a different sexual standard to her behavior than to his own. The many sexual women characters in *The Notebooks* overturn reader expectations and Rigoberto's previous reservations about their behavior. It would appear that the 1960s liberationist associations accruing to female sexuality have not disappeared after all.

The narrative of historical change provides one answer to this objection. As I have tried to insist throughout this book, such change is patchy so that there will be exceptions to any general tendency one identifies. Added to the regional diversity within Latin America (which I have stressed already as a cause of individual variations) is the chronological proximity to us of these works from the late 1980s and late 1990s, which makes historical perspective more difficult. Regarding Vargas Llosa and the case of these two particular erotic novels, separated by a decade, we are dealing with an author who often returns to previous characters and themes. Although *The Notebooks* may be the first sequel he has published, Vargas Llosa has made a habit of narrating different stories about the same or similar characters. It is not surprising that the Peruvian author would have wanted to continue Lucrecia's story. The twist comes from the fact that the Rigoberto character of *The Notebooks* is much more unpleasant than in *Praise;* it becomes difficult to care what he believes in or whom he has sex with. I found it impossible to sympathize with his self-pitying isolation. Thus Rigoberto's presumably positive switch in attitude toward the sexuality of the liberated woman is undercut at the source; his conversion to equal sexual standards for men and women has been made ironic and cynical, and his beliefs remain bereft of positive social implications. Lucrecia may win back Rigoberto, but no form of 1960s sexuality could be vindicated by a vote of confidence from such a corrupt source.

A second objection against choosing *Praise* could come from the fact that by the 1980s, Latin American women writers had gained a voice on a par with men on this topic of the sexual woman character. Why should I close *The Sexual Woman in Latin American Literature* with yet another male writer? Simply put, the reason is that most women writers have incorporated their new freedom to treat female sexuality realistically and moved on, presenting new images and fresh insights, contextualizing female sexuality within the contemporary lives of women characters. Perhaps women (writers) know from their own experience that expressing their sexual desire and acting upon it does not bring about a single, automatic reaction, such as liberation, but varied and multiple consequences depending on the moment and the situation. We saw this 1980s skepticism on the part of the woman writers foreshadowed in Clarice Lispector's *An Apprenticeship,* in which Lori's and Ulysses' euphoria and optimism are questioned by the novel's plot and the inscription of the dialogue. When we consider only those who produce a sexual fiction that revisits the social themes previously associated with the sexual woman character, male writers tend to predominate once again. *Praise* offers the irresistible advantage over other such works in that it treats narrowly and directly the promise of freedom that the 1960s writers thought inevitably accompanied the "newly sexed woman" in sexual fiction.

Although Lori from *An Apprenticeship* and Lucrecia from *Praise* share both a middle-class, urban, contemporary setting and elements of a liberated sexuality (which make them appropriate for consideration here), the experimentalism in each novel produces dramatically different meanings for female sexuality. *Praise* incorporates reproductions of paintings that are not assimilable to verbal discourse. In six chapters in which paintings are present, voices not tied to specific characters in the realistic frame story tell other narratives. That is, the Peruvian novel has an unusual multivocity and a visual-verbal heterogeneity affecting its message. In this chapter I show that through this multiplicity of discourses, Lucrecia is portrayed as a compliant feminine subjectivity: dominated, ever responding to the male other, and rarely resisting by asserting her own (sexual) desires. Progressively in action, thought, and imagination, Lucrecia is trapped through her sexuality in the web of male power relations, like the spider woman whose web grows from her body in Manuel Puig's *Kiss of the Spider Woman* (1979; *Beso de la mujer araña* 1976).

In contrast, *An Apprenticeship* has an apparent univocity in which the narrator and characters sound and think similarly about a philosophy of sexual liberation. Together they explicitly promote the idea that liberty results from a woman's active pursuit of meaningful sex. Additionally, Lori's increased social awareness at the end of her apprenticeship and Ulysses' socialism throughout mark them as characters who struggle against their own imperfections and for a better world. As we have seen, this essayistic message is deconstructed on the level of diegesis and in the scriptural qualities of the text, but never negated by a voice. The arrangement of the narrative questions the premise of an associated freedom for the woman's sexuality and provides a countermovement making evident the self-congratulatory satisfaction on the part of the characters and the gender hierarchy that they unconsciously reproduce. The characters seem unaware of the "unfreedoms" in which they live, the very ones that lead readers to understand *An Apprenticeship*'s ending as a pyrrhic victory over Lori's fear of domination. In Vargas Llosa's *Praise,* there is no such victory for a freedom achieved through female sexuality, pyrrhic or otherwise, since female sexuality is dramatically exorcized in the final pages. In the denouement, paradise is envisioned by Rigoberto as an asexual freedom *from* women, rather than sexual freedom *for* women. The only woman left in the house in the denouement, Justiniana, Lucrecia's maid, sees her permanence in her job threatened by unwanted sexual overtures. She, too, rejects sexuality as dangerous.

Justiniana's fears and Lucrecia's shocking sex with her stepson reveal in the Vargas Llosa novel a return to several themes treated in *Mulata* by Miguel Angel Asturias. Sexual women in Asturias battled antagonists in culture wars waged over the place of Native Americans and their cultures within modernity. Within the Guatemalan novel, female sexuality razed antiquated social structures and felled the people and spirits maintaining them. Basically, Asturias assigned the plotting of the struggle for sexuality for women almost exclusively to narrator comments and to the arrangement of events. Individual characters did not have access to a vision of the entire epic panorama. A destructive force, the Mulata was herself split and reduced until her immortality was lost; but the loss of the Mulata and her functions was to be mourned: it meant a victory for the senseless accumulation of goods and dead souls, without end. Balance was lost, and the world became the delirium of a priest with leprosy. The final apocalypse, seen through diseased eyes, retranslated female sexuality back into the excluded and evil excess it had most often been in Latin American fiction.

In broad strokes, it can be said that *Praise* revisits this sense of female sexuality as a destructive supplement, a dangerous resistance to priestly purity, that men may dally with at their own risk. Eduardo Béjar, for instance, attributes the final disaster to the female antagonist: "Lucrecia, unfaithful and incestuous wife, transgressing and monstrous, is the disturbance in Rigoberto's symbolic order" ["Lucrecia, esposa infiel e incestuosa, transgresora y monstruosa, es el trastorno del orden simbólico de Rigoberto" (253)]. While Asturias ridicules and undermines this anti-woman ideology, Vargas Llosa represents it as a reasonable reaction. Among critics, Béjar attempts more than most to give a positive spin to Vargas Llosa's plot, but even his sympathetic interpretation recognizes the danger Lucrecia's sexuality presents to her conservative family structure: "loving . . . constitutes in this way the calamity to the system of pleasures and retributions on which the husband's well-being as the controller and the consumer is founded" ["amar . . . constituye asimismo el descalabro del sistema de placeres y retribuciones en el que se funda el bienestar del marido en tanto controlador y consumidor" (253)].

Although the female sexuality in *Praise* has a thematic resemblance to that in *Mulata*, and though they both experiment formally in remarkably original ways, the novels' similarities should not be exaggerated. Other than their vision of female sexuality as destructive and their daringly creative novel forms, the two novels coincide in very little. The striking experiment of *Praise* comes from its mixing of kinds of "texts," especially of paintings and narratives within a single fiction. The reader passes from word to visual image and back to word, mentally adjusting the paintings to make them part of the fiction. As a consequence of the reader's search for a global understanding of the work, the paintings are temporarily read as elements of Vargas Llosa's story. No longer are they primarily paintings by Jacob Jordaens, Titian, François Boucher, Francis Bacon, Fernando de Szyszlo, or Fra Angelico—they are not extratextual. The art has been reassigned, reclassified, as text that communicates to the reader regarding Rigoberto, Lucrecia, Rigoberto's son Alfonso, and Lucrecia's maid, Justiniana.

The heterogeneity of *Praise* is even greater than it first appears because of two crucial differences between the Fernando de Szyszlo painting and the other five paintings reproduced for the reader. The Szyszlo pertains to the origin of the novel, and, in the frame story, the Szyszlo is the painting owned by the family and hanging in their living room. According to Vargas Llosa in a 1989 interview with Leopoldo Bernucci, the idea for *Praise* came from the painter Szyszlo himself, Vargas Llosa's good friend, who suggested they do a book together (Vargas Llosa "Entrevista" 373). In the interview Vargas Llosa reports that their plan was for Szyszlo's drawings to be more than mere illustrations of the writer's words, and for the verbal discourse to do more than merely describe or explain the other's drawings. Instead, the book would be created by the two together, reciprocally, in a constant process of mutual dialogue and influence. Vargas Llosa asserts that when the project with Szyszlo fell through, he resolved to write an erotic story in which "painting would have the role of a protagonist" ["la pintura tendría un papel protagónico"("Entrevista" 373)]. The single Szyszlo that is reproduced in *Praise* is *Road to Mendieta 10* [*Camino a Mendieta 10*], an abstract piece that plays a crucial role in the strategies for giving female sexuality a voice.

Reading the texts and the six paintings and understanding them as a novel is a process analogous to the surrealist technique of "communicating vessels" that Vargas Llosa has frequently discussed. Enkvist summarizes it in this way: the "procedure of *communicating vessels* consists of two or more stories told simultaneously, jumping from one to the other in order to obtain, consciously, the effect that they mutually influence each other. One receives the impression that there are secret and invisible ties between them."[4] The paintings reproduced for the reader, the narrations of the painting chapters, and the realist frame story interact in a nonexplicit manner through their juxtaposition: "The communicating vessels allow for making comparisons without saying so, for making contrasts, for showing that a character lies; they permit making the narration more dense and efficient. They involve the reader in the process of creation because the reader has to discover the game, judge the eventual contradictions, and draw his or her own conclusions, and all these things must be accomplished without obtaining, in general, any confirmation from the author that the reader has understood correctly."[5] The openness created by this technique constructs ambiguous meanings and makes readings vary from one reader to another.

Added to the heterogeneity of the visual and verbal texts, the purely verbal portions of the painting chapters contain vocabulary and syntax that, in some sense—emotional, moral, or aesthetic—approximate the images, historical period, or architecture of the individual paintings reproduced. In the first three paintings, from the sixteenth, seventeenth, and eighteenth centuries, for example, allusions to classical Greece and Rome freeze narrative moments. The paintings from the twentieth century—the fourth and fifth, respectively—partake of the abstract and nonallusive, yet manage to signal discourses, like those of psychology and pre-Columbian Peru, other than those of the classical world. The final painting, from the fifteenth century, inserts an iconic moment from Christian narrative into *Praise*. A constantly modulating verbal "language" approximating aspects of the paintings compounds the mixing of styles and imagery.

In each of the six chapters containing paintings, a first-person voice speaks as if it emanated from the painting itself. At times this ekphrastic voice is closely identified with a named figure in the painting and/or one from the realistic frame story. At the end of chapter 1, for instance, Rigoberto tells Lucrecia that he imagines her to be the wife of Candaules, King of Lydia. Rigoberto does not say more because he is already "lost in his dream" (11T) ["perdido en su sueño" (23)]. In chapter 2 we see first the Jacob Jordaens painting *Candaules, King of Lydia, Showing His Wife to Prime Minister Gyges*, then we read a first-person story told by Candaules about his wife. There is no text stating that we are reading Rigoberto's dream—no narrator commentary or peritextual material anchoring the voice of the Jordaens painting chapter in the frame—but it is logical to assume a connection between the Jordaens voice named Candaules and Rigoberto. The story told by Candaules is a separate, free-floating narrative, but it "communicates" with the contemporary, realist frame. The novel's strategy for the construction of meaning allows for the verbal portions of painting chapters to be closely associated with the dreams of a frame character *and* a free-floating narrative related to these characters only thematically, metaphorically. The paintings themselves also communicate primarily through comparison, but as part of Rigoberto's collection of erotica, they also have a metonymic relation to the frame story. Neither the similarity between Rigoberto's dream about being Candaules and Candaules' monologue, nor the fact that he is the frame character who knows who Candaules is, and who may have seen the Jordaens painting, is sufficient to prove that chapter 2 is in fact Rigoberto's dream, however. The paintings (or reproductions of them in books) belong to Rigoberto and are seen primarily by him, but this information does not definitely attribute all the painting monologues to his imagination.

The exact relation between each painting's voice and realist frame is an example of another of Vargas Llosa's frequent techniques: that of the "hidden fact" ["el dato escondido"], which the author describes thus:

"This method consists of *narrating by omission, or through meaningful omissions, in silencing temporarily or definitively certain facts of the story in order to give more emphasis or force to these very facts that have been momentarily or totally suppressed.* This premeditated emptiness suggests, that silence speaks, that mutilation perturbs, intrigues, contaminates the rest of the story with a certain enigmatic quality, a certain anxiety, and obligates the reader to intervene in the narration to fill the meaningful hole, adding, guessing, inventing, in active complicity with the narrator."[6] Philosopher Roman Ingarden's phenomenological theories of literature discuss the inevitability of reader participation to fill in gaps in all literary works necessitated by the nature of language. But Vargas Llosa is speaking about something more specific: a creative choice he makes as an author to withhold certain information in order to ensure greater reader participation than would normally exist in a story of facile comprehension. With *Praise,* what is unique is that one of the several highly significant omissions is not information about plot but form, that is, about the relation of the embedded narratives to the frame. On the one hand, this technique of omission ("hidden facts") of information prevents interpretations that treat all the ekphrastic voices as dreams of the frame characters from being convincing; we should resist the temptation to apply information about Candaules to Rigoberto. On the other hand, the author's technique of association ("communicating vessels") encourages interpretations that forge bridges across the silenced information, that compare disparate entities and read the text allegorically.

Many readers presume that all the voices in all the painting chapters are dreams of characters in the frame story because the first such voice seems so clearly to be Rigoberto's dream. As I suggested above, this presumption on the part of the reader is largely justified; in the case of experimental works, readers must put aside acquired habits of reading and simply learn how to read the new work in the process of doing so, from metatextual clues and from rereadings. Especially in those experimental works which, from the nature of the experiment, refuse to explain, clearly and from the beginning, how they construct their meaning, one often must use trial and error to discover how to endow them with sense. One experimental aspect of *Praise* lies precisely in such a lack of metafictional guidance, in not naming the exact relation between characters from the realistic frame story and those characters, like Candaules, occurring in the painting chapters. We readers sense they secretly converse with each other in what Béjar aptly calls a "semantic space of intertextual plurality" ["espacio semántico de pluralidad intertextual"(249)], but we must work to discover what is communicated and not assume it is information about the personality of frame characters.

It might be justified to subordinate the painting chapters to the frame story, owing to the prevalence and continued nature of the realist frame. Including the epilogue (which may be counted as either inside or outside the book), there are fifteen chapters, nine of which narrate the contemporary tale of Rigoberto's Lima family. Accordingly, some critics have assumed it is necessary to hypothesize possible characters in the realist frame story who dream or imagine the voice of a painting; whether Lucrecia dreams and speaks the three female ekphrastic monologues, for example. But in the process of subordination and focus on the realistic frame story, a significant portion of the novel's richness would be relegated to ornament or not taken into consideration.[7] Because attributing ekphrastic voices in the painting chapters to frame characters is so speculative and ultimately unproveable, my analysis relies sparingly on such argument. Another reason to resist the natural impulse to subsume the ekphrastic voices as mere dreams or fantasies of the frame characters is that in a narrative written at the end of the twentieth century, there can be little theoretical justification for giving priority to a tale set in contemporary times (the frame) over one set in historic times (for example, Candaules), based on the realist style in which the frame story is told. Realism is not truer than other styles; it only seems so.

Mario Vargas Llosa argued in *The Perpetual Orgy* (1986; *La orgía perpetua* 1975), his book on Flaubert: "The technique of objectivity [or realism] is aimed at reducing to an absolute minimum the 'imposition' [of a particular view] that every work of art inevitably entails. I do not maintain, naturally, that Flaubert's novels are free of all ideology, that they do not set forth a particular vision of society and humanity. I do maintain however, that in his case these ideas are not the cause but the effect of the work of art, which for the creator is not merely the consequence of a prior truth that he possesses and transmutes into fiction but the precise opposite: the search through artistic creation for a possible, and previously unknown, truth. Where Brecht and Flaubert differ is that in the latter the ideology is implicit in the fiction."[8]

My analysis aims to recognize that, while *Praise* is weighted toward the use of the objective for its power to convince, overvaluing the frame and undervaluing the embedded narratives and the paintings themselves is an unacceptable distortion of the novel as a whole. Vargas Llosa may want the typical reader to add his or her supplement in order to make sense across the silences of the "hidden facts," but the critic's task lies in signaling the text's silences more than in filling them in. Hence my search to name the novel's functionings in such a way as to compensate for the tendency to place greater emphasis on the realist frame than on the other types of texts within its mixture of styles.

In practice, if not in his conscious musings on his writings, Vargas Llosa's fiction combines realism with other genres, as if objective third-person narration were insufficient to tell the full tale. Like many of Vargas Llosa's late works, *Praise* alternates realism with other styles, as *Aunt Julia and the Scriptwriter* did with the radio soap operas and *The Storyteller* with the Machiguenga myths. Although in *Praise* Vargas Llosa appears to have moved away from a total dedication to the position that naturalness and objectivity ("realism") allow the reader the greatest freedom to interpret, the author still prefers little explicitness of authorial comment. When Vargas Llosa diverges from realism, as in the Bacon monologue, he adopts techniques of twentieth-century *implicit* conceptualization, such as surrealism or stream-of-consciousness, rather than a Brechtian alienation from mimesis for educational purposes. Both surrealism and stream-of-consciousness techniques aim at more inclusive definitions of the real, so that it includes psychological reality.

Postmodern writers today are wary of realism because "of the rhetorical subservience of language to the sway of forces that seek to validate . . . power by an ideology for which they claim a natural sanction" (Krieger 235). Keith Booker hypothesizes that even though Vargas Llosa "is ambivalent regarding the ultimate power of his art to effect radical social change, this ambivalence need not indicate surrender to the powers that be so much as a desire to avoid repeating the authoritarian gestures of those powers. In postmodernist culture, commitment and ambivalence need not be mutually exclusive" (186). During the period in which Vargas Llosa wrote *Praise,* and the time immediately afterward, he was the most directly involved in Peru's politics that he had ever been. Paradoxically, *Praise* manifests very few signs of the author's engagement of this sort; indeed, it may be categorized as the least involved with Peruvian politics of all his works to date. With its disaffected, individualistic, and hedonist protagonist, the novel and its sequel delve into personal politics, power within intimate relations, but there is no comment on the Peruvian political crisis its author would soon enter as a presidential candidate. In terms of sexual politics, in contrast, it is difficult to find ways in which the ambivalence of *Praise* does not "indicate surrender to the powers that be."

Murray Krieger has written intelligently in "A Postmodern Retrospect:

Semiotic Desire, Repression in the Name of Nature, and a Space for the Ekphrastic," a chapter in *Ekphrasis,* of the "semiotic desire for the natural sign," that is, about the justification and evaluation of cultural production in terms of its closeness to "nature," to that which exists. A preference for realism in the novel, like Vargas Llosa's or Flaubert's, may result from the desire for literature to appear lifelike, real, as if from "nature." Krieger warns that such an aesthetic theory "can use the aesthetic for subliminal political persuasiveness. Our desire to read the sign as natural can have effects that are dangerous as well as illuminating: it may reveal the idols of our culture but may also enslave us to them" (258). Though Krieger's argument is broader than I have space to take into account here, he suggests that by seeking to represent reality as objectively as possible, by trying to appear not to be literature at all, literature relinquishes its ability to convince readers that things could be otherwise than how they are. To gain this illusion of objectivity, literature must repeat the status quo. Hence, a realist style, an implicit and "objective" ideology, relies on conventionality and subtle, unconscious persuasions, rather than on engaging a reader's critical sense and conscious belief.

With this warning about the seductions of realism in mind, we must decide how best to read *Praise.* Overall interpretation, never easy in this novel, becomes particularly difficult because of the nonrealist embedded narratives. If we are to ascertain the role of the sexual woman characters—Lucrecia and the others—we must analyze all six interpolated ekphrastic stories as well as the frame. Additionally, the paintings often provide the best clues to understanding aspects of the painting stories and vice versa. The result of leaving out the painting monologues, or of only considering them less important, would be a distortion of the themes and a misunderstanding of the languages in which the novel constructs its meanings. In fact, to explain the textual strategy at work, it is best to start with a discussion of the paintings.

The first three paintings, those by Jordaens, Boucher, and Titian, exhibit a female body before the viewer's gaze. The first painting by Jacob Jordaens, in addition, points to male bonding occurring at such a moment of viewing a naked female body: Candaules, king of Lydia, shows his prime minister, Gyges, that his wife has an extraordinarily beautiful and sensual backside.[9] The king and prime minister in Jordaens's painting stand close together, united when they spy on the queen, and mistakenly believe that Candaules' wife has not seen them, in this scene based on ancient history as told by Livy. The painting placed second in the novel, François Boucher's *Diana at the Bath* [*Diana después de su baño*], prominently displays the naked goddess Diana and a nymph, as they dry off after a bath in a river. Titian's *Venus with Cupid and Music* [*Venus con el Amor y la Música*] features another naked goddess, reclining on a divan, with a fully dressed organist staring at her and stretching toward her while he keeps his hands on the organ's keys. The Titian closes the series of paintings relying on both Greek and Roman allusions for their narrative situation and the naked female body as the center of focus.

In the subsequent paintings, the female body is missing, made abstract, or deemphasized. At the same time, the latter three paintings are less readable as erotic. Painting number four, Francis Bacon's *Head I,* does not contain a body—female or male. Peruvian contemporary artist Fernando de Szyszlo painted the fifth, *Road to Mendieta 10* [*Camino a Mendieta 10*], which features abstracted forms, two of which are likely to be interpreted as human forms: one headless and legless, filled with curves and sticks as if a drawing of internal anatomy; the other more rectangular than a human body, as if the figure were wearing a costume, uniform, or protective and ornamental armor. The sixth and final painting, *The Annunciation,* by Fra Angelico, reverentially represents the fully clothed Virgin, who with beauty and grace, and without opulence, harmonically fills an elevated space. Hence four of the visual works treat a woman concretely, as a principal figure; the exceptions are the Bacon and the Szyszlo, although a case could perhaps be made for the latter as also containing a feminine form in the headless trunk covered (or filled) with curves.

The voices accompanying the paintings tend to parallel this pattern, in that the Bacon ekphrastic narrative is the one that mentions women (or a woman) less than the other five. The Szyszlo voice identifies itself as female and as the curvilinear headless trunk; in other words, the Szyszlo monologue concretizes the painting's abstract form by feminizing one of the figures in it as the female subject from which the voice emanates. That a male voice comes from a head with no body (in the Bacon monologue) and a female voice from a body with no head (in the Szyszlo monologue) is only one of the indicators that traditional gender hierarchies and paradigms are at work in the novel. The other ekphrastic voices identified as female come from the Boucher Diana figure, named Diana Lucrecia, and the Fra Angelico Madonna, while the Jordaens, Titian, and Bacon voices are male.

Each of the six painting chapters begins and ends a new narrative, with its own set of characters and its own space and historical setting. These monologues become *mises en abîme* of the frame story through their homologies, and yet their antitheses and allegories differentiate them from and comment on the frame. Additionally, they develop thematic material through form (especially the first-person monologue), and they furnish new content, introducing items not seen before into the narrative. For instance, in the Jordaens monologue, Candaules uses the metaphor of sex as knowledge: "I have studied her [his wife] as scholars ponder the ancient volumes of the Temple, and though I think I know her by heart, each day—each night, rather—I discover something new about her that touches me" (15T) ["Yo la he estudiado como hacen los eruditos con los viejos infolios del Templo, y aunque creo saberla de memoria, cada día—cada noche, más bien—descubro en ella algo nuevo que me enternece" (29)]. We learn from the Titian monologue that the speaker, Love, is a pornographer: "kindling the lady's bodily joy, poking up the ashes of each one of her five senses till they burst into flame, and peopling her fair-haired head with filthy fantasies" (70T) ["despertar la alegría corporal de la señora, avivando las cenizas de cada uno de sus cinco sentidos hasta volverlas llamarada y en poblar su rubia cabeza de sucias fantasías" (98)].

The strategy *Praise* employs to construct its ideology of the "newly sexed woman" is that of the discovery. In *The Oxford English Dictionary*, one of the earliest meanings of *discovery* still used is the "unraveling or unfolding of the plot of a play, poem, etc." This sense of *discovery* applies to the ending of the novel, when the plot is fully revealed and poetic justice does or does not become apparent. A second meaning of *discovery* as a strategy employed in *Praise* is the word's legal sense: the setting forth of facts or explanation, especially the disclosure of information necessary to maintain a claim to a title to property. Alfonso's school essay, "In Praise of the Stepmother," would be such a legal "discovery" because he reclaims his father's attentions and removes his stepmother from consideration. *Discovery* also contains within it the sense of "dis-cover-y," or the process of revealing secrets, as in the novel's climax of Rigoberto's sudden knowledge of his wife's affair with his son, but also (and more frequently), in the sense of uncovering the body, disrobing, in preparation for the nightly amours of husband and wife, for bathing and going to the toilet. In the past, the word *discovery* also meant a manifestation, a displaying, as when "Diana at the bath" or Lucrecia in her bath discovers herself. As an entity, a "discovery" would be Vargas Llosa's "hidden fact," which exists long before it is known. As a process of agency, a "discovery" detects the unknown, such as how juxtaposed elements communicate. As a process of resistance, a discovery fights the attempt to "cover," to close or to hide. *Praise* discovers female sexuality as a source of resistance and agency that males manipulate in their struggles for control.

In naming the novel's strategy the "discovery," I have been forced to discard some very apt alternatives for the way *Praise* combines themes, plot, and characterization, including the invention, the dream, the improvisation, the embodiment, and the performance. I decided not to call the strategy any of these in large part because of the silenced nature of the relation between the painting narratives and the realist frame. I discussed above the suggestion that Candaules is "really" Rigoberto imagining or dreaming, and that accepting this mere possibility as definitive sacrifices the fullness of the embedded narrative and gives unjustified priority to the contemporary tale over the ekphrastic monologue. The identification of Lucrecia with the Szyszlo voice causes similar difficulties for the same reasons. On the one hand, Lucrecia does tell her invented story of the Szyszlo painting to Rigoberto. We read: "She explained and he understood" (116T) ["Ella se lo explicó y él entendió" (152)]. On the other hand, chapter 12, "Labyrinth of Love" ["Laberinto de amor"], need not be the story she invented and explained to him. An alternative explanation — admittedly suggested by the strategies of the sequel, *The Notebooks of Don Rigoberto* — are that all the painting voices come from Rigoberto, that he pretends to be or dreams all the ekphrastic voices, no matter which characters seem most analogous to them. According to this theory, Rigoberto in his own way imagines Lucrecia inventing the Szyszlo painting and speaks or fantasizes as if he were she. But this possibility cannot be affirmed or denied. Such identifications come from reader associations rather than metafictional text or peritext, and I want to name what the text does and does not do, including the text's attempt to force the reader to jump to unsubstantiated conclusions. The other possible names for the novel's functioning suffer from the same tendency of being propitious for such an identification of sources for the ekphrastic voices in specific frame characters.

The alternatives for "discovery" present further difficulties beyond falling for the text's seductive web of analogies without textual confirmation. A strategy of "improvisation" would overly emphasize oral qualities, and a freedom in the arrangement of the plot, whereas more than most novels, *Praise* incorporates visual qualities and a fixed sequence of events with little ambiguity about what is said by whom or where. There is a great deal of mystery about what happened in Alfonso's mind and why, but this enigma is caused by the omission of information, not by free or changing versions of one story. Alfonso's interior at the end remains as unknown to the reader as at the beginning, a "hidden fact" ["dato escondido"] never discovered. Another discarded name for the novel's strategies, "embodiment," explains well one kind of relation between the paintings and the painting chapters, but this denomination could lead one to fall victim to prejudices that favor the visual over the verbal, the figural over the abstract, the realist over the nonrealist, and that which is embodied in characters over that which is free-floating in discourse and thus not embodied. In other words, while "embodiment" may have everything to do with fantasy versus reality, in that Rigoberto did not expect Lucrecia to act upon his fantasies for or about her, causing Rigoberto's dilemma and Lucrecia's tragedy, the idea of "embodiment" does not provide a neutral ground or context for understanding how the binaries like fantasy and reality are manifested. "Performance" comes very close to focusing on such a ground for comprehension of the plot and themes in both the realist and nonrealist narratives, but it must be discarded for reasons similar to that of the improvisation. "Performance" emphasizes the misleading idea that the theatrical is primary. It is true that the ekphrastic voices are performative, inventing the worlds they narrate, but on a literal level that is true of all fiction and does not help to describe how *Praise* acts in particular. If I called the novel's strategy for constructing its world the "performance," the major theme of freezing time in the visual would be lost as well. Thus it is unhelpful for describing *Praise* in its thematic specificity.

So, what do we discover about female sexuality and the "newly sexed woman"? That the danger of female sexuality pervades the language of *Praise* in every chapter, affecting both men and women. For Lucrecia, who comes to believe in freely expressing and acting on her sexual desires through Rigoberto's urging, the danger lies in the trap her new sexuality sets for her, because she is not really as free to act as she believes. For instance, Lucrecia worries: "No, Fonchito couldn't have any intimation that he was playing with fire; those effusions were doubtless prompted by a vague instinct, an unconscious tropism. They were dangerous games, nonetheless, weren't they Lucrecia?" (34T) ["No, Fonchito no podía sospechar que aquello era jugar con fuego, esas efusiones se las dictaba sin duda un oscuro instinto, un tropismo inconsciente. Pero, aun así, no dejaban de ser juegos peligrosos ¿verdad, Lucrecia?" (54)]. Rigoberto and his son Alfonsito incite her to sex, but characters are not the only elements of the novel's discourse that contribute to this portrait of entrapped female sexuality; the omniscient narration, the paintings, and the voices from them urge women characters to be sexual and also suggest the sexual woman's demise. This suggestion of catastrophe for sexual women manifests itself through varied allusions to the high art of the West. Considering the novel's discourse as a whole, including women in addition to

Lucrecia—Justiniana, who fears for her job, and the female ekphrastic voices—the "new" female sexuality proves to be bad business all around for the woman who is "newly sexed."

In comparison to the other two works I have analyzed in detail, however, it would not be accurate to say that female sexuality endangers the entire fictive world of *Praise* as it did that of Asturias's *Mulata,* because Rigoberto's middle-class world is represented as monumental and impervious to assault. Only individuals within it can be harmed or modified. Considering only the effect of female sexuality on individuals, few readers could disagree that Lucrecia and her attitude toward sex receive the novel's blame for destroying her husband's happiness. Critic Rafael Lampugnani, for instance, writes that she is "a weak but sensual character who exploits her sexuality to win acceptance in the family" (211). For Rigoberto, the danger of female sexuality lies in its disruption of his patriarchal family unit, in its threat to his domination of Lucrecia, when female sexuality is not adequately controlled by him. Some critics and readers (rightly) fault Alfonso for his part in the quasi-incestuous affair, but the novel portrays him as extremely young and never gives unassailable evidence as to his culpability.

There should be no doubt that female sexuality in *Praise* touches social issues of gendered sex relations. Speaking generally, Sara Castro-Klarén wrote: "Women, who in the novels f Vargas Llosa act out stereotypical roles of the place of woman in the most patriarchal of societies, seem to have a single desire: to have relations with the man who turns out not to be too cruel or evil. The rate of exchange charged for this negation of self is equivalent to all the services that a woman with her body and social being can give to that man inside and outside the home."[10] Regarding this particular novel, another critic wrote: "it is precisely Don Rigoberto's drive for mastery over the physical that informs Lucrecia's relationship with the boy. The phrase 'I have won sovereignty' . . . comes to Lucrecia's mind when she thinks of this relationship, and this echo of Chaucer's Wife of Bath indicates that her relationship with Alfonsito may be a subconscious reaction against the domineering attitude of her husband" (Booker 175). *Praise* sympathizes with Rigoberto when he expels the duplicitous Lucrecia. Nonetheless, it should be pointed out from the start that Lucrecia's expulsion from his house "may also be considered positive as freedom from her role of serving and dependence" ["puede ser también considerada positivamente como su libertad del rol de servicio y dependencia" (Béjar 253)].

An important example of the novel's use of allusions from Western art and history to refer to the struggles for control of female sexuality is Lucrecia's name, which draws attention to the political nature of the dangers that await the character. In Ovid's *Fasti* and Livy's *The History of Rome,* Lucretia's famous story begins when Roman soldiers off at war console themselves by speaking to one another about the purity and chastity of their wives at home. The soldier-husbands begin to compete with one another, each claiming to possess the most chaste wife. Returning home to check on the wives, the husbands discover that Collatinus's wife, Lucretia, is the only woman who was chaste. The leader of the soldier-husbands engaged in the wager and son of the tyrant, Sextus Tarquin, next "conceived a villainous desire to force Lucretia's virtue; not her beauty alone but her proven chastity pricked him on" (Livy 1.57). At the first opportunity, Tarquin forces himself on her. Lucretia dramatically reveals to her husband and to her father that Tarquin has raped her and, to prove her innocence, commits suicide in front of them. Together with Lucretia's family, Brutus broadcasts the perfidy of the rapist, and war against the tyrant begins. The republic of Rome is eventually founded when this war ends the reign of the Tarquins.

According to Nancy Vickers, Shakespeare "conceives the precipitating causes of the rape—Collatine's boast of his wife's chastity and Tarquin's reaction to her beauty—within the poetic tradition of the blazon, 'shaped predominantly by the male imagination for the male imagination . . . in large part, the product of men talking to men about women'" (Vickers, quoted in Kahn 144). Like the proverbial locker-room boasting of sexual conquests, male bonding reveals itself in the Lucretia story as rivalry, and results in Tarquin's predatory behavior.[11] Lucrece is the direct victim of Tarquin's violence, but important for almost all versions of the tale, Tarquin also violates male solidarity by transgressing against the husband's proprietary relationship to his wife. Collatine's property is sullied. Tarquin's rape of Lucrece is a transgression against Collatine's friendship, honor, and property, and thus a metaphor for the dictatorial and brutal nature of Tarquin's ruling family.[12] Additionally, in Shakespeare, "the inner consistency and dramatic intensity of Lucrece's verbal struggle against her assailant arises from its anatomy of marriage as the institution that effects male control of women's sexuality and thus determines the sexual politics of Roman (and English) society" (Kahn 150–51). Like Shakespeare's Lucrece, Vargas Llosa's Lucrecia is first and foremost a wife caught between two males.

The ancient history of Lucretia shares certain elements with that of Candaules' wife, the narrative moment displayed in the first painting,

Candaules, King of Lydia, Showing His Wife to Prime Minister Gyges, by Jacob Jordaens. In the Greek historian Herodotus' telling, Candaules' wife discovers that her husband has invited Gyges to her room to see her naked backside: her body has been discussed by the men and then put on show by one for the other.[13] Both Candaules' wife and Shakespeare's Lucrece suffer from male speech about their sexuality: in the former, Candaules brags about his wife's body to his prime minister; in the latter, Collatine brags about his wife's virtue to other soldiers. Furthermore, two kingdoms fall because male solidarity is later altered by female revenge: Candaules' wife delivers an ultimatum (kill the king or be killed by the queen) to Prime Minister Gyges; Lucrece asks Collatine to avenge her rape then kills herself. Rigoberto would like to have that kind of solidarity with another man (or, in this case a boy, his son), but only in fantasy, as a sexual goad. Later, Rigoberto discovers that his son is indeed a "Tarquin" or a "Gyges," that is, a sexual male ready to violate his "property," and not merely a fantasy available as a sexual stimulus as he had wanted.

Although similar in the betrayal of marriage and in having political consequences, there are several important differences between the narratives of Shakespeare's Lucrece, Candaules' wife in Herodotus, and Vargas Llosa's Lucrecia. In the two other literary works, Shakespeare's Lucrece and Candaules' wife are astute, political women not interested in the pleasures of sexuality. Not so in Vargas Llosa. Candaules' wife in the Jordaens painting smiles to the viewer with worldly amusement; in the Jordaens monologue, Candaules' wife is "never so eager to take the initiative, to respond, never so bold at biting, kissing, embracing" (21T) ["nunca tan ávida en la iniciativa y en la réplica, tan temeraria en el mordisco, el beso y el abrazo"(36)], as when Gyges is watching. While for Shakespeare's Lucrece sexuality was equal to shame, for Vargas Llosa's Lucrecia sexuality is a matter of a developing pride cultivated in her by her husband. Like Ulysses teaching Lori in *An Apprenticeship,* Rigoberto has an apt pupil in "liberated" sexuality for a wife. At the crucial point in the novel when Lucrecia is about to narrate her own fantasy based on the painting by Fernando de Szyszlo, Rigoberto asserts his surprise at her increased sexual awareness and inventiveness: "How much you've changed, Lucrecia. Not only do I love you with all my heart and soul now. I also admire you" (116T) ["Cuánto has cambiado, Lucrecia. Ahora no sólo te quiero con toda mi alma. También te admiro" (153)]. His admiration is for her ability to verbalize explicitly and inventively about her sexual desires. At this moment, flattered by Rigoberto's admiration, Lucrecia is suffering her greatest delusions, blissfully unaware that her happiness is about to end.

In addition to its allusions to sullied innocence in the sexual dealings of married women with the names Lucrecia and Candaules' wife, the story of *Praise* reminds us of the famous Greek myth of Phaedra: the story of a stepmother's love for her stepson. Euripides' tragedy *Hippolytus* closely balances in a stalemate Phaedra's grand passion and Hippolytus's grand virginity—there is no corollary to Lucrecia's thoughtlessness and Alfonso's seeming lack of understanding. In Racine's *Phèdre,* the French tragedian prefers the heroic battle between desire and taboo to be internal; Racine's stepmother is doomed to love her stepson despite her own internal, verbalized struggles against it. In Vargas Llosa, sexual passion appears to have no antagonist other than a discounted prudery.[14] Extreme youth (Alfonso in the minds of his father and stepmother) and shame (Justiniana) are ineffective palliatives to sexuality as motivator and controller of actions. Different from both Phaedra antecedents, Lucrecia converts to Rigoberto's sexual philosophy with very little resistance, verbalized or internalized. An inversion of her Roman namesake, Lucrecia falls victim to her belief that when her husband incites her to fantasize infidelity, he was encouraging her to partake of sexual freedom, free love, in her actions as well. *Praise* displays little contradiction between the early Lucrecia—who had refused to marry Rigoberto for a time because she worried she would not be accepted by his son—and the Lucrecia who receives the son's inexpert advances as if she were a prostitute contracted for the purpose of his sexual education. She does not understand that Rigoberto wants her freedom to be a shared fantasy, not a reality. Encouraged by her husband, Lucrecia becomes perpetually ready, open to any and all sexual advances, and to lust for lust's sake. In her lack of understanding, there is a lack of psychological depth in Lucrecia's characterization consistent with the schematic quality of the other characters, who, with the exception of Rigoberto, are more typical of pornography or popular literature than high art.[15] Lucrecia rapidly loses her sense of appropriateness, her moral values. From Rigoberto's point of view, however, her action of attributing to herself the sexual freedom he prizes transforms her from a beloved wife into a rebel and a traitor. He discovers his mistake too late, losing his wife, his sexual philosophy, and even finding it difficult to love his son.

Dangerous Discoveries

> According to Foucault, the preferred strategy is to "desexualize"
> sexuality by multiplying and diffusing pleasures, in order to can-
> cel the now-obsolete understanding of it as a circumscribed do-
> main fundamentally opposed to power and the law.
> **Winifred Woodhull, "Sexuality, Power, and the Question of Rape" (169)**

Sexuality expresses power, channels it; sexuality cannot be free from the grasp of power relations because it is a discourse about human relations, and power is intrinsic to human interaction. In this section, "Dangerous Discoveries," I trace one extended and implicit discovery made by readers about Lucrecia to demonstrate how it affects the construction of female sexuality. Then in the next section, "Discovering Power," what is discovered by several female characters is compared and analyzed. A detailed commentary on the Szyszlo chapter and on Lucrecia's feeling of sovereignty in the realist frame story again brings to light this strategy of discovery and the catastrophe foretold by the nature of what characters discover. But first, a few brief examples to illustrate the frequency of the textual maneuver of the discovery.

Some stories within *Praise* reflect the danger to men of discoveries of information. Alfonsito begins the revelation of his sex with his stepmother with an ingenuous question (the answer to which he already knew): "What does orgasm mean, Papa?" (126T) ["¿Qué quiere decir orgasmo, papá?" (168)]. Rigoberto is incredulous that Lucrecia could have talked to the boy about her orgasms, and cannot even imagine that the orgasm she talked to Alfonso about was actually from having made love to him: "They were products of Fonchito's imagination," Rigoberto thought, "something quite typical of his age: he was *discovering* wickedness, his sexual curiosity was surfacing, his awakening libido was prompting fantasies so as to bring conversations around to the fascinating taboo" (129T, emphasis added) ["Eran fantasías de Fonchito, algo muy típico de su edad: *descubría* la malicia, afloraba la curiosidad sexual, la líbido le sugería fantasías a fin de provocar conversaciones sobre el fascinante tabú" (171–72, emphasis added)]. Facing the bait Alfonso placed within his reach, however, Rigoberto has as few defenses as Lucrecia. He wants to know the whole story. Not only is Rigoberto's resistance to Alfonsito's manipulations as slight as Lucrecia's, his feelings at the moment of greatest danger are described similarly as "malaise" (129T, 131T) ["malestar" (171, 173)].[16] Rigoberto cannot resist asking Alfonsito to reveal more; thus he learns the truth. In this most obvious example of discovery, Rigoberto discovers too late that Alfonso is indeed sexual. As Rigoberto waits for Alfonsito to bring him his composition, the father laughs nervously, "with a grin that the glass of the bookcase full of erotica beamed back at him" (131T) ["naciendo una mueca lastimosa que le devolvió el cristal del estante libidinoso" (174)]. This reflection suggests that another "hidden fact"—hidden from Rigoberto, if not from the reader—is the extent to which he sows the seeds for the affair that causes him such pain.

Other examples are the voice of the Fra Angelico chapter, Maria, and the two Justinianas, who speak of their discovery that, in a world without clear morals, consisting of parodic righteousness and bourgeois conventionality, female sexuality is a locus where women are manipulated. It is true that Maria does not manage to learn exactly what has happened to her, nor what it means, when she is visited by the angel. But through her questions and her sense of alarm, we can ascertain that Maria has discovered to her chagrin that she is not in control of her life: "Why did I discover a gleam of tears in his eyes when he prophesied that I would suffer? Why did he call me mother if I am a virgin? What is happening? What is going to become of me after this visit?" (140T) ["¿Por qué descubrí un brillo de lágrimas en sus ojos cuando me vaticinó que sufriría? ¿Por qué me llamó madre si soy virgen? ¿Qué está sucediendo? ¿Qué va ser de mí a partir de esta visita?" (186)]. In the epilogue that follows Maria's questions, the narrator informs us that Justiniana of the frame story suffers from the similar realization that she is surrounded by more powerful forces, lying in wait to catch her: "Since Doña Lucrecia's departure, she [Justiniana] had had a foreboding that some sort of danger lay in wait for her here, and was on the edge all the time, with the constant feeling that if she let down her guard even for a moment, she, too, would fall into a trap and come out of it in worse shape than the stepmother" (146T) ["Desde la partida de doña Lucrecia tenía el presentimiento de que también a ella la acechaba un peligro aquí y vivía sobre ascuas, con la permanente sensación de que si se descuidaba un instante caería también en una emboscada de la que saldría peor que la madrastra" (194–95)]. Justiniana has discovered that Alfonsito may be one of those people setting sexual traps into which she may fall. The other Justiniana, the nymph who accompanies the goddess Diana Lucrecia in the Boucher ekphrastic chapter, like the maid of the realistic frame, discovers a male voyeur watching her mistress taking a bath. In these three examples of female characters, the women discover unwanted, unsolicited male intervention in their lives due to sexuality.

Michel Foucault "maintains that to designate sexuality as the locus of our freedom—as if it stood outside and against power—is to fall victim to a ruse of power" (Woodhull 168). Vargas Llosa's "liberated" woman, Lucrecia is fooled at least twice by the "ruse of power" that says repression is the only way power manifests itself in sexuality. First Lucrecia believes that Alfonsito is asexual, that he means her no harm, and that he cannot force her to do what he wants. Since she believes that his sexual provocations (kissing, petting) cannot cramp her freedom, she blames only herself for her sexual excitement upon receiving his attentions. Second, she never suspects that Rigoberto's influence on her may indeed be power over her, forming her and initiating the resistance she eventually shows to him. By expressing and practicing the sexuality Rigoberto encourages in her, she believes she can become more free, independent, and conscious; instead, she loses perspective and transgresses her own limits. With both males, Lucrecia is pressured to produce sexuality, and she (mis)understands the pressure and manipulation as a greater freedom to act as she wishes. She never makes the realization that power over her can provoke genuine sexual desire in her, in addition to repressing it at other times. Even the desire to fight against a power can be induced by that power. Similarly, the reader is likely to see Lucrecia's blindness to her manipulation by others as a lack of judgment, an immorality and an inability to act on her moral beliefs, as Rigoberto eventually does.

Before Alfonso interprets the Szyszlo painting, Lucrecia's initial resistance to him is primarily a denial that there could be anything sexual in his advances: "When the thin lips brushed hers, she clenched her teeth in confusion. Did Fonchito know what he was doing? Ought she to push him away? No, of course not. How could there be the least perversity in the mad fluttering of those mischievous lips that twice, three times, wandering over the geography of her face, alighted on hers for an instant, hungrily pressing down on them" (7T).[17]

Lucrecia sees him as an angel, genderless and sexless, with his head of blond curls and aura of innocence. Lucrecia worries that she misinterprets Fonchito's overtures as sexual; she thinks: "Would she one day become a hot-to-trot older woman, like some of her bridge cronies? Was that what was meant by the devil at midday, the passion of women of a certain age?" (35T) ["¿Se volvería un día una vieja fragorosa, como algunas de sus compañeras de bridge? ¿Sería esto el demonio del mediodía?"(55)]. In a process that repeats itself, Lucrecia considers the idea that Alfonso is coming on to her, but rejects the prospect, because of his age, because of her age, or simply because it is a reality his physical appearance seems to deny.

In fact, his childlike attractiveness provides him a "cover" from which to act without the negative consequences that would be normal in such a situation. Lucrecia's image of Alfonso's innocence as fragile, her idea that sex is an act free of power relations, and her concern that she might invade her stepson's purity, all rely on the "ruse of power" that says freedom inhabits sex, while domination manifests itself as repression. Lucrecia becomes angry when she learns that Alfonsito is on the roof peeping on her while she takes a bath. She displays herself obscenely to him because: "she had the presentiment that what she was doing was also a subtle way of punishing the precocious libertine crouched in the darkness up above, with images of an intimacy that would shatter, once and for all, that innocence that had served him as an excuse for his boldness" (43–44T).[18]

According to Lucrecia's Repressive Hypothesis, Alfonso must be on the roof because he is repressing his sexual urges; he is afraid to speak to her directly and so his libido seeks other outlets instead, such as spying on her. When Lucrecia exhibits herself to him aggressively, she forces him to deal with greater urges that still have no outlet, that is, she forces him to repress himself more. Hence she thinks she punishes him. Another interpretation, however, is that his spying is an unwanted act of sexual aggression in which he forces himself on her. When in response she displays herself more luridly, she in fact does his bidding, rewarding and encouraging his behavior. In this way, Lucrecia unknowingly teaches Alfonso that his manipulations may bear fruit and what those delicious fruits might be like. The "ruse" of Alfonso's power is that it appears to Lucrecia as powerlessness, and thus temporarily prevents her discovery that, through her production of sexuality, through her active disclosure of her body to Alfonso (and to Rigoberto), she loses her inner-directedness. Rather than gaining liberation through sex, Lucrecia forfeits her other, previous pleasures (her marriage, her home, her love) in a network of power relations that seek her progressive sexualization.

Meditating after her ostentatious display to Alfonso in her bath, Lucrecia first blames herself, then Rigoberto, then Alfonso: "Could it be because she'd turned forty? Or a consequence of those nocturnal fantasies and bizarre caprices of her husband? But it was all Alfonsito's fault. That child is corrupting me, she thought, disconcerted" (44T) ["¿Serían los cuarenta años? ¿O algún efecto de esas fantasías y extravagancias nocturnas de su marido? No, la culpa era toda de Alfonsito. 'Ese niño me está corrompiendo,' pensó, desconcertada" (64)]. Consciously or not, the child Alfonsito plays Lucrecia like a musical instrument: first worrying Justiniana enough with the thought of his suicide so that she tells Lucrecia, next worrying Lucrecia enough so that she is reconciled to him. After trying to resist, then having kept Alfonsito at a distance, in a different tactic of punishment for spying on her from the bathroom roof, suddenly she "embraced and caressed him, free of all constraint, a stranger to herself, and as though caught in the eye of a storm" (84T) ["lo abrazó y lo acarició, libre de trabas, sintiéndose otra y como en el corazón de una tormenta" (114)]. She feels odd, not herself, and attacked as if by forces of nature. A few moments later, responding to his avid kisses, "she hugged the boy to her, and with no inhibitions, went on kissing him with an impetuousness and a wantonness [freedom] that mounted step by step with her desire" (84–85T) ["estrechó al niño contra sí y, sin inhibiciones, siguió besándolo con un ímpetu y una libertad que crecían al ritmo de su deseo" (115)]. The narrator's language, speaking of her surrender to Alfonso as done with "a freedom" ["una libertad"], betrays the belief—so common that it is invisible in our way of speaking—that participation in sex, unlike any other act, cannot be coerced, that her kissing and making love to her stepson must be done of her free will. Alfonsito's advances lead to an explosion of her uncontrolled desire, but this so-called freedom is from her own sense of self and what she wants.

One should question whether there is indeed a self, an authentic, original core of an individual, that guides behavior, because it obscures our ability to see the context in which the individual moves as a significant factor in his or her behavior. But realist characters are normally portrayed as having such a "sense of self." This sense of self includes most significantly the subject's awareness of the way in which its various subject positions can be reconciled (at that time, in that place). In terms of Lucrecia, her sense of self is represented as precisely a reconciliation of the contradictions between her beliefs before meeting Rigoberto and Alfonso and the values they encourage in her. She progressively discards her previous moral standards and adopts the pro-sexuality stance of Alfonso and Rigoberto. Lucrecia hears an inner voice of restraint but ignores it in favor of the new desire Rigoberto and son have taught her.[19] After her truce with Alfonsito is interrupted by Rigoberto's arrival, she recovers her composure but for the rest of the evening hears inside her a warning voice that something is amiss: "there was a hidden malaise in Doña Lucrecia that did not leave her for an instant, an edginess that, every so often, made her shiver and her stomach feel hollow" (86T) ["había en doña Lucrecia un escondido malestar que no la abandonó un instante, una desazón que, de tanto en tanto, le producía un escalofrío y le ahuecaba el vientre" (116)]. Alfonso's manipulations have produced an inner discord and sense of guilt; Rigoberto, meanwhile, diligently works to rid her of the remaining inhibitions that curb her full enjoyment of pleasure.

By the climax of the novel, Lucrecia no longer has faith in marriage's tenets of masculine sexual prerogative and male authority; she discovers it intensifies her pleasure to imagine transgressing marriage's limits, and she has been taught in her marriage to place pleasure above all else. By "breaking" what Lucrecia has learned to regard as repressive social limits on her sexuality, those weighted toward female constraint and passivity, she believes she becomes more powerful. As she is about to follow lovemaking with Alfonsito by lovemaking with Rigoberto, to follow dinner with "dessert" (the "sobremesa" of the chapter title), for instance, there is little doubt that she feels strong: "She felt neither shame nor remorse. Nor did she consider herself a cynic. It was as though the world were docilely submitting to her" (109T) ["No sentía remordimiento ni vergüenza. Tampoco se consideraba una cínica. Era como si el mundo se plegara a ella, dócilmente" (145)]. When transgressing against the very sexual mores she had formerly believed in, against the personal obstacle of her internalization of Western culture's codes of behavior for women, Lucrecia feels a thrill from the risks she is taking: "It had been more powerful than her sense of danger, an uncontrollable ecstasy" (108T) ["Había sido más fuerte que su sentido del peligro, un arrebato incontenible" (144)].

Lucrecia indeed has been prepared for the night with Rigoberto by Fonchito's desperate kissing. She cannot get the boy out of her mind: "that intruding proximity, that curious angelical presence did not detract from her pleasure, but, on the contrary, enhanced it with a feverish, disturbing piquancy" (86T) ["esa vecindad intrusa, esa presencia mirona y angelical no empobrecía, más bien condimentaba su placer con una esencia turbadora, febril" (117)]. As Vargas Llosa explains, Georges Bataille "maintained that it was very important for there to be taboos, certain brakes, because he said that the transgression of those brakes, when there was a risk that one took, not only was the pleasure much, much greater, but it also produced in the individual a spiritual, intellectual, and moral enrichment. In this I coincide a great deal with Bataille."[20] Being married increases the commitment of a couple to each other and augments the negative social consequences of sexually transgressive acts; thus, in Vargas Llosa's interpretation of Bataille, marriage simultaneously increases the eroticism of extramarital affairs and the personal "enrichment" gained from them. Whatever the gain in autonomy from eroticism, however, the person who continues to pay a heavier price for marital indiscretions is the woman.[21]

Lucrecia is contaminated in her thoughts by Rigoberto's language, his job, his erotic pictures.[22] She wants to believe in Rigoberto's illusions of immortality and sovereignty. She worries that their happiness may come to an end, but since it has not yet, she tells herself that perhaps it never will (113–16T; 149–50). If it continues, she was convinced that her husband, and not her stepson or herself, would be the "fortunate beneficiary of her happiness" (115T) ["dichoso beneficiario de su felicidad" (150)], as if she had bought one of his insurance policies against the loss of her happiness, and signed the benefits over to him. But then doubts intrude: "Sooner or later, the whole thing will end badly. Reality is never as perfect as fiction" (114T) ["tarde o temprano, acabará mal. La realidad nunca era tan perfecta como las ficciones" (150)].

The most important discoveries made by a female character, however, occur in part symbolically and require explication. Lucrecia does not suspect any danger lurking in the Szyszlo painting *Road to Mendieta 10*, but she discovers there, and in herself, the landscape of her domination. Little Alfonso declares to his stepmother, mysteriously, that the Szyszlo painting is simultaneously Lucrecia's portrait and "something dirty" (105T, 112T): "'So I know now what's meant by an abstract painting,' the youngster reflected, without raising his head from the pillow. 'A dirty picture!'" (107T) ["'Entonces, ahora ya sé lo que quiere decir un cuadro abstracto' —reflexionó el niño, sin levantar la cara de la almohada—'¡Un cuadro cochino!'" 143]. *Road to Mendieta 10*, Szyszlo's painting reproduced in *Praise*, exhibits abstract forms that suggest figures associated with pre-Columbian Peru, including an altar of sacrifice. Lucrecia's first reaction to Alfonso's declaration is to rediscover the living room painting, which has suddenly become vaguely dangerous for having previously hidden its capacity to involve her: "It was as if she had never seen it before, as if the painting, like a serpent or a butterfly, had changed appearance and nature" (115T) ["Fue como si nunca lo hubiera visto antes, como si el cuadro, igual que una serpiente o una mariposa, hubiera mudado de apariencia y de ser"(151)]. Her new vision of the painting causes Lucrecia to be afflicted by inner presentiments of her future tragedy: forebodings assail her. Plus Lucrecia begins to suspect a sinister character beneath Alfonsito's angelic exterior: "something perverse like those tentacled creatures that dwell in the depths of ocean paradises" (112T) ["algo perverso, como esas bestias tentaculares que anidan en lo profundo de los paradisíacos océanos" (148)].[23] She has an intimation of evil within him because he attributed sexuality to this abstract work he has decided is her portrait.

For all his young age and supposed innocence, Alfonsito changes Lucrecia's way of viewing the Szyszlo painting and herself. Provoked by his declaration, Lucrecia examines the painting again, eventually agreeing with her stepson, seeing it differently than before. But she does not see it exactly as he does. She conceptualizes it as a sexual allegory for the love triangle of herself, the father, and the son. Nevertheless, it is significant that Alfonso manipulates Lucrecia's interpretation of the Szyszlo painting, just as his threats of suicide, his peeping on her in her bath, and his unseemly caresses have aggressively intruded on her intimate space and affected her relationship with Rigoberto.

This contradiction that Alfonsito's power over her, his ability to manipulate her to achieve his goals, is precisely the force that allows her to begin to resist the imposition of his will and is an example of Butler's "paradox of subjection," in which the powers that dominate are also those that form a subject, including the subject's powers of resistance and agency. In her introduction to *The Psychic Life of Power: Theories in Subjection,* Judith Butler writes:

> To be dominated by a power external to oneself is a familiar and agonizing form power takes. To find, however, that what "one" is, one's very formation as a subject, is in some sense dependent upon that very power is quite another. We are used to thinking of power as what presses on the subject from the outside, as what subordinates, sets underneath, and relegates to a lower order. . . . But if, following Foucault, we understand power as *forming* the subject as well, as providing the very condition of its existence and the trajectory of its desire, then power is not simply what we oppose but also, in a strong sense, what we depend on for our existence and what we harbor and preserve in the beings that we are. . . . Subjection consists precisely in this fundamental dependency on a discourse we never chose but that, paradoxically, initiates and sustains our agency. (1–2)

The paradoxical process of the subject's domination as that which also prepares and begins the subject's resistance to domination can be seen in Vargas Llosa's characterization when characters discover limitations on their own freedom to act and are inspired by that discovery to transcend those limitations. Concretely, the female characters, including female ekphrastic voices, discover how dangerous it can be to act on their sexual desires. Some of them resist being punished for a sexuality others have encouraged in them.[24]

This paradox, that the forces that dominate Lucrecia are precisely those that provide her with the ability to resist, becomes easier to see with Rigoberto, her main teacher, than with Alfonso. Lucrecia's resistance to

Alfonsito's interpretation of the Szyszlo combines with Rigoberto's nightly fantasies until it affects how she plays the sex games Rigoberto has taught her: she wants to tell Rigoberto her sexual fantasy, rather than listen when he tells his. According to Bataille, one may not be fully "sovereign" until one invents an erotic narrative. Julia Kristeva puts it succinctly: "The sovereign subject [in Bataille] can only be someone who *represents* experiences of ruptures; his *themes* evoke a radical heterogeneity. His practice: to write the themes of eroticism, of sacrifice, of social and subjective rupture. This series of themes will resemble the erotic novel or the philosophical essay—it matters little; what is important, is that the violence of thought be introduced there where thought loses itself" (247). One key to Lucrecia's feelings of sovereignty is the moment in which she "tells" the Szyszlo painting to Rigoberto, confronting him and representing to him the violence of her transgression.

From Rigoberto's reaction, it is clear Lucrecia had never before asked to speak her fantasy: "There was an astonished pause, like a freeze frame in a film" (115T) ["Hubo una pausa atónita, como el congelamiento de un film" (152)]. From the narrator's comments, it is also clear that she *should not* speak, according to Rigoberto's conception of their nocturnal games. Lucrecia's turning the tables on Rigoberto was "an answer that broke the tacit pact" (115T) ["una respuesta que transgredía el pacto tácito" (152)]. The pact between the lovers had been Rigoberto's undisputed leadership in the nightly rituals and dominant voice in the fantasies.

Additionally in the ekphrastic monologues, Béjar notes "the inscription of the husband as a controlling, critical agent, and of the wife as a ground of unlimited erogenous potential" ["la inscripción del marido como agente crítico controlador, y la de la esposa como campo de potencial erógeno ilimitado" (250)].[25] In imagery reminiscent of *An Apprenticeship* by Lispector, for example, the female Szyszlo voice summarizes: "We have lost name and surname, face and hair, our air of respectability and our civil rights. But we have gained the power of magic, mystery, and bodily enjoyment. We were a woman and a man and now we are ejaculation, orgasm, and a fixed idea. We have become sacred and obsessive" (120T) ["Hemos perdido el apellido y el nombre, la faz y el pelo, la respetable apariencia y los derechos civiles. Pero hemos ganado magia, misterio y fruición corporal. Eramos una mujer y un hombre y ahora somos eyaculación, orgasmo y una idea fija. Nos hemos vuelto sagrados y obsesivos" (160)]. The female voice of the Szyszlo painting explains how this transformation has occurred: "An exciting ceremony, with delightful and cruel reverberations, has just taken place, and what you see are its vestiges and its consequences" (118T) ["Acaba de oficiarse una ceremonia excitante, de reverberaciones deliciosas y crueles y lo que ves son sus vestigios y sus consecuencias" (158)].[26] In sum, she reports, "That woman is what I am, slave and master, your offering" (119T) ["Esa soy yo, esclavo y amo, tu ofrenda" (159)]. The figure on the left, she says (for example, stage right), is a warrior and a priest: he officiates over the voice of the Szyszlo painting, the victim: "Those reddish patches on the feet of the diluvial form are my blood and your sperm flowing forth and coagulating" (118T) ["Esas manchas de rubor en las patas del diluviano ser son mi sangre y tu esperma manando y helándose" (158)].[27] We are further told by the Szyszlo voice that the figure on the right lying on the sacrificial altar/stage may represent the speaker,[28] but that the figure is merely one aspect of herself, as seen by the male addressee: "myself, seen from inside and from below, when you calcine me and express me. Myself, erupting and overflowing beneath your attentive libertine gaze of a male who has officiated with competence and is now contemplating and philosophizing" (118T) ["yo, vista de adentro y de abajo, cuando tú me calcinas y me exprimes. Yo, erupcionando y derramándome bajo tu atenta mirada libertina de varón que ofició con eficiencia y, ahora, contempla y filosofa" (158)].

In a marked parallel to the Szyszlo monologue, the narrator of the frame story also defines a magic space for Rigoberto that is an altar or stage. His special room is the bathroom, a comic parody of the sacred:[29] "The bathroom was his temple; the washbasin, the sacrificial altar; he was the high priest and was celebrating the Mass that each night purified him and redeemed him from life" (98T) ["El cuarto de baño era su templo; el lavador, el ara de los sacrificios; él era el sumo sacerdote y estaba celebrando la misa que cada noche lo purificaba y redimía de la vida" (132)]. Between the ekphrastic chapter of the Bacon painting and Alfonsito pointing to the Fernando de Szyszlo painting in the family living room, a chapter is devoted to Rigoberto's bathroom ritual on Thursdays. At this point in the frame story, Rigoberto comments on Johan Huizinga's book *Homo Ludens* (1950). Huizinga—and his more currently fashionable partner Bataille—provide an intellectual bridge between the disparate ideas about eroticism, art, and politics in the novel. Huizinga stresses play in religion and Bataille religion in sexuality. These theories prepare the reader for the Latin American painting that follows the "initiation" of the copulation between stepmother and stepson. Rigoberto decides that Huizinga has a delightful theory about the "irresistible human propensity for game playing" (99T) ["irresistible propensión humana a jugar" (133)]. Despite his general approval of Huizinga's theory, however,

Rigoberto finds it to be mistaken, at least in part because "the decorous humanist" (99T) "el púdico humanista"(133)] had not gone far enough, in the final analysis neglecting to deal with the realm that could confirm his intuition. All the signs indicate that Rigoberto means the sexual realm, that constant of his imagination, and the particular subject of his bathroom reveries.[30]

The Szyszlo voice, in contrast to Rigoberto's dedication to theories, complains about the male figure's intellectualizations: "Now you would like to dissolve me in a theory" (119T) ["Ahora te gustaría disolverme en una teoría" (159)], like that of Bataille or Huizinga. The result, she says, is a painting where all can see her, not as she is, but as she is for him: "That is my face for you, at the hour of the senses. I am that when, for you, I shed my everyday skin and my feast-day one. That may perhaps be my soul. Yours" (119T) ["Esa es mi cara para ti, a la hora de los sentidos. Esa soy yo cuando, por ti, me saco la piel de diario y de días feriados. Esa será mi alma, tal vez. Tuya de ti" (159)]. The Szyszlo voice cooperates, she contributes, she accepts, but she protests she does not appear in the painting as she is to herself. In homologous fashion, Lucrecia has not been "herself"; instead she has been compliantly becoming an example of Rigoberto's theories, even to herself: a ventriloquist of male voices about female sexuality.

The Szyszlo voice reads the painting as the scene of her theatrical, magical sacrifice on the altar of art and love, where she performs three roles: "I have been the fortunate victim; the inspiration, the actress as well" (118T) ["he sido la dichosa víctima; también, la inspiradora, la actriz" (158)]. In the painting as "victim," the Szyszlo voice is sanctified by ancient pre-Columbian religious sacrifice, and yet seduced into/by her personal catastrophe, hence a "fortunate victim" ["dichosa víctima"]. As "inspiration," she feels transformed into art. In the frame story, Lucrecia fantasizes about ending the degeneration of her body, about bringing aging to a halt—not merely retarding or disguising the wrath of time. Such "immortality" may be achieved in art's simulation of the flesh, and she identifies herself with art in its supposed timelessness. The Borgesian chapter "The Labyrinth of Love," like the other painting chapters, also thematizes the aestheticization of the mimetic, the substitution of the freeze frame of art for the reality of the diachronic. In the same vein, Szyszlo said: "the pre-Columbian tradition is . . . a completely unpublished language of shapes that fulfill the purpose of mediating between the reality of the human group that developed them and the hidden forces promising to defeat the human condition. It was a matter of overcoming precariousness, fugacity, a question of promising paradises and eternal lives beyond death" ("Reflections" 43). In her third role, "actress," the Szyszlo voice admits to becoming gradually more conscious she is performing in the male figure's rituals.

The Szyszlo voice's feeling of "supreme egotism" is related to Lucrecia's "sovereignty," a word which Bataille uses in relation to "erotism" in a special way, as already noted. In addition, eroticism, especially as discussed by Georges Bataille ("erotism"), is Szyszlo's label for his own work. Painting and love provide contact with the sacred and life, with evil and death. In an interview, Ana María Escallón asked him: "Are you speaking about a special kind of love?" To which Szyszlo replied: "Only man can feel erotism, experience sensuality without fertility. This contact with the darkest forces is what is actually important. Because it is surely there where the forces that struggle fiercely against death may be found. However, Bataille also taught us that love is a battle that demands transgression in order to be complete" ("Reflections" 36). These opinions about Bataille could well have been spoken by Mario Vargas Llosa; they do not contradict the writer's views as expressed in "Sobre Bataille," "El placer glacial," "Bataille y el 'elemento añadido' en *Tirant le Blanc*" and elsewhere.

In "Bataille, Experience and Practice," Kristeva stresses the active nature of Bataille's eroticism, which, like his conception of laughter, is a reaching beyond the self into the extradiscursive. Erotism never is that-which-is-beyond-the-self, what Kristeva calls "the heterogenous," but always is the act of going from the self to that which is no longer self, the "traversal" from one to the other. In Vargas Llosa, this movement to transcend the "unary" (the unit, or self) may be seen, for instance, in the character of Lucrecia. In response to discovering from her stepson that she "is" the Szyszlo painting, the narrator immediately connects her perception of "inner experience" to Bataille's eros, which is "life beating, life living" (108T) ["la vida latiendo" (144)]. The Szyszlo voice continues to speak of an absolute time of sexuality when nothing else matters: "Everything that might have distracted us or impoverished us at the hour of supreme egoism that the hour of love is has disappeared. Here, as is true as well of the monster and the god, nothing restrains or inhibits us" (120T) ["Ha desaparecido todo lo que hubiera podido distraernos o empobrecernos a la hora del egoísmo supremo que es la del amor. Aquí, nada nos frena ni inhibe, como al monstruo y al dios"(160)]. Through these allusions to Bataille's vocabulary, the Szyszlo voice's understanding of her situation closely approximates Lucrecia's understanding of her own. In other words, values and meanings placed on a set of terms in the

French thinker's theory of erotism make apparent that the voice is using words which, in Bataille, are synonyms for many of the same things said by Lucrecia in the frame story, giving them a double thematic resonance in the novel as a whole.

Lucrecia's discovery of her feelings of sovereignty begins her disappearance as an individual into the heterogeneous as defined by Kristeva. It is a paradoxical movement in which she crosses from her self, constituted in discourse as stable and authoritative, able to speak and represent eroticism, to the unrepresentable, the beyond: "The 'I' affirmed only in order to disappear through eroticism and desire is the only 'sovereign I': sovereignty, which in essence is possibility for non-discursive communication, passes through the affirmation of the paranoid 'I' which is the 'I' of desire. Sovereignty is a return to the heterogeneous by traversing, through the desire that reestablishes continuity, the stasis of the knowing 'I'" (Kristeva 245). Lucrecia

> couldn't understand it, and made no attempt to do so. She preferred to bow to this contradictory situation, in which her acts challenged and violated her principles as she pursued that intense, dangerous rapture that happiness had become for her. One morning, on opening her eyes, the phrase "I have won sovereignty" came to her. She felt fortunate and emancipated, but could not have said what it was that she had been freed from. (110T)

> no podía comprenderlo, pero tampoco se esforzaba por conseguirlo. Prefería abandonarse a esa contradictoria situación, en la que sus actos desafiaban y transgredían sus principios en pos de esa intensa exaltación riesgosa que se había vuelto para ella la felicidad. Una mañana, al abrir los ojos, se le ocurrió esta frase: "He conquistado la soberanía." Se sintió dichosa y emancipada, pero no hubiera podido precisar de qué. (146)

In terms of power, "the sovereign subject refuses all positions, all fixations. This trans-Oedipus, as opposed to an anti-Oedipus, only takes on a position in order to engage in revolt: 'sovereignty is revolt, it is not the exercise of power. Authentic sovereignty refuses'" (Kristeva 251–52; the internal quotation from Bataille is from *Méthode du méditation* 221).[31]

Paranoia is a stage through which the sovereign subject passes. This paranoia or dissolution of the self is narrated by the Szyszlo voice. She says there is an another active agent in addition to the male figure of the warrior-priest. An unidentified, external group has worked on the male and female figures: "They" have taken off the skin from both the priest figure and his victim; "they" have softened their bones; "they" have left the two of them without secrets (119T; 159). "They" represent the male figure and the female speaker "in that picture that so many look at and so few see" (121T) ["nos representaron en ese cuadro que tantos miran y tan pocos ven" (161)]. The onlookers acting upon and watching the two Szyszlo figures may be the readers of *In Praise of the Stepmother;* the new topic their presence provides is a fear of being watched, the underside of the elsewhere thematized pleasures of exhibitionism.[32]

According to Kristeva, Bataille's concept of sovereignty describes an ephemeral moment of transition, in which the self is on its way to dissolution: "One must give strong emphasis to this moment in Bataille's work: desire and the heterogeneity to which it leads do not constitute a 'this side of' of knowledge and its unary subject but their traversal; carnal organicity, erotic orgies, and obscenity exist only as contradictions, as struggles, between the violent materiality external to the subject, and the affirmed authority of this very subject" (245). Humanity can be tragic because it falls into the trap or ruse of the self, the "unary," or unit, the illusion of invulnerability, indivisibility, perfection, stasis: it has many names.[33] In the frame story, "An incomprehensible feeling of pride came over Lucrecia" (109T) ["La poseía un incomprehensible sentimiento de orgullo" (145)], at the moment she experiences sovereignty.

Lucrecia feels the hubris of a tragic hero in that her new pride makes her blind to the fate that awaits her. But the nature of her personal qualities and the social context in which her fall is plotted betray the emptiness of bourgeois values rather than the fullness of heroic values. One finds, in Julio Ortega's words, "the ambivalence, the vital paradox; that is, the intimate tension of the individual who destroys him- or herself without being able to control his or her own destiny. That destiny, which was clear to the heroic character, is replaced in this manner by chance and nomadism; and the uncertainties only suppose the tragic norm of a distorted reality. The individual acts in the face of codes that the society pretends to assume, but the mirrorings and the real no longer correspond to each other. The codes are already parodic: they reiterate, like a miserable caricature, the great values that were the rhetoric of a bourgeoisie that no longer requires them."[34] Thus it is that the antiheroes Lucrecia and Rigoberto misunderstand the situation they face, misinterpret the signs that indicate danger ahead, and misalign their sexual practices. The sexual codes they follow, like those that led Emma Bovary astray, lead them to tragedy. Acting in a manner they believe will lead to felicity, they destroy their lives.

It is not an exaggeration to say that *Praise* constructs female sexuality as a tragic flaw. But the telling of Lucrecia's discovery in the full Aristotelian sense of the anagnorisis, the tragic hero's sudden knowledge that s/he has caused her/his own destruction, is elided, so that empathy and catharsis on her behalf are displaced. Instead, the voice of Szyszlo chapter discloses metaphorically woman's blindness to the power that soon will expel her from the story. The Szyszlo voice declares: "Altruistic sentiments, metaphysics and history, neutral reasoning, good intentions and charitable deeds, solidarity with the species, civic idealism, sympathy toward one's fellow have also been done away with; all humans who are not me and you have been blotted out" (120T).[35]

Freedom is the only illusion to persist on the Szyszlo stage, where sex alone exists. "Are we without shame? We are whole and free, rather" (119T) ["¿Somos impúdicos? Somos totales y libres, más bien" (159)]. The concept of freedom from an unknown limitation relates to eroticism in Bataille's theory as the only ideals not abandoned; Vargas Llosa separates from female sexuality and denounces this last altruism because sexual liberation for women is too threatening to the males in the novel.

If Lucrecia's sovereignty is to have full significance in Bataille's sense of the term, she must reject her domination by Rigoberto and her manipulation by Alfonsito, to the extent she is aware of them. The experience of sovereignty "is the site where power is contested, a site constituting the subject who is not the subject of power (as it has been thought and lived by society and, in particular, by Occidental society), but a free, contesting subject" (Kristeva 252). Butler's vision of the subject's paradoxical relation to power applies to Bataille's "sovereign subject" as a special case, a moment in which the subject becomes it *as* revolt, in revolt. This conception is particularly apt for Lucrecia's new consciousness at the moment she comes to feel sovereign, because it occurs at the very time when Rigoberto's and Alfonsito's effect on Lucrecia is greatest. By having suggested greater eroticism to her, by having prodded her into fantasies and acts, they "subject" her in the sense of subordination; to the extent they are successful, paradoxically, Lucrecia is unaware of their influence. When aware of the possibility of their influence, she rejects it and would deny it ever had transpired. The man and boy mold her as a subject who will be what they want: the "autonomous" subject who "refuses." In this revolt against the powers that have changed her, Lucrecia denies her *new* sense of self, that is, she represses the internalized domination that occurred during the formation process. That revolt against her subjection causes her dissolution as a unified subject. Lucrecia learns to rebel against the tame fantasies of eroticism Rigoberto teaches; she accepts the reality of sex with her stepson that is violent to her morals and to her husband's. She has repeatedly lost herself in the "labyrinth of love." She loses the self she was before marrying Rigoberto by becoming the transgressive self who learned from Rigoberto to rebel; then in her revolt, she loses the eroticism she learns from her husband in order to sleep with both father and son. Left with a divided self, with a conflicted position, having acted following a model of transgressive eroticism that brings with it feelings of sovereignty without any actual power, her actions cause her to be expelled from the family picture.

Discovering Power

> Instead of sidestepping the problem of sex's relation to power by divorcing one from the other in our minds, we need to analyze the social mechanisms, including language and conceptual structures, that bind the two together in our culture.
> **Winifred Woodhull, "Sexuality, Power, and the Question of Rape" (169)**

As we have seen, *In Praise of the Stepmother* manifests its "newly sexed woman" characters following a Bataille-influenced model of the destruction of the self and the transgression of culture; another way of saying the same thing is that the female characters Lucrecia, Justiniana, Diana Lucrecia, the Szyszlo voice, and the others experience the erotic as an inner voyage toward some common biological nature. Kristeva calls Bataille's idea of nature "heterogeneity," which expresses the idea that eros for Bataille consists of a transcendence of the individual. But male sexuality in the novel is not constituted in the same fashion. The male experience of eros is tinged with visions of hegemony and the domination of nature (and culture). *Praise* thus distinguishes between the genders in the way sexuality reflects power for men and women, in what they transgress against and what the transgression means. This gender differentiation, ascribing to males domination and to females compliance, distances the novel from Bataille's theory of erotism. This difference between female and male sexuality determines the plot outcome and provides an ideological context for the specifics of the meaning of female sexuality. In this section, I discuss the Boucher, Titian, and Bacon ekphrastic monologues, and the chapters on Rigoberto in his bathroom, within the novel's overall strategy for inscribing female sexuality. I compare male and female voices about eros to clarify the organization of thematic material and the ideology regarding sexual women and social change.

François Boucher's bucolic scene shows the goddess Diana and a nymph, both naked, surrounded by vegetation, drapery, her bow, the results of her hunt, a quiver of arrows, and two hunting dogs. Viewing the painting, readers discover the goddess Diana at her toilet. In Greek and Latin myth, viewing Diana naked was tantamount to a death sentence. Diana killed Acteon for spying on her in such a way by turning him into a stag that was hunted by his own dogs. In the Boucher monologue, the first-person voice calls herself Diana Lucrecia. She is accompanied by a nymph called Justiniana, her "favorite," just as in the frame story Lucrecia is helped by Justiniana, whom Lucrecia "promoted . . . to the status of personal maid" (32T) ["promovida . . . a la categoría de doncella" (52)]. The implication of analogies such as these is that the Boucher chapter parallels Lucrecia's dream; the narration also suggests that Alfonsito's spying inspired her dream. But whether or not the reader makes this connection, female sexuality in this ekphrastic chapter is voluptuous, polymorphously perverse, exhibitionistic, and told by a female voice. The nymph, Justiniana, begs: "Have pity on him, Diana Lucrecia. Why don't we play games with the little goatherd? By amusing him, we shall amuse ourselves as well" (47T) ["Compadécete de él, Diana Lucrecia. ¿Por qué no jugamos con el niño pastor? Divirtiéndolo, también nos divertiremos nosotras" (71)]. In the spirit of Boucher's painting, and in contradiction to the myths of Diana/Artemis, Diana Lucrecia seeks pleasure in exhibiting herself before the young goatherd-voyeur Foncín, instead of killing him right off for spying on her. Female homosexual acts are performed for the viewing pleasure of the peeping goatherd.

The art of François Boucher has long been considered "feminine," that is, related to female concerns of the boudoir, in part owing to his subject matter and in part owing to the artist's friendship with Madame de Pompadour, mistress and adviser to Louis XV. Influenced by Watteau, and a teacher of Fragonard, Boucher frequently painted mythological subjects in his works. Long described as frivolous, artificial, and decorative, the Rococo paintings like *Diana at the Bath* (1742) have been seen, in recent shows and through revisionist studies, not as feminine in themselves or as pandering to a feminine sensibility, but as eighteenth-century male views of what the feminine must be.[36] In a perceptive article, Carter Ratcliff wrote: "Boucher indeed appears to offer us a woman's world, or perhaps a womanly world (he avoided male figures whenever he could), but his vision of femininity looks thoroughly male to me. . . . Boucher often flatters the masculine self with an image of the world as an overabundance of female surfaces already aroused by proximity and needing, to feel complete, only the entry of a male principle in some form—explicitly phallic in pornography, implicitly phallic when that principle becomes the examining eye of the connoisseur who considers himself qualified to judge women and paintings as objects" (94). He adds: "Boucher's coyness, then, is that of a man who thinks he knows what women want—women like Madame de Pompadour, the king's best-known mistress" (Ratcliff 94).

Correspondingly, in the Boucher monologue the lesbianism between the goddess Diana Lucrecia and her favorite Justiniana is described as for the benefit of the boy watching, as if the pleasure of the women were validated and enhanced by the male presence. The Boucher voice explains: "It makes my ecstasy the keener to know that as I near climax beneath the diligent hands of my favorite, he is doing the same, at the pace I set, along with me" (49T) ["Aumenta mi éxtasis saber que mientras gozo bajo las diligentes manos de mi favorita, él goza también, a mi compás, conmigo" (73)]. Furthermore, Diana Lucrecia's pleasure mirrors a gender and a class hierarchy, a relation of serving and being served—never lovers giving pleasure to each other as equals: "There is no exercise or function, no wanton ritual of body or soul that we have not performed for him, the privileged freeholder [owner] enjoying our privacy from his errant hiding places. He is our buffoon; but he is also our master. He is in our service and we in his" (50T) ["No hay ejercicio o función, desenfreno y ritual del cuerpo o del alma que no hayamos representado para él, privilegiado propietario de nuestra intimidad desde sus escondrijos itinerantes. El es nuestro bufón; pero también es nuestro dueño. Nos sirve y lo servimos" (74)]. The two women describe analogous hierarchical scenarios between the two of them; Justiniana serves Diana Lucrecia, waits upon her desires, and massages her so that she orgasms. These actions are not reciprocated. Ratcliff argues that Boucher's frozen images of sensuality are, in art, what "absolutist Louis XV could not be in the theater of history": "With an iron will he invented a world whose politics are all of fleshy delight, where all delight submits to a control so rigid it can never transform itself into melancholy or doubt" (Ratcliff 96). Implicit in Diana Lucrecia's status as goddess is an abyss of power over others, separating her from them. Foncín recognizes this superiority and it attracts him. Despite the visual similarity of the two female figures in the Boucher painting, distinguished only by Diana's crown and foregrounding, Diana Lucrecia inspires poetry in Foncín, but Justiniana does not. This class hierarchy is another of the disclosures made by female voices: that (male) power favors those with wealth or high rank in society.

In the frame story we are repeatedly told of Rigoberto's wealth: his bathroom counter is of "ocher marble" (62T) ["mármol ocre" (89)], he has many servants and a large house. Lucrecia seems to have no other occupations than charities, purchasing goods, and pleasing her family. In this configuration, a woman may be an additional adornment, part of the payoff to a man for his sacrifices to conformity and commercial success. Like Bataille's prostitute discussed in the context of *An Apprenticeship*, a wife or mistress of this type who is loved less for her personality than for her looks and status, as an accoutrement of elite society, must be always ready for sex, always available, as if she were another object for the husband. A marriage between a wealthy man and his trophy wife is not a relation between equals. Lucrecia does appear to have some money of her own, but that is about all one can deduce from the information given. The lack of information about her background, possible career aspirations, or her family is typical of sexual women in literature, no matter the economic class from which they come.

Class differences become important on several occasions. In Vargas Llosa's extended interview with Ricardo A. Setti, the author describes with obvious distaste the kind of sexual advance made by Fonchito with Justiniana: "There were among my companions those who discovered it [sex] with housemaids. It is something that I never could accept, perhaps because very young I discovered the social problem.[37] Since I was a child, the idea that were some terrible social inequalities in my country was something that made me rebel. So the idea that the boys would take advantage of the servant to have their first sexual experiences was something that always seemed repugnant to me."[38]

Justiniana's position as an employee makes her rightly fear a "kill-the-messenger" reaction when she warns Lucrecia that Alfonso has climbed onto the roof of the bathroom to spy on her while she bathes. Annoyed with the message, Lucrecia does accuse Justiniana of inventing the story that Alfonso is in love with his stepmother. Additionally, in the epilogue, Justiniana is especially cognizant of her vulnerability to Alfonso as a maid.

Luxurious wealth also characterizes the visual landscape of the Titian painting that follows the Boucher. But the new discoveries to be made in the Titian chapter pertain more to gender differences than to those of class. The male voice, Love (Cupid), states he and the organist (Music) must accomplish the task of seducing the female figure, of convincing her to leave aside her thoughts of morality and to approach her "señor" avidly: "Our task consists of kindling the lady's bodily joy. . . . That is how Don Rigoberto likes to have us hand her over to him: ardent and avid, all her moral and religious scruples in abeyance and her mind and body filled to overflowing with appetites. It is an agreeable task, though not an easy one; it requires patience, cunning, and skill in the art of attuning the fury of instinct to the mind's subtlety and the heart's tender affections" (70T).[39]

The little god, like the father and his library in the frame narrative, is a source of "corruption," telling Venus sexy tales from his imagination. Love tells Venus fictions about hermaphrodites, androgynes, and playful sex: "Fictions that distract her and make her smile, fictions that shock and excite her" (72T) ["Ficciones que la distraen y hacen sonreír, ficciones que la sobresaltan y enardecen" (100)]. Furthermore, in all this foreplay and preparation for sex with the Titian Don Rigoberto, Love states that Venus cannot be blamed, for she is only following the orders of her husband: "she is an obedient wife who reluctantly goes along with these soirees that are a prelude to the conjugal night, out of respect for her husband, who programs them down to the last detail. She is, then, a lady who bows to the will of the master, as a Christian wife should" (74T) ["es una esposa obediente que se somete a estas veladas preparatorias de la noche conyugal por respeto a su esposo, quien las programa en sus mínimos detalles. Se trata, pues, de una dama dócil a la voluntad de su dueño, como debe serlo la esposa cristiana"(103)].

In the Titian monologue, Love's perorations detail the kind of lurid stories he tells Venus, the husband's arrangement with the religious, ascetic organist, and the Titian Don Rigoberto's requirements for the physical and emotional state his wife is to be in when she goes to his bed. The little god further describes for the reader the stages of Venus's gradual excitement and the sensuous beauty of her body that causes the organist such conflict with his religious vocation. But Venus is never seen to have an independent desire, she never presents resistance to the control of her emotions, she never says that she is a willing devotee of these rituals. Her wish to be "prepared" in such a way is not considered. Lucrecia's sovereignty, with its contestation of power, does not enter the mix. The justifications given by Love for Venus's submissive interactions with her husband and his allies are both her personality and the better to save her soul: "if these sensual love feasts are sinful, it is to be supposed that they will blacken only the soul of the person who, for personal pleasure, conceives them and orders them" (74T) ["si hay pecado en estos ágapes sensuales, es de suponer que ennegrecerán únicamente el alma de quien, para su deleite personal, los concibe y los manda" (103)]. The contribution of this chapter as alternative narrative parallel to the frame story is severalfold: that one possible outcome of Alfonso's teasing is merely Lucrecia's greater excitement when she is making love to her husband; that if she had remained faithful to Rigoberto, he could perhaps be made happy by her obedient, docile acceptance of Alfonso's provocations; that Rigoberto may be behind, indeed, in active favor of Alfonso's actions up to the point when the son has sex with Lucrecia; and that Rigoberto, not Alfonso or Lucrecia, deserves blame for an affair that he initially encourages. Later his blindness to possible outcomes does not allow him to prevent what happens.

Similarly, the Titian painting anticipates elements of the frame story, such as Alfonso's active role; and other aspects, such as Lucrecia's sovereignty, are given alternative outcomes. David Rosand suggests that the traditional ordering of the Titian derivatives into three generations—first without any musician, then with an organist, then finally with a lute player—shows that "the role of the female protagonist changes [within the series], becoming increasingly active, as Venus is transformed from passive object of the serenade—first as object for the outside observer alone and then for the musician courtier [the organist] as well—to full participant [with the lute player" (380)]. In terms of elite women in sixteenth-century Venice, Rosand argues: "Titian's pictures, in fact, fully document the relationship between woman and music" (380). In later versions, when the Reclining Venus goes so far as to pick up an instrument, she becomes a full participant in the courtly scene represented. Earlier members of the series, such as *Venus with Love and Music,* reflect a historical period before it was appropriate for women to perform. The particular Titian painting chosen by Vargas Llosa for the novel is the one of the series that shows a woman who remains passive but has begun to be active; more than merely serenaded, she has been invited to participate, but she has not yet assumed a full role as a performer of music, as she will in the culmination of Titian's series. In this historical, symbolic way, in the novel this picture foreshadows the active female role as a performer.

Returning to the Titian monologue, Venus's sexuality constitutes the main element of her characterization. She is constructed as if she were some simple machine that only needed priming before her sexuality flows freely. Like Candaules' monologue that supplements the frame story with the obedient vassal Gyges who adds the spice of exhibitionism to the king's pleasure; like Diana Lucrecia's monologue that adds lesbianism and voyeurism to the other sexual activities, Love's monologue subordinates everyone's desires to those of the "master." According to Titian's Venus, when her master Don Rigoberto makes love to her, he says: "You are not you but my fantasy" (75T) ["Tú no eres tú sino mi fantasía" (103)].[40] Love dissents with the master's conception of Venus as never exceeding Rigoberto's fantasy of her, however: "Perhaps that is how she is, in Don Rigoberto's elaborate imaginings. But she is nonetheless real, concrete" (75T) ["Tal vez sea así, en las alambicadas quimeras de don Rigoberto. Pero ella sigue siendo real, concreta" (103–4)]. Rigoberto's view of Venus, his fantasy of her, is contested by Love; the reader discovers through this process that the novel, with its repetitions and contradictions, never constructs her as fully known, only as she is to another character or a narrator. Perspectives on Venus are partial and loaded, both incomplete and contextual.

The most important implication of this phenomenological presentation of information is that we are missing Venus's conception of herself, just as the novel is largely short on information about Lucrecia's self-image. The Szyszlo voice also stressed that the sexual woman figure in the painting was an exclusively male idea of her, the theories about her held by her male lover. The Szyszlo voice does not part with the secret of what she is like to herself, or what she may have been like when not around, or influenced by, a corrupting man. In terms of discoveries of power, then, the Titian monologue reinforces an interpretation of *Praise* as a novel about both men's domination of women and men's fantasies/theories about women, within the sexual realm. With the painting by twentieth-century artist Francis Bacon, *Head I*, and "Profile of a Human Being" ["Semblanza de humano"], the Bacon monologue, not only is the male in control of the woman's sexuality, but he is also arrogant about it.

The Head in the Francis Bacon painting's monologue asserts: "Women even come to love me, in fact the youngsters become addicted to my ugliness. In the depth of her soul, Beauty was always fascinated by the Beast, as so many fantastic tales and mythologies recount" (91T) ["Las mujeres llegan a amarme, incluso, y los chicos a enviciarse con mi fealdad. En el fondo de su alma, a la bella la fascinó siempre la bestia, como recuerdan tantas fábulas y mitologías" (123–24)]. The relevance of fable and mythology to a novel about sexual fantasies has not been rejected in this monologue as much as redefined. References to "a great fire," to medical accidents and technology, replace the allusions to a luxurious palace, the Greco-Roman pantheon, an exaltation of nature, or Renaissance worship of humanity as God's greatest creation. Consistent with the high-art status of Jordaens, Boucher, and Titian paintings, and the classical references and literary allusions found in the monologues that correspond to them, the novel's prose before the Bacon voice had been weighted toward an erotic (high-art) model, rather than a pornographic (low-art) model. In a perceptive article on a large 1986 Bacon retrospective,[41] Donald Kuspit writes that: "In Bacon, ambivalence toward the authority of the past is used to undermine it, or at least to bring it into doubt" (59). Here the Socratic union of the beautiful and the good has been abandoned.[42] The grotesque in this portion of the novel forces the reader to struggle as best she can to discover the role of such contraries. Antithesis as a technique becomes strikingly evident pictorially and at the level of language, as with other important binaries in the novel: male and female, master and servant, young and old. From the Bacon painting on, the novel borrows surrealist (shock) techniques, or, in a more general sense, mixes them into a postmodern pattern of pastiche: a text that is fragmentary, aesthetically, and morally questioning rather than affirming, and not fitting into the genres as traditionally defined.

The male Bacon voice tells a first-person narrative of a lascivious, mutilated being, without arms or legs, missing one eye and one ear, and covered with boils in a futuristic and apocalyptic setting. No effort is made to hide the dictatorial, arrogant nature of this voice. The Bacon monster "trains" women to desire him: "No one has ever regretted being my lover. Males and females alike thank me for having given them advanced instruction in the fine art of combining desire and the horrible so as to give pleasure" (92T) ["Nunca lamentó alguno de mis amantes haberlo sido. Ellos y ellas me agradecen haberlos instruido en las refinadas combinaciones de lo horrible y el deseo para causar placer" (124)]. According to the Bacon voice, his lovers were taught that "everything is and can be erogenous and that, associated with love, the basest organic functions, including those of the lower abdomen, become spiritualized and ennobled" (92T) ["Conmigo aprendieron que . . . la función orgánica más vil, incluidas aquéllas del bajo vientre, se espiritualiza y se ennoblece" (124)]. The monster changes the predilections of all around him, teaching them the pleasures of the grotesque. Kuspit emphasizes that "Bacon's paintings . . . show off the figures' blatant exhibitionism" (60). He cites Anthony Storr, who explains that hysterical exhibitionism is a "defense against recognition of the lack of ideal persons in the world" (Kuspit 60); Bacon paintings paradoxically display and dissect that exhibitionism, showing the emperor to be without clothes.

The Bacon voice's sadism and arrogance compares to the Baconian figure which, according to Kuspit, is "peculiarly self-possessed rather than owned by the world. Its existence in the limbo of the space confirms its self-realization and its authenticity" (56). The voice of Bacon's *Head I* says: "Eating flesh is a prerogative of the gods" (92T) ["Comer carne es una prerogativa de los dioses" (125)], affirming at once his view of the violent nature of the human animal and his superiority among them.[43] The monster arrogantly, hysterically, claims authority over all who would be his lovers. This air of brutal corporeality and the idea of human sacrifice link the Bacon chapter to the Szyszlo ekphrasis. The theme of victimizer and victim, raised by the male Bacon voice, and repeated by the subsequent female Szyszlo voice, constitutes a matched erotic fantasy of sex-gendered domination. The author's departure from traditional realism in the painting chapters may be a desire for a more inclusive "sur"-realism, in order to dramatize an ultimate nightmare implied by the male and female social scripts of gendered eroticism.

The tone of Vargas Llosa's prose in the Bacon chapter, for instance, corresponds to the British painter's histrionic figure, so common in Modern art: "dissatisfied, rebellious, angry, violent, and violative, an incisive reflection of the discontents of civilization" (Kuspit 55). When Concepción Reverte Bernal compares this novel to certain fictions of Spanish American Modernism, she correctly draws our attention to its anachronistic language, and misfit, aestheticist protagonist. Nevertheless, Reverte Bernal recognizes that the embellishments and *art pour l'art* ideas are not found in all the chapters, and are not found uniformly in any of them: "The naturalist effects that splatter the modernist prose are principally in the chapters about the Bacon and Szyszlo paintings, and in those in which don Rigoberto does his philosophizing on the toilet" ["Los efectos naturalistas que salpican la prosa modernista están principalmente en los capítulos de los cuadros de Bacon y Szyszlo, y en aquellos en que D. Rigoberto hace sus consideraciones sobre el excusado" (573)]. In the Bacon chapter, the outdated language—"young fellow" (91T) ["apuesto jovenzuelo" (123)], "good-looking youth" (91T) ["mozalbete" (124)]—and the New Age goal to make ignoble body parts and practices more spiritual and more noble contrast with the grotesque setting and apocalyptic plot. The spiritual goals parallel Rigoberto's bathroom meditations and prefigure the rejection of sexuality at the novel's end.

It is only a short step (albeit a comic one) to Rigoberto's musings when he concentrates on beautifying his nose in the chapter after the Bacon ekphrasis: "At this instant he felt himself to be—snip snip snip snip— incorruptible, and soon now, in the arms and between the legs of his spouse, he would feel himself to be a monarch. He thought: a God" (98T) ["En este instante se sentía-chas chas, chas-incorruptible; y, pronto, entre los brazos y piernas de su esposa, se sentiría un monarca. Pensó: 'un dios'"

(132)]. Rigoberto's bathroom reveries in the frame story produce a sexual discourse with philosophical pretensions that have similar political implications. Encompassing anality and the unaesthetic, the domination of self and of others, his nightly meditations are glosses of and are glossed by the Bacon ekphrastic chapter in a mutually compounding intertwining of themes. Sex with Lucrecia, like Rigoberto's nightly bathroom rituals, makes him feel superior, in large part because of his submission to an arbitrary discipline and his development of aesthetic theories he believes alien to common folk.

In an interview about psychoanalysis and *Aunt Julia and the Script-writer*, Vargas Llosa asserted that themes of male sexual display and grotesque sexuality were aspects of his realism in portraying Peruvian society: "Now, those themes that you [Forgues] mentioned, [i.e., virility, castration, sexuality, homosexuality, comradery, violence,] are themes intimately tied to a society like the Peruvian or the Latin American one, that is, machista societies, for example, where the topic of sex is a central theme. Then to speak about machismo in a written fiction, in a world like one of these, is something that reflects an experience, a reality."[44] In Vargas Llosa's (probable) intention, Rigoberto's intense concentration on sexual display and sexual play, especially his visual and verbal fantasies, would have evolved in him from his involvement with machista society.

Rigoberto's embracing of the grotesque and the eccentric within the erotic is the familiar story of a bored bourgeois's search for something more spicy in his life. The novel justifies Rigoberto's obsessions with the idea that some private escape from the suffocating conformity of existence and empty public displays must be found in the reservoirs of emotional depth that come from extramarital affairs or transgressing against other prohibitions. His "flight of fancy" (87T) ["el vuelo de su fantasía" (117)] is the way he compensates for his gray and monotonous life as manager in an insurance company. He congratulates himself: "Just a pinch of wisdom to use as a momentary antidote to the frustrations and annoyances that seasoned existence" (104T) ["pequeña sabiduría para oponer un momentáneo antídoto a las frustraciones y contrariedades de que estaba adobada la existencia" (138)]. The frame story displays this self-congratulatory attitude as ironic, when what he calls wisdom proves to be lack of foresight and insight.

Like the Bacon monster, like Titian's Love, Rigoberto fancies himself a woman's sexual teacher, and he is, though differently than he realizes. He shows her how to expand her sexual horizons, her techniques, her imaginings—in short, how to channel her energies into increasing sexual pleasure. Rigoberto would like to be Lucrecia's sexual instigator: the one who steers her away from a discriminating morality and leads her toward the pursuit of pleasure without consideration of consequences. But pleasure only with him, of course. Until he is shocked into recognizing the full consequences of his lessons, he is happy that, regarding her sexuality, Lucrecia is becoming less shy and more verbal, less self-conscious and more open as a result of her time with him. Speaking generally of Vargas Llosa's fiction, Julio Ortega writes that "Borges said that Swift had proposed 'denigrating the human species.' That happy phrase could not be applied to Vargas Llosa, because his negation eludes totally the allegoric and didactic design; for that reason in his novels, it would be appropriate to say that humanity denigrates itself. . . . In his essay about Bataille we have seen how he declares directly that literature comes from a perception of evil . . . and also how he intends to assume that declaration in a totalizing perspective."[45]

The narrator thus makes explicit the connections between politics and Rigoberto's personal obsession with hygiene; Rigoberto "had so completely mastered the rite that his attention could be divided and be partially devoted, as well, to a principle of aesthetics, a different one each day of the week, one extracted from that manual, tablet of the law, or commandments drawn up by himself, in secret also, in these nocturnal sessions which, on the pretext of cleanliness, constituted his particular religion and his personal way of bringing about a utopia" (62T).[46] Rigoberto himself joins the idea of personal hygiene with that of the soul. He finds it easier to have "perfect" bowel movements that clean his digestive system than to have a clean conscience. The superiority of his system over an ethical perfection relies in part on its being visual; Rigoberto looks into the toilet bowl and sees his success (56T; 82), whereas after confession one cannot see the pestilence that has been removed from one's soul.

He has become "like an artist" (53T) ["como un artista"(79)]. Rigoberto's rituals of bathing and perfuming and grooming "feminize" him, make him share in stereotypically female culture of physical beauty and overweening concern with the appearance of the body.[47] Like the scriptwriter of *Aunt Julia and the Scriptwriter*, Rigoberto is a caricature of artists and intellectuals who (re)create; he becomes a comic parody of them because he creates no object for others to see. In a sense, Rigoberto's sexual fantasies replicate the self-centeredness and guilty consciences of the bourgeois milieu in which he is found, like Alberto, who produced pornography within the barracks of Leoncio Prado in *The Time of the Hero* (1966; *La ciudad y los perros* 1962).[48] At the same time, Alfonsito parallels an Alberto from a time before Leoncio Prado, because Rigoberto's young son is a writer of birthday notes in the first chapter and an essayist "in praise of" his stepmother near the end of the book.

Several of the painting monologues reveal that the female figures are/ will be controlled by a painter-dreamer. In the Boucher chapter, Diana Lucrecia speaks of the "eternal immobility" ["eterna inmovilidad"] in which she finds herself. Shortly it will "come to life and be time, history" (50T) ["se animará y será tiempo, historia" (74)], but until then, she waits for the painter who will be inspired to paint the three of them, who "will imprison us in dreams and, pinning us to the canvas with his brush, will believe that he is inventing us" (51T) ["nos aprisione en sueños y llevándonos a la tela con su pincel, crea que nos inventa" (76)]. In the Szyszlo chapter, the voice affirms: "You now know that, even before we knew each other, loved each other, and married, someone, brush in hand, anticipated what horrendous glory we would be changed into by the happiness we learned to invent" (121T) ["Ahora ya sabes que, aun antes de que nos conociéramos, nos amáramos y nos casáramos, alguien, pincel en mano, anticipó en qué horrenda gloria nos convertiría, cada día y cada noche de mañana, la felicidad que supimos inventar" (161)].

When in the frame story Rigoberto discovers his wife's affair, when his house of cards collapses violently in a moment, his delusions of domination and control of others disappear. Immediately his fetishistic eroticism transmutes to an ideal of chastity. After his dramatic discovery of Lucrecia's sex with Fonchito, Rigoberto's wants to become a monk. In his mind now, "he was a solitary being, chaste, freed of appetites, safe from all the demons of the flesh and sex. Yes, yes, that was how he was. The anchorite, the hermit, the monk, the angel, the archangel who blows the celestial trumpet and descends to the garden to bring the glad tidings to pure and pious maidens" (134T) ["Era un ser solitario, casto, desasido de apetitos, a salvo de todos los demonios de la carne y el sexo. Sí, sí, ése era él. El anacoreta, el santón, el monje, el ángel, el arcángel que sopla la celeste trompeta y baja al huerto a traer la buena noticia a las santas muchachas" (176–77)]. Rigoberto's sudden asceticism highlights his inauthenticity, shortsightedness, and selfish nature; his fantasy of being a monk demonstrates the persistence of his delusions of perfection and his evasion of guilt, not an authentic, sudden agreement with religion's attitudes toward sex.[49] Previously the novel and Rigoberto had promoted a favorable image of female sexuality as supremely malleable and controllable; his discovery that female sexuality cannot be sufficiently dominated surfaces in Rigoberto as a horror of it in all forms. It is as if having discovered the evil in his son and the complicity of his wife made Rigoberto yearn for an independence from others, especially for an isolation from all that is sexual. In effect, Rigoberto suffers from not realizing that his deployment of strategies of power inevitably meets with resistance.

For many readers, *Praise* traces the evil in his wife and the complicity of his son, and not Rigoberto's own guilt, however. The opinion that Lucrecia, and not Alfonsito, is responsible for their affair is based on the reasonable belief that her greater age places the burden on her to act morally. Rigoberto's role has not generally been taken into account. In stressing her role as victim of both father and son over that as victimizer of the son, I do not intend to defend Lucrecia's infidelity or her lack of judgment. But the novel's embedded narratives, and to a lesser extent the paintings themselves, construct female sexuality as manipulated, passive, and held in check until worked on by the males, young and old. The six ekphrastic chapters of embedded monologues supplement the nine chapters of the frame story and make the novel a combination of stories, indeed a series of commentaries on narrative possibilities. These monologues expose a dominated condition for female sexuality. In them, female sexuality is entrapped: the sexual woman is trained to transgress against her inner moral limits, led to believe that the result is more and greater pleasure for all sexual partners in the game, then blamed and castigated for having transgressed. The frame story, in contrast, suggests a lesser degree of culpability for Rigoberto and Alfonsito.

Female sexuality is not told from a woman's subjective experience in the Bacon monologue any more than in the other ekphrastic voices. In all, the male voices may be differentiated from the female voices largely by the former's more powerful condition. The discovery that males dominate, sometimes arrogantly but always thoroughly, over women in the painting monologues delivers the message that the genders in *Praise* have not benefited by the freedom thought to accrue to a developed and active sexual woman. Although Lucrecia has delusions of making decisions and controlling her own life, the sovereignty that she feels merely leads her to be susceptible to Alfonsito's machinations. Since the autonomy she feels comes from her increasing sexualization, in order to continue to feel it, she needs to produce a discourse of sexuality (or to have sex). This need in turn leads her to a search for ways to be sexual. Fonchito provides her such an outlet. This condition is not sexual freedom but sexual addiction, not autonomy but resistance, not the overcoming of personal obstacles blocking her from expressing her sexuality, but merely the changing from one male to another for whom she performs a role.

Dis-Closure

Well, Bataille was against the permissive society, for example.

Bueno, Bataille estaba en contra de la sociedad permisiva, por ejemplo.
Mario Vargas Llosa, *Sobre la vida* (116–17)

Vargas Llosa's realism relies on conventions, including those about gendered sexual behavior, for its believability. To recognize the conventional sexual politics of the frame story, for example, one need only imagine the novel with the genders reversed. Such a novel, "In Praise of the Step*father*," would tell the story of a recently married forty-year-old husband who comes to have sex with his very young and seemingly asexual, angelic stepdaughter, who in (feigned) innocence reveals the affair to her mother. During the affair, the mother had instigated the reticent stepfather through example and edict to develop and indulge his sexual fantasies, to the extent that he is convinced that his wife would accept his not-quite-incestuous relationship with her daughter. Once discovered, however, the man is thrown from the house and the mother watches the daughter in horror. In our imagined novel's epilogue, the daughter begins to seduce the male servant who recoils from her. Such a sex-changed version requires at least two unusual circumstances: a woman who encourages her husband to be more sexual, and more verbal about his sexuality, whereas society already expects men to be more sexual than their wives; and a mother who owns the house the family lives in, and thus can act as the judge and jury who finds against the offending male, whereas women usually have less property and less authority with regard to material possessions than their husbands. The context for such a sex-inverted story is exceptional, in contrast to the transparency and normalcy achieved in the frame story of *Praise*.

In realist fiction, exceptions to society's norms must be indicated as such — highlighted, emphasized, commented — in order for them to be situated within the limits of probability and normality. *Praise* treats the young Alfonso as such an exception to social expectations. All the other characters remark and wonder about him. But we are never privy to what goes on in his head. The narrator does not report what the boy thinks or feels; he informs only what other characters speculate about him. The title of his school essay, "In Praise of the Stepmother," may be literal or ironic as a consequence, and we are given little criteria by which to decide.[50] Other evidence as to Alfonso's character, such as comparisons to the ekphrastic Titian voice named Love, who parallels Alfonso's point of view, sex, and age, have been mined by some critics for clues to his personality. However, the Titian monologue follows Rigoberto's chapter in the bathroom and could more easily be the father's fantasy or dream than the son's.

Along a continuum of the way men influence women in the novel, the character of Titian's Love lies in the middle between the clearly dominant role Rigoberto plays in fomenting Lucrecia's fantasies and the understated, ambiguous role Alfonso plays in doing the same thing. In the Titian narrative, the young boy/god is employed by a husband to incite his wife sexually, exclusively for the husband, as Rigoberto of the frame story would have wished for his wife. Music and Love churn Venus's fantasies to produce in her an undiscriminating desire for her husband: "That is how Don Rigoberto likes us to hand her over to him: ardent and avid, all her moral and religious scruples in abeyance and her mind and body filled to flowing with appetites" (70T) ["Así le gusta a don Rigoberto que se la entreguemos: ardiente y ávida, todas sus prevenciones morales y religiosas suspendidas y su mente y su cuerpo sobrecargados de apetitos" (98)]. This alternative narrative path, whereby a young boy excites the desires of a married woman and yet does not sleep with her, diverging from the frame story in which the youth also takes his pleasure with her, discloses a chink in Rigoberto's armor, a silenced facet not developed in the frame story. Love is obedient and his sexuality is discounted. In the frame story, however, Alfonsito's attitudes toward sex with his mother-substitute are never disclosed unequivocally, though Justiniana suggests he purposefully meant to dislodge Lucrecia from his father's affections.[51]

The contrasts between Love's and Alfonso's loyalty (and sexuality) again highlights how little we readers know of Alfonso's motivations and qualities. Is he truly pre-Oedipal and angelical? Or is he a modern Oedipus who "kills" his father and sleeps with his (step)mother, despite his best efforts to avoid such a fate? Or is he merely evil? Oversexed, despite being underaged? Out of control or acting consciously out of spite? Interpretation of the frame story revolves around this ultimate ambiguity, yet we are not given access to Fonchito's thoughts and motivations, nor are we guided by peritextual information. Because Alfonso remains unknown, his story and the novel must be open to multiple interpretations. It may not have an open ending in the normal sense of the term, but the novel's secrets never are fully disclosed.

The knowledge the reader has about Alfonso is primarily visual: he had "the startled little face of a child Jesus" (4T) ["una carita de Niño Jesus" (16)]. Lucrecia thought: "What a lovely child! A born angel, one of those court pages in the elegant erotic etchings that her husband kept under

quadruple lock and key" (5T) ["¡Qué bonito niño! Un ángel de na-
cimiento, uno de esos pajes de los grabados galantes que su marido
escondía bajo cuatro llaves" (17)]. By reason of a visual association with
(popular) art, Lucrecia mistakes Fonchito as asexual: "it seemed impossible to Doña Lucrecia that the small blond head of this exquisite beauty
posing as a shepherd in the Christmas tableaux at the Santa María School
for Boys could harbor dirty, scabrous thoughts" (34T) ["a doña Lucrecia
le parecía imposible que la cabecita rubicunda de aquel primor que posaba
de pastorcillo en los Nacimientos del Colegio Santa María pudiera alber-
gar pensamientos sucios, escabrosos" (54)]. While on top of Rigoberto,
during the sexual act, Lucrecia thinks of Alfonsito as an angel (or literally
sees him out of the corner of her eye): "At the bottom of the pleasant
maelstrom that she found herself, found life to be, as though appearing
and disappearing in a mirror that is losing its silver backing, an intrusive
little face, that of a rosy-cheeked angel, was discernible from time-to-
time" (10T) ["En el fondo del torbellino placentero que eran ella, la vida,
como asomando y desapareciendo en un espejo que pierde su azogue, se
delineaba a ratos una carita intrusa, de ángel rubicundo" (22)]. These
angelic images are Lucrecia's repeated impression of him.

In contrast to Lucrecia, Rigoberto and Justiniana change their initial
opinions about his angelic exterior for certainties about his demonic interior. At first, Justiniana also concurs with Lucrecia's angelic diagnosis:
"Fonchito doesn't have the least idea he's doing something bad. I give you
my word he doesn't. He's like a little angel; he doesn't know good from
evil" (39T) ["Fonchito ni siquiera se da cuenta que hace mal. Palabra que
no se da. El es como un angelito, no diferencia lo bueno de lo malo" (59)].
But in the epilogue, Justiniana is no longer fooled by his angelic looks: "I
am not her. You can't buy me, or fool me with that angelic smile of yours"
(142T) ["Yo no soy ella. A mí, con esa carita de niño santo no me compras
ni me engañas" (190)]. She has completely changed her mind by the end.
In the final pages, she calls him "little devil" (143T) ["diablito" (191)] and
a "bandit" ("devil" 143T) ["bandido"(192)]. With reason, Justiniana
fears his duplicity at the moment he looks most like an angel; she knows
he is "someone more perverse and devious than all the grown men she
knew" (146–47T) ["alguien con más mañas y retorcimientos que todos
los viejos que ella conocía" (195)].

One time, however, the narrator briefly reveals Alfonso's malignance,
when the narrator presents not only Justiniana's opinion of Alfonso, but
also contrasts her mistaken point of view with the reality (of the fiction).
In the boy's play after he asks for a kiss good night, "she didn't see him as

the cruel, cold devil he had inside him, but as the pretty little boy he was on the outside" (148T) ["no parecía el diablillo cruel y frío que llevaba dentro, sino el niñito lindo que era por fuera" (196)]. Refusing clear confirmation of Alfonsito's evil nature to the reader, however, the narrator comments during the conversation with Justiniana that "Fonchito's head had moved toward her, the golden cone of lamplight surrounding it like a crown" (144T) ["la cabeza de Fonchito se había adelantado hacia ella y el cono dorado de la lamparilla la circundaba igual que una corona"(192)].

For Rigoberto, moments before reading the essay, Alfonsito is still "A cherub, an adorable child, an archangel in a first communion holy picture" (125T) ["Un querubín, un pimpollo, un arcángel de estampita de primera comunión" (167)]. When Rigoberto finally lifts his eyes from Alfonso's composition that breaks the illusion of his marital happiness, he still sees the same Fonchito on the outside, but he interprets his son as a fallen angel: "with his beautiful, beatific face. That's what Lucifer must have looked like, he thought" (132T) ["con su bella cara beatífica, 'Así debía ser Luzbel,' pensó" (175)].

Father-and-son relationships are normally portrayed by Vargas Llosa with all the poison he can muster, as his readers know.[52] Such relationships usually occupy the foreground of a story, whereas those with women recede into the background. Roy C. Boland finds parricide to be the most common form of father-son interaction in Vargas Llosa's writings: "What is at risk is paternal authority that is being defied by rebellious sons, avid to establish their own masculine autonomy. In these confrontations, women—whether mothers, cousins, aunts, maids, girlfriends, wives or stepmothers—are no more than sexual playthings, prizes or trophies for the possession of which fathers and sons fight each other, if not always to the death, almost always until either a sexual or a psychological castration occurs."[53] According to Boland's thesis, *Praise* manifests a son's attack on his father through the woman he loves most. Consequently, Lucrecia would be little more than a pawn in a game for control played by father against son.[54]

The voice of the final painting, by Fra Angelico, is Maria, "the chosen one" (136T) ["la elegida" (183)], whose simple joys are to clean the house, water the garden, and prepare her parents' food. Unlike the women in the earlier chapters—Lucrecia, Candaules' wife, Diana Lucrecia, Venus, Szyszlo's sacrificial victim, the monster's women—Maria does not understand or tolerate sexual talk, "The modest young girl that I am" (136T) ["La modesta muchacha que soy" (182)]. Rather than pleasure from sex, she wants children. Maria says: "What I ask of life is an upright husband, healthy children, and a peaceful existence, without hunger and without fear" (139T) ["Lo que le pido a la vida es un marido honrado, unos hijos sanos y una existencia tranquila, sin hambre y sin miedo" (185)]. In her preference for agape over eros, Maria represents both Christianity's undervaluation of eroticism and Rigoberto's overreaction to being betrayed. In fact, the life Maria wants is like Rigoberto's perspective on his household without Lucrecia; Justiniana will cook and clean for him but not be interested in sex with him.[55]

From Maria's perspective, however, the visit by "the rosy youth" (135T) ["el joven rosado" (179)] is neither consoling nor reassuring.[56] Maria is confused by her conversation with the angel. The "rosy youth" treats Maria as a married woman, although she is single. He calls her mother, although she is a virgin. She fears the abyss before her that threatens to change her life; she fears the future awaiting her because she does not understand or control it. The other girls, her neighbors and friends, have some sense of their sexual desires and tease Maria for ignoring her own; but Maria willfully pursues being good. She resists the lessons of love that would place the pursuit of pleasure first among her values; furthermore she does not acquiesce or immediately silence her wishes when confronted by those who would have her be otherwise. She might be considered self-directed if it were not for the visit of the angel, who is in ultimate control of her sexuality, her body, and her choices. There is no defense here of sexual women or of female sexuality as liberation.

In the sequel to *Praise, The Notebooks of Don Rigoberto*, Lucrecia recovers Rigoberto's love through Alfonso's continued trickery and manipulation, just as she lost it through this means in *Praise*. Lucrecia does not change or learn from having been discovered and thrown from her house. Indeed, she had been happy while the lover of her stepson and very easily, once again, falls under Alfonso's spell. Justiniana, her faithful double, reveals a more insightful and wary attitude than Lucrecia in this book as well. A major transformation between the first volume and the subsequent one has occurred in Rigoberto, however, who in *The Notebooks* eventually wants and tries to accept an indiscriminate sexuality for Lucrecia, in actual fact and not just in fantasy. Rigoberto repents having sent Lucrecia away, when they may have been reconciled. He imagines her in lesbian affairs, as a prostitute, in perverse sexual scenarios. Through writing fictions, essays, and diatribes, Rigoberto discovers an ability to tolerate her infidelity. Here Rigoberto's fantasies verge on popular written pornography, and the reader of *The Notebooks* discovers gradually his authorship of (many of) the intercalated texts. Painting and drawing play the role of mirroring Alfonso's obsessive personality, his unconscious desires, and his conscious plans for reconciling Rigoberto and Lucrecia, rather than the father's fantasies.

In this second novel about the characters in the frame story of *Praise*, readers still have little access to a baseline personality for Alfonso, and little confirmation by a narrator or peritextual indication of the relations between the frame story and the embedded narratives and essays. But there is a turnabout on Rigoberto's ideas regarding the question of gender equality in sexual mores. The new idea is that either a couple should agree to be faithful or agree not to be; one morality should not apply to males and another to females, nor should a mutually agreed upon ground rule for a couple be condemned by others as immoral if there is no coercion or physical harm involved. This mutual tolerance and gender equality is a minimal, nonliberationist 1990s treatment of themes of female sexuality. This tolerant attitude toward the sexual woman may turn out to be the principal legacy of the 1960s liberationist models of sexuality, eroticism, feminism, and sexual fiction.

What is unique about *Praise*, then, compared to *Mulata*, an *An Apprenticeship*, and *The Notebooks*, is the blame placed on those women who succumb to sexuality's illusions and enticements. This throwback to prefeminist times returns to the literature about prostitution and its criminality for metaphors, imagery and associations with which the portrait of the sexual woman is painted. Sexual women in *Praise*, unlike their literary predecessor the prostitute, do not symbolize or effect social change of any sort. *Praise* would seem to say that the erotic vein of sexual fiction has Vargas Llosa's approval, but not the social and political promises that have often been associated with it.

Rigoberto's attitude at the beginning of *Praise* was that sexual women were superior to other women; his final attitude, that (women's) sexuality is nefarious, equally conveys self-centered delusions. He loved Lucrecia for her sexuality, and in his overreaction to her infidelity it can be seen that he still does love her. What is truly rejected by the novel is not Lucrecia but the freedom from domination that was thought to accompany female sexuality in the 1960s model. In the process of extracting the sexual woman from sexual liberation, however, even the idea of woman's sexual *equality* has been jettisoned. *Praise* negates an equal place for female and male desire. It is almost as if Vargas Llosa had decided to protect the genders from the threat of equal treatment in sexual fiction.

Furthermore, any feminist idea of women's equality within love relationships with men becomes so entangled with Lucrecia's lack of judgment that a woman's inept attempt to extricate herself from male domination is made to appear as, at the very least, unfaithfulness and naïveté. In the epilogue, Justiniana reacts with warranted fear after the boy's lurid unscrupulousness is uncovered. Like Rigoberto, who promotes Lucrecia's sexual fantasies, a female friend early on tells tales of sexual excitement with children.[57] But unlike Rigoberto, who hypocritically approves in fantasy[58] but then condemns in practice, the friend first praises the practice: "And all of a sudden there came back to her the memory of a licentious friend who, at a benefit tea for the Red Cross, had given rise to flushed cheeks and nervous titters at her table when she told them that taking afternoon naps naked, with her young stepson raking her back with his nails, made her hot as a firecracker" (8T).[59] Female solidarity here is not moral, but rather another influence on her future acceptance of transgressive behavior.[60] The utopian idea of a new female sexuality with revolutionary social impact has shrunk to hedonism, from the outset. The social implications are not debated; they are revisited to be denied.

Lucrecia is a superficial ghost of a "newly sexed woman," just as Rigoberto caricatures the sensuous New Man. An appropriate partner for Rigoberto, however, Lucrecia sports many of the traits desired by the old-style conservative men who have desired sexual women, not because they wanted sex with an equal who also enjoyed herself, but because they wanted to be able to orchestrate sex the way they want it to be without a woman's inexperience or reticence getting in the way. At the same time, Lucrecia's gullibility verging on stupidity, her desire to please, singles her out as a certain literary type, a modern sexual woman. Lucrecia has given in very quickly to Alfonsito, yet she cannot believe what she has done. She continually resists the *idea* of what happened, though she resists sex little, if at all. In addition, we never see Lucrecia with a desire to hurt Rigoberto, or without feelings for him. There is a subtle but important difference between someone who has made mistakes through immoral acts and someone who acts in order to cause pain or in utter disregard for the pain of others.

Sexual women are dangerous in literature, and interesting to feminism, for several reasons: sexual women threaten patriarchal control because they ascribe to themselves the freedoms that pertain only to men and boys. The gender hierarchy intervenes unmistakably in this heterosexual fiction, adding social sanctions and the weight of cultural traditions to a woman's desire to give pleasure to a male partner. In the micropolitics of encounters within marriage, the construction of female sexuality is affected both by this discourse of male power and by female resistance to it. Vargas Llosa's novel treats the social question of how the "newly sexed woman" fits into the (middle-class) family as it is most commonly constituted in modernity, a married couple with few children, and then extirpates her from its midst. We do not read of Lucrecia's speech after Rigoberto is aware of the affair. She may be repentant or unrepentant. Lucrecia is silent; she does not respond to Rigoberto after he reads Alfonso's essay. Any sense of political change or of power is separated from the image of the sexual woman. Through Rigoberto, Candaules, Alfonsito, Love, and the other male characters, *Praise* denies female sexuality's revolutionary potential. To the extent it is social and juridical, marriage functions as a lens, coloring all relations seen through it in terms of a gender power imbalance, in which the power of the husband is recognized in general and resisted by few.

Candaules, King of Lydia, Showing His Wife to Prime Minister Gyges (1648), oil on canvas, by Jacob Jordaens. Reproduced by permission of the Nationalmuseum, Stockholm.

Diana at the Bath (1742) by François Boucher. Oil on canvas. Reprinted by permission of the Louvre, Paris. Photo: RMN—Herve Lewandowski.

Venus with Cupid and Music (sixteenth century) by Titian. Oil on canvas. Reproduced by permission of the Museo del Prado, Madrid.

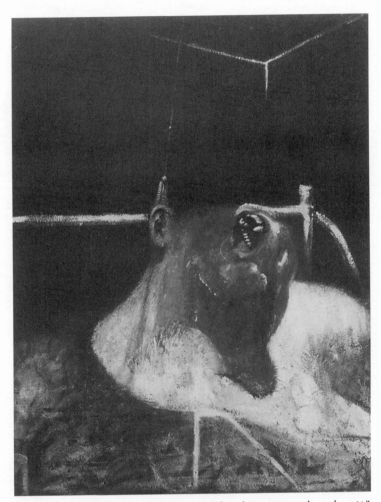

Head I (1947/1948) by Francis Bacon. Oil and tempera on board. 39½" x 29½". Reprinted by permission of Richard S. Zeisler, private collection.

The Annunciation (c. 1437) by Fra Angelico, fresco, Museo de San Marco, Florence. From *Fra Angelico: The San Marco Frescoes* by Paolo Morachiello. Reproduced by permission of the Ministry of Culture of Florence.

Notes

Chapter 1. Dangerous (to) Women: Introduction

1. "La literatura fue para ellas frecuentemente cárcel; cuando comienza a transformarse en instrumento desalienante, es corriente que quien lo esgrime—todavía torpemente—frente a una sociedad armada, estalle en pedazos" (Rama *Aquí la mitad del amor* 7).

2. In Liliana Trevizan's study of the Latin American short story by women in the 1980s, she asserts that before that decade, sexuality was merely suggested, not explored: "It is clear that the cultural transformations of the last decade have permitted the medium to grant freedoms to the Latin American woman writer to treat, without censorship, themes like infidelity, eroticism, and politics, which were avoided by previous generations" ["Es claro que las transformaciones culturales de la última década permiten que el medio otorgue libertad a la escritora latinoamericana para tratar, sin censura, temas como la infidelidad, el erotismo y la política, los cuales fueron eludidos por las generaciones anteriores" (11)].

3. "Así pasó con Delmira Agustini por quien comienza a existir un arte femenino en el Uruguay, y que muere cuando entran en pugna dentro de ella las dos funciones dispares que la nueva sociedad novecientista le impone: la mistificación de la burguesa convencional y su independencia como ente de la sensualidad amorosa" (Rama *Aquí la mitad del amor* 7).

4. Some men who wrote sexual texts also suffered from public scandal or from the negative reactions of intimates, but to a lesser degree than women.

5. "Las escritoras de hoy saben que si desean llegar a ser buenas escritoras, tendrán que ser mujeres antes que nada, porque en el arte la autenticidad lo es todo. Tendrán que aprender a conocer los secretos más íntimos de su cuerpo y hablar sin eufemismos de él. Tendrán que aprender a examinar su propio erotismo y a derivar de su sexualidad toda una vitalidad latente y pocas veces explotada" (16).

6. In addition to the male predecessors Gamboa and Andrade, discussed later in this chapter, some examples of twentieth-century treatments of the sexual woman, especially the prostitute, before the 1960s can be found in the works of the Argentines Roberto Arlt and Leopoldo Marechal, the Uruguayan Juan Carlos Onetti, and the Mexican Juan Rulfo.

7. Inside *Prostibulario,* a third collection was announced, *El arte de amar: la mujer,* but I have not been able to confirm through electronic or print sources that it indeed appeared. Since this was intended to be writings by men about women's sexuality, it is tempting to speculate on why it did not appear or had little circulation. Were women's desires somehow more dangerous?

8. Foster is considering only those writers who have obeyed the mandate in Foucault's theory to write about sexuality, rather than considering the entire picture of those who have and those who have not. In the next section, I make a similar move to discuss the theme of female sexuality as it has occurred.

9. Sexual liberation, in the sense of an individual's freedom to sleep with whomever he or she may wish, appears occasionally as an issue in novels from the 1960s on, but "free love" had limited appeal. Nevertheless, by positing a sexuality in which girls and women can claim for themselves the sexuality men have previously practiced—one separated from marriage, children, and even from love—writers who treat the theme questioned culture as currently constituted.

10. "De denunciar la situación de la mujer peruana . . . y al mismo tiempo burlarme de los patrones femeninos convencionales . . . y al mismo tiempo quería decir, más o menos, 'éstas son las verdaderas posibilidades de relación de una mujer' o 'una mujer debe atreverse a todo, absolutamente a todo'" (67).

11. "El discurso erótico de la escritora latinoamericana abre nuevos horizontes literarios y culturales en su uso de lo sexual como vehículo para un crítica audaz del sexo y la política.

"Es parte de un proceso revolucionario cuyo objeto es el de desenmascarar las categorías culturales del sexo y el género en la búsqueda de una verdadera liberación y concientización que conduzca a la restauración total de la dignidad de la mujer latinoamericana" (xxiv).

12. See the special issue, "Sexual Politics in Latin America," *NACLA Report on the Americas* 31.4 (Jan./Feb. 1998) for recent articles on abortion, reproductive rights, AIDS prevention, and lesbian and homosexual liberation movements.

13. "The term 'gender' was adopted by feminists to emphasize the social shaping of femininity and masculinity, to challenge the idea that relations between women and men were ordained by nature. Sometimes a distinction is made between 'sex' as the biological differences between male and female and 'gender' as the cultural distinction between femininity and masculinity along with the social division between women and men. . . . Not all feminists accept this distinction. Some think that it denies the importance of the physical body, while others argue that our understanding of the anatomically sexed body is itself socially constructed. . . . We ourselves endorse the latter view" (Jackson and Scott 2).

14. For an excellent collection of articles about the challenge for feminism of the differences between women, that is, the dangers of eliding or ignoring race, class, ethnicity, age, and other factors that distinguish people of the same gender from each other, see Meese and Parker, *The Difference Within* (1989).

15. For reasons of history and culture, during the same period women's groups, political parties, labor unions, and loose coalitions rarely accept the designation "feminist," although that has changed in the 1990s. Even women's groups whose raison d'être is to promote better wages for women, gender equality before the law, free education for girls, and so forth often have preferred not to be called "feminist." Nor do individual Latin American women writers normally welcome this

designation. Luisa Valenzuela, a widely translated Argentine known for ironic gynocentric narrative touching on issues of gender equality, autonomy, and sexuality, in 1998 felt it necessary to clarify before an English-speaking audience that she is not a feminist (November 12, 1998, in Columbia, Missouri, at the conference: "Spanish American Women Writers: Luisa Valenzuela, Albalucía Angel"). Although in the English-speaking world a group's or an individual's lack of acceptance of this term would indicate a rejection of activism on behalf of women, the history of Latin American women's movements that Francesca Miller and others tell, and the socially committed books Valenzuela writes, signal that something quite different is occurring. See Seminar on Feminism and Culture in Latin America (1990), Francesca Miller (1991), Audrey Bronstein (1982), Jane Jaquette (1991), and Asunción Lavrin (1994) for other histories of Latin American feminism. I highly recommend Debra Castillo's *Talking Back* (1992) for a full discussion of these issues. In *Latin American Women and the Search for Social Justice* (1991), Miller makes explicit the history of a twentieth-century feminism that went by other names. Much more than a problem of translation for the present study, the effect of this reticence is to hide the similarities between women's activism in Spanish-speaking, Portuguese-speaking, and English-speaking America, and to place a spotlight on the differences. If one cautiously disregards the effect of labeling, however, and recognizes homologies of interests where they exist, one finds enough similarities in the discourses themselves across languages and cultures to be able, when we discuss in English Latin American literature, to call some works "feminist."

16. I do not mean to suggest that greater numbers of sexually willing females would force prostitution's demise. The history and future of the practice are affected by economic motivations (female poverty) and many other factors, making it more complex than anything which a single action or factor could cause to disappear.

17. The change from the earlier representation of love as socially unifying in romance to sex as empowering to women and therefore threatening to society in its current form comes about gradually and can be seen in its purest form only in groups of novels beginning in the 1960s. Nevertheless, the portrayal of sex as a crucial social issue for women is not confined to one part of the twentieth century. It can be found in early avant-garde texts from the beginning of the century and in some of the latest postmodern ones at century's end.

18. For some of the best of the many new collections of articles on the connections in literature between sexuality and politics, see Hunt, *Eroticism and the Body Politic* (1991); Foster and Reis, *Bodies and Biases* (1996); and Bergmann and Smith, *¿Entiendes?* (1995). These last two deal with Latin American literature.

19. *Erotism*, the English title of Bataille's work *L'Erotisme*, appears to be a word invented by Bataille's translator. It is in any case convenient for denoting the French thinker's particular conception of eroticism.

20. "Impedidos, salvo en la forma poema, que es terreno privilegiado y no

sustituye la narrativa salvo por falencia, timidez o hipocresía, de dar el salto formal y expresivo hacia la conquista e ilustración del erotismo en el verbo, hacia su incorporación natural y necesaria, que no sólo no envilece la lengua del deseo y del amor sino que la arranca a su equívoca condición de tema especial y a sus horas para articularla en la estructura de la vida personal y colectiva, en una concepción más legítima del mundo, de la política, del arte, de las pulsaciones profundas que mueven el sol y las demás estrellas" (84).

21. By erotic poetry or prose, Cortázar means language which "sexualizes" without describing sexual acts, that is, which plays freely with sexual vocabulary and sexual attitudes without necessarily representing bodies in motion. In nonerotic texts, sexual pleasure is a referent, a matter of allusion; in erotic texts, pleasure inhabits language as well.

22. Interestingly, the anonymous editors of this volume decided not to attribute individual stories to their authors. Instead, a list of all the stories is accompanied by a list of all the authors, several of whom are women. Perhaps this move was in part to protect the authors of the most salacious works; the reason the editors give, however, is to let the reader play games as they read, just as the authors have had fun as they were writing.

23. For a polemic about Bataille's work between Mario Vargas Llosa and the younger Mexican Juan García Ponce, see Vargas Llosa's introduction to the 1978 Spanish translation of Bataille's brief *Histoire de l'oeil,* republished as "El placer glacial" in *Contra viento y marea,* vol. 2 (1972–1983).

24. "Instead of trying to applaud a protagonist who is cowardly and conservative in her actions, and trying to make her more heroic than she really is, we need to recognize that Bombal and not her narrator-protagonist is the brave one. This author has not given anything other than the revelation of a feminine consciousness which surrenders and conforms. But the denouement is appropriate given what has preceded it. The novel and not the principal character, in my opinion, represents a brave voyage toward the edge of literary approval, and beyond this frontier, toward the avant-garde" ["En vez de tratar de aplaudir una protagonista un poco cobarde y conservadora en acciones, y de tratar de hacerla más heroica de lo que verdaderamente es, debemos reconocer que es la Bombal y no la protagonista-narradora la intrépida. Esta autora no ha dado una revelación de la conciencia femenina a través de la novela como otra cosa que no sea una rendición y conformidad. Pero el desenlace es apropiado a todo lo anterior. La novela y no el personaje principal, en mi opinión, representa un viaje valiente hasta la frontera de la aprobación literaria, pasada esta frontera, hasta la vanguardia"(54)].

25. Francine Masiello correctly argues that "In the novels where Bombal emphasizes marriage and heterosexual fantasy, she still insists that the only plausible relationship is the bonding between female friends. Once again, *La última niebla* communicates this strategy insofar as the protagonist seeks the support of her secret comrade, Regina. Because of its strength as a secondary text, this clandestine relationship manages to undermine the heterosexual dynamic of the novel" (41).

While I agree that the protagonist wants Regina's "support," she never breathes a word about it. This "clandestine relationship" in *La última niebla* is also hidden from the protagonist; she has no real, dynamic friendships—not even with Regina. Regina represents what the protagonist would like to be and like to have; the reader may interpret Regina's character as the alternative to the protagonist's life half-lived, in terms of ethics; as her double in a Jungian reading; or as the desired other, submerged by fear of lesbianism, in a feminist reading.

26. About female short-story writers in Mexico (and not only those dealing with erotic themes), Seymour Menton wrote: "As a result, between 1970 and 1988, conditions for Mexican women short-story writers have greatly improved. Several of them have received grants from the Centro Mexicano de Escritores and from the Instituto Nacional de Bellas Artes; some have been university professors and their works have been published by prestigious publishing houses. However, taking into consideration that the majority of university students in letters are women, it is surprising the relatively small quantity of women who have distinguished themselves since 1970" ["Total que, entre 1970 y 1988, las condiciones para las cuentistas mexicanas han mejorado mucho. Varias de ellas han sido becarias de los talleres del Centro Mexicano de Escritores y del Instituto Nacional de Bellas Artes; algunas han sido catedráticas y otras periodistas; y sus obras han sido publicadas por casas editoriales de prestigio. Sin embargo, teniendo en cuenta que la gran mayoría de los estudiantes universitarios de letras son mujeres, sorprende la cantidad relativamente pequeña de mujeres que se han destacado en el cuento desde 1970" (139)].

27. In the aftermath of the upheavals of the 1960s, *The Girl in the Photograph* (1983; *As meninas,* Brazil, 1973) by Lygia Fagundes Telles offers a striking contrast between the 1940s and 1970s treatment of the sexual schoolgirl in novels of female development. In the later work, a female student loses her life to sexual debauchery and drugs. The novel indicts 1960s hedonism, while protesting against a society in which young girls suffer greater consequences from sex than boys, just as *As três Marias* had done in 1939.

28. Perhaps the logical impossibility of the title in Portuguese is the reason the English translator changed Andrade's title to *Fräulein* (1933); the idea of a love so abstract it could exist without a beloved can barely be imagined.

29. See Debra Castillo, "Meat Shop Memories: Gamboa," in *Easy Women* 37–62. My chapter was already written when I found that Castillo had said: "Gamboa's novel does not approach an understanding of female sexuality, it offers the first step toward such a discussion in that it raises the issue in a form impossible to marginalize. *Santa,* then provides an opening for other discussions, gestures toward other conceptualizations in which the question of women's sexuality can be raised in a different way, and serves as the forerunner for other texts in which later authors can rethink and revise the manner in which female sexuality will be understood in Mexican culture and represented in Mexican fiction" (62).

30. "No creo que de heroísmo, pero sí cierto satisfactorio desplante de

irreverencia ante los mitos en la literatura provocativa. Y pienso que si de un incendio saliera un pájaro envuelto en llamas, como vi en una ocasión propagarse el fuego en este lugar boscoso, y para cazar el ejemplar y tratar de salvarlo hubiera que quemarse con él, eso sería lo que el escritor con agallas intentase, inmolarse por un tema espectacular, sexistas y antisexistas aparte" (1157).

31. Media reports on the pill were often about technological discovery even though the technology had been available for a long time. What was actually occurring in the early 1960s was the marketing of the product after long efforts by various national birth control movements.

32. The meaning of the mother-daughter pair is here inverted from the negative treatment in earlier novels like *Aura* or *Doña Bárbara*; in Puig, it is a positive, central experience.

33. In contrast, in popular literature the promotion of woman's sexual liberation has quickly become codified and produced for mass readership. Such works promote the rules limiting and defining female sexuality that the society in which they are so popular is enforcing at that time. Compare this to the situation in the United States in Ann Barr Snitow. Although the phenomenon has been less studied in specific Latin American contexts, the generalization appears accurate.

34. "La escritura sería, pues, para mí, un modelo de sexualidad. Pero ¿qué escritura? Y ¿qué sexualidad?

"*Mi elección I.* Una escritura que no piense en el desenlace sino en las zonas intermedias; . . . una escritura de sentidos libres . . . ; una escritura que no le saque el cuerpo a la abstracción y que sepa soltar, a la manera de un flujo o de una linfa, sustancias significantes sin temor a dejar agujeros de lectura por la corrosión de su avance. Creo que esa escritura, cada vez que me he entregado a ella, como a una secreta seducción, es el colmo del erotismo. . . .

"*Mi elección II.* Una sexualidad que no se conciba con un final, tan lejos de la consumación como de la estrella matutina que cierra la noche de los amantes; un ideal de encuentro en el que no hay llegadas, sino permanencias; una cópula inaugural en la que no se sabe, en la que se balbucea un texto; un encuentro puntuado, con interrogaciones que se abren y se cierran, con puntos y comas, con suspensivos y admirativos, sin punto final; una sexualidad desobediente e irreverente.

"La escritura 'masculina' ha de ser seguramente como la sexualidad masculina sobre el cuerpo femenino: dominadora, indiscriminada, sin reconocimiento de las diferencias, metida en un guante o en un preservativo simbólico: escritura de representación y de reflejo más que de indomable deseo, seguramente desplazará sobre el texto una idea de la mujer ideologizada, una idea de la narración ideologizada, marcada incluso por esos temibles rasgos o trazas de la clase, el género, la raza, el color, marcada por esos terribles rasgos del crudo realismo que pegan la palabra al referente y no dejan ni una lucecita entremedio; esa literatura o esa escritura masculina la hacen tanto hombres como mujeres; esa literatura, en cierto modo, es la línea comatosa que registra la lenta desaparición de la literatura." (Mercado 12–13)

35. The representational (masculine sexuality) and the discursive (female sexuality) camps do not divide along gender lines, in my view. Many women authors are interested in representing a female character's sexuality without connecting style or language to woman's experiences of sexual pleasure, just as male authors are making such connections in greater and greater numbers.

36. To add a Latin American example to those Bell analyzes, one only need look as far as Boom writer par excellence Gabriel García Márquez. In his 1972 short story, the barely adolescent Eréndira represents the victimization (Santa) half of the dyad, while the grandmother (a retired whore) is the empowered (doña Bárbara) side. The resolution of García Márquez's story violently breaks the cruel slavery keeping the two sides of the dichotomy bound together, allowing Eréndira's autonomy, but only at the cost of the Abuela's death and Ulises's abandonment.

37. "La celebración de la amistad-solidaridad femenina, que tanto ha sido tema de la escritura femenina en Europa, Estados Unidos o Australia durante los 70, está ausente en la narrativa mexicana, tanto como la exploración de la relación madre-hija en búsqueda de una comprensión mutua de generaciones de mujeres" (130).

38. In speaking of women of Latin American background in the United States, Oliva M. Espín (1984) wrote: "In fact, Latin women experience a unique combination of power and powerlessness which is characteristic of the culture. The idea that personal problems are best discussed with women is very much part of the Hispanic culture. Women in Hispanic neighborhoods and families tend to rely on other women for their important personal and practical needs" (155).

39. Speaking of gay liberation, Queer theory, and transvestism, Jean Franco summarizes an additional caution that we, too, should not forget: "It is important, however, to stress the historical and regional differences which give these terms a different inflection in Latin America, where a tradition of paternalism secured by male bonding and expulsion of the feminine is only recently being transformed by modernization" ("From the Margins to the Center" 201).

40. In *Gay and Lesbian Themes in Latin American Writing*, David William Foster analyzes the following four novels from the 1960s: Miguel Barbachano Ponce's *El diario de José Toledo* [The Diary of José Toledo] (Mexico, 1964); Mauricio Wácquez's *Toda la luz del mediodía* [All the light of midday] (1964); the famous José Donoso's "Hell Has No Limits"; and José Ceballos Maldonado's *Después de todo* [After all] (Mexico, 1969); none about lesbian themes, and none by women. The 1980s, in contrast, produced quite a few lesbian texts which he studies and to which I refer the interested reader.

Chapter 2. Miguel Angel Asturias and the "Newly Sexed Woman"

1. Much excellent scholarship on the Mayans and on Asturias has recently become available, greatly facilitating serious study of the novel. A critical edition of *Mulata* from Colección Archivos is said to be in the works. (A note is appended

to that effect in the edition of Asturias's *El árbol de la cruz,* published in 1993 by Archivos.)

2. Luis Harss, whose interview and scholia are widely cited in the critical literature, though sympathetic to Asturias's project, sees as personal or stylistic weaknesses some elements that in fact are purposefully mimetic of Mayan texts. (See Harss 97, for example.) Some may label the novel's density as elitist when in fact it was a calculated political move on Asturias's part, designed to force Westerners to learn something about the ancient and modern Maya of Guatemala. It is not wrong of an author, fed up with those who rub elbows with the contemporary Maya and yet remain ignorant of their culture, to try to make them understand their kinsman. Nor is it wrong for the reader who may never go to Guatemala or Mexico, who may never meet a living Maya, to complain about the effort required to make sense of *Mulata.* But it is definitely worth the effort.

3. To praise the impossibility of pigeonholing *Mulata* in terms of understood Western antifeminist or feminist ideologies is not to say that, in order to study women, one should always look at works favoring a seemingly inconsistent image of them. Nor do I mean that somehow women are necessarily more authentically portrayed in fiction not written from a feminist perspective. But I do believe that if one wants to find the place where traditional gender paradigms have been "given the slip," so to speak, where difference can enter into writing, then a book laden with sensory images, but hesitant to explain or to tame them, is not a bad place to begin the search. Some early feminist writers of the second wave, in the 1960s at least, too often attacked sex roles frontally and thus, despite all their efforts, were doomed to repeat many of the sexist clichés in reverse (Butler, *Gender Trouble*).

4. Doubts have arisen as to Asturias's ability to understand Quiché Mayan (or any other Mayan language) at the time of his first studies at the Sorbonne and shortly thereafter, when he cotranslated the *Popol Vuh* and wrote *Leyendas de Guatemala* (Prieto *Archeology* 31–32).

5. Despite the importance of Asturias's "neo-Mayan" stylistic innovations in *Mulata,* I will not be entering as a full player in the game of identifying this or that detail as authentic or adapted Indian material. Throughout the rest of this chapter on Asturias, I explain certain obscure references, of course, but not as a goal in itself. Rather, I provide explanations as may be necessary as a means of conveying my understanding of Asturias's writing of the sexual woman. Nor do I ask why the author may have chosen this allusion rather than that one—a biographical question—as much as I construct my own edifice for representing his novel within the debate of feminist ideas at the time it was written and, most of all, today.

6. In this brief article Asturias summarizes the ideas of a Dra. Goldenberg who spoke at the Consejo Argentino de Mujeres Israelitas. If she indeed existed (and I have no reason to doubt it), Dra. Goldenberg argues the new increase in so-called "working women" is not a temporary distortion of reality, but a permanent shift in the workplace. The article has been republished in a collection of Asturias's journalism entitled *América, fábula de fábulas,* hereinafter *América.*

7. "El concepto semidivino o semidiabólico que nuestros antepasados tenían de la mujer ha ido quedando guardado entre las ropas viejas y sólo de vez en vez se oye todavía a los que se refieren a ella como a un ser situado en un pedestal, fuera de la vida diaria, fuera de la lucha cotidiana, aislada en las cuatro paredes de su casa" (Asturias *América* 348).

8. "Far from hurting her, in her feelings toward her husband, they humanize her, they make her transform herself completely into what she should be, the collaborator of man, not against man, but with man, the woman who, in the middle of the necessities of life, in the violence of daily happenings, has arrived at a comprehension of the falsity of the antithesis 'man-woman' (*Man* capitalized, *woman* with a very, very small *w*), has begun to feel responsible like her husband, she also, and on the same level as he in everything that is beneficial, for the two of them, for their house, and principally for their children" ["lejos de perjudicarla, en sus sentimientos hacia el marido, la humanizan, la hacen transformarse plenamente en que debe ser, la colaboradora del hombre, no contra el hombre, sino con el hombre, la mujer que en medio de las necesidades de la vida, en el embate de los acontecimientos diarios, ha llegado a comprender la falsedad de la antítesis 'hombre-mujer' (Hombre, con mayúscula, y mujer con una 'm' minúscula, muy, muy, minúscula), a sentirse, como su esposo, responsable, ella también, y a la par que él en todo lo que es beneficioso, para ellos dos, para la casa y principalmente para sus hijos"] (Asturias *América* 349).

9. "Hay que repetir que en la actualidad la mujer ha llegado a ser, en un plano superior a todos los tiempos, un factor económico tan importante, si no más, que el hombre, y esta salvedad no es, queridas lectoras sino una galantería de mi parte, que sin tal no podría despedirme de vosotras que sois además tan bellas, tan graciosas, tan amables y seductores, cuando no erais factores económicos, pero qué horror . . . estoy volviendo al pasado . . . cuando erais . . . de nosotros, pues ahora, como factores económicos que sois, ya sois vuestras, y disponéis de vuestras vidas sin tomarnos en cuenta!" (Asturias *América* 350).

10. The *lox* probably refers to both the vulva and the vagina, because of the image of it as a "throat" ["garganta"].

11. "¡A la preciosa garganta que es prenda de amor, a la caja de pedernales rojos, la luna los derrama mes a mes, a la virgen ofrenda, al rugoso caracol, a la estrella-serpiente, tragadora y sustentadora, la que ordena la vida labrada en ejes de esperanza, la gran carnicera, sueño colgado del cielo de la boca de los perversos, soga alrededor del cuello del señor que conduce la existencia, y mala y baldía como carne de moscas, para los que la toman de lugar de placer . . . de pasatiempo!" (259–60).

12. There are Guatemalans and Argentines of African descent, of course, but their numbers are small, much smaller than in other parts of Latin America, such as in Brazil or the Caribbean. Certain gods of the Classic Maya are represented as having black skin or black-painted skin, however.

13. A piece of Asturias's journalism from the period of the composition of

Mulata seems to confirm his statement to Harss. In a 1960 review of the Spanish translation of Brazilian novelist Jorge Amado's *Gabriela, cravo e canela* (*Gabriela, Cloves and Cinnamon*), Asturias describes Gabriela, Amado's "mulata," in terms similar to those of his own Mulata. She is "like an apparition" ["como una aparición"], with "fascinating beauty" ["belleza fascinante"], and a "Woman with birdwings, with eyes of running water, who escapes, with a head of black hair, so nocturnal, appropriate for dreams and daydreams" ["Mujer con alas de pájaro, con ojos de agua que corre, que se escapa, con cabellera negra, de tan nocturna, propia para el sueño y el ensueño"] ("Jorge Amado: *Gabriela, clavo e canela*" in Asturias *América* 171).

14. René Prieto writes that the Mulata is "the incarnation of all that Asturias abhors and condemns" ["la encarnación de todo lo que Asturias aborrece y condena"] (Prieto "El papel político del erotismo en *Mulata de tal*" 89), but in the Harss and Dohmann interview, the novelist makes plain that she has positive qualities he seeks to exploit.

15. Caridad Jiménez has pointed out to me that "Já" in Spanish *caló* means "woman." (Private communication. See Rosensweig "*Caló*": *Gutter Spanish* 69).

The special place of the Salvajos deserves more attention but would be inappropriate for this study, since female Salvajos are not portrayed as sexual. It is clear that the Salvajo society, despite their activities as chicken thieves, is positively portrayed, distinctly in contrast to the hellish characters filling up most pages.

The relation of humans to animals within the Mayan worldview is complex and important but also only indirectly related to my subject here. For one thing, every human has a *nahual,* an animal self, with whom he or she is intimately connected. *Nahuales* play important roles in the final battle between the spider and the porcupine, who are the transformed and spirit-possessed priest Chimalpín and sorcerer Yumí, as well as in many lesser scenes.

16. In "A Note on Gender Iconography: The Vagina," Shirley Ardener gives several examples from African society in which groups of women unite to punish a man who has offended women by insulting a woman's sexual parts or by being unfaithful to her. Ardener remarks that such women's rituals are more frequent than we know, because they are rarely recorded in patriarchal societies. It is fair to say that we shall never know whether, in its inspiration, *any* of the scenes of woman's violence to men in *Mulata* were purely invented or at least partially inspired by events Asturias may have witnessed, in addition to legends he may have heard or read. I show that, whatever the source, the novel contains many analogies to Mayan culture as represented in anthropological discourse.

17. It also might be seen as a grotesque intuition of woman's doubleness, a meditation on the "sex which is not one," the image which Luce Irigaray proposes as representing woman's potential for resistance against patriarchy.

18. The reader may also wish to consult Victor Bravo (82–89) and Susan Willis.

19. A new source for Asturias's mythic details, *Los chortis de Guatemala* by Charles Wisdom, unmentioned by previous critics, lends considerable weight to

my thesis that the sexual women are radically ambivalent portraits, woven into his narrative because they are constitutive of the Mesoamerican contextual substrate. Although the Spanish translation was his likely source, the English original *The Chorti Indians of Guatemala* (1940) has been reprinted.

20. According to Giuseppe Bellini, this focus on the corrupting power of money is one of the main analogues to Quevedo's themes. In a difficult-to-acquire article, Bellini makes explicit the homologies between Quevedo's prose and *Mulata*: "The presence of the *Divine Comedy* in this 'demonological' conception in *Mulata de tal* has already been mentioned, but improperly. Dante is an easy and exterior reference for Asturias, [and] despite his late predilection for the *Comedia*, one totally alien to this novel. What really is evident in the work is the presence of Quevedo's *The Dreams*, not due to a 'taste for domination' denounced in the Castillian author by [Miguel de] Unamuno, but rather resulting from moral motivations, the powerful play of fantasy creating unforgettable and hallucinating figures and constructions, the power of language in its vigor and plastic value, prodigious mental ability to renovate and transform language. In this sense, Asturias represents in the Spanish of America a role of the same importance as that of Quevedo in the Castillian of Spain in the seventeenth century." ["Ya se habló de una presencia, en esta concepción 'demonológica' de *Mulata* . . . , de la *Divina Comedia*, pero impropiamente. Dante es referencia fácil y exterior a Asturias, a pesar de su tardía predilección por la *Comedia*, totalmente ajena a esta novela. Lo que sí es patente en ella es la presencia de *Los sueños*, no ya por el 'dejo de dómine' denunciado en el escritor castellano por Unamuno, sino por el dominante motivo moral, el juego poderoso de la fantasía, creadora de figuras y construcciones imborrables y alucinantes, el poder del lenguaje, su vigor y valor plástico, la facultad prodigiosa de renovación y transformación del idioma. En este sentido Asturias representa en el castellano de América un papel de la misma importancia que el de Quevedo en el castellano de la España del siglo XVII" (Bellini, "Miguel Angel Asturias y Quevedo" 65)].

21. Tazol says: "with no need for any hangings, they will remain with me, thanks to your efforts, and what better tribute, since I will use those bodies to ferment liquors that I will sell later at high prices to those who feed on human flesh" (45T) ["sin necesidad de ahorcamientos, se quedarán conmigo, gracias a tu gestión, y que mejor tributo, ya que esos cuerpos me servirán para fermentar licores que después venderé a precios de oro, a los que se alimentan de carne humana" (45)].

22. Harss harshly criticizes the novel: "Asturias relies too heavily on his senses. He is not a thinker, and his work tends to be conceptually weak. There are times when he seems not to know too well what he is doing or where he is going. He lets the irrational get out of hand, and then meanings are lost. In *Mulata* he lumbers and strays. But his impish humor carries many good pages" (Harss and Dohmann 99). One reason the novel appears "conceptually weak" to Harss is because he does not suspect the functioning of a female devil contract, among other things.

23. "—Si te devuelven el sexo (¡sangre de cacao su anuncio, sangre virginal su anuncio, el hijo de su sangre su anuncio!), si te lo devuelven envuelto en el suelo, ¿te lo llevará?

"—Si me lo devuelven envuelto en el suelo, me lo llevaré—contestó la mulata—; en el suelo que es la piel de la tierra, lo enrollaré . . .

"—Si te lo devuelven (¡Fuego es, serpiente es, es devorador de hombres!), si te lo devuelven en el camino de los esposos, ¿te lo llevarás?

"—Si me lo devuelven en el camino de los esposos, me lo llevaré. En el esposo, que es la piel de la esposa, lo enrollaré. . . ." (252).

24. "'¿Dónde estaban los grandes brujos?' Estarían al pie del árbol de cacao, . . . y en las axilas peludas, enmascarados de tecolotes, los intérpretes de lenguas pintadas, verde la lengua del que hablaba quiché, añil la del zuhutil, roja la del cacchiquel, blanca la del quekchí, amarilla la del mame, morada la del pocomame, negra la del que hablaba pocochí" (300).

25. "Some years ago the late Sir Eric Thompson proposed that the Central Area of the Mayan region was inhabited by Cholan-speakers during the Classic period—with Chontal and Chol in the low hills and plains in the northwest, and Chorti in the southeast—it seems certain that Cholan once predominated across a great arc extending right through the Central Area, . . . it can hardly be coincidental that Chol is still spoken around the great Classic site of Palenque, and Chorti in the vicinity of Copán; phonetic readings of the Classic texts support this fact" (Coe *The Maya* 26).

26. The hieroglyphs of the "table of astronomies" ["mesa de las astronomías"] are mentioned in the novel (346T; 351) as are the *chacs* (242T; 246), the gods (GI or GII) who, according to Schele and Miller, appear in reptilian or anthropomorphic form, wear shell jewelry, and are associated with the sun or Venus (48–49). In the last thirty years, there has been new life infused into the study of the ancient Maya by the great progress that has been made since 1965—three years after the publication of *Mulata*—when a Russian linguist first cracked the phonetic code.

27. Asturias was more likely to have seen the Spanish translation of Wisdom, which says: "Todos los seres sobrenaturales poseen, en grados variables, las características siguientes: 1, neutralidad o dualismo moral; 2, dualismo sexual; 3, multiplicidad, 4, bilocalidad en el cielo y en la tierra; 5, personalidad dual, integrada por partes nativas y católicas. El concepto de lo dual es tan fuerte que los indígenas lo adscriben, sin vacilar, a cualquier ser, incluso cuando el carácter doble pudiera no servir para ningún propósito; en tales casos simplemente afirman que el ser en referencia 'debe' ser hembra y macho, bueno y malo, etcétera." (*Los chortis de Guatemala* 462)

28. Further examples pertinent to Asturias's works are "The deer god . . . is dual sexed, the male being the protector of female deer, and the female, of male deer" (400) ["el dios venado" . . . "Sexualmente es dual: el macho protege a las venadas y viceversa" (452)]. The same is true of the god of medicines and "the guardian of the milpas" (401) ["el guardián de las milpas" (452–53)].

29. This circumstance associates the female Sisimite with Felicito Piedrasanta (a drunk condemned to turn into a stone and roll down the mountain), whom Yumí and Zabala seek out early in their wanderings in their attempt to restore Zabala to her full stature.

30. There appears to be a controversy (or confusion at any rate) regarding the linguistic or cultural family of the Huastec group. The language is spoken in the region of Veracruz, Mexico, and, according to the *Atlas Cultural de México: Lingüística* (Castañeda 1988), belongs to the Mayan family of languages (56). English reference works tend to agree. But Pérez Botero and *The Flayed God* say Tlazoltecoatl/Tlazolteotl is either Aztec, which does not appear to be true, or Mexican, which would be literally true, but misleading.

31. Professor John Scott of the University of Florida suggests that Tazol may be a Mayanized form of Tlazol, since the *teotl* ending merely refers to "deity." Private communication.

32. See Mercedes de la Garza, *El universo sagrado de la serpiente entre los mayas* [The sacred universe of the serpent among the Mayas], especially the chapter "La serpiente y las deidades femeninas" [The serpent and the female deities], pp. 209–17, in which riches and fertility are attributed to serpents; and *Poesía Indígena [Indigenous poetry]*, "Canto a la Mujer-Serpiente (Cihuacóatl)" ["Song to the woman-serpent (Cihuacóatl)] 15–16, in which a broom (the Mulata's weapon against Zabala/Giroma) is featured.

In *Arts mayas du Guatemala* [Mayan arts in Guatemala], the book accompanying a large exhibit of Mayan art at the Grand Palais in Paris in 1968 for which Asturias was consulted, Ixchel is described as follows: "Malevolent in some of her aspects, benevolent in others, she is generally represented with the traits of an old woman, her head crowned by a coiled serpent" ["Maléfique dans certains de ses attributions, favorable dans d'autres, elle est généralement représentée sous les traits d'une vieille femme, la tête surmontée d'un serpent lové" (xxxiii)].

33. Previously unpublished drafts of an early chapter of *Mulata,* titled by Asturias "Tierrapaulita," have recently appeared that apparently are an early version of this episode of sleeping with a snake. Dorita Nouhaud argues in the notes that this episode was the seed for the novel as a whole (29 n. 1). The idea is convincing.

34. See Schele and Miller (306 n. 3) for a fuller discussion. For our purposes here, it is most important that neither when Asturias wrote, nor today, was/is the issue settled.

35. Prostitution is not unique to capitalist societies, and is known to have existed among the precapitalist Maya during the early conquest: "In both highlands and lowlands, [Mayan] boys and young men stayed apart from their families in special communal houses where they presumably learned the arts of war, and other things as well, for Landa says that the prostitutes were frequent visitors" (Coe *The Maya* 158). Landa is Archbishop Diego de Landa, author of *Relación de Yucatán* [Story of the Yucatán], an important sixteenth-century source for information on the Maya.

36. Other important associations of these two goddesses, according to Thompson, are with the monkey, representing the arts as well as salaciousness, and in the Mexican tradition, death; and, with the spider, in the Mayan tradition associated with the weaver Ixchel, whose web supports the sky and whose husband or partner was a poet or singer. In Asturias's novel, the spider is not associated with the Mulata but is the *nahual* of Zabala and later also of the priest Chimalpín.

37. Regarding the Mulata's hermaphroditism in the novel, her mysterious and disturbing body further indicates that the Mulata probably is an underworld deity. Schele and Miller remind us that many underworld deities are "transformational, combining male and female figures" (268).

38. "—Celestino—le dijo la enanita [Zabala/Juana Puti]—, ésta tu mujer, para que vos veas, no tiene sus *perfeuciones* de mujer, pero tampoco tiene *perfeuciones* de hombre. Has de saber que yo la fuide a espiar, mientras se bañaba, y no es mujer, porque no es mujer, te lo garantizo, si me conoceré yo mis *perfeuciones,* pero tampoco es hombre cabal, porque no tiene tus *perfeuciones* que también conozco
. . .

"Y dicho esto, se frotó contra Yumí.
"—Me vas a decir entonces que es . . .—se tragó la palabra Celestino.
"—No sé lo que es, pero no es hombre y no es mujer. Para hombre le falta tantito tantote y para mujer le sobra tantote tantito" (66).

39. "We say the sun and the moon cannot share the same bed because if they did the sun as a male and the moon as a female would breed monstrous children. That's why when the Mulata marries the protagonist, Yumí, she never shows him her face when they make love. She always gives him her back. We don't know why, whether because she has abnormal tastes or for some other reason. The Indian texts say the gods dealt out severe punishments to those who made love 'facing the wrong way.' We don't know whether the reference is to homosexuality or simply to abnormal posture" (Asturias, in Harss and Dohmann 97).

40. In "the Kekchi-Mopan-Maya legend of the sun and the moon, the moon is the first woman to have sexual intercourse" (Thompson 133), but "Moon had no vagina. With the aid of the deer this was remedied. Thereupon Sun and Moon were the first to copulate" (Thompson 169). Because of the Moon Goddess's lack of a vagina, perhaps she could only have anal sex.

41. "Hasta caer fuera del tiempo, en una eternidad roedora, dos lunas de alquitrán sus pupilas inmensamente abiertas, dos coágulos solitarios en medio del espanto absoluto, el pavor, el miedo, la congoja, el llanto a gritos, llanto de alguien sin dueño, sin asidero, y allí mismo, el furor suicida, el querer deshacerse de su imagen presente a cambio de una futura imagen, golpeándose la cara contra lo infranqueable, y allí mismo el aullido, el más angustioso aullido al encontrarse de nuevo con su yo lunar, vertebral, horadado, pasivo, climatérico" (58).

42. In Asturias's translation their names are Pluvioso (Rain), Sembrador (Seeder), and Volcán (Volcano).

43. The *Popol Vuh* tells that human twins fail several tests upon entering the

nether realm, for instance, being fooled into calling manikins by the name of the Underworld Lords. A second pair of twins sends ahead Mosquito as a scout; when Mosquito bites the manikins and they do not respond, he discovers they are a trick. Mosquito learns the names of all the Lords for these semi-divine twins and communicates his reconnaissance. The twins use the information to call the Lords by their names and thus gain an advantage over them.

44. "Reading any account of Mesoamerican ritual activity makes chillingly clear that the blood needed to maintain the universal system was provided. There seem to be endless numbers of sacrificial rituals running the gamut from symbolic bloodletting and animal sacrifice to autosacrifice to the ultimate sacrifice of human life itself. Autosacrifice, as depicted in the Aztec and Mixtec creation myths, was most common. Throughout Mesoamerica the bleeding of ears, tongues, and genital organs by members of the priesthood was a daily ritual occurrence, sometimes reaching ghastly proportions" (Markman and Markman 180).

45. All four Mayan visual formats should remind us of the importance of stylization and line which, if Asturias wanted to imitate Mayan art in a verbal text, would have no exact equivalent. For example, "Maya art, both painting and sculpture, showed a marked sensitivity to the boundaries of the pictorial field, notably through the many innovative devices artists used to break them" (Schele and Miller 37). For example, Asturias's bizarre chapter breaks, which rarely coincide with moments of transition or summary, may result from an attempt to use his chapter titles in parallel fashion to the bands, often glyphic or scriptural, which frame Mayan visual art.

46. "'¿Y qué le pasó a tu madre?,' atrevió la voz 'Sábana,' espantándose una nube de moscas negras, pegajosas de luna. '¿No supo?, la despedazaron los coyotes.' 'Pero quedó usted . . .,' apicaró la voz 'Sábana,' en tono casi amoroso. . . . pero ella no se dio por aludida del piropo encubierto de aquél. . . . Ahora me tiene afuera, pensaba la mulata, una mulata de barro sin quemar, pero como cuando me tenía adentro, porque estamos en el mismo temblor" (345).

47. Coyotes have played an important role in Mayan belief and in Asturias's previous Neo-Indigenist novel, *Men of Maize*.

48. "And that Giant stink even reached the Huasanga, impelled by her bridal desires. . . .

"'My Gigantic,' she squeaked at him in the frying talk of her great desire, 'I don't know what's happening to your Huasanguita, but I want to try a Giant!'" (149T)

["Y hasta aquella hediondez de gigante pretendía llegar la Huasanga, impulsada por su deseo de recién casada. . . .

—¡Gigantón mío—chirriábale el hablar frito en la salida de su gran deseo—, no sé qué le pasa a tu Huasanguita, pero quiero probar gigante." (152)]

49. "La Huasanga, [estaba] montada en el Cadejo, el sexo de Giroma, como una flor, en el ojal de la solapa de su chapetilla de amazona" (201).

50. Antonio Cornejo Polar points out that indigenist fiction could never be

"authentic" because it was written in Spanish and because the native literatures consisted of poems and epics, not novels. Poetic techniques, though, could be approximated, more than the other cultural forms at least, if only for the brevity of a novel's internal poems and incantations.

51. "¡Este taimado extranjero concibe al hombre como carne de infierno y procura, cuando no exige, la multiplicación de los seres humanos aislados como él, orgullosos como él, feroces como él, negociantes como él, religiosos a la diabla como él, para llenar su infierno! ¡Por eso deshizo el vaho de espejo que el Corazón del Cielo había regado sobre los sexos, vaho de espejo en el que el hombre y la mujer, en el mágico instante de dar la vida dejaban copia de sus imágenes confundidas en el nuevo ser, cuyo ombligo ofrecían a la comunidad, significando con ello que éste no iba a ser ajeno a la existencia de todos, sino parte de sus existencias que a la vez son parte de la existencia de los dioses!" (203).

52. "—¡Lo que es difícil—suspiró al hablar el curial—es darle batalla al Angel Portaluz que se ha mezclado con el progreso humano, adaptándose a maravilla con las costumbres modernas, como todos nosotros, por otra parte, porque, para mí, el demonio, por el pecado original, entra en la formación natural del hombre, en un sesenta o setenta por ciento, y me quedo corto!" (209).

53. The standard text by Michael Coe speculates that images of the underworld found in art of the Classic period in a certain cave, show queer sex: "Deep caverns have always been conceptual entrances to Xibalbá for the past and present Maya. One such cave, now named Naj Tunich, was discovered in 1979 by local residents in karst terrain near Poptun, in the southeastern Petén. The importance of Naj Tunich lies in its extensive hieroglyphic texts (altogether comprising about 400 glyphs) and scenes, all executed in carbon black on the cave walls. The latter include depictions of the ball game, *amorous activities which are probably of a homosexual nature,* and Maya deities, which not unexpectedly include the Hero Twins, Hunahpu and Xbalanque" (Coe *The Maya* 169, emphasis mine). Coe asserts that this cave's paintings reflect not just beliefs about the divine but also actual sexual practices among the elite, owing to the parallelisms often found between gods and royalty. Since this cave was discovered after *Mulata* was written, I am not arguing that its paintings were a source. At most they corroborate what Asturias found elsewhere or invented.

54. In Asturias's novel, Yumí suffers from a "moon from the back" ["luna de espaldas"] instead of the honey*moon* he was anticipating when he married the Mulata. Humorously, Yumí laments how nice it would be to see the face of the person to whom you are making love. Thus he may be complaining about vaginal intercourse from behind. A second rejection of sex from behind occurs when the peons turn from the Mulata in the scene in which she dances dressed only in bananas. But it would be a mistake to assume that these preferences for frontal sex in the novel are antihomosexual, just as it would be jumping to conclusions to presume that the preference must have belonged to Asturias rather than to the story he is telling, as a strategy within the Mayan Game.

55. Jerónimo comments to Chimalpín later, "smallpox for you and delight for her, because you can't tell me that a woman who chooses a hedgehog [porcupine] for a husband isn't full of lust" (288T) ["la viruela para usted, Padrecito, y la delicia para ella, porque no me diga, mujer que escoge de marido a un puercoespín debe ser muy lasciva" (293)].

56. The aphrodisiac that really drove the Mulata wild in Quiavicús was the ticking of the Clock of Babylon. In a possible reference to the supposed Mesoamerican obsession with calendrics, the Mulata shouts: "It's the end of the world! . . . Why not take advantage of every free minute that passes by with lovemaking!" (65T) ["¡Pero si es el fin del mundo! . . . Cómo no aprovechar, en la entrega amorosa, cada instante que fluye gratuito!" (65)].

57. One of the many moments when the Mulata is linked through imagery to the moon, snails, and water is when Yumí says to the Mulata-as-Jerónimo: "A woman is a shirt of dreams the earth puts on. A shirt of water, if she's a woman as fresh and good as the rain. A shirt of mirrors, if she's a woman of the sun, a strong woman. And a shirt of forgetfulness, a shirt of erased faces, if she's a moon woman, a seashell [snail] woman with precious holes" (232T; alternative translation of *caracol* provided) ["la mujer es la camisa de sueños que la tierra se pone. Camisa de agua, si es mujer dulce y buena como la lluvia. Camisa de espejos si es mujer de sol, mujer bravía. Y camisa de olvido, camisa de borrar rostros, si es mujer lunar, mujer caracol de preciosos agujeros" (236)].

58. "Su Señoría Ilustrísima, el de la paciencia gastada, trenzaba las manos, torcía la boca, juntaba las cejas, fastidiado por la minuciosa relación que aquel viejo párroco reumático, deforme, con una pierna más larga que otra, le hacía de su lucha con las más primitivas formas del demonio en Tierrapaulita, la brujería más pestilente, el más enconado odio por Dios, las peores supersticiones. . . . En la curia nadie dio oídos a los relatos del cura de Tierrapaulita" (207).

59. "La artillería gruesa contra Satán: las obras completas de Santo Tomás de Aquino, una *Historia Eclesiástica Indiana,* por fray Diego de Mendieta; *El Criticón,* de Baltasar Gracián; la *Apologética,* del Obispo Las Casas; libro de predicadores, Bossuet a la cabeza, *Prontuario de Teología Moral* del Padre Larraga y, a Mayor Gloria de Dios, libros sobre cataclismos, huracanes, predestinación, diabolismo, sin faltar el *Manual de Exorcistas* de fray Luis de la Concepción, la Santa Biblia y, como libro de cabecera, el *Apocalipsis*" (210).

60. "VOCES: ¡Qué negra suerte la de los negros! . . . ¡Qué negra suerte la de los negros! . . .

"BARTOLOMÉ *(no sabe qué hacer y cae de rodillas)*: ¡Perdón! . . . ¡Perdón! . . . ¡No me acuséis sin oírme! . . . ¡Aconsejé llevar negros a las Nuevas Indias, pero ya el infame comercio existía! . . . ¡el sufrimiento de los indios me cegó hasta proponer que esos cirineos de color, también esclavos, también esclavos, vinieran a ayudar con la cruz de la conquista a mis pobres bestezuelas de barro que por su contextura física ya no soportaban más!" (Asturias, "La audiencia de los confines" 235).

61. Psychoanalysis would be likely to see the erosion of the borders between

self and other and between one social group and its enemy as problematic for the individuals involved. René Prieto writes at length of the ending of *Mulata* as a devastation of the self that leaves a void within. The sense of loss accompanying the breakdown of an individual's identification with a social group has often been mourned. Nevertheless, it can have some social value. Racial, sexual, and ethnic fanaticisms encounter an insurmountable obstacle when the idea is accepted that each of us can have only partial affiliation with any single group, because of the great number of antithetical ties each person has to aspects of her life and to the shifting definitions of such collectivities.

62. Pérez associates the Mule (*la Mula*) with the Mulata because their names are so similar.

63. Wisdom writes that "Chamer, the god of death, is both a giant male dressed in female's clothes and a male with a female consort, each dressed according to his [or her] sex, the male causing death to women, and the female, to men" (398) ["Chamer, el dios de la muerte, es al mismo tiempo un varón gigantesco vestido con ropas femeninas y un varón acompañado de su consorte (femenina), cada uno ataviado con ropa correspondiente a su sexo; en este caso él ocasiona la muerte a las mujeres y ella a los varones" (449T)].

64. "Bailaba con el cuello rodeado de un collar de bananitas de oro, del que pendía un banano manzana que al bailar le golpeaba los senos. Así la miraban los peones. Los mayorales. Los mozos. En redor de su cintura, y en sus antebrazos, bananas doradas y bananas moradas, en movimiento al compás de sus caderas, de sus glúteos, de sus pies, de sus tobillos" (57).

65. In a prose work associating Baker with time, analogous to Asturias with the Mulata, e.e. cummings wrote that Josephine Baker "enters through a dense electric twilight, walking backwards on hands and feet, legs and arms stiff, down a huge jungle tree — as a creature neither infrahuman nor superhuman but somehow both: a mysteriously unkillable Something, equally nonprimitive and uncivilized, or beyond time in the sense that emotion is beyond arithmetic" (on Baker's debut as Fatou in Paris in 1926, quoted in Hammond 41). The racist and sexist language used by cummings to describe Baker is consistent with the times in which Asturias may have seen her, and possibly with the image Baker wanted to promote for herself, according to biographers.

66. "—¡Una polvareda fue la creación y una polvareda queda de las ciudades que destruimos! . . . ¡Los hombres verdaderos, los hechos de maíz, dejan de existir realmente y se vuelven seres ficticios, cuando no viven para la comunidad y por eso deben ser suprimidos. ¡Por eso aniquilé con mis Gigantes Mayores, y aniquilaré mientras no se enmienden, a todos aquellos que olvidando, contradiciendo o negando su condición de granos de maíz, partes de una mazorca se tornan egocentristas, egoístas, individualistas. . . .

"—¡Plantas, animales, astros . . . , existen todos juntos, todos juntos, como fueron creados! ¡A ninguno se le ha ocurrido hacer existencia aparte, tomar la vida para su uso exclusivo, sólo al hombre que debe ser destruido por su pretender existir aislado, ajeno a los millones de destinos que se tejen y destejen alrededor suyo!" (202–3).

67. "El argumento y el desarrollo de los acontecimientos . . . aparecen hilados de manera caprichosa y abstrusa, y muchas veces se contradicen y enhebran de modo similar al discurso de un loco o de un niño o, simplemente, con la espontaneidad y falta de causalidad con que se cuentan las consejas y leyendas populares, dichas por boca del pueblo. Ello no impide que el mundo novelesco esté estructurado a la perfección" (462–63).

68. In a comparative study of leprosy as a disease in medieval literature, Saul Nathaniel Brody concludes that the "inaccurate and morally charged picture of leprosy was carried over into the twentieth century" (194–95). The 1933 *Oxford English Dictionary*, for example, "conveys moral and aesthetic distaste and mistaken medical information" in its definition of leprosy: "A loathsome disease (*Elephantiasis Graecorum*), which slowly eats away the body, and forms shining white scales on the skin." Brody explains: "Leprosy lesions are never white, except when there is scarring; the white scales are not the result of empirical reporting but can be traced ultimately back to the Bible (in II Kings 5:27, Gehazi is described as a 'leper as white as snow'; Leviticus 13:10 identifies 'a white color in the skin' as a sign of leprosy) and to the Greek word *lepros*, 'a scale,' which is the etymological source of Greek *lepra*, 'leprosy'" (194–95).

69. According to Schroeder, Sylvia Rendón published in Spanish most of Chimalpahin's Fourth Relation in 1949, then included this extract in her complete translation from Fondo de Cultura Económica later (Schroeder 246). Schroeder gives the complete reference to the early publication as: "La cuarta relación de don Domingo de San Antón Muñón Chimalpahin Quauhtlehuanitzin." *Anales del Instituto Nacional de Antropología e Historia* 3 (1949): 199–218. The later publication into which Rendón incorporated this piece was her *Relaciones originales de chalco Amaquemecan: Escritas por Don Francisco de San Antón Muñón Chimalpahin Cuauhtlehuanitzin*. Mexico City: Fondo de Cultura Económica, 1965.

70. "Invitan al señor de Tenochtitlan a una lucha donde sólo podrá triunfar el muy bien dotado sexualmente. La guerra se transforma en asedio erótico, acercamiento de contrarios, acto sexual con todos sus preámbulos; y el canto finaliza con la victoria de la mujercita de Chalco que, con sus encantos, logra hacer suyo al poderoso Axayacátl" (281).

71. In ancient Mayan art, the gods of the underworld were depicted as farting, defacating, and having pus oozing from sores. (See Schele and Miller 268, plate 109, also 281).

72. The 1960s women's movement, accused of liberal notions of private property and the priority of the individual over the group, was not a target for his ire. It was not really in his field of vision. In general, feminism means uniting as a group based on common grounds for political action, attitudes with which he sympathized.

Chapter 3. Clarice Lispector and the Promise of Freedom

1. There are also professors in *Wild Heart*, "The Crime of the Mathematics Professor" in *Family Ties* ("O crime do professor de matemática" in *Laços de família*), *Apple in the Dark,* and elsewhere in Lispector's works.

2. I was already working with the idea of the reflection when I discovered Kadota's book from 1998, very late in the revision process of this book.

3. "*Uma Aprendizagem ou O Livro dos Prazeres* . . . lembra um Manual de Iniciação Amorosa mas, na verdade, é uma crítica à linguagem romântica e quase um ensaio filosófico sobre o prazer, mas o prazer do autoconhecimento. . . . O prazer do *Livro dos Prazeres* está condicionado à aquisição de conhecimentos e lenta evolução do ser em relação à capacidade de amar. É um percurso atravessado por uma linguagem mutacional que salta das frases feitas ao discurso didático e se mascara em romântico" (113).

4. But Mazzara and Paris conclude that "not only existentialism but mysticism is a humanism. The greatest Christian mystics have preserved their humanity along the mystic way and in mystic union. Furthermore, after their times of spiritual anguish and delight, and because of them, they have enjoyed earthly ones, which range from the most commonplace to the most exalted" (714). While the enjoyment of earthly "times of spiritual anguish and delight" may be frequent among mystics, this delight does not define mystical experience. On the contrary, the Christian mystic in the mystical experience seeks *release* from such earthly delights and the death of his or her humanity in temporary divine ecstasy.

5. The opening comma of *An Apprenticeship* yokes the main text to the preceding peritexts. Preceding the comma are (in reverse order): a half-title page for part one, a full title page, three epigraphs, and a preliminary note. This note continues the regression back to an origin outside the text. In it, Clarice Lispector speaks to the reader in the first person, as author and source for the fiction to follow. Inscribed as "C.L.," she is indicated by her initials, like G.H., the protagonist of *Passion*. Thus, the prefatory note places *An Apprenticeship* in a complicated relation to Lispector's life and her other writings.

6. This prayer may be seen as a rebellion against Ulysses' teachings at the beginning of the apprenticeship. Ulysses suggests she pray to herself, that she ask more of herself than she feels capable of giving. Instead, she prays to God to give her what she has not given herself.

7. After the first edition of *A legião estrangeira,* the stories are published separately from the chronicles. I am using the collection of chronicles published after Lispector's death as *Para não esquecer: Crônicas.* The story collection retains the title *A legião estrangeira.* The title of the translation is *The Foreign Legion: Stories and Chronicles.*

8. During the years of writing *An Apprenticeship,* Lispector also contributed barely changed fragments of the novel to the newspaper *Jornal do Brasil,* some of which Richard Mazzara has discussed. "Another Apprenticeship: Clarice Lispector's *A descoberta do mundo* and *Uma Aprendizagem.*" The chronicles

Mazzara discusses are in *Descoberta* on the following pages: 30, 78–80, 99–101, 113–15, 132–33, 167–69, 170, 181–83, 203, 212–14, 225–26, 249–51, 663, 738–39, and 755–57. But the process does not end there. After *An Apprenticeship*'s publication in 1969, several additional fragments from it return—in *Felicidade clandestina* [Clandestine Happiness] (stories, 1971), *The Stream of Life* (1989; *Água viva* 1973), and *Onde estivestes de noite* (stories, 1974; Where you were at night, *Soulstorm* 1989).

9. Olga de Sá (1979) found two occasions when Lispector augmented, modified, and republished Lori's "state of grace" from *An Apprenticeship*: on April 1968 in the *Jornal do Brasil* (RJ) and in *The Stream of Life* (*Água viva* 104–107).

10. "É o que aqui se pretende mostrar de Clarice Lispector: uma postura consciente, de *reflexão* contínua, embora muitas vezes dissimulada em sua representação sígnica, alicerçada na linguagem poética e/ou paradoxal, no fluxo de consciência, que confunde/constrange o leitor pouco habituado a uma narrativa fragmentada que o atropela continuamente, acostumado que está ao relato linear e fatual" (20, emphasis added).

11. In an earlier fiction published in *Legion*, Lispector associates the image of oranges growing with a will to be happy, fecund, in possession of oneself, the opposite of Lori. "I can sense the patient brutality with which the sealed earth is opening up inside, and I know with what burden of sweetness the summer will ripen a hundred thousand oranges, and I know that those oranges are mine, because I am in love" ("Because I am in Love," *The Foreign Legion* 141–42T) ["sinto a paciente brutalidade com que a terra fechada se abre por dentro, e sei com que peso de doçura o verão amadurecerá cem mil laranjas são minhas, porque eu quero" ("Porque eu quero," *Para não esquecer* 53)]. I would argue with the translation of "eu quero" as "I am in love" because there is little in this text to indicate love. Better might be "because I want" or "because I desire."

12. The Sphinx reference could also allude to Machado de Assis, who used the image. (My thanks to Elizabeth Ginway for pointing this out.)

13. The satisfaction of sexual desire—the "little death" in French—plays only a small part in *An Apprenticeship*. Neither confirmed nor denied as meaning death in the novel, the orgasm would be an example, a specific case, of the general and multiple "deaths" that the living suffer.

14. "Também Lóri usava a máscara de palhaço da pintura excessiva. Aquela mesma que nos partos da adolescência se escolhia para não se ficar desnudo para o resto da luta. Não, não é que se fizesse mal em deixar o próprio rosto exposto à sensibilidade. Mas é que esse rosto que estivesse nu poderia, ao ferir-se, fechar-se sozinho em súbita máscara involuntária e terrível: era pois menos *perigoso* escolher, antes que isso fatalmente acontecesse, escolher sozinha ser uma 'persona.' Escolher a própria máscara era o primeiro gesto voluntário humano. E solitário" (92, emphasis added).

15. Note that the Portuguese does not indicate necessarily a male adolescent, merely an adolescent person.

16. Ulysses/Odysseus in Homer uses namelessness to fool Polyphemus, the man-eating cyclops who has Ulysses and his men trapped in a cave. When Polyphemus asks Ulysses his name, the hero responds "no one." Later, when Polyphemus's monstrous neighbors ask the giant who has blinded him, the cyclops responds "no one," and thus receives no help to pursue the fleeing sailors.

17. A spin-off from these paragraphs of *An Apprenticeship* appeared as a *crônica* in the *Jornal do Brasil* called "Diante do que é grande demais" (December 30, 1972: B2). The context is the same as in the novel (a search for lost papers), and several sentences are reproduced exactly with the change from the narrator speaking of Lori's sentiments in the third person to a first-person voice.

18. The importance of losing one's name is a repeated theme in Lispector. It appears in *Apple in the Dark* (1961) as "deheroization" and in *Passion* (1964) as "neutrality."

19. The image of maturity as wheat in the rain from *An Apprenticeship* was expanded by Lispector in the short text "Such Gentleness" (*Soulstorm* 160–61T) ["Tanta mansidão," *Onde estivestes de noite* 114–17] employing the same context of an interior growth newly understood by a woman watching the rain. The major change between the novel and the 1974 fragment is from the third to the first person. In the English translation in *Soulstorm*, as in the translation of *An Apprenticeship*, the word "wheat" does not appear.

20. Cixous has written extensively on Clarice Lispector and almost single-handedly is responsible for Lispector's popularity in France. In 1992, *An Apprenticeship* was published in French translation, and in the fall of 1993, Cixous was teaching the novel in her seminar.

21. "Loreley é o nome de um personagem lendário do folclore alemão cantado num belíssimo poema por Heine. A lenda diz que Loreley seduzia os pescadores com seus cânticos e eles terminam morrendo no fundo do mar, já não lembro mais de detalhes. Não, não me olhe com esses olhos culpados. Em primeiro lugar, quem seduz você sou eu. Sei, sei que você se enfeita para mim, mas isso já é porque eu seduzo você" (106).

22. Loreley

> I do not know what haunts me,
> What saddened my mind all day;
> An age-old tale confounds me,
> A spell I cannot allay.
>
> The air is cool and in twilight
> The Rhine's dark waters flow;
> The peak of the mountain in highlight
> Reflects the evening glow.
>
> There sits a lovely maiden
> Above, so wondrous fair,
> With shining jewels laden,

She combs her golden hair.

It falls through her comb in a shower,
And over the valley rings
A song of mysterious power
That lovely maiden sings.

The boatman in his small skiff is
Seized by turbulent love,
No longer he marks where the cliff is,
He looks to the mountain above.

I think the waves must fling him
Against the reefs nearby,
And that did with her singing
The lovely Loreley.
Heine (47–48)

Written in 1823–1824, "The Loreley" (and other poems) by Heine were called anonymous folk ballads and published without his name by the Nazis because of his Judaism. Lispector perhaps could have figured out the original German from her knowledge of Yiddish, or there may have been a Portuguese, English, or French translation available to her. (For more on Lispector's knowledge of languages, see my *Clarice Lispector*).

23. According to a 1986 compilation of biographical information, when Lispector was asked if the name Ulysses came from Homer, James Joyce, or her dog (whose name was Ulysses), she said it was none of them. She said the character was named for a professor of philosophy she met in France ("O que a crítica não viu" 1, 6).

24. The translation calls Lori a "jaguar," but we may also consider her a tiger, given in several Portuguese-English dictionaries as a translation for *tigre*. Lispector was not concerned with making the animal appear from the Americas, and the term "jaguar" may make it seem as if she were. Similarly, the choice of an apple as the most important fruit in the novel, like "tiger" rather than "jaguar," indicates not a regional flavor for the imagery but a biblical one. (Of course, there are no apples in the Bible, but much of Christiandom continues to assume that the fruit of the Tree of Knowledge was an apple.) The fact that apples must be imported to Rio de Janeiro and are much more exotic and expensive than bananas or guavas is important in this sense.

25. "Lóri se sentia como se fosse um tigre perigoso com uma flecha cravada na carne, e que estivesse rondando devagar as pessoas medrosas para descobrir quem lhe tiraria a dor. E então um homem, Ulisses, tivesse sentido que um tigre ferido não é perigoso. E aproximando-se da fera, sem medo de tocá-la, tivesse arrancado com cuidado a flecha fincada.

"E o tigre? Não, certas coisas nem pessoas nem animais podiam agradecer. Então ela, o tigre, dera umas voltas vagarosas em frente ao homem, hesitara, lambera uma das patas e depois, como não era a palavra ou o grunhido o que tinha importância, afastara-se silenciosamente. Lóri nunca esqueceria a ajuda que recebera quando ela só conseguira gaguejar de medo" (135).

26. "O que também salvara Lóri é que sentia que se o seu mundo particular não fosse humano, também haveria lugar para ela, e com grande beleza: ela seria uma mancha difusa de instintos, doçuras e ferocidades, uma trêmula irradiação de paz e luta, como era humanamente, mas seria de forma permanente: porque se o seu mundo não fosse humano ela seria um bicho" (44). In Lori's animal form as "a trembling radiation," it is hard not to remember the shimmering reflection of Ulysses by the swimming pool. Ulysses' aura is her love for him clouding her vision, and how she discovers her existence through the mirror of Ulysses' love, as if love were a complicated displacement of narcissism. Being an animal means having a permanent luminescence of love.

27. See the final chapter of Solange Ribeiro de Oliveira's *A barata e a crisálida*, "Sintaxe e Visão do Mundo," for a discussion of aspects of Lispector's expressive syntax in *Passion* and, occasionally, in *An Apprenticeship*.

28. "Se bem que podia acontecer uma coisa humilhante. Como agora no táxi acontecia com Lóri. É que, depois de anos de relativo sucesso com a máscara, de repente-ah, menos que de repente, por causa de um olhar passageiro ou de uma palavra ouvida do chofer-de repente a máscara de guerra da vida crestava-se toda como lama seca, e os pedaços irregulares caíam no chão com um ruído oco. E eis rosto agora nu, maduro, sensível quando já não era mais para ser. E o rosto de máscara crestada corava em silêncio para não morrer.

"Entrou em casa como uma foragida do mundo. Era inútil esconder: a verdade é que não sabia viver. Em casa estava bom, ela se olhou ao espelho enquanto lavava as mãos e viu a 'persona' afivelada no seu rosto" (93).

29. "Escute, Lóri, você sabe muito bem como conheci você e quero de propósito relembrá-lo: você estava esperando um táxi e eu, depois de olhar muito para você, pois fisicamente você me agradava, simplesmente abordei você com um começo de conversa qualquer sobre a dificuldade de encontrar táxi àquela hora, ofereci-lhe levá-la no meu carro para onde você quisesse, no fim de cinco minutos de rodagem convidei você para um uísque e você sem nenhuma relutância aceitou. Com os seus amantes você foi abordada na rua?" (52–53).

30. In the published translation, it is: "Because with her past lovers if she had given her body it was for her own pleasure. Nothing more or less" (77T); in Portuguese: "Pois com os amantes que tivera era como que apenas emprestava o seu corpo a si própria para o prazer, era só isso, e mais nada" (119).

31. In English the sexual double entendre of masturbation cannot (and perhaps should not) be avoided, even though it is not as strong in the Portuguese; Mazzara and Parris render the expression as "to be in touch with herself" (35T).

32. "—(Eu te amo)
"—(É isso então o que sou?)

"—(Você é o amor que eu tenho por você)
"—(Sinto que vou me reconhecer. . . . estou quase me vendo. Falta tão pouco)
"—(Eu te amo)
"—(Ah, agora sim. Estou me vendo. Esta sou eu, então. Que retrato do corpo inteiro)" (*Para não esquecer* 26).

33. "Claro que devemos comê-la, é preciso não esquecer e respeitar a violência que temos. As pequenas violências nos salvam das grandes. Quem sabe, se não comêssemos os bichos, comeríamos gente com o seu sangue. Nossa vida é truculenta, Loreley: nasce-se com sangue e com sangue corta-se para sempre a possibilidade de união perfeita: o cordão umbilical. E muitos são os que morrem com sangue derramado por dentro ou por fora. É preciso acreditar no sangue como parte importante da vida. A truculência é amor também" (107).

34. "Aspirou de novo a morte viva e violentamente perfumada dos peixes azulados, mas a sensação foi mais forte do que pôde suportar e, ao mesmo tempo que sentia uma extraordinariamente boa sensação de ir desmaiar de amor, sentiu, já por defesa, um esvaziamento de si própria" (109).

35. "Oh, não se assuste muito! às vezes a gente mata por amor, mas juro que um dia a gente esquece, juro! A gente não ama bem, ouça, repeti como si pudesse alcançá-la antes que, desistindo de servir ao verdadeiro, ela fosse altivamente servir ao nada. Eu que não me lembrava de lhe avisar que sem o medo havia o mundo" (*Legião* 111).

36. "Epiphany," Joyce's modified religious term, is often employed to describe moments of intensity and disorientation felt by Lispector's characters. Since a phrase from Joyce's *Portrait of the Artist as a Young Man*, "near to the savage heart," became the title of Lispector's first novel, *Wild Heart* (1943), critics have felt justified not only in calling the intense moments in Lispector "epiphanies" but also in attributing Joycean influence to her characterization. However, Lúcio Cardoso suggested the title to her when he read her still-untitled manuscript and, late in life, Lispector insisted that Joyce had had no impact on her, indeed that she had never read him. Olga de Sá devoted a large portion of *A escritura de Clarice Lispector* to a delineation of areas of comparison with Joyce, and I refer the interested reader to Sá's analysis. Sá affirms that Lori's state of grace, for instance, qualifies as an epiphany. Here I use "epiphany" sparingly and do not mean to imply either a religious/mystical experience for the character or the influence of Joyce on the author.

37. "A fruta do mundo era dela. Ou se não era, que acabara de tocá-la. Era uma fruta enorme, escarlate e pesada que ficava suspensa no espaço escuro, brilhando de uma quase luz de ouro. E que no ar mesmo ela encostava a boca na fruta e conseguir mordê-la, deixando-a no entanto inteira, tremeluzindo no espaço" (167).

38. The apple image attains a complex meaning in Lispector's 1961 novel, *Apple in the Dark*.

39. The epigraph of Joan of Arc's speeches from Arthur Honegger's 1935 *Jeanne d'Arc au bûcher* (*Joan of Arc at the Stake*) underlines the themes of death by fire and resurrection of the select. In the words by Claudel, the lyrics elaborate a trial for Joan in which the judge is a pig, and sheep and asses are allied in the decision to burn her alive. The simple lyricism of Claudel's poem, the static, undramatic verbal emphasis, plus the role of Brother Dominique and his book, who is friend, teacher, and keeper of the written word for a female protagonist, are similar to *An Apprenticeship*. Lispector's only dramatic work, "The Woman Burned at the Stake and the Harmonious Angels" (151–61T in *Legion*; "A pecadora queimada" *Legião*, only in the first edition, not collected in later editions of *Legião* or *Para não esquecer*), has many of the same parallels to Claudel's dramatic poem.

Other images in the novel that appear arbitrary are apocalyptic allusions. For example, those who rise from the dead are clothed in white robes (Revelation 7:9, 13), and Lori wishes to wear white after she dies: "When I am dead I shall wear only white. And I shall meet whom I want; the person that I want will wear only white also" (77T) ["Depois de morta andarei só de branco. E encontrarei quem eu quero: a pessoa que eu quero também estará de branco" (120)].

40. In a note to Ulysses, Lori writes that she has a "a shining black horse" (13T) ["cavalo preto e lustroso" (28)] inside her which is wild and free, tame and sweet. In a later, short prose piece published in "Study of the Diabolic Horse" (111–13; *Onde estivestes de noite* 1974, "Estudo do cavalo demoníaco" 51–54), the horse has the same characteristics: black, demonic, nocturnal, and stolen from a (mythical) king whom she has murdered; when she rides the diabolical horse, fifty-three flutes run behind and a clarinet goes before (see Marting, "Girl-Colt").

Lori's black horse is close to the black horse of the New Testament Apocalypse, with the significant change that her mount issues from the devil's throne instead of from God's book. Reconjugated in the feminine in *An Apprenticeship*, woman rides the horse of her own appetites. The connection to the horses of the Apocalypse changes Lori's horse from a symbol of wild abandon to that of cautious self-liberation. As the novel progresses, the horse fights the reins holding it back, as Lori's desires are held in check by her fear of love (e.g., 93T; 140). The cliché of woman as a horse that the virile man rides belongs to Lori's limited vocabulary (and Lispector's sense of humor). Despite her education and privileged background, Lori is not terribly sophisticated intellectually.

41. Diegetically, during the period before speech between them is easy, Lori sends notes and they speak briefly over the telephone. Lori's writings are reproduced as text, whereas Ulysses' poems and essays are merely mentioned. Following the note to him about the diabolic horse, she writes him a long letter about silence in the mountains of Spain, in Italy, and in Berne (19–21T; 32–39), emblems of her solitude. The texts about silence were published separately as chronicles in *Legion*.

Much later, Lori copies for him from the newspaper a Czech poem, "Voz Longínqua," whose theme about a sad love is similar to the Loreley poem cycle (84–85T;130–31). The poem is by Zdenek Rytir and the music by Karel Svoboda, a Czech songwriter and performer who visited Brazil in 1967. (*Uma Aprendizagem* was written 1964–1968.) Press notices for Rytir appeared in *Jornal da Bahia* (Salvador) November 1, 1967, and *Diário de Notícias* (Salvador) November 2 and 3, 1967. (My thanks to Pavla Lidmilová in Prague, who supplied the information about Rytir.)

Finally, Lori writes for herself a list of "things she can do." A heterogeneous text within a heterogeneous text, the paragraph of the list begins in the third person, "She sat down before a clean sheet of paper" (95T) ["sentou-se diante do papel vazio" (144)], and ends in the first person, "but I will not speak of the love of bodies" ["mas de amor de corpo não falarei"]. The published translation changes this last to the third person: "But she did not say anything about making love" (95T). Some items on the list of what she *can do* are in fact what she has already done: "wait impatiently for my lover" ["esperar o amado com impaciência"]; "hold hands" ["mãos dadas"]. Other items she wishes to do, as in "have love" ["ter amor"].

42. In *Wild Heart,* the scene of a woman "creating" the man lying in bed with her occurs in a failed relationship, a sterile creation without fruit. Sá has pointed out that the chapter "O banho" in *Wild Heart* is also a precursor to Lori's swim in the ocean (*Escritura* especially 155).

43. This is the title given to the section of *An Apprenticeship* republished in *Felicidade clandestina* (151–53).

44. On the contrary, if she became aware of *L'Erotisme* before or during the time of writing *An Apprenticeship,* she probably would have noted the great similarities between his ideas and her own as developed in her previous books. If Lispector had indeed read *L'Erotisme,* the evidence would be in the minutiae. But she would not necessarily need to read his book to write of eroticism as he defines it because, if Bataille is correct, all (male) eroticism follows his model. If Bataille is not correct, then Lispector had many of the same (mistaken) notions. Another possibility for influence rather than mere coincidence, however, may be Lispector's familiarity with works by Roger Caillois, who inspired Bataille.

45. Lori's various moments of comprehension precede any such decision on her part. Her sense of rootedness in the world is lost, Ulysses explains to her; there is a disarticulation ("desarticulação")—first a surprise, then a disorientation, a clumsiness in the way of proceeding, since one no longer knows the location of the obstacles in one's path. Speaking of their future love, Ulysses says to Lori: "But don't be afraid of the lack of articulation that will follow. That confusion is necessary so that you can see what, if it were articulated and harmonious, you would not see and would consider obvious. When that confusion occurs there will be a clash between you and reality" (67T) ["Mas não tenha medo da desarticulação que virá. Essa desarticulação é necessária para que se veja aquilo que, se fosse articulado e harmonioso, não seria visto, seria tomado como óbvio. Na desarticulação haverá um choque entre você e a realidade" (106)]. Her "human soul" ["alma humana"] intermeshes with her body like matched gears: "If her

gears were to stop for a fraction of a second, she would disintegrate into nothingness" (105T) ["A engrenagem falhasse por meia fração de segundo, ela se desmancharia em nada" (157)].

46. "Seu coração começou a bater forte, e ela se sentia pálida pois todo o sangue, sentiu, descera-lhe do rosto, tudo porque sentiu tão repentinamente o desejo de Ulisses e o seu próprio desejo. Permanece um instante de pé, por um instante desequilibrada. Logo seu coração bateu ainda mais depressa e alto porque ela compreendeu que não adiaria mais, seria agora de noite" (159).

47. It may be a simplification to say that in the patriarchal religions, male priests and diviners preside over ceremonies such as baptisms and marriages, and in matriarchal religions, women officiate in commemorations of crucial moments like births and the onset of menstruation.

48. One would never want to reduce the complex and rich imagery of *An Apprenticeship* to Lispector's biography, but her painful burns in 1967, that is, between *Paixão* (1964) and *Aprendizagem* (1969), may have increased her interest in tame fire and in fire which burns only in the imagination. In comparison to *Passion, An Apprenticeship* gives fire a diminished role and increases the healing powers of water (rain, ocean). The dry heat of hatred is replaced by the agreeable, warming fire in the fireplace on a cold, rainy day in Tijuca forest. The flames which kill St. Joan and the fires of Hell during the Apocalypse have been transformed into Prometheus's gift, tamed and put to use by humanity.

49. The published translation reads: "This book required such great liberty that I was afraid to give it. It is far beyond me. I tried to write it with humility. The person in me is stronger than the author" ("Preliminary Note," xiiiT).

50. The protagonist of Lispector's previous novel *Passion*, G.H., changes from a chrysalis to a larva, in reverse order from nature. According to Solange Ribeiro de Oliveira, this reversal of the biological process signifies G.H.'s acquisition of attributes of the cockroach, while she leaves behind her identity and beauty. G.H. will assume the name "cockroach" ("barata") as synonymous with hers (51–52).

51. "[Lóri:] '—Você acha que eu ofendo a minha estrutura social com a minha enorme liberdade?' [Ulisses:] '—Claro que sim, felizmente. Porque você acaba de sair da prisão como ser livre, e isso ninguém perdoa. O sexo e o amor não te são proibidos. Você enfim aprendeu a existir. E isso provoca o desencadeamento de muitas outras liberdades, o que é um risco para a tua sociedade'" (171–72).

The published translation reads: "[Lori:] 'Do you think that all my freedom goes against the structure of my social class?' [Ulysses:] 'Of course it does, fortunately. The fact is that you've just come out of prison as a free agent and no one can forgive you for that. Sex and love aren't forbidden to you anymore. You've finally learned how to exist. And this causes the release of many other liberties, which is a threat to your social class'" (115T).

52. "—Lóri, você e agora uma supermulher no sentido em que sou um super-homem, apenas porque nós temos coragem de atravessar a porta aberta.

Dependerá de nós chegarmos dificultosamente a ser o que realmente somos" (168).

53. Written while Castellanos lived in Tel Aviv and first published in the newspaper *Excélsior,* this article was collected in *El uso de la palabra.* A translation is available in *A Rosario Castellanos Reader* (264–66).

Chapter 4. Mario Vargas Llosa and the End(s) of Sexual Freedom

1. "Al transgredir el tabú contra el incesto, se concitan en la mente de doña Lucrecia imágenes sugestivamente reminiscentes de una terminología política libertaria, lo cual indica el carácter eminentemente político que tiene la prohibición en la novela: '"He conquistado la *soberanía*." Se sintió dichosa y emancipada'" (Reati, "Erotismo e historia" 146; emphasis Reati, 37).

2. "Entonces, conjeturó que el ideal de perfección acaso era posible para el individuo aislado, constreñido a una esfera limitada en el espacio (el aseo o santidad corporal, por ejemplo, o la práctica erótica) y en el tiempo (las abluciones y esparcimientos nocturnos de antes de dormir)" (80).

3. In contrast, her stepson, Alfonso, loves her because she is so physically beautiful: "contemplating her as though his stepmother had just descended from Paradise" (34T) ["contemplándola como si acabara de bajar del Paraíso" (54)]; and he says in conversation with Justiniana: "She's so pretty, so very pretty. [Tears come to my eyes, like when I take Communion]" (39T, tr. modified) ["Es tan, tan linda . . . Se me salen las lágrimas, igualito como cuando comulgo" (59)]. This difference in Rigoberto's and Alfonsito's stated reasons for loving Lucrecia are parallel to Love's differences from Don Rigoberto in the Titian monologue.

4. "El procedimiento de los *vasos comunicantes* consiste en dos o más historias contadas simultáneamente saltando de una a otra parte para obtener, conscientemente, el efecto de que se influyan mutuamente. Se obtiene la impresión de que hay lazos secretos e invisibles" (Enkvist 36, emphasis Enkvist's).

5. "Los vasos comunicantes permiten hacer comparaciones sin decirlo, mostrar contrastes, mostrar que un personaje miente, permiten hacer más densa y más eficaz la narración. Envuelven al lector en el proceso de creación porque el lector tiene que descubrir el juego, juzgar las contradicciones eventuales y sacar sus conclusiones, y eso sin obtener, en general, ninguna confirmación del autor de que ha entendido bien" (Enkvist 37–38).

6. "Este método consiste en *narrar por omisión o mediante omisiones significativas, en silenciar temporal or definitivamente ciertos datos de la historia para dar más relieve o fuerza narrativa a esos mismos datos que han sido monentánea o totalmente suprimidos.* Este vacío premeditado sugiere, ese silencio habla, esa mutilación turba, contamina al resto del relato cierto enigma, cierta zozobra, y obliga al lector a intervenir en la narración para llenar ese hueco significativo, añadiendo, adivinando, inventando, en complicidad activa con el narrador" (Vargas Llosa, quoted in Enkvist 34; emphasis Enkvist's).

7. This idea of the painting chapters as "free-floating" stories, not necessarily anchored in a character of the frame, reverses the stand I took in an earlier article, "Concealing Peru in Mario Vargas Llosa's *Elogio de la madrastra*," where I wrote, "The paintings are subordinated to the frame story, just as the first-person fantasies are subordinated to the paintings" (39). In that essay, I was trying to make sense of the uncharacteristic non-Peruvian places that prevail and the role of metonymy. Here, in contrast, I am looking at all the significant relations between characters, and such subordination has definite negative consequences in reducing the painting monologues excessively. A more meaningful sense of the relation to objective reality of the novel's ideology as fiction is gained by treating the realistic frame as constructed, just as much as the painting's voices are. They are all equally fiction.

8. "La técnica de la objetividad está encaminada a atenuar al máximo la inevitable 'imposición' que conlleva toda obra de arte. No digo, claro está, que las novelas de Flaubert carecen de ideología, que no proponen cierta visión de la sociedad y del hombre, sino que, en su caso, estas ideas no son causa sino bien efecto de la obra de arte; ésta no es para el creador mera consecuencia de una verdad previa que él posee y trasmuta en ficción, sino lo opuesto: la búsqueda, mediante la creación artística, de una posible e ignorada verdad. La diferencia con Brecht es que en Flaubert la ideología es implícita a la ficción" (208).

9. In chapter 1 of *Praise,* Rigoberto says that Alfonsito will probably have his first erotic dream the night that Lucrecia went to his room in a skimpy nightgown; the first dream (about Candaules) mentioned, though, certainly resonates most strongly with Rigoberto's character and predilections. However, the dream also parallels—converses with—the dream predicted for Alfonsito by his father. If Rigoberto dreams he is king, the suggestion is that Alfonso would dream he is Gyges. (See, for instance, the interview Vargas Llosa gives to Ricardo Setti in Vargas Llosa, *Sobre la vida* 119.)

10. "Las mujeres, que en las novelas de Vargas Llosa desempeñan papeles estereotipos [*sic*] del lugar de la mujer en las sociedades más patriarcales, parecen tener un único deseo: relacionarse con un hombre que no resulte ser demasiado cruel o malvado. La tasa de cambio por esta negación de sí misma equivale a todos los servicios que una mujer con su cuerpo y ser social pueda brindarle a ese hombre dentro y fuera del ámbito del hogar" (49).

11. A limited homosocial affectivity can be found in a tendency to form same-sex groups. This sociability among males appears in Vargas Llosa's other novels in friendships and in an emphasis on the male professions, such as the military, the police, the government. In *Praise,* it is a father-son rivalry.

12. Kahn concludes: "Given the continuity between Homer's, Vergil's, and Shakespeare's epic poems, it is difficult to regard Tarquin's violation of Lucrece as a departure from the heroic norm" (157).

13. The discoveries are threefold: Candaules dis-covers (reveals) his wife to Gyges; Candaules' wife discovers her mistreatment; through research, the reader

may discover Candaules' demise in Herodotus. As excerpted in the painting and ekphrastic chapter, the novel never narrates the third of these: the transfer of wealth, wife, and power from Candaules to Gyges found in the Greek historian. The Herodotus story metaphorically implicates Rigoberto in the destruction of his marriage; the tragedy is, in part, of his own making. Since Rigoberto is led to his Candaules fantasy by musing on the fact that his young son has just seen Lucrecia in her skimpy nightclothes, Alfonsito/Gyges would—eventually in the logic of metaphor—supplant the king with regard to the queen. Rigoberto is sexually excited by imagining himself the love-lost king and "forgets" the consequences of Candaules' actions. The source for the painting points to Rigoberto's inability to see the meaning of his own activities.

Additionally, if the full Candaules story had been told to the reader of *Praise,* there would have been good reason to suspect from an early moment that the source of evil in the household may be little Alfonso, anticipating too directly and too easily the surprise ending. So this part of the ancient story is withheld from the reader and may only be discovered extratextually.

14. The maid Justiniana gains an important symbolic value, beyond her purely functional role in advancing the plot and providing an ear for the others, as the correlate of chastity, otherwise missing from *Praise.* The prototypical virgin-and-whore division of earlier literature is subtly repeated in Justiniana and Lucrecia. Although both Justiniana and Lucrecia are wives and both are sexually active, the former has reserve and feels shame for sexual activities and the latter does not; Justiniana's embarrassment makes Lucrecia laugh. Justiniana is younger than Lucrecia, who has helped her servant to get the pill and who tries to imagine Justiniana in bed with her husband (35–36T; 55–56).

15. In a commentary on *Time of the Hero* (1966; *La ciudad y los perros* 1963), critic José Miguel Oviedo consolidates in a concise footnote many of Vargas Llosa's comments on eroticism, sex, and pornography from *The Perpetual Orgy* (1986; *La orgía perpetua* 1975) that are pertinent here: "Vargas Llosa has made various affirmations about his literary tastes that have an illustrative relation with the parody of literature that Alberto incarnates and with the importance of the erotic or frankly pornographic element in his work: 'I prefer Tolstoy to Dostoyevsky, realistic invention to the fantastic one, and among irrealities, the one that is closer to the concrete than to the abstract, for example, pornography over science fiction, romantic fiction over horror stories' [*Orgía* 19]; 'a novel has been more seductive for me to the extent to which in it appear, combined with laziness in a compact story, rebellion, violence, melodrama, and sex' [*Orgía* 20]; 'in my case, no novel produces in me great enthusiasm, fascination, or plenitude, if it does not have, in a minimum dosage, erotic stimulation. I have confirmed that the excitation is the most profound when the sexual is not exclusive or dominating, but rather when it is completed by other materials, when it is found integrated into a vital context that is complex and diverse, as it occurs in reality' [*Orgía* 35]." ["Vargas Llosa ha hecho varias afirmaciones sobre sus gustos literarios que

guardan relación muy ilustrativa con la parodia de la literatura que encarna Alberto y con la importancia del elemento erótico o francamente pornográfico en su obra: 'prefiero a Tolstoi que a Dostoievski, la invención realista a la fantástica, y entre irrealidades la que está más cerca de lo concreto que de lo abstracto, por ejemplo la pornografía a la ciencia-ficción, la literatura rosa a los cuentos de terror' (19); 'una novela ha sido más sedutora para mí en la medida en que en ella aparecían, combinadas con pericia en una historia compacta, la rebeldía, la violencia, el melodrama y el sexo' (20); 'en mi caso, ninguna novela me produce gran entusiasmo, hechizo, plenitud, si no hace las veces, siquiera en dosis mínima, de estimulante erótico. He comprobado que la excitación es más profunda en la medida en que lo sexual no es exclusivo ni dominante, sino se completa con otras materias, se halla integrado en un contexto vital complejo y diverso, como ocurre en la realidad'" (35). (Oviedo, "Tema del traidor" 57n.6; the internal quotations are from *La orgía perpetua,* quoted in Oviedo)].

16. It is ironic that Lucrecia and Rigoberto both perceive Alfonsito as an angel immediately before the boy is about to embark on devilish acts: to kiss his stepmother with sexual intentions and to inform his father about his sexual relations with Lucrecia.

17. "Cuando los delgados labios rozaron los suyos, apretó los dientes, confusa. ¿Comprendía Fonchito lo que estaba haciendo? ¿Debía apartarlo de un tirón? Pero no, no, cómo iba a haber la menor malicia en el revoloteo saltarín de esos labios traviesos que dos, tres veces, errando por la geografía de su cara se posaron un instante sobre los suyos, presionándolos con avidez" (19).

18. "Tenía el pálpito de que aquello que hacía era también una sutil manera de escarmentar al precoz libertino agazapado en la noche de allá arriba, con imágenes de una intimidad que harían trizas de una vez por todas esa inocencia que le servía de coartada para sus audacias" (64).

19. The order in which the events are given to the reader advances the affair beyond moments of doubt or resistence, fast-forwarding the narrated scenes to those in which the lovers have gotten acclimated to their new sexual intimacy. In chapter 11, "After Dinner" ("Sobremesa," literally, "Desert"), for example, we read that the illicit lovers spend their first night together before we hear about their first having had sex together; about their sneaking up to the bedroom while Rigoberto is away on a business trip before we hear about the way it happened that they could sleep together at all; we hear that Lucrecia has lost all vestiges of her inhibitions and feelings of guilt, before we find out how she lost them for the first time.

20. "Sostenía que era muy importante que hubiera tabúes, ciertos frenos, porque decía que la trasgresión de esos frenos, cuando había un riesgo, que uno invertía, no solamente el placer era muchísimo mayor sino que se producía un enriquesimiento de tipo espiritual, intelectual y moral en el individuo. En esto yo coincido bastante con Bataille" (Vargas Llosa, *Sobre la vida* 116–17).

21. Bataille was not concerned explicitly with the social sex-gender system that

invests men with authority and women with responsibility, as we saw in the chapter on Lispector's *An Apprenticeship*. His ideas do have gender-differentiated consequences, however.

22. Julio Ortega finds that a tension exists between the philosophies of Sartre and Bataille in the Peruvian's fiction: "With Sartre, Vargas Llosa seems to believe, or to have believed, that existence overpowers itself in critical lucidity; with Bataille, that that same existence, perversely, is irreducible to codified languages. But between Sartre and Bataille, Vargas Llosa does not appear to propose a continuity, or any type of synthesis, but rather the incorporation of a double intuition . . . [which] acts . . . as another of the internal tensions. . . . The 'negative' and the 'positive' do not annul each other, nor do they mix: they are given at the same time." ["Con Sartre, Vargas Llosa parece creer, o haber creído, que la existencia se sobrepone a sí misma en la lucidez crítica; con Bataille, que esa existencia, de modo perverso, es irreducible a los lenguajes codificados. Pero entre Sartre y Bataille, Vargas Llosa no parece proponer una continuidad, o cualquier tipo de síntesis, sino la incorporación de un doble acertijo . . . [que] actúa . . . como otra de las tensiones internas. . . . Lo 'negativo' y lo 'positivo' no se anulan, tampoco se funden: se dan a la vez"(Ortega 27)]. The tension between Sartre, who espoused a revolutionary role for literature, and Bataille, who proposed an erotic role, produces a fundamental conflict for *Praise*, which the characters resolve in favor of one philosophy or the other. Rigoberto, for instance, has long rejected Sartrian politics and sought Bataille's eroticism. Lucrecia, malleable and complaisant, does not so much consciously choose Bataille's values as imitate him and adapt.

23. The reader, however, has been tipped off earlier in the text. When Fonchito first kisses Lucrecia on the mouth sexually he is described as "a nervous little viper" (84T) ["una nerviosa viborilla" (114)].

24. Mexican poet and feminist Sor Juana Inés de la Cruz wrote in the seventeenth century:

> Misguided men, who will chastise
> a woman when no blame is due,
> oblivious that it is you
> who prompted what you criticize:
>   If your passions are so strong
> that you elicit their disdain,
> how can you wish that they refrain
> when you incite them to do wrong?
>   You strive to topple their defense,
> and then, with utmost gravity,
> you credit sensuality
> for what was won with diligence.
>
> [Hombres necios que acusáis
> a la mujer sin razón,

sin ver que sois la ocasión
de lo mismo que culpáis:
    Si con ansia sin igual
solicitáis su desdén,
¿por qué queréis que obren bien
si las incitáis al mal?
    Combatís su resistencia
y luego, con gravedad,
decís que fue liviandad
lo que hizo la diligencia.]
        (28–29)

25. Eduardo Béjar proposes a reading of *Praise* in which "woman—who in his plays *The Young Lady from Tacna* (1990; *La señorita de Tacna* 1981) and *Kathie and the Hippopotamus* (1990; *Kathie y el hipopótamo* 1983) had been established from a machista point of view as the historical material of the scribe (author) for the fictional arrangement of reality—now serves, being an irreducible body and exploratory desire, as a metaphor for the (literary or visual) text that is open and plural, full as Barthes (1973) says, of semantic sounds that expand the authorial a priori and actualize themselves in the spasms of pleasures from multiple readings." ["la mujer—que en sus obras de teatro *La señorita de Tacna* (1981) and *Kathie y el hipopótamo* (1983) había sido planteada desde una postura machista como la materia histórica del escribano (autor) para el arreglo ficcional de la realidad— sirve ahora, en tanto cuerpo irreducible y sentimiento exploratorio, de metáfora del texto (literario o plástico) abierto y plural, lleno como dice Barthes (1973) de ruidos semánticos que ensanchan el a priori autorial y se actualizan en los espasmos de gozo de múltiples lecturas" (Béjar 245)].

26. In his monograph on Szyszlo, Vargas Llosa writes similarly about the Peruvian's paintings in general: "The magic spaces are also theatrical stage sets and in them we watch a spectacle" ["Los recintos mágicos son también decorados teatrales y en ellos asistimos a un espectáculo" (*Fernando de Szyszlo* 21)].

27. In an interview by Ana María Escallón published in a book for which Mario Vargas Llosa wrote the foreword, Szyszlo commented: "What matters to me is that the counterpart of death is love, not life. Love engenders life, it originates before life. Love is poetry within everyone's reach; it is, therefore, the opposite face of death" (Szyszlo "Reflections" 36).

28. In the Escallón interview, Szyszlo said: "My spaces have always ranged between the landscape and the room. In closed spaces I represent interiors bearing the connotation of a sacrificial chamber or a nuptial room. . . . Space is important in my painting because it acts upon the images that have been represented there; it generates a kind of pressure" (Szyszlo "Reflections" 38).

29. Szyszlo: "Contemporary man has lost the sense of what used to be called religion. Nowadays, . . . the only remaining doors for us to escape from the ferocity of the human condition are art and love. These are the only possibilities that allow

us to get in touch with whatever sacred things are still within human reach" (Szyszlo "Reflections" 37).

30. Indeed, Huizinga addresses the erotic only briefly in *Homo Ludens,* and then to say that copulation itself is not play, but that everything before, after, or different from it may well be: "Caresses as such do not bear the character of play, though they may do so on occasion; but it would be erroneous to incorporate the sexual act itself, as love-play, in the play category. The biological process of pairing does not answer to the formal characteristics of play as we postulated them. Language also normally distinguishes between love-play and copulation. The term 'play' is specially or even exclusively reserved for erotic relationships falling outside the social norm. . . . We feel compelled to regard the erotic use of the play-term, universally accepted and obvious though it may be, as a typical and conscious metaphor" (Huizinga 43–44). Rigoberto dismisses Huizinga's exclusion of "the biological process of pairing."

31. Kristeva makes great claims for Bataille in this sense: "On the historical level, the fact that it has been possible to think such a subject [the sovereign subject] marks the end of a historical era that is fulfilled by capitalism. Shaken by social conflicts, revolutions, the claims for irrationality (from drugs to madness, claims that are in the process of being recognized and accepted), capitalism is making its way towards an *other* society that will be the achievement of a *new* subject" (252, emphasis Kristeva's).

32. The first three painting chapters share visual or verbal indications of one figure more than those actually pictured, a figure who is a viewer of the nude woman. In *Candaules, King of Lydia, Showing His Wife to His Prime Minister Gyges,* the viewer of the Jordaens painting plays such an important role that Rosemary Geisdorfer Feal has postulated from the level of both Candaules' and his wife's gaze that the onlooker they see must be a child. In the Boucher chapter, "Diana at the Bath," a hidden voyeur is clearly postulated in the monologue, adding one figure, the young goatherd, to those pictured. With the Titian "Venus with Cupid and Music," an additional person, the master Don Rigoberto, not seen in the painting, is also present in the subsequent monologue. Together with the organist (Music), the first-person speaker Love is preparing Venus for her husband's arrival. This husband and master, though visually absent, dominates the Titian verbal discourse.

33. Animal desires are part of the heterogenous, the violent, and the material, but "Nothing is tragic for the animal, which doesn't fall into the trap of the *self*" (Bataille, *Inner Experience* 73, quoted in Kristeva).

34. "La ambivalencia, la paradoja vital; o sea, la íntima tensión del individuo que se destruye sin poder controlar su destino. Ese destino, que era claro al personaje heroico, es reemplazado así por el azar y la errancia; y las certidumbres sólo suponen la trágica norma de una realidad distorsionada. El individuo actúa frente a los códigos que la sociedad finge asumir, pero los espejismos y lo real ya no se corresponden. Los códigos son ya paródicos: reiteran, como una caricatura

miserable, los grandes valores que fueron la retórica de una burguesía que ya no los requiere" (Ortega 29).

35. "Han sidos abolidos también los sentimientos altruistas, la metafísica y la historia, el raciocinio neutro, los impulsos y obras de bien, la solidaridad hacia la especie, el idealismo cívico, la simpatía por el congénere; han sido borrados todos los humanos que no seamos tú y yo" (160).

36. According to Ratcliff, major exhibitions of Boucher were at the Metropolitan Museum, the Detroit Institute of Arts, and the Grand Palais in Paris in 1986. This would have been when Vargas Llosa was in the process of writing *Praise*, published in 1988.

37. RAS [Ricardo A. Setti]: For you, the discovery of sex was then with prostitutes. . . .

MVLL: With prostitutes, naturally. It was customary.

[RAS: Para usted, el descubrimiento del sexo fue entonces con prostitutas. . . .

MVLL: Con prostitutas, naturalmente. Era lo acostumbrado]. (*Sobre la vida* 117)

Vargas Llosa seems unaware that prostitution is also a social "problem" and often a matter of class differences and/or economic necessities.

38. "Había entre mis compañeros quienes lo [el sexo] descubrían con las sirvientas. Es algo que yo no pude nunca aceptar, quizá porque yo descubrí muy joven el problema social. Desde muy niño, la idea de que había unas desigualdades sociales terribles en mi país era lo que a mí me sublevó. Entonces la idea de que los niños se aprovecharan de la sirvienta para tener sus primeras experiencias sexuales era algo que siempre me repugnó" (*Sobre la vida* 117).

39. "Nuestra tarea consiste en despertar la alegría corporal de la señora. . . . Así le gusta a don Rigoberto que se la entreguemos: ardiente y ávida, todas sus prevenciones morales y religiosas suspendidas y su mente y su cuerpo sobrecargados de apetitos" (98).

40. At another moment, he tells her: "You will not be Lucrecia today, but Venus, and today you will change from a Peruvian woman into an Italian one and from a creature of this earth into a goddess and a symbol" (75T) ["Hoy no serás Lucrecia sino Venus y hoy pasarás de peruana a italiana y de terrestre a diosa y símbolo" (103)]. The mention of both the names Lucrecia and Rigoberto could be thought of as evidence that this chapter is a dream or fantasy belonging to the frame story's Rigoberto, or possibly to Alfonso. But the coincidence of names does not prove any relation between the two stories. More important is the way the stories combine to create a single novel through separate, closely parallel, story lines.

41. According to Kuspit, the show was at the Tate Gallery in 1985 and traveled to Germany and elsewhere in 1986. It would be interesting to know if Vargas Llosa saw the exhibition.

42. As with the Jordaens, Titian, and Szyszlo monologues, correspondences exist between Rigoberto's divagations in the frame story and the narrative told by

the voice of the Bacon painting. The smell of musk excites both Rigoberto and the monster with no limbs, for instance, and Rigoberto's scatological bathroom meditations also return in different form. If it were necessary or advisable to see the Bacon chapter as an allegory of the frame story, it would imply the possibility of father-son incest: Lucrecia would symbolize Beauty in love with Rigoberto the Beast, and Alfonsito a good-looking youth with a perverse soul. Both are the monster's lovers.

43. The typical Francis Bacon painting suggests "the world is a slaughterhouse": the "space is an abyss, which, like a legendary monster, regularly needs a sacrifice to keep it quiescent. The meat is also the insignia of the figure; the trophy of a kill, it signals the figure's secret carnivorous authority" (Kuspit 55).

44. "Ahora, esos temas que tú has mencionado [la virilidad, la impotencia, la castración, la sexualidad, la homosexualidad, la camadería, la violencia] son temas íntimamente ligados a una sociedad como la peruana o la sociedad latinoamericana, es decir sociedades machistas, por ejemplo, donde el tema del sexo es un tema central. Entonces hablar del machismo en una ficción escrita, en un mundo de éstos, es algo que refleja mucho una experiencia, una realidad" (Vargas Llosa "La especie humana" 73–74).

45. "Borges dijo que Swift se había propuesto 'denigrar al género humano.' Esa frase feliz no podría ser aplicada a Vargas Llosa, porque su negación elude totalmente el diseño alegórico y didáctico; de modo que en sus novelas, cabría decir, esa humanidad se denigra a sí misma. . . . En su ensayo sobre Bataille hemos visto cómo declara directamente que la literatura proviene de una percepción del mal . . . y también cómo intenta asumir esa declaración en una perspectiva totalizadora" (Ortega 31).

46. "Dominaba de tal modo el ritual que su atención podía escindirse y parcialmente consagrarse, también, a un principio de estética, uno distinto cada día de la semana, uno extraído de aquel manual, tabla o mandamientos elaborados por él mismo, también secretamente, en estos enclaves nocturnos que, bajo la coartada del aseo, constituían su religión particular y su personal manera de materializar la utopía" (89).

47. The philosophy of physical perfection originates in a secret decision in Rigoberto's past, and he carries the rituals through more fully and with greater consciousness than Lucrecia, but she comes to share with him the desire for eternal life. She learns through love the most superficial level and the most noble aspects of several of his obsessions. For his part, Rigoberto performs the ritual of cleanliness in search of perfection and the slowing down of time, which is done for his own pleasure and salvation, and also in his wife's name "Like Amadís in the name of Oriana" (66T) ["Como el Amadís por Oriana" (93)].

48. Oviedo affirms that Alberto "creates for himself a revealing defense mechanism: in order to survive among the corrupt, he generates his own source of corruption; this one is a rather parodic manifestation of literary activity, a type of parody that will repeat throughout the length of the Vargas Llosa's work" ["se

crea un revelador mecanismo de defensa: para sobrevivir entre los corrompidos, genera su propia fuente de corrupción; ésta es una manifestación más bien paródica de la actividad literaria, un tipo de parodia que se repetirá a lo largo de la obra de Vargas Llosa" (Oviedo, "Tema del traidor" 55)].

49. This type of rejection of sexuality, according to Vargas Llosa, led the author away from religion: "So its [sex's] condemnation, its repression, its ethical or religious abolition is something that since I was a child—at first in a confused way, later in a reasoned manner—led me to question religion. I think that men have the right to pleasure, that pleasure is something very respectable and defensible in all its strange diversification, complexity, subtleties, and varieties, which have to do with the very complexity of the human being" ["Entonces, su condena, su represión, su abolición ética o religiosa es algo que desde muy niño—al principio de una manera muy confusa, luego de una manera más razonada—me llevó a cuestionar la religión. Creo que los hombres tienen derecho al placer, que el placer es algo muy respetable y defendible en toda su extrañísima diversificación, complejidad, matices y variantes, que tienen que ver con la complejidad misma del ser humano"] (Vargas Llosa, *Sobre la vida* 115). By coming to religion through a rejection of sexuality, Rigoberto follows a reverse trajectory from the one that Vargas Llosa traced in his life.

50. One piece of evidence is the chronology: Alfonso first seizes upon the "ready-made" artwork by Szyszlo to accuse Lucrecia of sexual misconduct, playfully and teasingly, to her face; then he produces his own discourse, writing his own text, to accuse her of sexual misconduct to Rigoberto, behind her back.

51. Rigoberto's first wife, Alfonso's mother, was named Eloisa, the namesake of Heloise, the unfortunate woman tutored by the equally unfortunate Peter Abelard in the twelfth century.

52. In his autobiographical writings, Vargas Llosa returns repeatedly to the topic of his dislike for his own father. Most recently, see *A Fish in the Water* (1994; *El pez en el agua* 1993).

53. "Lo que está en juego es la autoridad paterna, que está siendo desafiada por hijos rebeldes, ávidos de establecer su propia autonomía masculina. En tales enfrentamientos las mujeres, ya sean madres, primas, tías, sirvientas, novias, esposas o madrastras, no son más que juguetes sexuales, premios y trofeos por cuya posesión los padres e hijos se baten, si no siempre hasta la muerte, casi siempre hasta la castración, ya sea sexual o psicológica" (Boland 87).

54. In contrast to Boland, whose thesis is that fathers and sons perform special, Freudian scenarios in Vargas Llosa's novels, José Miguel Oviedo believes father-son conflicts should be subsumed within a general thematic tendency based on conflict and hierarchy: "His readers already know how this novelist's characters like to place themselves before others, disputing something at times very worthwhile, at other times despicable, many other times nothing at all, except the furor and naked intensity of the challenge. Life confronts them, throws them against one

another like dogs fighting over prey, and places them in perfectly recognizable groups: students/professors, fathers/sons, the military/the civilians, the strong/the weak, the bosses/the subordinated, the informers/the avengers, the 'dog' cadets/ the veteran cadets, those from Lima/those from the mountains, and so forth" ["Sus lectores ya conocen cómo los personajes del novelista gustan colocarse unos frente a otros, disputando a veces algo muy valioso, otras veces algo despreciable, muchas otras nada—salvo el furor y la intensidad desnuda del desafío—. La vida los enfrenta, los arroja a unos contra otros, como perros que pelean una presa, y los coloca en bandos perfectamente reconocibles: alumnos/profesores, padres/ hijos, militares/civiles, fuertes/débiles, jefes/subordinados, soplones/vengadores, cadetes 'perros'/cadetes 'veteranos,' limeños/serranos, etc." (Oviedo 50)]. Other sets of "perfectly recognizable groups" who fight for their place in the hierarchy are: men/women and adults/children.

55. An additional homology to Justiniana can be found in the Spanish "la calor" ("the heat" 135T), instead of "el calor." Maria's usage is an anachronism, which could reflect a lack of education in the speaker.

56. The angel is described by Maria in terms that remind one of Fonchito rather than Rigoberto, since Justiniana sees Alfonsito "with pink heels" (141T) ["de talones rosados" (189)] in the epilogue, and Love, a young boy (in the Titian chapter), is also "rosy" (69T) ["rosáceo" (97)].

57. Lucrecia's friends were correct, however, that the son would be the greatest obstacle to her happiness with Rigoberto (6T; 18).

58. "'Did Fonchito see you in your nightdress?' her husband's voice dreamed aloud, in passionate tones. 'You may have given the boy wicked thoughts. Perhaps he'll have his first erotic dream tonight.' She heard him laugh excitedly, and she laughed, too" (9T) ["—¿Fonchito te ha visto en camisón?—fantaseó, enardecida, la voz de su marido—. Le habrás dado malas ideas al chiquito. Esta noche tendrá su primer sueño erótico, quizás. Lo oyó reírse, excitado, y ella se rió también" (21)].

59. "Y de pronto le cruzó por la cabeza el recuerdo de una amiga licenciosa que, en un té destinado a recolectar fondos para la Cruz Roja, había levantado rubores y risitas nerviosas en su mesa al contarles que, a ella, dormir siestas desnuda con un ahijadito de poco años que le rascaba la espalda, la encendía como una antorcha" (20).

60. The location of the friend's erotic tale, a Red Cross benefit, is a satire of "polite," or elite, society.

Bibliography

Abrego, Carlos, and Samuel Gordon. "Una conversación con Miguel Angel Asturias." *Cuadernos Hispanoamericanos* 289, no. 90 (July–Aug. 1974): 326–33.

Aeschylus. "The Eumenides." *Aeschylus I: The Oresteia.* Tr. and introd. Richmond Lattimore. In *The Complete Greek Tragedies,* ed. David Grene and Richmond Lattimore. Chicago: University of Chicago Press, 1947, 1953. 133–71.

Albizúriz Palma, Francisco. *La novela de Asturias.* Guatemala City: Editorial Universitaria, 1975.

Alderfer, Hanah, et al., eds. *Diary of a Conference on Sexuality.* Proceedings of "The Scholar and The Feminist Conference: Toward a Politics of Sexuality," Saturday, April 24, 1982, Barnard College. New York: Faculty Press, 1982.

Allende, Isabel. *La casa de los espíritus.* 3rd ed. Mexico: Editorial O.M.G.S.A., Editorial Diana and Edivisión, Compañía Editorial, 1985. (First pub. 1985)

——. *House of the Spirits.* Tr. Magda Bogin. New York: Bantam, 1986.

——. "Isabel Allende." Interview by Magdalena García Pinto. *Women Writers of Latin America: Intimate Histories.* Tr. Trudy Balch and Magdalena García Pinto. Austin: University of Texas Press, 1988. 23–42.

——. "Mis líos con el sexo." In *Voces femeninos de Hispanoamérica: antología,* ed. Gloria Bautista Gutiérrez. Pittsburgh: University of Pittsburgh Press, 1989. 241–48. (*El País,* 27 julio 1988).

Alvarez, Sonia, et al., eds. *Cultures of Politics/Politics of Cultures: Re-visioning Latin American Social Movements.* Boulder, Colo.: Westview Press, 1998.

Amado, Jorge. *Dona Flor and Her Two Husbands.* Tr. Harriet de Onís. 1st ed. New York: Avon, Bard Books, 1969.

——. *Dona Flor e seus dois maridos.* 1st ed. São Paulo: Livraria Martins, 1966.

Amorim, Enrique, et al. *Prostibulario.* Colección Espejo de Buenos Aires. Buenos Aires: Merlín, 1967.

Andrade, Ana Luiza. "O Livro dos Prazeres: A Escritura e o Travesti." *Coloquio/Letras* [Lisbon] 101 (1988 Jan.–Feb.): 47–54.

Andrade, Mário de. *Amar, verbo intransitivo, um idílio.* Introd. Telê Porto Ancona Lopez. 10th ed. Belo Horizonte, Brazil: Itatiaia, 1982.

——. *Fraulein.* Tr. Margaret Richardson Hollingsworth. New York: Macaulay, 1933.

Ardener, Shirley. "A Note on Gender Iconography: The Vagina." In *The Cultural Construction of Sexuality,* ed. Pat Caplan. London and New York: Tavistock Publications, 1987. 113–42.

Arêas, Vilma. "A moralidade de forma." *Lembrando Clarice.* Special Issue of *Minas Gerais Suplemento Literário* 22, no. 1091 (Dec. 19, 1987): 12–14.

Arias, Arturo. "Algunos aspectos de ideología y lenguaje en *Hombres de maíz.*" *Hombres de maíz.* By Miguel Angel Asturias. Crit. ed. 1st ed. Coord. Gerald Martin. Colección Archivos, no. 21. Spain: Archivos; Nanterre, France: Centre de Recherches LatinoAmericaines (CSIC), 1992. 553–69.

Arts Mayas du Guatemala, Grand Palais. Paris: Ministère d'État Affaires Culturelles, Réunion des Musées Nationaux, June–Sept. 1968.

Asturias, Miguel Angel. "Acceptance Speech." *Miguel Angel Asturias, Jacinto Benavente, Henri Bergson.* Nobel Prize Library. New York: Alexis Gregory, 1971; and Del Mar, Calif.: CRM Publishing, 1971. 7–8.

———. "Algunos apuntes sobre *Mulata de tal.*" *Studi di Letteratura Ispanoamericana* [Milan] 5 (1974): 19–27. (Also in *Los novelistas como críticos, vol. II,* ed. Norma Klahn and Wilfredo H. Corral. Mexico City: Ediciones del Norte, Fondo de Cultura Económica, 1991. 310–17.)

———. *América, fábula de fábulas.* Comp. Richard Callan. Caracas: Monte Avila, 1972. Especially 170–71, 348–50, 351–52.

———. "El aporte de la novela a la sociología." *Novela y novelistas: reunión de Málaga, 1972.* Prol. Manuel Alvar. Málaga, Spain: Instituto de Cultura de la Diputación Provincial de Málaga, Servicio de Publicaciones, 1973. 139–51.

———. "Arte y magia." *Cuadernos Hispanoamericanos* 201, no. 34 (July–Aug. 1975): 93–96.

———. "La audiencia de los confines." In *Teatro 1.* 2nd ed. Buenos Aires: Losada, 1964. 179–249.

———. "Dissertazione sul tema: Paisije y Lenguaje en la novela hispanoamericana." In *Studi di Letteratura Ispano-Americano,* ed. Giuseppe Bellini. Vol. 7 of *Omaggio a Miguel Angel Asturias.* Milan: Cisalano-Goliardica, 1976. 45–54.

———. *Hombres de maíz.* Critical ed. Coord. Gerald Martin. Colección Archivos. Nanterre, France: Centre de Recherches LatinoAmericaines (CSIC), 1992.

———. *Leyendas de Guatemala.* 6th ed. Buenos Aires: Losada, 1975.

———. *Mulata.* Tr. Gregory Rabassa. New York: Bard (Avon Books), 1963, 1967.

———. *Mulata de tal.* Buenos Aires: Losada, 1963; Madrid: Alianza tres/Losada, 1983.

———. *"El problema social del indio" y otros textos.* Ed. Claude Couffon. Pages Oubliées, Pages Retrouvées. Paris: Centre de Recherches de l'Institut d'Études Hispaniques, 1971.

———. "Seminario presidido por el Sr. Miguel Angel Asturias sobre la ponencia del Jaime Díaz Rozzotto, '*El Popol Vuh:* Fuente estética del realismo mágico de Miguel Angel Asturias.'" *Cuadernos Americanos* 34, no. 201 (July–Aug. 1975): 97–106.

———. *Sociología guatemalteca: El problema social del indio/Guatemalan Sociology: The Social Problem of the Indian.* Tr. Maureen Ahern. Introd. Richard J.

Callan. Bilingual ed. Tempe: Center for Latin American Studies, Arizona State University, 1977.

———. "Tierrapaulita." Ed., notes, Dorita Nouhaud. *Co*Texts* 7 (Nov. 1984): 15–31.

Asturias, Miguel Angel, and J. M. González de Mendoza, tr. *Popol Vuh o Libro del consejo de los indios quichés.* 6th ed. Buenos Aires: Losada, 1965.

Aubrun, Charles V. "Aperçu sur la structure et la signification de *Mulata de tal.*" Hommage à Asturias. *Europe* 46, no. 473 (Sept. 1968): 15–20.

Bal, Mieke. *Reading "Rembrandt": Beyond the Word-Image Opposition.* Cambridge: Cambridge University Press, 1991.

Barbosa, Maria José Somerlate. *Clarice Lispector: Spinning the Webs of Passion.* New Orleans: University Press of the South, 1997.

Bassie-Sweet, Karen. *At the Edge of the World: Caves and Late Classic Maya World Views.* Norman: University of Oklahoma Press, 1996.

Bataille, Georges. *Erotism: Death and Sensuality.* Tr. Mary Dalwood. San Francisco: City Lights, 1986. Reprint of *Death and Sensuality: A Study in Eroticism and the Taboo.* New York: Walker, 1962. (Tr. of *L'Érotisme.* Paris: Les Editions de Minuit, 1957.)

———. "L'Histoire de l'érotisme." *Oeuvres complètes.* Vol. 8. Paris: Gallimard, 1976. 7–165.

Bayón, Damián. "La géométrie humanisée des Sud-Américains." Tr. from Spanish to French by Robert Marast. In *La peinture de l'Amérique Latine au XXe siècle: Identité et modernité,* ed. Damián Bayón and Roberto Puntual. Paris: Mengés, 1990. 102–8.

Béjar, Eduardo. "La fuga erótica de Mario Vargas Llosa." *Symposium* [Washington, D.C.] 47, no. 4 (winter 1993): 243–56.

Bell, Shannon. *Reading, Writing, and Rewriting the Prostitute Body.* Bloomington and Indianapolis: Indiana University Press, 1994.

Bellini, Giuseppe. "Miguel Angel Asturias y Quevedo (documentos inéditos)." *Homenaje a Sánchez Castañer.* Spec. issue of *Anales de Literatura Hispanoamericana* 6 (1979): 61–76.

———. "Un patibolario elogio di Vargas Llosa." *Rassegna Iberistica* [Rome] 35 (Sept. 1989): 17–28.

———. "Per una lettera de *Mulata de tal.*" In *Aspetti e problemi delle letterature iberiche: Studi oferti a Franco Meregalli,* ed. Giuseppe Bellini. Rome: Bulzoni, 1981. 41–49.

Benedetti, Mario, et al. *Cuentos de nunca acabar.* Montevideo: Trilce, 1988.

Bergmann, Emilie L., and Paul Julian Smith, eds. *¿Entiendes? Queer Readings, Hispanic Writings.* Durham: Duke University Press, 1995.

Boland, Roy C. "Padres e hijos en las novelas de Mario Vargas Llosa." In *Love, Sex, and Eroticism,* ed. Alan Kenwood. Melbourne and Madrid: Voz Hispánica, 1992. 85–97.

Bombal, María Luisa. *"House of Mist" and "The Shrouded Woman."* Tr. by the author. Foreword Naomi Lindstrom. Austin: University of Texas Press, 1995. (First pub. 1947).

———. *La última niebla.* 10th ed. Buenos Aires: Andina, 1978. (First pub. 1935)

Booker, M. Keith. *Vargas Llosa among the Postmodernists.* Gainesville: University Press of Florida, 1994.

Borinksy, Alicia. Preface to *Theoretical Fables: The Pedagogical Dream in Contemporary Latin American Fiction.* Philadelphia: University of Pennsylvania Press, 1993. ix–xii.

Bosco, María Angélica, et al. *El arte de amar: el hombre.* Buenos Aires: Merlín, 1967.

Brandão, Ignácio de Loyola. *Bebel que a cidade comeu.* 2nd ed. Rio de Janeiro: Codecri, 1978. (First pub. 1968).

Bravo, Victor. "La metamorfosis y lo festivo: *Mulata de tal.*" *Magias y maravillas en el continente literario.* Colección Zona Tórrida, Letras Universitarias. Caracas: Ediciones La Casa de Bello, 1988. 82–89.

Bronstein, Audrey. *The Triple Struggle: Latin American Peasant Women.* Boston: South End Press, 1982.

Brotherston, Gordon. "Indigenous Literatures and Cultures in Twentieth-Century Latin America." In *Latin America since 1930: Ideas, Culture and Society.* Vol. 10 of *Cambridge History of Latin America,* ed. Leslie Bethell. Cambridge: Cambridge University Press, 1995. 287–305.

Bruce-Novoa, Juan. "Eroticism in the Contemporary Mexican Novel." In *Studies in Romance Languages and Literature,* ed. Sandra Messinger Cypess. Lawrence, Kans.: Coronado Press, 1979. 77–90.

Bruner, Edward. "Ethnography as Narrative." In *Anthropology of Experience,* ed. Victor Turner and Edward Bruner. Urbana: University of Illinois Press, 1986.

Burns, Allan F. *An Epoch of Miracles: Oral Literature of the Yucatec Maya.* Tr. with commentaries by Allan F. Burns. Foreword Dennis Tedlock. Austin: University of Texas Press, 1983.

Butler, Judith. *Gender Trouble: Feminism and the Subversion of Identity.* New York and London: Routledge, 1990.

———. *The Psychic Life of Power: Theories in Subjection.* Stanford: Stanford University Press, 1997.

Cabrera, Vicente. "Ambigüedad temática de *Mulata de tal.*" *Cuadernos Americanos* 31, no.180 (Jan.–Feb. 1972): 208–18.

Caicedo, Andrés. *Qué viva la música.* 4th ed. Bogotá: Plaza and Janes Editores Colombia, 1990. (First pub. 1977).

Caillois, Roger. *L'homme et le sacré.* 2nd ed. Paris: Gallimard, 1950.

Callan, Richard. *Miguel Angel Asturias.* Boston: Twayne, G. K. Hall, 1970.

Campbell, Olga G. "*Elogio de la madrastra:* Alegoría del amor o novela erótica." In *Mario Vargas Llosa: Opera Omnia,* ed. Ana María Hernández de López. Colección Pliegos de Ensayo. Madrid: Pliegos, 1994. 23–29.

Campos, Jorge. "Lenguaje, mito, y realidad en Miguel Angel Asturias." *Insula* 22, no. 253 (Dec. 1967): 11, 13.

———. "Las nuevas leyendas de Miguel Angel Asturias." *Insula* 23, no. 254 (Jan. 1968): 11, 14.

Cano Gaviria, Ricardo. "Conversaciones con Mario Vargos Llosa." *El buitre y el ave Fénix, conversaciones con Mario Vargas Llosa.* Barcelona: Anagrama, 1972. 9–111.

Carpentier, Alejo. *The Kingdom of this World.* Tr. Harriet de Onís. New York: Knopf, 1957.

———. *El reino de este mundo.* Barcelona: Seix Barral, 1983. (First pub. 1949).

Carullo, Sylvia G. "Violencia y deseo mimético en *Elogio de la madrastra.*" *Hispanic Journal* [Indiana, Pa.]14, no. 2 (fall 1993): 157–66. [Also in *Texto Crítico* 1, no. 1 (July–Dec. 1995): 57–68.]

Carvalho, Lucia Helena de Oliveira Vianna de. "Clarice Lispector—um exercicio de decifração." Special issue of *Minas Gerais, Suplemento Literario* [Belo Horizonte, Brazil] 22, no. 1091 (Dec. 19, 1987): 10–11.

Castañeda, Leonardo Manrique, coord. *Atlas Cultural de México: Lingüística.* Mexico City: Departamento de Lingüística del Instituto Nacional de Antropología e Historia, Grupo Editorial Planeta, Secretaria de Educación Pública, 1988.

Castellanos, Rosario. "Clarice Lispector: La memoria ancestral." *Mujer que sabe latín.* Mexico City: Sep Diana, 1979. 127–33.

———. "The Eternal Feminine." Tr. Diane E. Marting and Betty Tyree Osiek. In *A Rosario Castellanos Reader,* ed. and intr. Maureen Ahern. Austin: University of Texas Press, 1988.

———. *El eterno femenino, farsa.* Mexico City: Fondo de Cultura Económica, 1975, 1986, 1993.

———. "Kinsey Report" and "Ninfomanía." *Poesía no eres tú, Obra poética: 1948–1971.* 2nd. ed. Letras Mexicanas. Mexico City: Fondo de Cultura Económica, 1975. 284, 317–20.

———. "Kinsey Report." Tr. Maureen Ahern. In *A Rosario Castellanos Reader,* ed. and intr. Maureen Ahern. Austin: University of Texas Press, 1988. 112–16.

———. "The Liberation of Love." Tr. Laura Carp Soloman. In *A Rosario Castellanos Reader,* ed. and intr. Maureen Ahern. Austin: University of Texas Press, 1988. 264–66.

———. "El movimiento de women's love." In *El uso de la palabra.* Prologue. José Emilio Pacheco. Mexico City: Ediciones de Excélsior-Crónicas, 1974. (Originally pub. in *Excelsior.*)

Castelpoggi, Atilio Jorge. *Miguel Angel Asturias.* Buenos Aires: La Mandrágora, 1961.

Castillo, Cátulo. "Prostíbulos y prostitutas." In *Prostibulario,* by Enrique Amorim et al. Colección Espejo de Buenos Aires. Buenos Aires: Merlín, 1967. 7–29.

Castillo, Debra A. *Easy Women: Sex and Gender in Modern Mexican Fiction.* Minneapolis: University of Minnesota Press, 1998.

———. *Talking Back: Toward a Latin American Feminist Literary Criticism.* Reading Women Writing Series. Ithaca: Cornell University Press, 1992.

Castro-Klarén, Sara. *Mario Vargas Llosa: Análisis introductorio.* Lima: Latinoamericana Editores, 1988.

Cixous, Hélène. "Apprenticeship and Alienation: Clarice Lispector and Maurice Blanchot." In *Readings: The Poetics of Blanchot, Joyce, Kleist, Lispector, and Tsvetayeva,* ed., tr., introd. Verena Andermatt Conley. Theory and History of Literature, vol. 77. Minneapolis: University of Minnesota Press, 1991. 74–109.

———. "Reaching the Point of Wheat, or A Portrait of the Artist as a Maturing Woman." *Remate de Males* [Campinas] 9 (1989): 39–54.

———. *Reading with Clarice Lispector.* Ed., tr., introd. Verena Andermatt Conley. Theory and History of Literature, vol. 73. Minneapolis: University of Minnesota Press, 1990.

———. *Vivre l'Orange/To Live the Orange.* Bilingual ed. Tr. Ann Lidle, Sarah Cornell, Hélène Cixous. Paris: Éditions des femmes, 1979.

Cixous, Hélène, and Catherine Clément. *The Newly Born Woman.* Tr. Betsy Wing. Minneapolis: University of Minnesota Press, 1986.

Coe, Michael D. *Lords of the Underworld: Masterpieces of Classic Maya Ceramics.* Photographs Justin Kerr. Princeton: Princeton University Press, 1978.

———. *The Maya.* 4th ed., fully revised. New York: Thames and Hudson, 1966, 1987.

Company Gimeno, Salvador. "Un *Elogio* Total." *Explicación de Textos Literarios* 25, no. 2 (1996–1997): 129–39.

Congrains Martín, Enrique. "Enrique Congrains Martín, ¿Homenaje a las limeñas?" April 4, 1971, interview in Caracas with Wolfgang Luchting. *Escritores peruanos, qué piensan, qué dicen.* Lima: ECOMA, 1977. 65–81.

———. *No una, sino muchas muertes.* Montevideo: Alfa, 1967.

Cornejo Polar, Antonio. "La profundidad histórica del indigenismo." *Literatura y sociedad en el Perú, la novela indigenista.* Biblioteca de Cultura Andina. Lima: Lasontay, 1980. 57–91.

Corrales Egea, J. "Tres escritores hispanoamericanos en Paris: II. Miguel Angel Asturias." *Insula* 197, no. 18 (April 1963): 12.

Cortázar, Julio. "/que sepa abrir la puerta para ir a jugar." *Ultimo Round.* 3rd ed. 1st pocket book ed. Mexico City: Siglo XXI, 1969, 1972. 2:58–85.

Costa Lima, Luiz. "A mística ao revés de Clarice Lispector." *Por qué literatura?* Nosso Tempo, 2. Petrópolis, Brazil: Vozes, 1966. 100–26.

Cotler, Julio. "Peru since 1960." Tr. Elizabeth Ladd. In *Latin America since 1930, Spanish South America.* Vol. 8 of *The Cambridge History of Latin America,* ed. Leslie Bethell. Cambridge: Cambridge University Press, 1991. 451–507.

Couffon, Claude. *Miguel Angel Asturias.* Paris: Seghers, 1970.

Dällenbach, Lucien. *The Mirror in the Text*. Tr. Jeremy Whiteley and Emma Hughes. Cambridge, England: Polity Press, 1989.

de la Garza, Mercedes. *El universo sagrado de la serpiente entre los mayas*. Mexico City: Universidad Nacional Autónoma de México, Instituto de Investigaciones Filológicas, Centro de Estudios Mayas, 1984.

Denser, Marcia, ed. *O prazer é todo meu*. Rio de Janeiro: Record, 1984.

———, ed. *Muito prazer*. Rio de Janeiro: Record, 1982.

Derrida, Jacques. "The Law of Genre." In *Acts of Literature*, ed. Derek Attridge. New York: Routledge, 1992. 221–52.

Díaz Rozzotto, Jaime. "*El Popol Vuh*: Fuente estética del realismo mágico de Miguel Angel Asturias." *Cuadernos Americanos* 165, no. 28 (July–Aug. 1969): 145–56.

Dicter, Midge. *The New Chastity and Other Arguments against Women's Liberation*. New York: Coward, McCann, and Geoghegan, 1972.

Domínguez, Nora. "New Fiction by Argentine Women Writers." *Review* 48 (spring 1994): 67–68.

Donoso, José. *Hell Has No Limits*. Tr. Suzanne Jill Levine. Los Angeles: Sun and Moon Press, 1995.

———. *Historia personal del Boom*. Barcelona: Seix Barral, 1983.

———. "Ithaca: The Impossible Return." Lecture presented in English, Feb. 1980, Barnard College, New York. In *Lives on the Line: The Testimony of Contemporary Latin American Authors,* ed. Doris Meyer. Berkeley: University of California Press, 1988. 179–95.

———. "José Donoso." In *Interviews with Latin American Writers*, ed. Marie-Lise Gazarian Gautier. Elmwood Park, Ill.: Dalkey Archive Press, 1989. 57–78.

———. *El lugar sin límites*. Mexico City: Joaquín Mortiz, 1966.

———. *La misteriosa desaparición de la marquesita de Loria*. 4th ed. Barcelona: Seix Barral, 1985. (First pub. 1980).

Dunkerley, James. "Guatemala since 1930." In *Cambridge History of Latin America,* ed. Leslie Bethell. Cambridge: Cambridge University Press, 1990. 7:211–49.

Enkvist, Inger. *Las técnicas narrativas de Vargas Llosa*. Romania Gothoburgensia xxxvi. Goterna, Kungälv, Sweden: Acta Universitatis Gothoburgensis, 1987.

Espín, Olivia M. "Cultural and Historical Influences on Sexuality in Hispanic/Latin Women: Implications for Psychotherapy." *Pleasure and Danger: Exploring Female Sexuality*. Ed. Carole S. Vance. Boston: Routledge and Kegan Paul, 1984. 149–64.

Etchenique, Nira. "Curriculum." In *Prostibulario,* by Enrique Amorim et al. 41–49.

Euripides. "Hippolytus." Tr. David Grene. *Euripides 1. The Complete Greek Tragedies*. New York: Washington Square Press, 1973. 170–230.

Facio, Sara, and María Cristina Orive. *Actos de fe en Guatemala*. Texts by Miguel Angel Asturias. Selection of texts by Manuel José Arce and María Cristina

Orive. Tr. of Asturias from Spanish to French by Andrés Camp. Tr. of Asturias from Spanish to English by Gerald Martin. 2nd ed. Buenos Aires: La Azotea, 1989.

Fagundes Telles, Lygia. *As meninas.* Rio de Janeiro: Nova Fronteira, 1973.

———. *The Girl in the Photograph.* Tr. Margaret A. Neves. New York: Avon, 1982.

Fares, Gustavo. Review of *Aventuras del desacuerdo,* by Ester Gimbernat González. *Revista Iberoamericana* 166–67 (Jan.–June 1994): 585–88.

Fernández Olmos, Margarite, and Lizabeth Paravisini-Gebert, eds. *El placer de la palabra: Literatura erótica femenina de América Latina, antología crítica.* Mexico City: Planeta Mexicana, 1991.

———. *Pleasure in the Word: Erotic Writings by Latin American Women.* Fredonia, N.Y.: White Pine Press, 1993.

Ferré, Rosario. "La autenticidad de la mujer en el arte" and "El diario como forma femenina." In *Sitio a Eros: trece ensayos literarios.* Mexico: Joaquín Mortiz, 1980. 13–27.

Ferreira, Teresa Cristina Montero. *Eu sou uma pergunta: Uma biografia de Clarice Lispector.* Rio de Janeiro: Rocco, 1999.

Fiedler, Leslie. "Postmodernism and Literary History." In *Postmodernism: A Reader,* ed. Patricia Waugh. London and New York: Edward Arnold, 1992. 31–48. (First. pub. in *Cross the Border—Close the Gap.* New York: Stein and Day, 1972. 61–85).

Fitz, Earl. *Clarice Lispector.* Boston: Twayne, 1985.

Foppa, Alaíde. "Realidad e irrealidad en la obra de Miguel Angel Asturias." *Cuadernos Americanos* 27, no. 56 (Jan.–Feb. 1968): 53–69.

Foster, David William. *Alternate Voices in the Contemporary Latin American Narrative.* Columbia: University of Missouri Press, 1985. 129–36.

———. "The Case for Feminine Pornography in Latin America." In *Sexual Textualities: Essays on Queer/ing Latin American Writing.* Austin: University of Texas Press, 1997. 39–63.

———. *Gay and Lesbian Themes in Latin American Writing.* Austin: University of Texas Press, 1991.

Foster, David William, and Roberto Reis, eds. *Bodies and Biases: Sexualities in Hispanic Cultures and Literatures.* Hispanic Issues, vol. 13. Minneapolis: University of Minnesota Press, 1996.

Foucault, Michel. *Histoire de la sexualité.* 3 vols. Paris: Gallimard, 1976, 1984.

———. *The History of Sexuality.* Vol. 1: *An Introduction.* Tr. Robert Hurley. New York: Vintage, Random House, 1978, 1980.

Franco, Jean. "Afterword: From Romance to Refractory Aesthetic." In *Latin American Women's Writing: Feminist Readings in Theory and Crisis,* ed. Anne Brooksbank Jones and Catherine Davies. Oxford Hispanic Series. New York: Oxford University Press, 1996. 226–37.

———. "Beyond Ethnocentrism: Gender, Power, and the Third-World Intelligentsia." In *Marxism and the Interpretation of Culture,* ed. Cary Nelson and Lawrence Grossberg. Urbana: University of Illinois Press, 1988. 503–15.

————. "From the Margins to the Center: Recent Trends in Feminist Theory in the United States and Latin America." In *Gender Politics in Latin America,* ed. Elizabeth Dore. New York: Monthly Review Press, 1997. 196–208.

Frazer, Sir James George. *The Golden Bough.* 1 volume, abridged ed. New York: Macmillan, 1963, 1972.

Freud, Sigmund. "A Special Type of Choice of Object Made by Men (Contributions to the Psychology of Love I)." In *The Standard Edition of the Complete Psychological Works of Sigmund Freud,* tr. and ed. James Strachey. London: Hogarth Press and the Institute of Psycho-Analysis, 1957. Vol. 9:163–75.

Fuentes, Carlos. *Aura.* 7th ed. Mexico City: Alacema, 1972.

————. "Aura." Tr. Suzanne Jill Levine. In *Triple Cross.* New York: E.P. Dutton, 1972. 5–144.

————. *La nueva novela hispanoamericana.* 6th ed. Mexico City: Joaquín Mortiz, 1969, 1980.

Gallegos, Rómulo. *Doña Bárbara.* 33rd ed. Colección Austral, 168. Madrid: Espasa-Calpe, 1975. (First pub. 1929).

Gamboa, Federico. *Santa.* 6th ed. Mexico City: Grijalbo, 1979. (First pub. 1903).

García Márquez, Gabriel. "La increíble y triste historia de la cándida Eréndira y de su abuela desalmada." In *La increíble y triste historia de la cándida Eréndira y de su abuela desalmada.* Bogotá: Oveja Negra, 1972, 1984. 83–142.

Garibay K., Ángel María. *Poesía indígena de la altiplanicie.* Mexico City: Universidad Nacional Autónoma de México, 1972.

Gaston, Robert W. "Pictorial Representation and Ekphrasis in *Elogio de la madrastra.*" *Antípodas* 809 (1996–1997): 219–29.

Geisdorfer Feal, Rosemary. "In Ekphrastic Ecstacy: Mario Vargas Llosa as the Painter of Desire." In *Painting and the Page: Interartistic Approaches to Modern Hispanic Texts.* Albany: State University of New York Press, 1995. 197–21.

————. "The Painting of Desire: Representations of Eroticism in Mario Vargas Llosa's *Elogio de la madrastra.*" *Revista de Estudios Hispánicos* 24, no. 3 (1990): 87–106.

Genette, Gérard. "Frontiers of Narrative." In *Figures of Literary Discourse,* tr. Alan Sheridan. Introd. Marie-Rose Logan. New York: Columbia University Press, 1982. 127–44.

Georgescu, Paul Alexandru. "Casualidad natural y conexión mágica en la obra de Miguel Angel Asturias." *Ibero-Romania* [Munich] n.s. 2 (Neue Folge, 1975): 157–75.

Giberti, Eva. "Cómo aman los argentinos." In *El arte de amar: el hombre,* ed. María Angélica Bosco et al. Buenos Aires: Merlín, 1967. 7–41.

Girard, Rafael. *Los chortis ante el problema maya.* Colección Cultura Precolombina. 5 vols. Guatemala City: Publicación del Ministerio de Educación Pública, 1949.

———. *Los mayas: su civilización, su historia, sus vinculaciones continentales.* Mexico City: Costa-Amic, Libro Mexicano, 1966.

———. *El Popol Vuh, fuente histórica.* Vol. 1 of *El Popol Vuh como fundamento de la historia maya-quiché.* Guatemala: Editorial del Ministerio de Educación Pública, 1952.

González del Valle, Luis. "Fantasía y realidad en *Mulata de tal.*" *Sin Nombre* 2, no.3 (1972): 65–74. (Also in *La nueva ficción hispanoamericana a través de Miguel Angel Asturias y Gabriel García Márquez,* ed. González del Valle and Vicente Cabrera. New York: Eliseo Torres and Sons, 1972.)

Graupera, Artura A. "Pejorative Connotative of *el tal* and *un tal:* A Comment." *Hispania* 64 (Dec. 1981): 601.

Grosz, Elizabeth. "Freaks." *Social Semiotics* [Sydney, Australia] 1, no. 2 (1991): 22–38.

Groth Kimball, Irmgard. *Mayan Terracottas.* Introd. José Dane Kimball. New York: Frederick A. Praeger, 1961.

Gudeman, Stephen. *The Demise of a Rural Economy: From Subsistence to Capitalism in a Latin American Village.* London: Henley; Boston: Routledge and Kegan Paul, 1978.

Guerlac, Suzanne. "'Recognition' by a Woman! A Reading of Bataille's *L'érotisme.*" *Yale French Studies* 78 (1990): 90–105.

Gutierrez, Angela Maria Rossas Mota de. "*Elogio de la Madrastra:* Alegoria dos Anos 80." *Revista de Letras* [São Paulo, Brazil] 34 [1994]: 121–30.

Hammond, Bryan, comp. *Josephine Baker.* Theatrical biog. by Patrick O'Connor. London: Cape, 1988.

Harss, Luis. "Mario Vargas Llosa o los vasos comunicantes." In *Los nuestros.* 9th ed. Buenos Aires: Sudamericana, 1981. 420–62.

Harss, Luis, and Barbara Dohmann. "Miguel Angel Asturias, or the Land Where the Flowers Bloom." In *Into the Mainstream, Conversations with Latin American Writers.* New York: Harper and Row, 1967. 68–101.

Heine, Heinrich. *Heinrich Heine: Lyric Poems and Ballads.* Tr. Ernst Feise. Pittsburgh: University of Pittsburgh Press, 1961, 1968. 47–48.

Helena, Lucia. "Aprendizado de Clarice Lispector." *Littera* [Rio de Janeiro] 5, no. 13 (Jan.–June 1975): 99–104.

Heresies (The Sex Issue) 12 (1981).

Herodotus. *The History.* Tr. and introd. David Grene. Chicago: University of Chicago Press, 1987.

Honegger, Arthur. *Jeanne d'Arc au bûcher.* Oratorio dramatique sur le poème de Paul Claudel. Vocal Score. New edition with texts in English and German. Paris: Salabert; New York: Polyglot, 1947. (First pub. 1935).

Hope, Charles. "Problems of Interpretation in Titian's Erotic Paintings." In *Tiziano e Venezia, convegno internazionale di Studi, Venzia, 1976.* Venice: Neri Pozza, 1980. 111–24.

Hudson, Glenda A. "Perspectives of the Feminine Mind: The Fiction of Clarice

Lispector and Katherine Mansfield." *Remate de Males* (Campinas) 9 (1989): 131–37.

Huizinga, Johan. *Homo Ludens: A Study of the Play Element in Culture.* Boston: Beacon, 1950, 1966.

Hunt, Lynn, ed. *Eroticism and the Body Politic.* Baltimore: Johns Hopkins University Press, 1991.

Irigaray, Luce. "This Sex Which Is Not One." Tr. Claudia Reeder. In *New French Feminisms: An Anthology,* ed., introd. Elaine Marks and Isabelle de Courtivron. New York: Schocken, 1981. 99–106. (From Irigaray, *Ce sexe qui n'en est pas un.* Paris: Minuit, 1977).

Jackson, Stevi, and Sue Scott. "Sexual Skirmishes of Feminist Factions: Twenty-Five Years of Debate on Women and Sexuality." Introduction to *Feminism and Sexuality: A Reader.* A Gender and Culture Reader. New York: Columbia University Press, 1996. 1–31.

Jameson, Fredric. "Periodizing the Sixties." In *Postmodernism: A Reader,* ed. Patricia Waugh. Kent, Eng.: Edward Arnold, 1992; New York: Routledge, Chapman and Hall, 1993. 125–52. (Also in *The Ideologies of Theory: Essays 1971–1986.* Vol. 2. Minneapolis: University of Minnesota Press, 1988. 178–202. Also in *The Sixties without Apology,* ed. Sonhya Sayres et al. Minneapolis: University of Minneapolis, and Social Text, 1984. Essay first pub. 1984).

———. "Pleasure: A Political Issue." In *The Syntax of History.* Vol. 2 of *The Ideology of Theory: Essays 1971–1986.* Theory and History of Literature, 49. Minneapolis: University of Minnesota Press, 1988. 61–74.

Jaquette, Jane. "Female Political Participation in Latin America." In *Sex and Class in Latin America,* ed. June Nash and Helen Icken Safa. Brooklyn, N.Y.: J. F. Bergin Publishers, 1980. 211–44.

———. *The Women's Movement in Latin America: Participation and Democracy.* 2nd ed. Boulder, Colo.: Westview Press, 1994.

Jaramillo Levi, Enrique. Prologue. *El cuento erótico en México.* Mexico City: Diana, 1975. 11–22.

Jardine, Alice. "Preliminaries." In *Gynesis: Configurations of Woman and Modernity.* Ithaca: Cornell University Press, 1985. 13–28.

Jervey, Jane Hammond. "Indian Thought and Mythology in Miguel Angel Asturias, Specifically in His *Mulata de Tal.*" M.A. thesis, University of South Carolina, 1972.

Job, Peggy. "La sexualidad en la narrativa femenina mexicana 1970–1987: Una aproximación." In *Mujer y literatura mexicana y chicana: culturas en contacto: Primer coloquio fronterizo; 22, 23, y 24 de abril de 1987,* ed. Aralia Lopez-Gonzalez, Amelia Malagumba, and Elena Urrutia. Tijuana: El Colegio de la Frontera Norte, 1988. 123–39.

Juana Inés de la Cruz, Sor. "A Philosophical Satire," "Sátira filosófica." In *Sor Juana Inés de la Cruz Poems: A Bilingual Anthology.* Tr. Margaret Sayers Peden. Binghamton, N.Y.: Bilingual Press/Editorial Bilingüe, 1985. 28–29.

Kadota, Neiva Pitta. *A tessitura dissimulada: O social em Clarice Lispector.* São Paulo: Estação Liberdade, 1997.

Kahn, Coppélia. *"Lucrece:* The Sexual Politics of Subjectivity." In *Rape and Representation,* ed. Lynn A. Higgins and Brenda R. Silver. New York: Columbia University Press, 1991. 141–59.

Kamisky, Amy. *Reading the Body Politic.* Minneapolis: University of Minnesota Press, 1993.

Kanneh, Kadiatu. "Sisters Under the Skin: A Politics of Heterosexuality." In *Feminism and Sexuality: A Reader,* ed. Stevi Jackson and Sue Scott. New York: Columbia University Press, 1996. 172–74.

Kantaris, Elia Geoffrey. *The Subversive Psyche: Contemporary Women's Narrative from Argentina and Uruguay.* Oxford: Clarendon Press, 1995.

Kaufmann, Thomas da Costa. *"Eros et poesia:* la peinture à la cour de Rodolphe II."* Tr. from the English by Jérôme Coignard. *Reveu de l'Art* 69 (1985): 29–46.

Krapp, John. "Figural Castration in Mario Vargas Llosa's *In Praise of the Stepmother." Hispanófila* 121 (Sept. 1997): 35–43.

Krieger, Murray. *Ekphrasis: The Illusion of the Natural Sign.* Baltimore: Johns Hopkins University Press, 1992.

Kristal, Efraín. *Temptation of the Word: The Novels of Mario Vargas Llosa.* Nashville: Vanderbilt University Press, 1998.

Kristeva, Julia. "Bataille, Experience and Practice." In *On Bataille: Critical Essays,* ed. Leslie Anne Boldt-Irons. Albany: State University of New York Press, 1995. 237–64.

Kuspit, Donald. "Hysterical Painting." *Artforum* 24 (Jan. 1986): 55–60.

Lampugnani, Rafael. "Erotic Parricide in Vargas Llosa's *Elogio de la madrastra." Antipodas* 1 (Dec. 1988): 209–18.

Landa, Fray Diego de. *Relación de las cosas de Yucatán.* 9th ed. Introd. Angel María Garibay. Mexico City: Porrúa, 1966.

Laquer, Thomas Walter. *Making Sex: Body and Gender from the Greeks to Freud.* Cambridge: Harvard University Press, 1992, c. 1990.

Lavrin, Asunción. "Women in Twentieth-Century Latin American Society." In *The Cambridge History of Latin America,* ed. Leslie Bethell. Cambridge: Cambridge University Press, 1994. Vol. 6, part 2: 483–544.

Latin American Subaltern Studies Group. "Founding Statement." *The Postmodernism Debate in Latin America.* Special issue of *boundary* 2 [20, no. 3 (fall 1993)] Ed. John Beverley and José Oviedo. Durham, N.C.: Duke University Press, 1993. 110–21.

Leal, Luis. "Myth and Social Realism in Miguel Angel Asturias." *Comparative Literature Studies* 5 (1968): 238–47.

León Hill, Eladio. *Miguel Angel Asturias, lo ancestral en su obra literaria.* New York: Eliseo Torres and Sons, 1972.

León-Portilla, Miguel. *Literaturas indígenas de México.* Mexico City: Editorial MAPFRE, Fondo de Cultura Económica, 1992, 1996.

Levi Calderón, Sara. *Dos mujeres*. Mexico City: Diana, 1990.

El libro de los libros de Chilam Balam. Tr. Alfredo Barrera Vásquez and Silvia Rendón. 12th ed. Mexico: Fondo de Cultura Económica, 1988. (1st ed. 1948).

Lispector, Clarice. *Água viva*. 5th ed. Rio de Janeiro: Nova Fronteira, 1980. (First pub. 1973).

———. *Apple in the Dark*. Tr. Gregory Rabassa. New York: Knopf, 1961, 1967; University of Texas Press, 1986.

———. *An Apprenticeship, or The Book of Delights*. Tr. Richard A. Mazzara and Lorri A. Parris. Austin: University of Texas Press, 1986.

———. *L'apprentissage*. Paris: Éditions des femmes, 1992.

———. *Uma aprendizagem ou o livro dos prazeres*. 8th ed. Rio de Janeiro: Nova Fronteira, 1969, 1980.

———. *A cidade sitiada*. 5th ed. Rio de Janeiro: Nova Fronteira, 1982. (First pub. 1949).

———. *A descoberta do mundo*. Rio de Janeiro: Nova Fronteira, 1984.

———. *Felicidade clandestina*. Rio de Janeiro: Nova Fronteira, 1971, 1975.

———. *The Foreign Legion: Stories and Chronicles*. Tr. Giovanni Pontiero. New York: New Directions, 1992; Manchester, England: Carcanet, 1986.

———. *A hora da estrela*. 6th ed. Rio de Janeiro: José Olympio, 1981. (First pub. 1977).

———. *The Hour of the Star*. Tr. Giovanni Pontiero. Manchester, England: Carcanet, 1986.

———. *A legião estrangeira*. Coleção Nosso Tempo. 3rd ed. São Paulo: Atica, 1982. (First pub. 1964).

———. *A maçã no escuro*. 6th ed. Rio de Janeiro: Nova Fronteira, 1982. (First pub. 1961).

———. *Near to the Wild Heart*. Tr. Giovanni Pontiero. New York: New Directions; Manchester, England: Carcanet, 1990.

———. *Onde estivestes de noite*. Rio de Janeiro: Nova Fronteira, 1980. (First pub. 1974).

———. "O sueter." *A descoberta do mundo*. 172. (First pub. *Jornal do Brasil* [3 Aug. 1968]: B2).

———. *A paixão segundo G.H.* Critical ed. Coleção Arquivos. Florianópolis, Brazil: CSIC, 1988. (First pub. 1964).

———. *Para não esquecer: crônicas*. 2nd ed. Coleção de Autores Brasileiros 20. Ill. Léo Amorim. São Paulo: Atica, 1979.

———. *The Passion According to G.H.* Tr. Ronald W. Sousa. Minneapolis: University of Minnesota Press, 1988.

———. *Perto de coração selvagem*. 8th ed. Rio de Janeiro: Nova Fronteira, 1988. (First pub. 1943).

———. *Soulstorm*. Tr. Alexis Levitin. Introd. Grace Paley. New York: New Directions, 1989.

————. *The Stream of Life.* Tr. Elizabeth Lowe and Earl Fitz. Foreword Hélène Cixous. Minneapolis: University of Minnesota Press, 1989.

Livy. *Livy: A History of Rome: Selections.* Tr. Moses Hadas and Joe P. Poe. The Modern Library. New York: Random House, 1962. Book 1: 57–60, pp. 72–76.

López Alvarez, Luis. *Conversaciones con Miguel Angel Asturias.* Colección Novelas y Cuentos. Madrid: Magisterio Español, 1974.

Lorand de Olazagasti, Adelaida. "*Mulata de Tal.*" In *Homenaje a Miguel Angel Asturias,* ed. Helmy F. Giocoman. New York: Las Américas, 1971. 264–77. (Also in *Asomante* 24 [July–Sept. 1968]: 68–79).

Lorde, Audre. "Uses of the Erotic as Power." In *Take Back the Night,* ed. Laura Lederer. New York: William Morrow, 1980. 295–300.

Lorente-Murphy, Silvia. "Lo diabólico en *Elogio de la madrastra.*" In *Mario Vargas Llosa: Opera Omnia,* ed. Ana María Hernández de López. Colección Pliegos de Ensayo. Madrid: Pliegos, 1994. 31–39.

Lorenz, Gunter W. "Diálogo con Miguel Angel Asturias." *Mundo Nuevo* 43 (1970): 35–51.

McClear, Margaret. "Charactonyms in Miguel Angel Asturias' *Mulata de tal.*" In *Naughty Names,* ed. Fred Tarpley. Publication #4, South Central Names Institute. Commerce, Texas: Names Institute Press, 1975. 39–44.

MacKinnon, Catharine A. "Feminism, Marxism, Method, and the State: An Agenda for Theory." In *Feminist Theory, A Critique of Ideology,* ed. Nannerl O. Keohane, Michelle Z. Rosaldo, Barbara C. Gelpi. Chicago: University of Chicago Press, 1982. 1–30.

Markman, Roberta H., and Peter T. Markman. *The Flayed God: The Mesoamerican Mythological Tradition.* New York: HarperCollins, 1992.

Martin, Gerald. "Estudio general." In *Hombres de maíz,* by Miguel Angel Asturias. Critical ed. Paris: Editions Klincksieck; Mexico City, Madrid, Buenos Aires: Fondo de Cultura Económica, 1981. Especially pp. clix–ccxliv.

————. Introduction to *Men of Maize,* by Miguel Angel Asturias. Critical ed. Coord. Gerald Martin. Pittsburgh Editions of Latin American Literature, Colección Archivos. Pittsburgh: University of Pittsburgh Press, Association Archives de la littérature latino-américaines, des Caraïbes et africaine du XXe siecle, UNESCO, 1993.

————. "*Mulata de Tal:* The Novel as Animated Cartoon." *Hispanic Review* 41 (1973): 397–415.

Marting, Diane. "The Brazilian Writer Clarice Lispector: 'I Never Set Foot in the Ukraine.'" *Journal of Interdisciplinary Literary Studies* [Lincoln, Neb.] 6, no.1 (1994): 87–101.

————. "Clarice Lispector's (Post)Modernity and the Adolescence of the Girl-Colt." *MLN* 113 (1998): 433–44.

————. "La crítica feminista literaria y la novela no-realista: María Luisa Bombal y Luisa Valenzuela." In *Segundo Simposio Internacional de Literatura: Evaluación de la Literatura Feminista en Latinoamérica, Siglo XX,* vol. I. San José, Costa Rica: Instituto Literario y Cultural Hispánico, 1985. 49–57.

————, ed. *Clarice Lispector: A Bio-Bibliography.* Westport, Conn.: Greenwood Publishing, 1993.

Masiello, Francine. "Women, State, and Family in Latin American Literature in the 1920s." In *Women, Culture, and Politics in Latin America: Seminar on Feminism and Culture in Latin America.* Berkeley and Los Angeles: University of California Press, 1990. 27–47.

Mathieu, Corina S. "Contenido y técnica en *Elogio de la madrastra.*" In *Mario Vargas Llosa: Opera Omnia,* ed. Ana María Hernández de López. Colección Pliegos de Ensayo. Madrid: Pliegos, 1994. 41–49.

Mazzara, Richard. "Another Apprenticeship: Clarice Lispector's *A descoberta do mundo* and *Uma aprendizagem.*" *Hispania* 70 (Dec. 1987): 946–48.

Mazzara, Richard, and Lori A. Parris. "The Practical Mysticism of Clarice Lispector's *Uma aprendizagem ou o Livro dos prazeres.*" *Hispania* 68 (Dec. 1985): 709–15.

Mead, Robert G., Jr. "A Myth for Mankind." Review of *Mulata de tal* by Miguel Angel Asturias, tr. Gregory Rabassa. *Saturday Review* 4 (Nov. 1967): 32.

Meese, Elizabeth, and Alice Parker, ed. *The Difference Within: Feminism and Critical Theory.* Amsterdam: John Benjamins Publishing, 1989.

Mendoza, María Luisa. *De Ausencia.* 2nd ed. Mexico: Joaquín Mortiz, 1975. (First pub. 1974).

Meneses, Carlos. *Miguel Angel Asturias.* Madrid: Júcar, 1975.

Menton, Seymour. "Las cuentistas mexicanas en la época feminista (1970–1988)." In *Narrativa mexicana (desde "Los de abajo" hasta "Noticias del imperio").* Serie Destino Arbitrario #4. Mexico City: Universidad Autónoma de Tlaxcala, Universidad de Puebla, 1991. 131–40. (Also in *Hispania* 73, no. 2 [May 1990]: 366–70.)

Mercado, Tununa. "Las escritoras y el tema del sexo." *Nuevo Texto Crítico* 2, no. 4 (2nd semester 1989): 11–13.

Michie, Helena. "Re-membering the Body: Contemporary Feminism and Representation." In *The Flesh Made Word: Female Figures and Women's Bodies.* New York, Oxford: Oxford University Press, 1987. 124–50, 160–65.

Miller, Francesca. *Latin American Woman and the Search for Social Justice.* Hanover, N.H.: University Press of New England, 1991.

Molina, Enrique. *La sombra donde sueña Camila O'Gorman.* 1st ed. Mexico City: Joaquín Mortiz, 1972.

Molloy, Sylvia. *Certificate of Absence.* Tr. Daniel Balderston with the author. Austin: University of Texas Press, 1989.

————. *En breve cárcel.* Barcelona: Seix Barral, 1981.

Morales Gómez, Antonio. *El Tlilamatl: o Libro de los dioses.* Mexico City: Editora Inter-Continental, 1944.

Nunes, Benedito. *Leitura de Clarice Lispector.* São Paulo: Edições Quíron, 1973.

"O que a crítica não viu. *A Hora da Estrela*: os críticos daqui e de fora estão reconhecendo o inegável: Clarice Lispector é nossa maior escritora." *Jornal do Brasil* (Oct. 25, 1986, Idéias): 1, 6.

Oliveira, Solange Ribeiro de. *A barata e a crisálida*. Rio de Janeiro: José Olympio; Instituto Nacional do Livro, 1985.

Ortega, Julio. "Vargas Llosa: El habla del mal." In *Mario Vargas Llosa*, ed. José Miguel Oviedo. Madrid: Taurus, 1981. 25–34.

Ossers Cabrera, Manuel A. "Justiniana: Un personaje secundario de pertinencia humana." In *Mario Vargas Llosa: Opera Omnia*, ed. Ana María Hernández de López. Colección Pliegos de Ensayo. Madrid: Pliegos, 1994. 51–56.

Ovid. *Ovid in Six Volumes*. Vol. 5: *Fasti*. Tr. Sir James George Frazer. Loeb Classical Library. Cambridge: Harvard University Press, 1926. Book 2, sections 685–852, pp. 107–19.

Oviedo, José Miguel. *Mario Vargas Llosa: La invención de una realidad*. 3rd ed. Barcelona: Seix Barral, 1970, 1977, 1982.

———. "Tema del traidor y del héroe: Sobre los intelectuales y los militares en Vargas Llosa." In *Mario Vargas Llosa*, ed. José Miguel Oviedo. Madrid: Taurus, 1981. 47–65.

Oyarzún, Kemy. "Edipo, autogestión y producción textual: Notas sobre crítica literaria feminista." In *Cultural and Historical Grounding for Hispanic and Luso-Brazilian Feminist Literary Criticism*, ed. Hernán Vidal. Literature and Human Rights, No. 4. Minneapolis: Institute for the Study of Ideologies and Literatures, 1989. 587–623.

Parker, Andrew, et al., eds. *Nationalisms and Sexualities*. New York: Routledge, 1992.

Payne, Judith A., and Earl E. Fitz. *Ambiguity and Gender in the New Novel of Brazil and Spanish America: A Comparative Assessment*. Iowa City: University of Iowa Press, 1993.

Peixoto, Marta. *Passionate Fictions: Gender, Narrative, and Violence in Clarice Lispector*. Minneapolis: University of Minnesota Press, 1994.

———. "Rape and Textual Violence in Clarice Lispector." In *Rape and Representation*, ed. Lynn A. Higgins and Brenda R. Silver. New York: Columbia University Press, 1991. 182–203.

Peñuela Cañizal, Eduardo. "Una dimensión del hispanismo: Mestizajes semióticos en el indigenismo." In *Teoría semiótica: Lenguajes y textos hispánicos*. Vol. 1 of *Actas del Congreso Internacional sobre Semiótica e Hispanismo celebrado en Madrid en los días del 20 al 25 de junio de 1983*, ed. Miguel Angel Garrido Gallardo. Madrid: Consejo Superior de Investigaciones Científicas, 1984. 761–83.

Pérez, Luis. "La terminología demonística de *Mulata de tal* por Miguel Angel Asturias y las convenciones en que se funda." In *International Congress of Romance Linguistics and Philology, Actes du XIIIe Congrès International de Linguistique et Philologie Romanes*, ed. Marcel Boudreault and Frankwalt Mohren. Laval, Quebec: Les Presses de l'Université Laval, 1976. 1:781–86.

Pérez Botero, Luis. "Carácteres demológicos en *Mulata de tal*." *Revista Iberoamericana* 38, no.78 (Jan.–Mar. 1972): 117–26.

Piñón, Nélida. *A casa da paixão.* 4th ed. Rio de Janeiro: Nova Fronteira, 1982. (First pub. 1972).

Poggioli, Renato. *The Theory of the Avant-Garde.* Tr. Gerald Fitzgerald. Cambridge: Belknap Press of Harvard University Press, 1968.

Popol Vuh, The Definitive Edition of the Mayan Book of the Dawn of Life and the Glories of Gods and Kings. Tr., notes, and introd. Dennis Tedlock. Revised and expanded ed. New York: Touchstone, 1996.

Prieto, René. *Miguel Angel Asturias's Archaeology of Return.* Cambridge: Cambridge University Press, 1993.

———. "El papel político del erotismo en *Mulata de tal.*" *Revista de Estudios Hispánicos* 22, no.2 (May 1988): 81–91.

Puig, Manuel. *Beso de la mujer araña.* Barcelona: Seix Barral, 1976.

———. *Kiss of the Spider Woman.* Tr. Thomas Colchie. New York: Knopf, Random House, 1979.

———. *Pubis angelical.* 4th ed. Barcelona: Seix Barral, 1981. (First pub. 1973).

———. *Pubis angelical.* Tr. Elena Brunet. New York: Random House, 1986.

Quintana, Epaminondas. Prologue. In *Sinceridades,* by Miguel Angel Asturias. Guatemala City: Académica Centroamericana, 1980. ix–xxxix.

Racine, Jean. *Phédre.* Ed. Christian Delmas and George Forestier. Paris: Gallimard, 1995.

Rama, Angel. "Los contestatarios del poder." In *Novísimos narradores hispanoamericanos en "Marcha," 1964–1980.* Mexico City: Marcha Editores, 1981. 9–48.

———. Prologue. In *Aquí la mitad del amor.* Montevideo: Arca, 1966. 7–10.

Ramazanoglu, Caroline, and Janet Holland. "Women's Sexuality and Men's Appropriation of Desire." *Up against Foucault: Explorations of Some Tensions between Foucault and Feminism.* New York: Routledge, 1993. 239–64.

Rank, Otto. "The Stepmother Theme." In *The Incest Theme in Literature and Legend.* Tr. Gregory C. Richter. Introd. Peter L. Rudnytsky. Baltimore: Johns Hopkins University Press, 1992. 92–130.

Ratcliff, Carter. "François Boucher, Absolutist Painter." *Art in America* 74 (July 1986): 93–97.

Real Academia Española. *Diccionario de la lengua española.* 18th ed. Madrid: Espasa-Calpe, 1956.

Reati, Fernando. "Erotismo e historia en *Elogio de la madrastra.*" *Quaderni Iberoamericani* [Turin, Italy] 78 (Dec. 1995): 33–43.

———. *Nombrar lo innombrable: Violencia política y novela argentina 1975–1985.* Buenos Aires: Legasa, 1992.

Reis, Roberto. "Representations of Family and Sexuality in Brazilian Cultural Discourse." In *Bodies and Biases: Sexualities in Hispanic Cultures and Literatures,* ed. David William Foster and Roberto Reis. Hispanic Issues, vol. 13. Minneapolis: University of Minnesota Press, 1996. 79–114.

Reverte Bernal, Concepción. "*Elogio de la madrastra* de Mario Vargas Llosa, un relato modernista." *Revista Iberoamericana* [Pittsburgh] 58, no. 159 (April–June 1992): 567–80.

Riedel, Dirce Côrtes. "O enunciado de uma aprendizagem." *Jornal do Brasil* 40 (Nov. 15, 1969). Suplemento do Livro: 9.

Rocha, Glauber. "El dulce deporte del sexo (como se ama delante de millones de personas)." Tr. Haydée M. Jofré Barroso. In *Nuevos cuentos del Brasil,* ed. Haydée M. Jofré Barroso. Buenos Aires: Ediciones de la Flor, 1972. 175–186.

Roffiel, Rosamaría. *Amora.* Mexico City: Planeta Mexicana, 1989.

Rosand, David. "Ermeneutica Amorosa: Observations on the Interpretations of Titian's Venuses." In *Tiziano e Venezia, convegno internazionale di Studi, Venzia, 1976.* Venice: Neri Pozza, 1980. 375–81.

Rosensweig, Jay B. *"Caló": Gutter Spanish.* New York: E. P. Dutton, 1973.

Royano Gutiérrez, Lourdes. "*Mulata de tal,* 1963." In *Las novelas de Miguel Angel Asturias desde la teoría de la recepción.* Valladolid, Spain: Universidad de Valladolid, Secretario de Publicaciones, 1993. 207–24.

Rulfo, Juan. *Pedro Páramo.* Ed. José Carlos González Boixo. 2nd ed. Madrid: Cátedra, 1984.

———. *Pedro Paramo.* Tr. Margaret Sayers Peden. Foreword by Susan Sontag. New York: Grove Press, 1994.

Sá, Olga de. "Clarice Lispector: A travessia do oposto." Ph.D. diss., Pontifícia Universidade Católica de São Paulo, 1983–1984.

———. *A escritura de Clarice Lispector.* Petrópolis, Brazil: Vozes; São Paulo: Faculdades Integradas Teresa Dávila, 1979.

Saénz, Jimena. *Genio y figura de Miguel Angel Asturias.* Buenos Aires: Editorial Universitaria de Buenos Aires, 1974.

Said, Edward. *Culture and Imperialism.* New York: Alfred A. Knopf, 1993.

Sánchez, Hernán. "Erotismo, cultura y poder en el *Elogio de la madrastra* de Mario Vargas Llosa." *Anales de la Literatura Hispanoamericana* 23 [Editorial Complutense, Madrid] (1994): 315–23.

Sánchez, Luis Rafael. *La guaracha del macho Camacho.* Havana: Casa de las Américas, 1985.

Sanjines, José. "La sensualidad de la forma y la forma de la sensualidad en *Elogio de la madrastra.*" In *Mario Vargas Llosa: Opera Omnia,* ed. Ana María Hernández de López. Colección Pliegos de Ensayo. Madrid: Pliegos, 1994. 57–70.

Sarduy, Severo. *De donde son los cantantes.* Mexico City: Joaquín Mortiz, 1967.

———. *Escrito sobro un cuerpo.* Buenos Aires: Sudamericana, 1969.

———. "From Cuba with a Song." Tr. Suzanne Jill Levine and Roberto González Echeverría. In *Triple Cross.* New York: E. P. Dutton, 1972. 233–329.

Sartre, Jean-Paul. *Being and Nothingness.* Tr., introd. Hazel E. Barnes. Secaucus, N.J.: Citadel Press, 1956, 1974.

Sawacki, Jane. "Foucault, Feminism, and Questions of Identity." In *The Cambridge Companion to Foucault*, ed. Gary Gutting. Cambridge: Cambridge University Press, 1994. 286–313.

Schaefer, Claudia. "Monobodies, Antibodies, and the Body Politic: Sara Levi Calderón's *Dos mujeres*." In *Danger Zones: Homosexuality, National Identity, and Mexican Culture*. Tucson: University of Arizona Press, 1996. 81–106.

Schele, Linda, and Mary Ellen Miller. *The Blood of Kings: Dynasty and Ritual in Maya Art*. Photographs Justin Kerr. New York: George Braziller; Fort Worth: Kimbell Art Museum, 1986.

Schmidt, Rita Terezinha. "Clarice Lispector: The Poetics of Transgression." *Luso-Brazilian Review* 26, no. 2 (winter 1989): 103–15.

Schrader, Ludwig. "Conejos amarillos en el cielo." *Ibero-Romania* [Munich] o.s. 2, no. 3 (Oct. 1970): 231–47.

Schroeder, Susan. *Chimalpahin and the Kingdoms of Chalco*. Tucson: University of Arizona Press, 1991.

Scott, John F. *Ancient Mesoamerica: Selections from the University Gallery Collection*. Gainesville: University Press of Florida, 1988.

Seminar on Feminism and Culture in Latin America. *Women, Culture and Politics in Latin America*. Berkeley and Los Angeles: University of California Press, 1990.

Shaw, D. L. "Notes on the Presentation of Sexuality in the Modern Spanish-American Novel." *Bulletin of Hispanic Studies* 59, no. 3 (July 1982): 275–82.

Shaw, Donald L. *The Post-Boom in Spanish American Fiction*. Albany: State University of New York Press, 1998.

Showalter, Elaine. "Introduction: The Feminist Critical Revolution." In *The New Feminist Criticism: Essays on Women, Literature and Theory*. New York: Pantheon, Random House, 1985. 3–17.

Sierra Franco, Aurora. *Miguel Angel Asturias en la literatura*. Ed. Merlinton Salazar. Guatemala City: Istmo, 1969.

Silva, Suleima Cury da, and Décio Orlando S. da Rocha. "*Aprendizagem*: Uma leitura psicanalítica." *Littera* [Rio de Janeiro] 16 (July–Dec. 1976): 72–79.

Snitow, Ann Barr. "The Front Line: Notes on Sex in Novels by Women, 1969–1979." In *Women, Sex, and Sexuality*, ed. Catherine R. Stimpson and Ethel Spector Person. Chicago: University of Chicago Press, 1980. 158–74.

———. "Mass Market Romance: Pornography for Women Is Different." In *Powers of Desire: The Politics of Sexuality*, ed. Ann Snitow, Christine Stansell, and Sharon Thompson. New York: Monthly Review Press, 1983. 245–63.

Somers, Armonía. "Carta abierta desde Somersville." *Revista Iberoamericana* 160–61, no. 58 (July–Dec. 1992): 1155–65.

———. *La mujer desnuda*. 2nd. ed. Montevideo: Arca, 1990. (First pub. 1950).

Sommer, Doris. *Foundational Fictions*. Berkeley: University of California Press, 1991.

Spivak, Gayatri Chakravorty. "Can the Subaltern Speak?" In *Marxism and the Interpretation of Culture,* ed. Cary Nelson and Lawrence Grossberg. Urbana: University of Illinois Press, 1988. 271–313.

Steele, Cynthia. *Politics, Gender, and the Mexican Novel, 1968–1988: Beyond the Pyramid.* Austin: University of Texas Press, 1992.

Stimpson, Catherine R., and Ethel Spector Person, eds. *Women, Sex and Sexuality.* Chicago: University of Chicago Press, 1980. 158–74.

Szyszlo, Fernando de. "Reflections with Fernando de Szyszlo: Interview with Ana María Escallón." In *Fernando de Szyszlo,* by Mario Vargas Llosa et al. Bogotá: Ediciones Alfred Wild, 1991. 15–52.

Taussig, Michael. *The Devil and Commodity Fetishism in South America.* Chapel Hill: University of North Carolina Press, 1980.

Tedlock, Barbara. "Mayans and Mayan Studies from 2000 B.C. to A.D. 1992." Review essay. *Latin American Research Review* 28, no. 3 (1993): 153–69.

Tedlock, Dennis. *Breath on the Mirror: Mythic Voices and Visions of the Living Maya.* New York: HarperCollins/HarperSan Francisco, 1993, 1994.

———, trans. Introduction. *Popol Vuh: The Definitive Edition of the Mayan Book of the Dawn of Life and the Glories of Gods and Kings.* Revised and expanded ed. New York: Touchstone, 1996.

Tejera, María Josefina. "Fantasía y realidad en *Mulata de Tal* de Miguel Angel Asturias." *Revista Nacional de Cultura* 182 (Oct.–Dec. 1967): 86–104.

Thompson, Sir J. Eric S. "The Moon Goddess in Middle America, with Notes on Related Deities." Carnegie Institute [Washington, D.C.], Publication #509. *Contributions to American Anthropology and History* 5, no. 29 (1939): 127–73.

Trevizan, Liliana. *Política/sexualidad: Nudo en la escritura de mujeres latino-americanas.* Lanham, Md.: University Press of America, 1997.

Ulate Rodríguez, María. "*Mulata de Tal* de Miguel Angel Asturias: Yumí y sus relaciones." *Káñina, Revista de Artes y Letras de la Universidad de Costa Rica* 3, no. 1 (1979): 57–67.

Valdivieso, Jorge H. "*Elogio de la madrastra:* Un discurso erótico de símbolos, máscaras y sensaciones." In *Estudios en homenaje a Enrique Ruiz-Fornells,* ed. Juan Fernández Jiménez, José J. Labrador Herraiz, L. Teresa Valdivieso. Homenajes 1. Erie, Pa.: Asociación de Licenciados and Doctores Españoles en Estados Unidos, 1990. 666–71.

Valenzuela, Luisa. *Cambio de armas.* Hanover, N.H.: Ediciones del Norte, 1982.

———. *El gato eficaz.* 1st ed. Barcelona: Seix Barral, 1982.

———. *Other Weapons.* Tr. Deborah Bonner. Hanover, N.H.: Ediciones del Norte, 1985.

Vargas Llosa, Mario. *Aunt Julia and the Scriptwriter.* Tr. Helen Lane. New York: Penguin Books, 1995.

———. "Bataille y el 'elemento añadido' en *Tirant Le Blanc.*" Introd. to *El combate imaginario: Las cartas de batalla de Joanot Martorell,* by Martín de Riquer. Barcelona: Seix Barral, 1972. 9–28.

———. *La chunga.* Barcelona: Seix Barral, 1986, 1990.

———. *La ciudad y los perros.* Definitive ed. Madrid: Alfaguara, 1997. (Orig. pub. 1963)

———. *Los cuadernos de don Rigoberto.* Madrid: Alfaguara, 1997.

———. *Elogio de la madrastra.* Bogotá: Arango, 1988.

———. "Entrevista a Mario Vargas Llosa." With Leopoldo M. Bernucci. *Hispania* 74, no. 2 (May 1991): 370–74.

———. "La especie humana no puede soportar demasiado la realidad: Entrevista a Mario Vargas Llosa por Roland Forgues." (Interview, Lima, 6 Aug. 1982). In *Les avatars de la première personne et le moi balbutriant de "La tía Julia y el escribidor" suivi de "La especie humana no puede soportar demasiado la realidad." Entrevista a Mario Vargas Llosa por Roland Forgues.* Toulouse: France-Ibérie Recherche, 1983. 67–80.

———. *Fernando de Szyszlo.* Colección Pintores Peruanos. Lima: Santiago Valverde, 1979.

———. *Fiction: The Power of Lies.* 1993 Meredith Memorial Lecture. Bundoora, Victoria, Australia: La Trobe University, 1993.

———. *A Fish in the Water: A Memoir.* Tr. Helen Lane. New York: Farrar, Straus and Giroux, 1994.

———. *El hablador.* Barcelona: Seix Barral, 1987.

———. *In Praise of the Stepmother.* Tr. Helen Lane. New York: Farrar, Straus and Giroux, 1990; New York: Penguin, 1991.

———. *Literature and Freedom.* CIS Occasional Papers 48. St. Leonard, Australia; Auckland, New Zealand: Center for Independent Studies, 1994.

———. *The Notebooks of Don Rigoberto.* Tr. Edith Grossman. New York: Farrar, Straus and Giroux, 1997.

———. *La orgía perpetua.* 2nd ed. Barcelona: Bruguera, 1975, 1978, 1983.

———. *The Perpetual Orgy.* Tr. Helen Lane. New York: Farrar, Straus and Giroux, 1986.

———. *El pez en el agua.* Barcelona: Seix Barral, 1993.

———. "La pintura de Fernando de Szyszlo." *Plural* 5, no. 7 (April 1976): 43–46.

———. "El placer glacial." *Contra viento y marea, II (1972–1983).* Barcelona: Seix Barral, 1984. 2:107–34. (First pub. as introd. to *Historia del ojo,* Spanish trans. of the novella by Georges Bataille).

———. "Sobre Bataille." *Caretas* [Lima] 574 (22 Oct. 1979): 40–40A.

——— . . . *Sobre la vida y la política.* 2nd ed. Mexico City: Kosmos-Editorial, 1989. Includes: "Diálogo con Vargas Llosa," interview by Ricardo A. Setti, and "Ensayos y conferencias" by Vargas Llosa.

———. *The Storyteller.* Tr. Helen Lane. New York: Penguin, 1990.

————. "Szyszlo y el paisaje de la costa." *Caretas* [Lima] 577 (12 Nov. 1979): 40F–40H.

————. *Three Plays: "The Young Lady from Tacna," "Kathie and the Hippopotamus," "La Chunga."* Tr. David Graham-Young. London: Faber and Faber, 1990.

————. *La tía Julia y el escribidor.* Barcelona: Seix Barral, 1977.

————. *Time of the Hero.* Tr. of *La ciudad y los perros* by Lysander Kemp. New York: Grove Press, 1966.

————. *A Writer's Reality.* Syracuse, N.Y.: Syracuse University Press, 1991.

Veloso, Caetano. "Língua." Sung by Caetano Veloso with Elza Soares on the album *Veló,* Polygram 824 024, 1984.

Williams, Raymond Leslie. *Mario Vargas Llosa.* New York: Ungar, 1986.

Willis, Susan. "Nobody's Mulata." *Ideologies and Literature* 4, no. 17 (1983): 146–62.

Wisdom, Charles. *The Chorti Indians of Guatemala.* Midway Reprint 1974. Chicago: University of Chicago Press, 1940.

————. *Los chortis de Guatemala.* Publicación del Seminario de Integración Social Guatemalteca, #10. Tr. to Spanish, Joaquín Noval. Ed. Jorge Luis Arriola. Guatemala City: Educación del Ministerio de Educación Pública, 1961.

Wittig, Monique. *Les guérillères.* Paris: Les Editions de Minuit, 1969.

————. *Les guérillères.* Tr. David Le Vay. New York: Viking Press, 1971.

Woodhull, Winifred. "Sexuality, Power, and the Question of Rape." In *Feminism and Foucault: Reflections on Resistance,* ed. Irene Diamond and Lee Quinby. Boston: Northeastern University Press, 1988. 167–76.

Wynne, Michael. "Masaccio and Beato Angelico at Fiesole." *Apollo* 120 (1984).

Index

Diane E. Marting received her Ph.D. in comparative literature from Rutgers University and has edited three major book-length reference works on Latin American women writers. The first, *Women Writers of Spanish America: An Annotated Bio-Bibliographical Guide* (1987), lists more than a thousand Spanish American women writers, with brief annotations of the works of more than two hundred of them. The second, *Spanish-American Women Writers: A Bio-Bibliographical Source Book* (1990), provides extensive information on more than fifty women writers, including their biographies and bibliographies. The third, *Clarice Lispector: An Annotated Bio-Bibliography* (1993), annotates the works by and about this major Brazilian author. In addition, Marting has held a fellowship from the American Council of Literary Societies and received two Fulbright grants, one to Colombia and one to Brazil. She has published numerous articles in academic journals and currently is a member of the faculty at the University of Florida.